MW01131440

The Iron Marshal

THE NAPOLEONIC LIBRARY

Other books in the series include:

1815: THE RETURN OF NAPOLEON
Paul Britten Austin

A SOLDIER FOR NAPOLEON
John H. Gill

LIFE IN NAPOLEON'S ARMY
The Memoirs of Captain Elzéar Blaze
Introduction by Philip Haythornthwaite

MEMOIRS OF A FRENCH NAPOLEONIC OFFICER
Maurice Barrès

THE MEMOIRS OF BARON VON MÜFFLING
A Prussian Officer in the Napoleonic Wars
Baron von Müffling

WATERLOO LETTERS
A Collection of Accounts From Survivors of the Campaign of 1815
Edited by Major-General H. T. Siborne

The Iron Marshal

A Biography of Louis N. Davout

John G. Gallaher

Frontline Books

To Maia

The Iron Marshal

A Greenhill Book

Published in 2000 by Greenhill Books
www.greenhillbooks.com

This edition published in 2018 by

Frontline Books
an imprint of Pen & Sword Books Ltd,
47 Church Street, Barnsley, S. Yorkshire, S70 2AS
For more information on our books, please visit
www.frontline-books.com, email info@frontline-books.com
or write to us at the above address.

ISBN: 978-1-52673-832-5

Publishing history
The Iron Marshal was first published in 1976 by Southern Illinois University Press (Edwardsville). A hardback edition containing a New Preface by the author was published by Greenhill Books, London, in 2000. This 2018 edition is reproduced complete and unabridged by Frontline Books.

CIP data records for this title are available from the British Library

Printed and bound by CPI Group (UK) Ltd, Croydon, CR0 4YY

CONTENTS

List of Maps and Illustrations · vi

New Preface · vii

Preface · ix

1 / The Early Years · 3
2 / The Volunteer · 13
3 / The Republican General · 26
4 / The Sands of Egypt · 37
5 / A Marshal's Baton · 62
6 / The Austerlitz Campaign · 95
7 / Military Glory · 116
8 / The Administrator · 151
9 / The Wagram Campaign · 172
10 / The Good Years · 204
11 / The March to Moscow · 219
12 / The Retreat from Moscow · 253
13 / The Siege of Hamburg · 273
14 / The Minister of War · 298
15 / The Declining Years · 335

Notes · 347
Bibliography · 397
Index · 407

List of Maps and Illustrations

MAPS

The Egyptian Campaign · 44–45

Campaigns of 1805 and 1809 · 98

Battle of Austerlitz · 108

The Jena Campaign · 122

The Battle of Jena-Auerstädt · 129

Battle of Eylau · 144

Battle of Wagram · 194

The Russian Campaign · 222

Battle of Borondino · 244

ILLUSTRATIONS

Louis N. Davout at age twenty-two · 9

Louise-Aimée-Julie Leclerc · 73

The Davout château at Savigny-sur-Orge · 79

The Battlefield of Austerlitz · 107

Louis Friant · 120

Charles Etienne César Gudin · 121

Louis Charles Antoine Alexis Morand · 121

Louis N. Davout, Duke of Auerstädt, Prince of Eckmühl · 131

The Lion of Eckmühl · 189

NEW PREFACE

THE CAREER OF Louis N. Davout continues to interest and fascinate all who are interested in the Napoleonic period. Only Marshal André Massena can rival Davout for the title of Napoleon's most capable lieutenant. Never defeated in battle, he was a superb strategist, tactician, organizer and administrator. Only the Imperial Guard surpassed the troops he commanded. His defeat of the Prussians at Auerstädt, his role in the battles of Austerlitz, Eckmühl, Wagram and Borodino, and his defense of Hamburg, singled him out among the marshals of the Empire.

The primary sources for a study of Davout have neither changed nor have there been additions in twenty-four years since the publication of *The Iron Marshal*. The one hundred cartons of the K^1 series ("Donation Davout") in the war archives (Service Historique de l'Etat-Major de l'Armée) at the Château de Vincennes are still the principle primary source for studying the Marshal's military career. The multi-volume publication by his daughter, Adélaïde-Louise, Marquise de Blocqueville (*Le Maréchal Davout: Ranconté par les Siens et par Lui-Même*), remains the essential source for his private life and his relationship with his wife and family.

While *The Iron Marshal* was in press, the late Daniel Reichel published *Davout et l'Art de la Guerre* (Neuchâtel, Switzerland: 1975). This is a serious study of Davout's military career up until 1805. Reichel planned a second volume, but he never finished the work. F.G. Hourtoulle's *Davout le Terrible*, also published in 1975, is respectable but does not add to our knowledge or understanding of Marshal Davout. In the past quarter of a century there have also been published books and articles on the various campaigns and battles in which Davout played a major role. But these do not add to Davout's role, or change my opinion of him, or my evaluation of him as a military leader or a man.

Thus I have chosen not to undertake a re-writing of *The Iron Marshal*. I believe that this study has stood the test of time in its present form. I leave it to the next generation of scholars to improve on the current literature to produce the elusive "definitive" work on Louis N. Davout.

I wish to thank Lionel Leventhal and Greenhill Books for making *The Iron Marshal* again available to the public.

JOHN G. GALLAHER

Mercer Island, WA
January 2000

PREFACE

THE NAPOLEONIC PERIOD has attracted historians for more than one hundred and fifty years. Virtually every principal figure has had detractors and apologists. Still the last words are yet to be written. Considering this vast wealth of literature, Marshal Louis N. Davout has not received adequate treatment. His detractors have gained a wider following than his apologists. Moreover, he has not been adequately studied by English-speaking historians although they have done a great deal of work on the Napoleonic era. The reason for this seems to be that he did not serve in Spain or Portugal and he did not take part in the Waterloo campaign. Thus he has been neglected by English historians. Furthermore, he was not as colorful as King Joachim Murat, nor was he as close to Napoleon as Marshal Louis Alexandre Berthier, nor was he executed by a French firing squad like Marshal Michel Ney. The result is that no biography of Davout has been written in the English language. It it true that Charles de Mazade published a large portion of the Marshal's correspondence (*Correspondance du Maréchal Davout,* 4 vols.), his daughter, Adélaïde-Louise de Blocqueville, wrote five volumes (*Le Maréchal Davout*) to prove that he was a good father and husband, and his grandson, Joseph Vigier, wrote a biography (*Davout: maréchal d'empire*). However, the latter two studies were undertaken in order to counter the generally unfavorable picture of Davout which had emerged in the first three quarters of the nineteenth century. What I have attempted to do in the pages that follow is to give an accurate and unbiased account of Marshal Davout and to place him in proper perspective in the Napoleonic Era.

Louis N. Davout was one of the most capable military commanders and administrators of the Empire. His defeat of the Prussian army at Auerstädt (1806) ranks as one of the great victories of the period. The service he rendered at Austerlitz, Eylau, Wagram, and

Borodino contributed substantially to those victories upon which the Empire rested. It might further be pointed out that he was not with the army at Leipzig or Waterloo when Napoleon suffered his two great defeats. His administrative work in Germany and Poland contributed greatly toward holding together the Empire. He was hard working and honest, and he pushed those under him almost to the breaking point. He was totally intolerant of sloth, neglect, and incompetence—traits which did not mar his own character. The result was an excellent army corps but an unpopular commander. He was not attracted by the Parisian social life which accompanied his titles and position, and was incapable of the type of light conversation which dominated the salon. His relationship with Napoleon was good during the years of the Consulate and through most of those of the Empire. However, he began to fall from favor in 1812 while in Russia and there was coolness on the part of Napoleon in 1813 and 1814. Nevertheless, Davout remained loyal to the end and served as Minister of War during the Hundred Days.

This study could not have been undertaken or completed without assistance from many quarters. However, I must first express my indebtedness to the late Professor Thomas P. Neill of St. Louis University who first introduced me to the marshals of Napoleon and kindled the flame which led to this study. I sincerely regret that he did not live to see its completion. I wish also to acknowledge the cooperation of the staff members of Lovejoy Library of Southern Illinois University at Edwardsville, the Bibliothèque Nationale at Paris, the Service historique de l'état-major de l'armée at the château de Vincennes, the Archives nationales at Paris and the Archives départemental de l'Yonne, at Auxerre. In addition I wish to thank the Office of Research and Projects of the Graduate School of Southern Illinois University at Edwardsville and the American Philosophical Society for financial support which made possible my work in French archives and libraries. I wish to thank Barbara Long for the maps.

My pleasure is sincere in further acknowledging the contributions of my friends and colleagues. I wish to thank Professor Robert F. Erickson of Southern Illinois University at Edwardsville for reading the manuscript and making helpful suggestions. I also would like to thank Jane Peterson for her skillful typing and proofreading of the manuscript. In particular, I wish to express my deepest gratitude to Professor Donald D. Horward of Florida State University for the very valuable suggestions and comments which he made after spending many hours with this manuscript. His assistance was indispensable. Finally, I am indebted to my wife Maia Gallaher for her encouragement and moral support throughout the years I worked on this study.

JOHN G. GALLAHER

Edwardsville, Illinois
May 1975

THE
IRON MARSHAL

1

The Early Years

THE CHATEAU OF ANNOUX, which dominated the Burgundian countryside north of l'Isle-sur-Serein, witnessed the birth of Louis Nicolas d'Avout on the tenth day of May in the year 1770. His father, Jean François d'Avout, although of modest means, could boast of an ancient noble family dating back into the middle ages. This noble blood was to prove both an embarrassment and hindrance to young Louis during the Revolution, but it also enabled him to acquire the best military education available under the old regime and launched him on a career which need not embarrass any man.

The house of d'Avout was one of the most noble in Burgundy. It took its name from the village of Avot in the canton of Grancey-le-Chateau, some twenty-three miles north of Dijon. Various spellings of the name appear throughout the high middle ages and early modern period: Avou, Avo, Avoud, Avoult, and Avot can be cited between 1283 and 1516.[1] The origins of the house can be traced back to the early fourteenth century with a high degree of reliability, and to the first half of the thirteenth century if less substantial evidence is accepted.[2]

The earliest reliable historical evidence of the family appears in October of 1278 in the form of a transaction between Guillaume de Mello, Lord of Epoisses, and the Abbey of Fontenay. The name of Monsignor Mille Davou appears as a witness on this document.[3] At that time the family holdings consisted of the fief of Avot. Primarily through advantageous marriages in the late fourteenth century several additional fiefs were added, and the family became well established. The fifteenth century witnessed the acquisition of the fief of Vignes, and the family left Avot to reside on their newer and more prosperous estate twelve miles east of Avallon. In the mid-seventeenth century the cadet branch of the family came into existence. Nicolas d'Avout (d. 1661) had two sons: François Jacques, who became the Lord of Vignes and head of the older branch of the family, and his younger brother Nicolas, who became Lord of Annoux. It was this younger branch of the family from which Louis Nicolas d'Avout[4] descended.[5]

Louis d'Avout came by his military talents quite naturally. His father, Jean François d'Avout, was a lieutenant in the La Rochefoucauld regiment (later the Royal-Champagne) and served in the Seven Years' War. At the Battle of Minden (1759) he was wounded while distinguishing himself under fire. Capitan-Major Cesar d'Avout was killed at Landau in 1743, while a century earlier one Nicolas de Davot, seigneur de Romanet, served under Gaston d'Orleans in the campaign of 1644 and his son Nicolas was named lieutenant in the regiment of Bligny in 1677. It was this military heritage, which can be traced back into the fourteenth century, that gave rise to the old Burgundian expression: "When a d'Avout is born, a sword leaves its scabbard."[6]

Little is known of Davout's father. Jean François d'Avout was born in 1739 on the family estate of Annoux. His father, Nicolas d'Avout, had married Catherine de Somme, whose family was from Givet on the upper Meuse. At the age of twenty-nine Jean François married Marie Adelaïde Minard despite the reluctance of her mother. But Madame Minard quickly became fond of d'Avout as he proved to be a good father and thoughtful husband. Mademoiselle Minard had been born on October 3, 1741, of a family hardly less noble or illustrious than that of her husband. Her father, Etienne Minard de Velars, had married his cousin, Marie-Louise Minard.[7] He was a lieutenant colonel in a regiment of *Forêt-infanterie* and *chevalier de l'ordre royal et militaire de Saint-Louis*. The Minard family also traced its origins into the middle ages. Perhaps its most illustrious member was Antoine Minard, Lord of Mongarneau, Bilemain, and so forth. In 1544 he had been appointed president of the *Parlement de Paris*, a position he held until his assassination at the hand of a Huguenot on December 12, 1559.[8] Other members of the Minard family served with honor in the armies of France in the seventeenth and eighteenth centuries. Thus the future Marshal had a long-standing military and administrative tradition on both sides of his family.

Shortly after the birth of Louis Nicolas, the d'Avout family moved from Annoux to nearby Etivey where they resided some ten years. It was while living at Etivey that Madame d'Avout gave birth to her other three children. On September 16, 1771, a daughter, Julie,[9] was born. Two years later Alexandre[10] was born and in 1776 a fourth child, Charles.[11] Within three years of the birth of their last child, tragedy struck the d'Avout family. On March 3, 1779, Jean François was killed in a hunting accident. Young Louis was not yet nine years of age when his father was struck down in his prime of life. His mother was forced to assume the heavy responsibility of raising and educating the four children. In order to conserve the adequate, but by no means lavish, inheritance left by her husband, Madame d'Avout sold Etivey, which was too costly for her to maintain, and purchased the chateau and grounds of Ravières. Ravières was less pretentious and more suitable to the means and needs of the widow d'Avout. She was to maintain her residence there throughout the Revolution and Empire, and the estate remained in the family into the twentieth century.

In the years following her husband's death Marie Adelaïde d'Avout was greatly aided by her mother, who had also been deprived of her husband early in life. Madame Minard de Velars was an intelligent and well-educated woman. She was high spirited and extremely capable—as evidenced by the fine education of her children and the careful manner in which she managed the rather modest fortune left her upon the death of her husband. She not only aided her daughter in the financial management of her affairs, but also was a major influence in the education of the children. Louis Davout formed an attachment to his maternal grandmother which survived her death in 1784 and became most apparent when upon his suggestion his youngest daughter was given her name.[12]

In the fall of 1779 young Louis entered the *Ecole royale militaire* at nearby Auxerre. Here it was that he received the basic education which prepared him for the military academy at Paris and a life of service under the King, the Republic, and the Empire. The military school of Auxerre had been established in 1777 by royal decree. It was one of the twelve such institutions[13] designed to improve the French army, which came into existence as part of the military reforms initiated by Louis XVI's active Minister of War, Claude Louis de Saint-Germain. The humiliations of the Seven Years' War had clearly indicated the need for reform. It was hoped that the establishment of these military schools—and the reestablishment in the same year (1777) of the *Ecole militaire* at Paris, the forerunner of St.-Cyr—would provide the officers necessary for this rebuilding of the army. Admission to the school was based upon the student's ability to pay the tuition, not upon his birth, and an ability to read and write. But to obtain a royal scholarship one had to prove four generations of nobility, financial need, as well as the ability to read and write. The six-year course of study included history, geography, languages, mathematics, drawing, and such extracurricular activities as fencing and dancing.[14]

The *Ecole militaire* of Auxerre was located in the buildings of the "college" which had been founded by Amyot and operated by the Jesuits until the Society was expelled from France in 1763. At the time Davout entered, the school was in the hands of Benedictine monks.[15] Young Davout was only nine years of age when he left his family to become a boarder at Auxerre. Discipline was severe and the work hard. Louis had some difficulty adjusting to the new environment, as his parents had not been strict disciplinarians and the boy had been accustomed to a considerable amount of freedom. Yet, with the aid of the assistant principal, Dom Charles-Marie Laporte, who was also his mathematics teacher, the boy was able to make the necessary adjustments, and benefited greatly from his years at Auxerre.

Davout appears to have been no better than an average student. Languages were his weakness. He did poorly in English; and it might be added that although he spent a number of years in German-speaking districts in later life, he never mastered that language. On the other hand, he excelled in mathematics. When awards were given out at the school in September 1783, Louis Davout received honorable mention for achievements in geometry. The following year he again received honorable mention for his achievements in mathematics—this time in algebra. Other than these two awards the future Marshal received no distinctions, military or academic, while at Auxerre.

The direction and influence of the Benedictines came to an end in September of 1785, when Davout entered the *Ecole royale militaire* in Paris. Marshal de Belleisle and Paris Duverney had founded this West Point of France in 1751 as a means of attracting the sons of the poorer nobility into the service of the King. Admission was by appointment upon recommendation by the directors of the provincial military schools. Davout's appointment was signed by Louis XVI—as were all appointments—and by his Minister of War, de Ségur. Virtually nothing is known of *Cadet gentilhomme* Davout during the two years he spent at the *Ecole militaire*. However, he received the same general education as every cadet. The subjects taught included history, geography, mathematics, French and German grammar, drawing, fortification, fencing, and dancing. For those cadets who might serve at foreign courts, there were lectures on ethics and law. For those who were considered in need of them, there were writing classes. Outside of the classroom there was instruction in shooting and riding. The riding school was reputed to be the finest in Europe in the years before the Revolution. There was also religious training which was considered the backbone of any educational program under the Old Regime and formed an intricate part of the education of the cadets at the military academy. Chapel services were held three times every day. All cadets began their day with mass at 6:00 A.M. Confession was heard on Saturday and all received communion together six times a year. Each Sunday there were catechism classes. This spiritual guidance did not always have the desired results. Napoleon Bonaparte emerged from it practically an atheist. Louis Davout, while he did not lose his faith, was never what one could call a religious man.

The *Ecole militaire* had an aristocratic and royalist tone. This is best seen in the fact that the vast majority of its former students went into self-imposed exile during the early years of the Revolution. Davout's ready acceptance of the principles of 1789 becomes even more unusual in the light of his aristocratic heritage and royalist education. It is perhaps easier to understand why a Napoléone de Buonaparte, the son of a poor Corsican nobleman, would embrace a political and social revolution; but a descendant of the proud and noble d'Avout family—with its military tradition of service in the King's army—this was quite another matter.

While at the *Ecole militaire* in Paris, Louis Davout was the classmate of future prominent men, the most noteworthy of them being Raymond-Jacques-Marie de Narbonne.[16] He was not, however, as has been alleged, a classmate of cadet Bonaparte. Napoleon left the *Ecole* on September 1, 1785, while Davout did not arrive until the twenty-seventh of September. Had Bonaparte spent the customary two years at the Paris school, instead of one, their paths would have crossed thirteen years earlier than that fateful day in March 1798 on the eve of the Egyptian campaign.

The two and a half years which Davout studied at the *Ecole militaire* were somewhat longer than the average student spent at Paris. Upon his successful completion of the "passing out" examinations, the young man of eighteen received a commission as *sous-lieutenant* and joined the Royal-Champagne cavalry regiment. This was the same regiment in which his father and his uncle had served with distinction, and in which his cousin, François Claude d'Avout, was presently serving. At the time Second Lieutenant Davout joined the regiment it was commanded by the brother of Madame Du Barry, Colonel comte d'Hargicourt. Shortly after his arrival the Marquis de Fournes took command.

The regiment was stationed at Hesdin, in the province of Artois, when Davout joined it in the winter of 1788. In these early years of his career the young lieutenant was financially pressed, and only by depriving himself of all luxuries was he able to live on his army pay. Upon receiving his commission, the King had made him a present of a horse to help with the burdensome expense of equipping a newly created cavalry officer. But interestingly enough, this generosity on the part of the Crown, which included all of his education and military training, did not suffice to make a royalist out of the young Burgundian. When revolution broke over France in the summer of 1789, Lieutenant Davout embraced the new doctrines of liberty and equality. In the years following the fall of the Bastille, he became very interested in political and social affairs. This is perhaps

LOUIS N. DAVOUT at age twenty-two. Born d'Avout at Annoux in 1770, he changed the spelling of his name to Davout in the early years of the French Revolution. Educated at the military schools of Auxerre and Paris, he entered the army of Louis XVI. He fought in the wars of the Revolution, during which period he rose to the rank of general. In the Napoleonic years he served in most of the major campaigns and became a marshal of the empire.—From Blocqueville, *Le Maréchal Davout prince d'Eckmühl: raconté par les siens et par lui-même*, vol. 1

best seen in the criticism made to him at this time by his uncle, Major Jacque-Edme d'Avout, who was serving in the same regiment: "My nephew Davout will never amount to anything; he will never be a soldier. In place of working on [military] theory, he occupies himself with Montaigne, Rousseau and the other philosophers." [17] Rousseau unquestionably had his influence on the young officer, and he became an ardent republican in the early years of the Revolution.

In embracing the new revolutionary ideas, Davout opened the door to many troubled days, which he could otherwise have avoided. It led to his imprisonment and discharge from the army, and what must have seemed at the time to the end of his military career. In his regiment as a whole the vast majority of officers were royalists and in complete discord with the basic assumptions of the Revolution. These sentiments were shared by the local municipal government of Hesdin. But a small group of officers in the regiment, mostly the young junior officers, accepted the changes of 1789 and looked upon them as a means of improving government in particular and society in general. The rank and file of the regiment was enthusiastic in its support of the National Assembly and all for which it stood. They were also impatient to see the decrees of the new government carried out without the delays and circumventions which they correctly traced to the predominantly antirevolutionary officer corps. In the town of Hesdin itself, the majority of the inhabitants also supported the new government in Paris.

The first indication that there would be trouble at Hesdin came in April of 1790. On the twenty-seventh of that month a proposal was drawn up by the newly created National Guard for a federative union between itself and the King's royal regiment. The proposal was accepted by most of the junior officers and by the men of the Royal-Champagne. On the other hand, the federation was strongly opposed not only by the majority of the officer corps of the regiment, including all of its high-ranking members, but also by the municipal government of Hesdin. Despite this opposition, the supporters of the union met before the city hall, and swore an oath of adherence to the federation. This document, announcing the federation, was sent to the National Assembly where it was read and approved on May 7, 1790. It bore, among others, the signature of Second Lieutenant Louis Davout.

There were neither reprisals nor repercussions as a result of the formation of this federation, but clearly it indicated the division which existed in the army. Other signs of disunity were not long in making themselves visible. On the first of August the officers of the regiment gave a dinner for the officers of the National Guard; but in doing so, they excluded all junior officers. Then a noncommissioned officer of radical royalist views was promoted to the rank of second lieutenant despite an order from the King that no promotions should be made until new regulations governing such promotions should go into effect in late October. On this occasion Davout felt it was his duty to protest the action of his superiors—even though the promotion was in accordance with the law which would become effective in the near future—because it did not conform with existing regulations.

The breaking point came in the second half of August. As the result of a disturbance in the town, which involved men from the Royal-Champagne regiment, the first actual reprisals were taken. Knowledge of the affair which took place on the night of August 1, following the dinner given for the officers of the National Guard, reached the highest quarters; and the Minister of War, La Tour du Pin Gouvernet, directed that the men responsible should be discharged from the army. This order was carried out on August 21; and forty-nine enlisted men were dismissed from the regiment, among them veterans of more than twenty years of service. They were not given a trial but were simply discharged and ordered to return to their respective departments. Davout was enraged. His protest against this arbitrary action was both loud and strong. So incensed was he that he wrote a fiery protest to the government. His reward came in the form of a letter of *cachet* from the Minister of War, and Davout was imprisoned at Arras.

Protest demonstrations were also staged by the rank and file of the regiment and members of the National Guard, and a letter was sent to the National Assembly. In its meeting on September 4, the Assembly passed a resolution which dispatched two commissioners to Hesdin to investigate the actions of the Royal-Champagne regiment. They spent two months at Hesdin and took testimony from over two hundred persons. Their findings were then dispatched to the Assembly. In this report representative Salle de Choux wrote the following: "I point out in passing, . . . that M. Davout, *sous-lieutenant* of the Royal-Champagne, who had defended the opinions of the soldiers, has found himself enveloped in their disgrace; he has been secretly put in a cell in the fortress of Arras, by a letter of *cachet;* he was only released upon the presentation of a second letter of *cachet,* and during his detention he was discharged from the army. I do not submit to you this offense; M. Davout proposes to demand that action be taken against the minister." [18]

Davout had been released from prison after six weeks, but only after he had been stripped of his commission and dismissed from the army. Upon regaining his freedom, he immediately protested his discharge and was reinstated in the army with his former rank. He had planned to make a personal attack against La Tour du Pin Gouvernet; but upon his release from prison he discovered, much to his disappointment, that the Minister had fallen from power. Even though he was restored to rank in the Royal-Champagne, he could hardly rejoin that regiment after all that had happened. He, therefore, asked for and received a prolonged leave of absence and returned to his mother's home at Ravières.

Ravières was not the same as when he had last visited his family. His mother, deprived of the sound judgment and good council of Madame Minard, had remarried. In a ceremony which had taken place on August 31, 1789, she became Madame Louis Turreau de Linieres.[19] The entire Davout family disapproved of her marriage to the young lawyer, who was twenty years her junior, and they displayed their disapproval by their refusal to attend the ceremony which had been held in the local parish church. For their part, the Turreau family, a mixture of bourgeois and petite nobility, fully approved of the match and were well represented at the church. Though Louis Davout did not approve of his mother's remarriage, he did not continue to oppose it after the ceremony. He accepted the *fait accompli* and reestablished good relations with his mother and new stepfather, whom he had never disliked personally. The marriage lasted only a few years, during which time Davout remained on good terms with Turreau, who was to have an active, if brief, political career. He was elected an alternate deputy to the Legislature but was never seated. Then in 1792 he was elected from l'Yonne to the Convention, where he voted for the execution of Louis XVI and the purge of the Girondins. When the Thermidorian reaction set in, he was sent on a mission to the Army of Italy as a military administrator. He met his untimely death in Italy, from natural causes, with General Bonaparte's army.

2

The Volunteer

THE MONTHS which Davout now spent in forced leisure at Ravières were not spent in idleness. He read extensively in both modern and ancient history, and political philosophy. During this period his acceptance of the new revolutionary doctrines became even more complete. His association with his stepfather, an acknowledged republican who was taking an active part in national and local politics, helped to strengthen his acceptance of the Revolution. He had no desire to enter the political arena himself; consequently, when the opportunity again presented itself for him to resume his military career, he did not hesitate. With the formation of the 3rd Volunteer Battalion of Yonne, Davout enlisted as an ordinary soldier.

The decree calling for the formation of volunteer battalions throughout France was passed by the National Constituent Assembly in September 1791. The growing international tension and the flight of Louis XVI from Paris to Varennes (June 22) caused the representatives to think in terms of strengthening the army. One hundred thousand men were to be enlisted and trained as a supplement to the dwindling regular army. Desertions had depleted the ranks of the army as more than half of the nine thousand officers had already resigned and/or emigrated. Accordingly, recruits were signed up through the fall of 1791, but all did not go as planned. There was jealousy on the part of the regular army which envied the better pay and more rapid promotions to be had in the volunteer units. This feeling was made even stronger by the firm conviction—not without justification—that the volunteers were inferior to the regular troops.

The regular army was also jealous of the volunteers' privilege of electing their officers. It was this particular feature of the new battalions that gave Davout his first opportunity to display his abilities. Because of his military education at Auxerre and Paris, his previous military service, and his acceptance of the Revolution, he was first elected captain of the 8th Company of the 3rd Volunteer Battalion of Yonne (September 23),[1] and three days later *lieutenant-colonel en second* of the Battalion.[2] Davout received four hundred votes, just sixty fewer than François Dubois (formerly du Bois), who was elected *1er lieutenant-colonel* of the battalion.[3]

The Revolution had opened up the ranks of the army to men of ability rather than to those of nobility. Under the old regime it would have been unlikely that Davout would have ever reached the rank of lieutenant colonel; and this despite his noble birth and good schooling. His uncle Jacques-Edme d'Avout, whose military career was considered to have been a successful one, had only attained the rank of major; while his father, a veteran of the Seven Years' War, had still been a lieutenant at the age of forty. Davout's younger brother Alexandre, who had been elected a lieutenant in the 3rd Battalion on September 23, 1791, was chosen to succeed Louis as Captain of the 8th Company when his brother became second in command of the battalion.[4]

During the course of the year which Davout had spent at Ravières with his family, he had fallen in love with Marie-Nicolle-Adelaïde de Seuguenot, the daughter of Charles-Elie de Seuguenot and Marie-Magdelaine Cassons. The Seuguenots lived in the vicinity of Dijon; but their attractive daughter often visited with her cousin, who was married to a cousin of Madame Davout. The romance blossomed through the summer of 1791; and despite the fact that she was two years his senior, they were married on November 8, 1791, with the blessings of both families.

Shortly after the marriage Davout rejoined his battalion, which was stationed at Joigny. On December 16 he marched north with his unit to join the Army of the North. With the outbreak of war in the spring of 1792, he was unable to obtain a leave to return home until September of the following year. Upon his arrival at Ravières he learned that his wife had been unfaithful, and he began proceedings for a divorce, which had been legalized by the decree of September 20, 1792. Without opposition from his wife, Davout easily obtained the divorce on grounds of "incompatibility and character" on January 3, 1794.[5] The former Madame Davout's health failed during the next eighteen months and she died on August 3, 1795.

At the time Davout had rejoined his battalion early in November 1791 France had still been at peace with Europe and Louis XVI on his throne. Then in rapid succession France went to war with Austria and Prussia, the monarchy was overthrown (August 10, 1792), a republic was proclaimed (September 22), and the King executed (January 21, 1793). In preparation for the outbreak of war, which all of Europe generally believed would occur in the spring of 1792, the 3rd Volunteer Battalion of Yonne began a rigorous training program. Few of the men had had any previous military experience, so that it was necessary to begin with the most elementary aspects of military training. The work was slow and hard for both officers and men; nevertheless, the majority of both were willing and eager. As might be expected, the long winter, hard training, and military discipline caused some of them to prefer the comforts of home to the barracks life at Dormans, where the battalion was quartered. By the end of January 1792 it was necessary for Lieutenant Colonel Davout to write the administrators of the Department of Yonne asking that they take the necessary steps to round up deserters and send them back to the battalion.[6]

Shortly before the battalion was ordered east from Dormans at the outbreak of hostilities, Davout became involved in a domestic affair and was largely responsible for saving the lives of seven men—among them the former Bishop of Mende, M. de Castellane. Accusations had been brought against M. de Castellane by the Legislative Assembly, and he was attempting to flee into exile when the townspeople of Dormans became aware of his presence. A crowd quickly gathered before the inn in which he was spending the night with his six companions. As the crowd became a mob, cries went up of "to the lamp post." At this point Davout moved in with soldiers and informed the people that before they could assassinate those in the inn they would have to begin by assassinating the troops. Tempers had risen to a high pitch, and it was only at the end of three hours of turmoil that tranquility was restored and de Castellane was safely escorted from the inn. Placing the ex-bishop under arrest Davout escorted him to jail for safekeeping through the night. The next morning he sent him to Orléans to stand trial; but, whether with Davout's knowledge or without it, he never arrived at his destination. Reaching Lyon shortly after leaving Dormans, he made good his escape across the frontier.[7]

The 3rd Battalion of Yonne received orders on April 21, the day after war was declared, to break camp and march to Verdun where it would join the army commanded by General Lafayette. However, before reaching its destination these orders were countermanded; and the battalion was instructed to proceed to Sedan, where it went into quarters—still as part of Lafayette's army. Then in mid-July Davout and his battalion of volunteers went into the entrenched camp at Maulde. Here it was that he received the news of the attack on the Tuileries and the fall of the monarchy. The establishment of the Republic on September 22 was welcome news for the young aristocrat. Having supported the revolutionary ideas from the beginning, he showed no sympathy for the royal cause during the period of the Constitutional Monarchy. He had been forced out of the King's army after being imprisoned by the King's minister. It was the Legislative Assembly which had given him a new start in the "people's army" of volunteers. Thus he rallied to the new government and inspired his troops with republican aspirations.

The first casualties of the Yonne battalion were reported to the departmental administrators by Lieutenant Colonel Davout in a letter dated August 16, 1792.[8] A detachment of some four hundred men, which included twenty-two men from Davout's battalion, had been surprised while en route to relieve an outpost. In the fighting which took place as the French fell back they lost ten men. Two of them were from the 3rd Yonne: a captain, believed to have been captured; and a drummer who was killed. In this letter Davout also expressed concern about replacements. "Of all the recruits whom you have announced, we have received only fifty-one of them, and, in order to bring the battalion up to full strength, two hundred and thirty more are needed; we have all that is necessary to equip them."[9]

In mid-August Davout's battalion was ordered to Condé. On his arrival he learned that his commander, General Lafayette, had fled France and asked for asylum in the enemy camp.[10] This was somewhat of a shock to the young lieutenant colonel, who was himself filled with patriotic zeal and had believed Lafayette a strong supporter of the Revolution.

Davout now came under the direct orders of General O'Moran, while General Dumouriez was placed in command of the Army of the North. O'Moran gave the 3rd Battalion of Yonne the assignment of maintaining communications between Condé and Valenciennes. In a letter to the administrators of Yonne Davout wrote of a major engagement which took place on the afternoon of September 1. In it he told of his volunteers driving off an enemy corps of some six thousand men. He spoke of the enemy leaving four hundred dead on the field but said nothing of his own losses.[11]

The major enemy invasion, launched in the late summer of 1792, came southeast of Condé. A Prussian army under the command of the Duke of Brunswick crossed the Rhine at Coblenz, entered French territory at Longwy, and attacked Verdun in the last week of August. This stronghold, one of the keys of the French chain of defenses, surrendered on September 1 after only a token resistance. Brunswick had not intended to march on Paris. His army of forty-two thousand Prussians was deemed too small for such an ambitious undertaking, and he could expect little support from the Austrian forces on his flanks. Nevertheless, he found himself at Verdun with no more than an undisciplined mass of *Fédérés* at Châlons between himself and the French capital. Hence, after some delay, he advanced westward into the Argonne forest. Here it was that General François Etienne Christophe Kellermann supported by Dumouriez halted his advance in the Battle of Valmy on September 20.

Davout did not take part in the Argonne campaign; he remained at Condé. Kellermann escorted the Duke of Brunswick across the frontier, and French soil was again free of foreign troops. This evacuation on the part of the Prussians freed the Army of the North to invade the Austrian Netherlands. General O'Moran advanced into Belgium against some of the stiffest enemy resistance. Just to the north of Condé the Austrians vigorously defended the hermitage of Peruwelz. During this heavy fighting Davout distinguished himself by personally leading his volunteers in an assault which captured the fortified position on October 24, 1792.

The 3rd Battalion of Yonne formed part of the left flank of the army advancing into Belgium. On its right was the main body of troops, directly under Dumouriez, which fought the victorious Battle of Jemappes on November 6. This battle opened the way for the occupation of all the territory on the left bank of the Rhine. That Dumouriez did not push the Austrians east of the Rhine, and instead held up along the left bank of the Meuse, has been considered a strategical error. Davout did not take part in the Battle of Jemappes. His battalion advanced on Brussels where it took part in the siege of that city. When Brussels fell some five hundred to six hundred French prisoners of war were freed. Among those released were members of the 3rd Yonne.[12] The battalion concluded the campaign at the siege of Antwerp.

The greater part of Belgium was now occupied. Dumouriez put his army in winter quarters and went himself to Paris, where the trial of the King was in progress. The General was in sympathy with the more moderate Girondins and while in the capital worked for the acquittal of Louis XVI. Though he was unsuccessful in this endeavor since Louis was executed on January 21, 1793, he was able to achieve his other goals. The Convention declared war on England and Holland on February 1, 1793, and authorized Dumouriez to invade the Netherlands. The trial of the King had made clear to the world the direction in which the Revolution was moving. The declaration of war on England was merely in anticipation of Parliament's declaring war on France. On March 7 France also declared war against Spain; and in rapid succession the Holy Roman Empire, the Pope, Naples, and Portugal fell in line with the First Coalition. Only the Scandinavian kingdoms, Switzerland and Russia, remained neutral. To cope with the pending danger of invasion from all sides the Convention decreed the levy of three hundred thousand men on February 24, 1793. "All French citizens between the ages of eighteen and forty inclusive," the law read, "not married, or widowers without children, are on call until the quota . . . has been filled." [13] The first meaningful universal draft of modern times was thus introduced, and the foundation for the concept of total war was laid down.

Dumouriez crossed the Dutch frontier with a mere sixteen thousand men (later reinforced by five thousand),[14] but the force was quite insufficient to obtain any serious objective. The Allies launched an offensive at the same time aimed at the reconquest of Belgium. With his rear threatened by this counterattack, Dumouriez rushed south leaving the so-called Army of Holland on Dutch soil. About midway between Brussels and Liège the French commander decided to give battle. On the eighteenth of March he attacked the Prince of Coburg, who had taken up a defensive position near the village of Neerwinden. Davout and his volunteers handled themselves with distinction as the center of the line successfully advanced. The right also scored early gains; but the French left broke, and the battle was lost. Along with the battle all of Belgium was also lost, and the French army fell back on the line of fortified towns designed to protect the country from invasion.

The defeat at Neerwinden brought Dumouriez's military career to a rather abrupt end. Following the battle he opened negotiations with the enemy for the first time. The Austrians allowed him to withdraw his army from Belgium—and Holland—unmolested. Fearing the growing power of the Jacobins and disgusted by their treatment of the Belgians, he came to the decision that the only way the war could be successfully carried on and France restored to some form of normality would be for him to march on Paris with his troops and restore the constitutional monarchy of 1791. He made his plans known to the Austrians, who promised not to attack while the coup was being carried out. At the same time the Convention had lost all confidence in the commander of the North and sent four commissioners and the Minister of War, Pierre Beurnouville, to place Dumouriez under arrest and bring him to Paris for trial. But Dumouriez, surrounded by loyal troops, was able himself to arrest the commissioners and Minister and to turn them over to the enemy.[15] However, he misjudged the sentiment of the rank and file of his army, which refused to turn against the government. The decisive moment came when Lieutenant Colonel Davout ordered his volunteers to fire on their treasonous commander.

Davout had fallen back on the fortified camp at Louvain following the defeat at Neerwinden. As the entire army withdrew from Belgium, the 3rd Yonne moved south across the frontier into the camp at Condé. There was much confusion in the army and both officers and men spoke loudly of treason. As Dumouriez's plans for marching on Paris became known throughout the army a group of commanders of volunteer battalions met to discuss what course of action they should follow. There was much indecision stemming from a conflict of personal interest and patriotic duty. Then with the arrival of a new delegation of deputies from the Convention at the front, who issued a warrant for Dumouriez's arrest and encouraged the volunteer commanders to support the government, Davout became determined to act. He set out for Saint-Amand, the general headquarters of the army, with volunteers from his battalion on the morning of April 4. On the road from Condé to Saint-Amand, Davout met Dumouriez, who was returning from a meeting with the Austrian commander. Dumouriez first tried to win over the Lieutenant Colonel and his men. Then realizing that this was impossible and that his plans were being thwarted, he fled toward the enemy's camp under a hail of bullets. Twice during the chase that ensued Davout nearly captured Dumouriez. The General's horse refused to jump a ditch at one point, and he only escaped capture by jumping on to the horse of the Duke of Chartres and riding double. Again at the river Escaut the fugitives barely made good their escape by leaving behind Dumouriez's secretary. Davout returned to Condé with the General's horse and his secretary as proof of the effort which had been made. The plot had been broken up even if its chief architect had escaped; the grateful government was not long in showing its gratitude to the commander of the volunteer battalion who had delivered the *coup de grâce.*[16]

Dumouriez's treason and desertion had a profound effect on the army and its relationship with the government in Paris—to say nothing of the course of the Revolution itself. The General's close ties with the Girondins enabled the Jacobins to accuse their political opponents of treason by association. This was one of the final strokes which brought about the fall of the moderate republican faction in the Convention. Of an almost equal importance was the effect upon the army. The defection of the royalist officers from the army during the early years of the Revolution was understandable if not expected. Even the desertion of an officer like Lafayette did not have major repercussions, as he was known to have supported the King and the constitutional monarchy. But Dumouriez was considered a patriot, a republican, a supporter of the Convention, and an advocate of the revolutionary war. His defection was a blow to many members of the government and the army. If Dumouriez could turn against the Convention, then whom could the deputies trust? Was not every commanding general a suspect? Could any military man be trusted? The answers to these questions were to be found by the Jacobin-controlled government who sent an endless number of representatives of the people to the front. These civilians, deputies of the Convention, were to have absolute power. They could, and often did, interfere in the strategy of campaigns and tactics of battles. They had the power to, and often did, arrest generals, who were sent to Paris for trial—with the usual result of being condemned to death. Not until the victorious General Bonaparte's Italian Campaign in 1796–97 was a commander able to act with any substantial independence.

Order in the Army of the North was only gradually restored. General Dampierre, who had resisted Dumouriez's attempts to win his support, was named the new commander. He immediately reorganized the forces under his command. On May 1, 1793, in gratitude for actions of April 4, Davout was promoted to the rank of colonel and given command of a demi-brigade. His demi-brigade was composed of the 2nd Battalion of the 104th Infantry Regiment, the 3rd Battalion of Volunteers of Aube, and his own 3rd Battalion of Yonne. Davout now came under the direct orders of General Charles Joseph Kilmaine and took an active part in the fighting in the Saint-Amand forest and the defense of the camp at Famars. As the French were forced back Davout's troops formed the rear guard and in constant contact with the enemy they suffered between thirty and forty casualties daily. Then in early July Davout was abruptly transferred to the Army of the West.

As early as 1791 there were signs of dissatisfaction in the west-central portion of the country. The proclamation of the Republic and the trial and execution of the King coupled with the religious settlement drove the western departments—particularly the Vendée—into open rebellion against the Paris government. By the winter of 1793–94 not only had the Vendée revolted, but Lyon, Bordeaux, Marseille, and numerous other sections of southern and western France refused to recognize the republican government in Paris. During the course of 1793–94 the Jacobin government was able to reestablish its control over the greater part of the nation, but the Vendée remained a problem throughout the Directory.

Davout was not a Jacobin—nor was he in sympathy with the Jacobin leaders. This is best illustrated in a scene which took place toward the end of April 1793. He was with General Auguste Henri Marie Dampierre at the latter's headquarters when two agents, who were actually spies of the Minister of War, paid the General a visit. In the course of the conversation Davout and the General's aide-de-camp, who was also present, expressed their dislike for Marat, Danton, and Robespierre, while at the same time they praised the Girondins, Pétion, Brissot, and Guadet, who were being attacked by those extreme factions of the left which included the War Minister. "At dinner one of the agents, to draw the officers on, said Paris no doubt would not be quiet for long, as the Convention had sent Marat before the *Tribunal révolutionnaire*. Falling into the snare, Davout and the staff officers replied that Marat well deserved the fate that they thought awaited him. The agent professed his surprise at the conduct of Davout. Was he not the man who had been driven from his regiment and imprisoned in the citadel of Arras? It was he who in 1790 had taken the side of the patriot soldiers, who had given the example of a *pacte fédératif* between the citizens and the soldiers of the line. The agent went on to express his astonishment at seeing him so prejudiced against Marat, Robespierre, and the Jacobins. Was it not Robespierre and Marat who had defended him when he had been the victim of arbitrary power? Davout replied, 'I am not prejudiced against those who were my defenders in 1790. Then I refused to serve the plans of a King who was my benefactor. Now, for the same reason, I refuse to serve the Jacobins and to support their plans, which seem disastrous to me.'"[17] This affair resulted in Davout's being denounced by the agents to the Minister of War.

It was most likely his close friendship with General Dampierre coupled with the energetic actions he took against Dumouriez that saved him at this time. Nevertheless, it would also seem that his transfer from the northern front to the Vendée was not by chance; it was because there were those in the government who had their doubts about this son of a Burgundian nobleman. Though he was now a suspect from the Jacobins' point of view, he still had influential friends. These supporters secured for him, on July 3, 1793, a promotion to the rank of general of brigade.

Davout joined the corps of General La Baroliere in the vicinity of la Rochelle immediately after receiving his promotion and took part in the Battle of Vihiers (July 18). In this general engagement Davout commanded a small detachment of cavalry, which formed a protective shield for the government's troops when they fled from the battlefield before the Vendeans. The lack of discipline on the part of officers and men alike must surely have had an effect on Davout. In his brief stay with this motley mass of men referred to rather loosely as an army, he witnessed what should have been a victory turned into a complete rout because of the absence of discipline.[18]

After Vihiers Davout was ordered to Niort, and then to escort a detachment to reinforce General Tuncq at Sables-d'Olonne. Upon his arrival at Tuncq's headquarters he received a dispatch from Paris dated July 30 which announced his promotion to general of division and ordered him back to the Army of the North. Returning to Paris for his specific orders, Davout was informed that he was being given command of the "camp of the Madeleine" at Lille. But rather than accepting the appointment and the promotion Davout astonished the Minister of War by refusing both. He pleaded that he was too young (twenty-three years old) and lacked the experience required for the assignment. This action was both dangerous and wise. Dangerous because it increased the suspicion of the government, but wise because a mishap in such a position, even if through no fault of his own, could have led to the scaffold.

Once again it became impossible for him to remain in the army. The Jacobins were rapidly gaining complete control of the government and through it the army. Realizing that he would soon be forced out of the service, Davout submitted his resignation on August 29, 1793, and prepared to retire to his mother's home at Ravières. While he was still settling his affairs in Paris, the Convention passed into law an ordinance forbidding any nobleman to reside or even travel within twenty leagues of Paris, the army, or the frontier. Davout, therefore, sought permission from the Minister of War, Bouchotte, to return to Ravières and make his residence with his mother. This permission was granted as the result of intercession on the part of Davout's good friend General Pille, with whom he had served while attached to the Army of the North.[19] Once again the young general found himself in forced retirement; and once again, not despairing of a return to his military career, he put his time to good use by reading military history and engaging in civic activities. The rest he had hoped to get at Ravières, however, was soon interrupted.

Shortly after his return home there came a knock on the door and a local administrator, accompanied by two police officers, served

Madame Davout with an arrest warrant.[20] She was immediately taken into custody to be transported to Auxerre, the departmental seat of government. As a special favor to Davout he was allowed to accompany his mother on the journey. The distance being too great to be covered in one day, it was necessary to spend the night at Tonnerre, twenty-two miles due east of their destination. Neither Davout nor his mother had been informed of the reason for her arrest at the time it had been made. At Tonnerre his mother was required to spend the night in the local jail; but Davout was able to make sufficient inquiry to ascertain the charges which would be brought against her at her trial. What he found was that his mother had been denounced as being in correspondence with *émigrés.* If this charge could be proven Madame Davout would certainly have been condemned to death.

The accusation stemmed from a transaction between Madame Davout and friends of hers, the La Rochefoucaulds. When the La Rochefoucaulds emigrated before the Terror had begun, Madame Davout, as a favor to them, had taken some of their belongings for safekeeping. They had gone through the formality of a sale for purposes of deception, and there had been correspondence relative to the whole affair during the months after the departure of the La Rochefoucaulds. This correspondence, which was in Madame Davout's secretary at Ravières, was all the evidence needed by the prosecutor to send her to her death. Thus it became imperative that these letters be destroyed before they could fall into the hands of the authorities—who would soon search the house.

Davout had taken a room at an inn in Tonnerre for the night. When all had quieted down he slipped out a back door and made his way back to Ravières on foot. Scaling the garden wall he awakened his sister and gained entrance to the chateau without being noticed by the household servants. Going directly to his mother's quarters he found the damaging evidence in a secret hiding place behind her secretary and burned it. He then returned to the inn before dawn so that his actions were completely unnoticed in Tonnerre.[21]

The next morning he accompanied his mother on to Auxerre, where, a few days later she appeared before the Revolutionary Tribunal. But much to the astonishment of the prosecutor he was not provided with sufficient evidence against the accused. Thus no formal charges were brought, and Madame Davout was set free at once. This would seem to have been the happy ending for this nightmare of a melodrama, but despite the lack of evidence she still remained a suspect; and in April 1794, at the height of the Terror, she was again arrested and imprisoned. This time Davout himself was to share his mother's fate, and they both remained three months in prison. Only the fall of the Jacobins from power on the ninth of Thermidor brought their captivity to an end, and they once again returned to Ravières.

His expulsion from the army, his mother's narrow escape from the guillotine, his own three months in prison, and the general conditions in France and in the army caused Davout to become a bitter opponent of Jacobinism and to have grave doubt about the merits of Republicanism. Jacobinism, in his eyes, became synonymous with the Terror, with corruption in government, and with mismanagement of military affairs. He had little understanding and even less sympathy with the problems facing the central government; he saw only its faults and its errors. Before the Revolution the young nobleman had supported the King, to whom he owed his education. During the early years of the Revolution he had become a republican, accepting the basic principles of liberty and equality. However, the unhappy experiences of 1793–94 turned him against Jacobinism and, as in the case of so many other Frenchmen, enkindled a deep desire for order without fear and oppression. When General Bonaparte seemed to offer such a government, Davout welcomed it with enthusiasm and became one of the strongest supporters of the imperial dictatorship.

3

The Republican General

THE THERMIDORIAN REACTION began at the end of July 1794. Robespierre, Saint-Just, and Couthon went to the guillotine July 28, and the so-called Thermidorians picked up the reins of government. Gradually the Jacobins and their supporters lost power and influence, while those whom they had persecuted were reinstated in good grace with the government.[1] The Davouts were not restored at once to favor after the fall of the Jacobins. They were still members of the old nobility, and, even if to a lesser extent, still subject to suspicion. It was only with some difficulty that Davout was restored to his rank and given employment with the Army of the Moselle.

Davout's recall was largely the work of two of his good friends. Though Louis Turreau was no longer living with Madame Davout, he had remained on good terms with her son. It is impossible to ascertain what influence, if any, he may have had in preventing the Davouts from being executed during the last months of the Terror. He had been a Jacobin in the Convention, though with limited influence. The Thermidorians sent him as a commissioner to the Army of Italy, which was a form of exile. Nevertheless, Turreau still had friends in Paris. Before leaving the capital he interceded on Davout's behalf by recommending to Carnot, who still directed the French armies, that he be placed on active duty.[2] Davout's other champion was General Louis-Antoine Pille, who was now Commissioner of the movements of the Land Army (commissaire des movements de l'armee de terre) at the Ministry of War. Davout wrote to him on October 2 imploring his intervention.[3]

Davout had received word, though not through official channels, that he was to be restored to the rank of general of brigade and given employment with the Army of the West, stationed at Brest. There was no serious action in the west at this time, and what fighting there might be would consist of putting down rebel uprisings. As he wished to serve on the frontier he again sought the aid of Pille. On October 13, Pille placed before the *Comité de Salute Public* a report[4] recommending that General Davout be sent to the Army of the Moselle rather than the Army of the West. The explanation for the request, as Davout himself put it, was that he was best suited to command cavalry and there was little with the army at Brest. Furthermore, the Army of the Moselle was in need of two generals of brigade. Thus Davout was assigned to the "Moselle." Auxious to rejoin the army, he set out at once for the north. The Army of the Moselle was commanded by General Jean René Moreaux in the fall of 1794. Part of his forces was besieging the city of Luxembourg while the main portion pushed on to the Rhine.

The military situation had changed drastically in the north during Davout's absence. On June 26, 1794, General Jean Baptiste Jourdan had won the Battle of Fleurus and opened the way for the reconquest of northern and western Belgium. In September his Army of the Sambre and Meuse crossed the Meuse and captured Aix-la-Chapelle on the twenty-second; and following the Battle of the Roer, October 2, it pushed on to the Rhine. This feat accomplished, the armies of the Moselle and the Rhine became active. The Army of the Moselle pushed north to Treves and then down both banks of the river arriving at Coblenz by October 23. In this push General Moreaux had left behind one division at Luxembourg to besiege that city in which the Austrians had left a strong, well-supplied garrison.

The winter of 1794–95 was spent by the French besieging cities on the left bank of the Rhine. The most important of these were Mayence, Mannheim (that is, the bridgehead which was on the left of the Rhine—the city itself being on the right bank), and Luxembourg. The siege of Luxembourg was already in progress when Davout joined the army. He was given command of a brigade in the division of General Debrun, and almost at once he began to make his arrival felt.

On the night of November 24, Davout led a daring raid into the enemy-held territory known as Grünwald. Three storehouses of badly needed supplies were burned because they could not be carried away under the heavy enemy fire.[5] It was unfortunate that the French could not save the supplies as they could have made good use of them. The winter was extremely cold and the besieging troops suffered intensely. Food, munitions, clothing, and housing were all lacking in sufficient quantity. Nevertheless, the siege went on. The death of General Moreaux of fever, and his replacement by General Ambert had no effect on the operation.

By the end of the winter the Austrian forces, under Marshal Blaise Colomban Bender, were running short of food. To hasten their capitulation Davout suggested to Ambert that an attack be made on the last mill which remained in the hands of the enemy. With the commanding general's approval, Davout made preparations to destroy the mill of Eich, which was situated in the lower part of the city. Hearing of a recent deserter from Bender's defending garrison who was being held at Thionville, Davout sought for and received permission to use the man as a guide in return for his freedom. The prisoner, Joseph Gund, accepted the offer, and on the night of March 4, 1795, Davout led a raiding party through the enemy's lines. It was a bold undertaking, and at one time Davout was actually in the hands of the Austrian defenders. Nevertheless, the mill was burned and the small party of Frenchmen returned having suffered only two casualties.[6] Then on the nineteenth of the same month the Austrian garrison made a sortie in force. Marshal Bender threw virtually the entire garrison against the section of the besieging line held by Debrun's division. Once again Davout was in the thick of the battle and was highly praised for his conduct by his commanding general. Unfortunately, he did not see the city surrender on June 7, 1795. For the day after the great sortie General Ambert and the divisions under his command, which formed part of the Army of the Moselle, marched off to the Rhine to take part in the siege of Mayence, leaving others[7] to finish the task they had started at Luxembourg.

The besieging forces at Mayence formed the nucleus of the newly created Army of the Rhine and Moselle. It was also responsible for the Rhine south to the Swiss frontier and north to Coblenz where it was flanked by the Army of the Sambre and Meuse. Davout most likely spent very little time before Mayence, if indeed he took part in the siege at all. On the eighteenth of May he was at Speyer, some fifteen miles south of Mannheim on the Rhine. From this city he wrote a lengthy letter to his good friend Bourbotte, a representative in the Convention, in which he expressed the hope that peace would soon be made.[8] There was good reason for optimism. The Prussians had signed a peace treaty at Bâle on April 5, 1795, and the Spanish had quickly followed their example along with some of the lesser German principalities. Thus there remained in the field only the armies of Austria which received virtually no support from the lesser states of the Holy Roman Empire. England, to be sure, was also still at war with the Republic, but she gave little aid in the form of troops committed to the Continent.

At the beginning of July, Davout was still at Speyer and war continued. Writing to General Marceau he now pessimistically looked forward to another winter of combat.[9] He had first met Marceau while in the Vendée during the summer of 1793. They had become very good friends and plans had been made for Marceau to go home with Davout to Ravières where preliminary arrangements were being made for the general to marry Davout's sister Julie. The continuation of the war now upset these plans, and the affair was soon dropped. Julie was never officially engaged to Marceau. In 1801, six years later, she married General Beaumont.[10]

Command of the Army of the Rhine and Moselle had passed into the hands of General Jean Charles Pichegru in April 1795. He had gained something of a reputation in Holland where he had driven out a British army during 1794–95, and had, more recently, saved the Thermidorians from an attempted *coup* by the Jacobins on *12ᵉ Germinal* (April 1) 1795. Though in command of the newly formed army, he allowed a great amount of freedom to his divisional commanders. He spent the summer of 1795 near Strasbourg and seldom even visited his army, which was mainly besieging Mayence and Mannheim. The new commander possessed little real military talent, as became evident in the campaign of 1795. Furthermore, his personal habits had been deteriorating steadily since 1793. By the summer of 1795 he had "abandoned himself to disgraceful debauches." [11] But while his personal weaknesses and lack of ability could have been forgiven him, that which could not be forgiven was the treasonable act against his country and his comrades in arms. As early as August 1795 he began to negotiate secretly with the enemy.[12]

Toward the end of the summer Davout moved south to join in the siege of Mannheim as part of the division of General Dufour.[13] He was thus before the city when it capitulated on September 20, 1795. But even as the siege was being brought to a successful conclusion, the campaign of 1795 was opening on the lower Rhine. On September 5 the Army of Sambre and Meuse, still commanded by Jourdan, but strongly seconded by General Jean-Baptiste Kléber, crossed the Rhine and captured Düsseldorf. From this bridgehead Jourdan pushed the Austrian forces up along the right bank of the river. The master strategy of the campaign now called for the Army of the Rhine and Moselle to cross the river in force and support Jourdan. To this end Pichegru launched an attack on Heidelberg, which was one of the main bases of supply for the Austrian army. However, he himself did not take command of the divisions on the Neckar but rather appointed General Ambert while he remained on the left bank of the Rhine. Then instead of sending one strong force up the left bank of the Neckar so as to make a direct attack upon the town, Pichegru divided his force and sent General Dufour's division up the right bank and Ambert's division, in which Davout commanded the forward brigade, up the left.[14] The whole affair turned into a fiasco. On September 24 Ambert lost contact with Davout who advanced more rapidly than had been expected. Then the Austrians fell on Dufour's force at Quasdanowich and defeated it. Dufour fell back in confusion and was only saved when Ambert stopped his own advance to aid him in recrossing the river. This left Davout, who had engaged the enemy at Wieblingen, without support and without artillery. Seeing his dangerous position, the Austrians attacked and forced him to fight a retreating action. The two French divisions were forced to seek safety under the guns of Mannheim. The complete failure of Pichegru's movement against the right flank and rear of the Austrian army enabled General François Sebastien Charles Joseph Clairfayt, its commander, to launch a full-scale attack against Jourdan. Unsupported, Jourdan was forced back into the fortified camp he had prepared at Düsseldorf. As it was now obvious that the campaign had failed, the French army, leaving a strongly garrisoned bridgehead on the east bank of the Rhine, withdrew to its former position.

Early in October 1795 command of the troops at Mannheim was given to General Louis Charles Antoine Desaix, who had previously been on the Upper Rhine. Then on the sixteenth Ambert became ill and was replaced by General Nicolas Charles Oudinot, who had just joined the 6th Division. Although Oudinot's promotion to general of brigade was dated June 14, 1794, he was still considered a senior general over Davout because the latter (promoted to general of brigade in July of 1793) could only claim seniority from September 24, 1794, when he was recalled to the army. Despite this technicality, which could have generated jealousy, Davout and Oudinot became, and remained throughout the Empire, good friends. The command which Oudinot assumed was not destined to be a happy one. While Clairfayt was attacking Jourdan in the north, he left General Dogobert Siegmund Würmser to check any possible threat that might arise from Pichegru in his rear. However, the energetic Würmser could not be content with a negative role, and on October 18 he attacked Oudinot's forces before Mannheim. Though Pichegru had substantial strength available under Desaix (two divisions, some 12,979 men) [15] he chose not to use it. Desaix's forces merely prevented a complete disaster. Left on his own, Oudinot followed the only course of action open to him. After a stubborn battle, in which Oudinot himself was wounded and taken prisoner,[16] his troops fell back to Mannheim. Davout had held firm in the center of the line before Mannheim but was eventually forced back into the city under cover of a screen provided by twelve squadrons of cavalry led personally by Desaix.[17] Würmser immediately laid siege to Mannheim. Not content to wait for further developments, the Austrian general opened trenches on November 11 and bombarded the city with siege artillery. The garrison was commanded by General Ann Charles Basset de Montaigu. There had been no real preparations for a siege, and both food and military supplies were scarce. Thus on November 21, Montaigu surrendered the city and its garrison to the Austrians.

Davout became a prisoner of war for the first and only time in his long military career. Nevertheless, he was much more fortunate than the majority of his brother officers. General Würmser had been a friend of his uncle Major Jacques-Edme d'Avout, when the Austrian General had been serving in France before the Revolution. In remembrance of this friendship Würmser permitted Davout to return to France on his word of honor that he would no longer take part in the war. Thus for the third time in five years Davout found himself with forced leisure. As in the past he did not waste the months he now spent at Ravières.

Davout had exhausted the modest family library during the long months he had spent at home on two previous occasions. He was now fortunate enough to obtain permission to use the library of Madame de Louvois. This library at the chateau of Ancy-le-Franc was one of the finest in Burgundy. During the first eight months of 1796 Davout read extensively in ancient history, familiarizing himself with the military strategy and tactics of the Greeks and Romans. It was not until October, 1796, that he was allowed to rejoin the Army of the Rhine and Moselle at Kehl as a result of an exchange of officers.

During Davout's absence from the army conditions had changed both on the Rhine and in Paris. The Directory had been established in October 1795, shortly before the surrender of Mannheim. This led to the end of the Convention and the Committee of Public Safety. In their place were created the Chamber of Five Hundred and the Chamber of Ancients, with an executive made up of five directors.[18] France was tired of the war and exhausted from the supreme sacrifice which had been required. The new government offered to the people the hope of a return to normality—whatever that might be—after the six years of upheaval. To accomplish this end it was necessary to bring the war to an honorable conclusion, which hopefully meant the attainment of France's "natural frontier"—the Rhine. The annexation of Prussian territory on the left bank of the Rhine could be compensated for by giving the Prussians lands on the right bank of the river. This would serve two purposes: it would satisfy the Hohenzollerns; and it would offend Austria, whose Emperor considered himself the protector of the lesser German states and wished to control them. Furthermore, Belgium had been Austrian territory, and it was this nation which stood to lose the most if France was to be allowed to keep the left bank of the Rhine. It might also be pointed out that England too objected to the annexation of Belgium—in particular the excellent port of Antwerp from which they feared an invasion of the island kingdom could best be launched. Thus the main obstacle to peace from the Directory's point of view was Austria supported by England. Austria would have to be defeated on the battlefield before she would accept peace on the basis of the "natural frontiers."

3 / The Republican General

The strategy for the campaign of 1796, which was designed to end the war, was a two-pronged drive on Vienna. The main French force was to strike across the Rhine and down the Danube valley. The Army of Italy, under the command of General Bonaparte, was to strike across the Lombard plains and advance on the Austrian capital from the southwest. Both operations got off to a good start. The Army of the Sambre and Meuse, still under the command of Jourdan, drove through Frankfort, Bamberg, and Amberg to the river Naab on the Bohemian frontier. To the south the Army of the Rhine and Moselle, under Moreau, struck through Stuttgart and Augsburg reaching a point east of Ingolstadt. But at these points their advances were checked. The Archduke Charles fell on Jourdan with the main Austrian force and drove him back. The retreat was not halted until the French army was safely behind the Rhine. This exposed the left flank of Moreau's force and actually threatened to cut the army off from its bases on the Rhine. Moreau had no alternative but to withdraw up the Danube through the Black Forest to Freiburg and back across the Rhine. Bonaparte, on the other hand, was much more successful in Italy. He had advanced to the Po and moved down that river to lay siege to Mantua.

Davout did not rejoin the Army of the Rhine and Moselle until after the campaign of 1796 had been concluded.[19] In November 1796 he was at Kehl, one of two footholds the Army of the Rhine and Moselle held on the right bank of the Rhine. Moreau had given command of the defenses of Kehl to General Desaix, who had three divisions under Ambert, Duhesme and Sainte-Suxanne. Davout was given command of the 3rd, 10th, and 31st Infantry Demi-brigades. This appointment apparently was not made until after the major sortie of the garrison on November 22. There is no mention of Davout in the reports of this frustrating failure. Then on December 9, General Beuronville, who had recently taken command of the Army of the Sambre and Meuse, concluded an armistice with the Austrians. This enabled the Archduke Charles to send some thirteen battalions from the lower Rhine to take part in the siege of Kehl. By January 9, 1797, the network of trenches opened by the Austrians reached dangerously close to the French positions; and it became evident that a strong attack could not be beaten off if enthusiastically pressed. On that day Moreau authorized Desaix to negotiate a capitulation and to withdraw his forces to the left bank of the Rhine. Thus on January tenth the French evacuated Kehl with the honors of war and all of their baggage. The Austrians entered the city the same night.

As the winter drew on, the armies along the Rhine began to make preparations for a spring campaign which, in coordination with the movements of the Army of Italy, were to bring the war to a successful conclusion. The strategy for 1797 differed little from that of the preceding year. The two armies on the Rhine would advance to the Danube and then down the river to Vienna where they would be joined by the Army of Italy which would have come up from the south. There was, of course, a basic problem which existed throughout the Revolutionary wars—a lack of unity of command on the Rhine. Paris mapped out the master strategy which included the movements of all the armies, and in Italy there was no problem, for General Bonaparte was in full command of all troops. On the Rhine, however, it was a different story; there were two commanders—neither being capable of imposing his will upon the other. The obvious result was a virtual disregard for one another. This may be seen in the armistice that had been signed by the commander of the Army of the Sambre and Meuse without consulting the commander of the Rhine and Moselle—an action which led to the loss of the latter's footholds on the right bank of the Rhine (Kehl and Huningue).[20] Had Beurnonville continued to be a threat on the lower Rhine, the Archduke could not have sent support to the siege of Kehl. Without the added support in the enemy camp the Army of the Rhine and Moselle could have held a footing from which to launch its spring offensive. As it was, Moreau would have to cross the river in the face of strong enemy opposition.

The first push on Vienna came not from the Rhine, where the major French forces were mustered, but from Italy. The defeat of the Austrian army and the surrender of Mantua opened the way for Bonaparte. By the second week of March he was moving in force eastward out of the Po valley into southwestern Austria. This action was meant to take place simultaneously with the offensive in Germany; however on the Rhine there were delays, and it was not until the thirteenth of April that General Hoche, the new commander of the Sambre and Meuse, denounced the armistice. The Archduke Charles had been transfererd to Italy in February, too late to make any difference there, and was succeeded by General Latour as commander of the Austrian armies in Germany. When the French attack came, Latour fell back before the superior forces of the Sambre and Meuse. Hoche's advance guard, under the command of the dashing General Michel Ney, crossed the Lahn at Giessen and led the attack.

Further up the Rhine, Desaix, in temporary command of the Army of the Rhine and Moselle, planned his crossing at Diersheim, ten miles north of Strasbourg. Although Moreau returned from Paris the day before the crossing took place, it was Desaix who actually commanded. The river was to be crossed by three columns, one under General Dominique René Vandamme, a second under General Jardy, and the third under Davout.[21] The crossings were made on April 20, two days after General Bonaparte had signed a general armistice with the Austrians at Leoben (April 18). Due primarily to a delay in gathering the necessary boats for the crossings, it was daybreak before the operation could actually begin. Rather than postpone it and lose the element of surprise which had been attained, Moreau and Desaix decided to make the crossings in broad daylight. Difficult as the task was, and despite heavy losses, the French established a foothold. Davout's column attacked the town of Diersheim and drove out the Austrian defenders; but his success was shortlived. Returning in superior numbers the enemy recaptured the town and prepared to hold it. A seesaw battle raged the entire day with the town changing hands seven times. By evening Davout, having been reinforced twice during the battle, was in possession of Diersheim and the Austrians had been thrown back in disorder. The bridgehead established, the main forces of the Rhine and Moselle poured over the river, and attacked the enemy along the entire perimeter. Davout led the offensive on the right, Vandamme moved up the Kinzig through Offenburg to Gengenbach, while the left, under General Claude Joseph Lecourbe, pushed to the river Rench.

Moreau's forces were ready to strike in force when the campaign was abruptly halted. On April 23 the Austrian commander sent a messenger to Moreau announcing to him that an armistice had been signed between their two nations at Leoben. Because of their tardiness in opening the campaign in Germany, the two armies on the Rhine were deprived of playing an important role in the conclusion of the peace. The active and energetic Bonaparte was rightly able to claim the victory for himself and the Army of Italy. Had Moreau and Hoche passed the Rhine three weeks earlier, they would have been on the Danube somewhere in Bavaria and could have claimed a major share of the glory.

4

The Sands of Egypt

THE FRIENDSHIP which had developed between Davout and Louis Desaix was one of the most significant relationships which affected the career of the future Marshal. Not only did Desaix introduce him to General Bonaparte and secure for him a place with the Army of Egypt, but he was also instrumental in Davout's warm reception upon their return to France in 1800. Perhaps even more important, though not so concrete and much more difficult to determine, is the change in Bonaparte's attitude toward Davout. Desaix would write to Bonaparte in glowing terms of the exploits of Davout during the campaign of Upper Egypt, and, there can be little doubt, spoke well of his friend in his conversations with the Commander in Chief. It is impossible to measure such influence, but it certainly existed until Desaix's untimely death on the battlefield of Marengo in June of 1800. This influence must be taken into consideration to understand the good favor in which Davout stood during the early years of the Consulate.

Louis Desaix de Veygoux was born on August 17, 1768, at Saint-Hilaire d'Ayat in Auvergne. Like Davout, he was of noble birth. Also like Davout, he entered one of the newly created military schools—at Effiat—on a scholarship made available to the sons of poor nobles. But unlike Davout, Desaix was probably the worst student in his class. When he had completed the courses of instruction at Effiat at the age of fifteen, he applied for admission to the naval academy. His application was turned down, undoubtedly because of his poor scholastic record, so he entered the Bretagne infantry regiment (*Regiment Bretagne-Infanterie*) as a second lieutenant. At the time the Revolution broke out six years later he was still a lieutenant. Like many of the younger members of the nobility, he saw in the Revolution an opportunity for advancement based on merit rather than social standing, and embraced it. With the outbreak of war in 1792, and the unlimited possibilities for promotion which accompanied it, Desaix rose, in seven months, from a lieutenant to a general of brigade. He distinguished himself while serving with the armies of the Rhine, but he was not content to remain under General Moreau after the armistice of Leoben was signed in April 1797.[1]

During the summer of 1797 Desaix traveled in Italy to study at first hand the victorious campaign which had just put an end to hostilities, but what was even more important in his mind was to meet the victorious General Bonaparte. As he himself put it in a letter to a friend; "I am convinced that Moreau will never accomplish anything great and that we must always play an inferior role under his command; whereas the other one [Bonaparte] is destined to rise to such fame, to acquire so much glory, that some of it will have to reflect on his lieutenants." [2] There is no doubt but that Desaix deliberately sought out, and attached himself to, General Bonaparte. There is also no doubt but that he took Davout with him. Had Desaix lived, he would surely have ranked high among the marshals of the Empire.

Desaix was not an easy man to know. He tended to conceal his thoughts and never took a strong political stand. Having little use for politicians, his relationship with the various governments during the Revolution was stormy. Yet he always seemed to survive. During the early years of the war his noble birth had been a handicap. His brothers and cousins were fighting with the *émigrés* against France, and his mother and sister were in prison. His own military career was almost ended in January 1797 when the government ordered his arrest as a political suspect. Only the bayonets of his own troops prevented the commissioners from carrying out their orders, and he eventually persuaded the Directors of his loyalty.

Desaix not only made the acquaintance of General Bonaparte on his Italian visit, but he also impressed him rather favorably. His fame had preceded him to Italy where Bonaparte was always seeking good divisional commanders. The two men seemed to recognize their mutual need for one another, and a friendship of respect sprang up almost at once. When Bonaparte returned to Paris, he was well received and given command of the Army of England with the task of invading the British Isles. Realizing that without control of the Channel an invasion was out of the question, he dismissed such a plan from his mind. Then in the spring of 1798 he was given command of an army which at first designated the Left Wing of the Army of England, to mislead the enemy. In reality it was the Army of Egypt, or as it was sometimes referred to, the Army of the Orient. The chief author of the Egyptian expedition was the newly appointed Minister of Foreign Affairs, the defrocked Bishop of Autun, Charles-Maurice de Talleyrand. Bonaparte also favored the expedition from the beginning, but it was Talleyrand, supported by "the spokesmen of French commercial interests overseas," who convinced the Directors of its desirability.[3]

Thus it was that General Bonaparte was recruiting officers for an army whose destination was so secret that it was known to few others than the commanding general. Desaix was, quite naturally, one of the first to join the expedition. Then, on March 22, 1798, he brought General Davout to the rue de la Victoire and introduced him for the first time to Napoleon Bonaparte. The commander of the mysterious expedition could hardly have been very impressed with the appearance of the young general, for Davout did not make a good first impression. He was extremely careless about his dress which to some extent might be attributed to the influence of Desaix; the latter being known for his shabby appearance.[4] But the extremely neat Bonaparte was not in a position, nor in a habit, of judging a man by his appearance, particularly if that man was presented by General Desaix. In fact, Bonaparte was somewhat limited in his choice of high-ranking officers. There was first of all the problem of a limited number of experienced officers of the rank of general, and then the question of their willingness to serve under the brash new conqueror of Italy. With respect to this latter limitation it should be noted that many of the generals were Bonaparte's senior both in age and length of service. These drawbacks did not affect Davout. He was in no way Bonaparte's senior and was more than willing to make himself available. There is no evidence that Bonaparte had heard of Davout before 1798—unless, of course, it was from Desaix during his visit the previous year. What reputation he had gained up to that point was limited to the men with whom he had served in the armies on the Rhine. His acceptance by Bonaparte was based exclusively on the recommendation of Desaix, and it would be in Desaix's division that Davout would hold his first command.

Davout was not given a particular command at the outset of the expedition but was assigned to General Headquarters. He went to Marseilles, which was one of several ports where the army was being organized in preparation for its departure. On May 8, 1798, Bonaparte joined the army at Toulon; and on the nineteenth it sailed south—to a destination still unknown to the vast majority of soldiers and sailors aboard the four hundred vessels. The army alone numbered about thirty-two thousand men, most of whom came from the best regiments of the Army of Italy. As Bonaparte moved south from Toulon he was joined by contingents from Marseilles (which carried Davout), Genoa, and Corsica. The men and materials which had been assembled at Civita Vecchia under the command of Desaix did not join the rest of the expedition until it reached Malta.

The English squadron which was sent to investigate the French preparations along the northern Mediterranean coast was commanded by Admiral Horatio Nelson. He had sailed from the Spanish port of Cadiz on May 2 with a small force of three ships of the line, two frigates, and a sloop; a force which was quite inferior to the thirteen ships of the line escorting the French armada. Nelson arrived off Toulon just after the French had departed. He immediately set a southerly course in hopes of overtaking his enemy. But Bonaparte, who was heading first for Malta, sailed down the west coast of Corsica, then turned eastward between Corsica and Sardinia and on south along Sardinia's eastern shore. Nelson, on his part, continued straight south along the opposite side of Sardinia. Thus when a violent storm broke over the western Mediterranean, it struck the English fleet with its full fury, but did relatively little damage to the French who were on the leeward side of the island. Nelson's ships were not only scattered over miles of sea, but several were severely damaged. His flagship, the *Vanguard,* was dismasted and forced to put in to San Pietro for repairs, while his frigates returned to Gibraltar to be refitted. The French thus arrived undetected at their destination off the coast of Malta on June 9. Here they joined the task force from Civita Vecchia which had been waiting three days.

The island of Malta is strategically located between Sicily and North Africa and dominates the central Mediterranean Sea. By the end of the eighteenth century the Knights of Malta, or the Order of the Knights Hospitaler of St. John of Jerusalem as they were officially known, had controlled the island for almost three hundred years.[5] While they continued in theory their perpetual crusade against the Moslems, they were completely unable to cause the Turkish Empire any real harm. Their "perpetual war" had degenerated into little more than perpetual piracy, and the knights lived off the spoils of captured Turkish merchant ships. The defenses of the island [6] had fallen into decay, and the majority of the knights had lost any real desire to defend Malta against overwhelming odds.[7]

The French landed on June 10, and the following day the Grand Master, Baron von Hompesch, sent an emissary to Bonaparte aboard *l'Orient* to ask for a truce. Davout took an active part in the landing and in what little fighting that did occur. Bonaparte set about reorganizing the government at once. He pensioned the knights, strengthened the fortifications, and took on fresh supplies for the second leg of the journey. Then leaving thirty-five hundred French troops under General Charles Henri Vaubois to hold the island against possible English attack, Bonaparte departed on June 18–19 for Egypt. During the few days he spent at Malta, he had recruited some five hundred of the knights' best soldiers; and even some of the knights themselves joined the expedition.

While Bonaparte was sailing to Malta, Nelson repaired his ships and received reinforcements. Eleven ships of the line joined him on June 7, bringing his force to fourteen capital ships in all. The English fighting force was now equal in number and firepower to the French ships of the line and superior to them in the quality and experience of its men—a fact that is born out in every major naval engagement of the revolutionary period. However, Nelson's frigates had not returned from Gibraltar. This left him without the means of properly scouting the Mediterranean as he pursued the enemy. In his efforts to locate and give battle to the French fleet, Nelson passed through the Straits of Messina on June 20. On that same day Bonaparte was informed of the size and intentions of the English and decided to sail somewhat north of the usual course from Malta to Alexandria. Thus it was that Nelson, who guessed correctly the destination of the French, passed to the south of the slower and more cumbersome armada during the foggy night of June 22–23 and arrived off Alexandria first. The English had sighted a few French sails to the north on June 22; but lacking swift frigates for reconnaissance and unwilling to divide his force, Nelson sailed onto the east, leaving the French unmolested at their most vulnerable period of the entire expedition.

Egypt was nominally a part of the Ottoman Empire in 1798. However, all real control of the country had long since slipped out of the hands of Constantinople. The rulers of the Nile were the Mamelukes, who formed a feudal type of nobility. The Mamelukes were not themselves Egyptian, nor for the most part Turks. Bought as slaves in the Caucasus mountain districts, they were Georgians, Armenians, and Circassians. Coming to Egypt between the ages of eight and ten, they were trained as warriors; but they remained slaves until such time as they were given a military command. They then became full-fledged members of the ruling class. There were about ten thousand Mamelukes in Egypt at the time of Bonaparte's arrival. Though they were in control of the country, they gave lip service to Turkish sovereignty and received the Sultan's representative with much ceremony. They further provided him with a palace, but they did not allow him any voice in government. Bonaparte, on his part, recognized the sovereignty of Constantinople and considered the Mamelukes as foreign tyrants who held the Egyptian people in bondage. In this way he could pose as an ally of the Turks and the great liberator of the Egyptian people.

After six weeks aboard ship, the weary and seasick French troops came in sight of Alexandria. Nelson had found the harbor empty and so sailed to the north in hopes of finding his quarry at Crete or along the eastern coast of the Mediterranean. Bonaparte feared that the English might reappear at any time. Therefore, he ordered the army to land immediately on the beaches at Marabout—six miles to the west of Alexandria. Despite bad weather and the coming of night, the French executed the amphibious operation, for which neither sailors nor the soldiers had had any experience or practice, with an amazingly slight loss of life. During the morning of July 2 Bonaparte led his weary army along the sandy beaches to Alexandria. The town was ordered to be taken by assault when it refused to open its gates to the French. As had been the case at Malta, the defenders had no real hope of withstanding the invading force.

However, the French had neither artillery nor cavalry, nor what was even more important, water. A serious effort on the part of the defenders would certainly have prolonged the siege for some days. As it was, the French carried the city in one day with few casualties on either side.

Davout was still attached to general headquarters during the landing and the assault on Alexandria. Having taken part in the fighting he entered the city with the first French troops. Then on July 11 he was given a definite command in Desaix's division.[8] He replaced General Mireur as commander of the cavalry when the latter's body was found south of Alexandria in the desert near Damanhur. Mireur had either been killed by the Arabs or had taken his own life.[9] He had been with Desaix when the division set out from Alexandria at the head of the army on its march to Cairo.

The road led southward from the coast through Damanhur and east to the Rosetta leg of the Nile at Rahmaniya. On the march to Damanhur the troops had suffered severely from the heat and from lack of water. The army had not been issued canteens and the few wells they passed along the way scarcely sufficed to keep the men alive. From Damanhur to the Nile it was only slightly less miserable. The cavalry had no horses and so suffered even more than the infantry because of the additional equipment they carried. Once they reached the Nile at Rahmaniya their greatest enemy—thirst—was conquered and the men began to prepare to meet the Mameluke army. It was here at Rahmaniya, which the army reached on July 11, that Davout took up his new command.

The first encounter with the Mameluke army occurred just south of Rahmaniya at Shubra Khit on July 13. The proud and arrogant Murad Bey had led a force of four thousand horsemen and between two and three thousand foot soldiers north from Cairo to meet the invaders. Bonaparte was aware of their presence, and on the night of July 12 he marched his entire army up the Nile until, by the first glimmers of morning, it came within sight of Shubra Khit. He then formed his four divisions into squares reminiscent of the Swiss tactics of the fifteenth century. Each side of a square was six ranks deep. In the center of the squares the baggage and what little cavalry there was sought protection from the superior numbers of the enemy horsemen. Bonaparte placed his artillery at the corners of each square. These preparations completed, the troops were given a brief

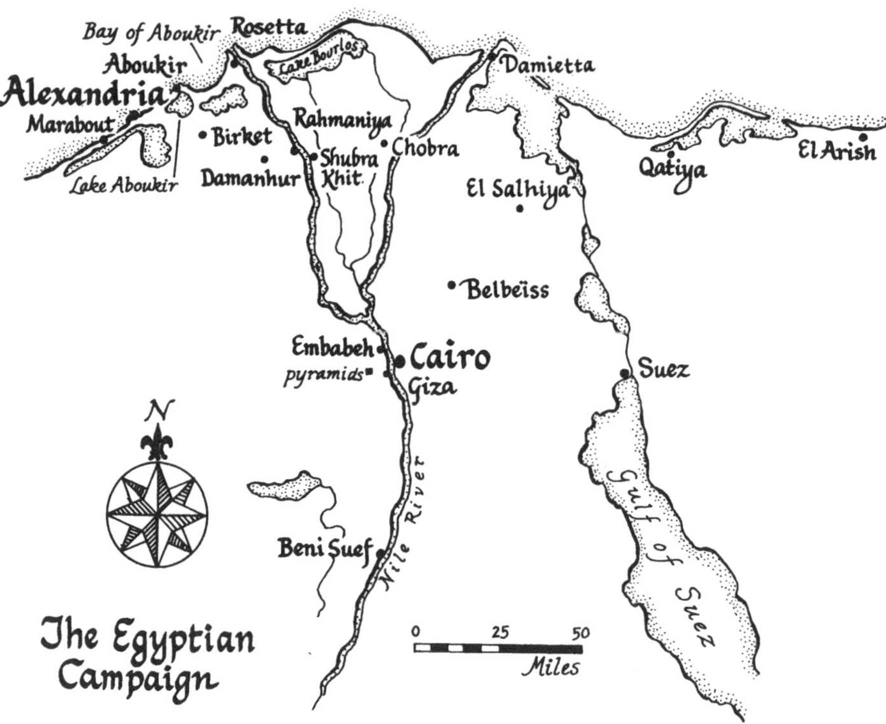

rest as the Mamelukes had not yet assembled for the battle. The action which followed can hardly be called a "battle" in the Napoleonic sense of the word. Each time the Mamelukes came within range of the French guns they were driven back with heavy losses. Finding the same deadly fire on all sides of the squares, the Mamelukes returned to their original position after a blood-letting which lasted about an hour. At this point, Bonaparte ordered his divisions forward. The Mamelukes waited only long enough to see their infantry being routed, and then they turned and fled into the desert. While this fighting was taking place along the left bank of the Nile, two flotillas were fighting a life-or-death struggle in the middle of the river. The gunboats which had accompanied Murad Bey from Cairo had met the boats carrying supplies for the French. The river battle proved to be a much closer match; and, in fact, the Egyptians were on the verge of victory when their largest gunboat

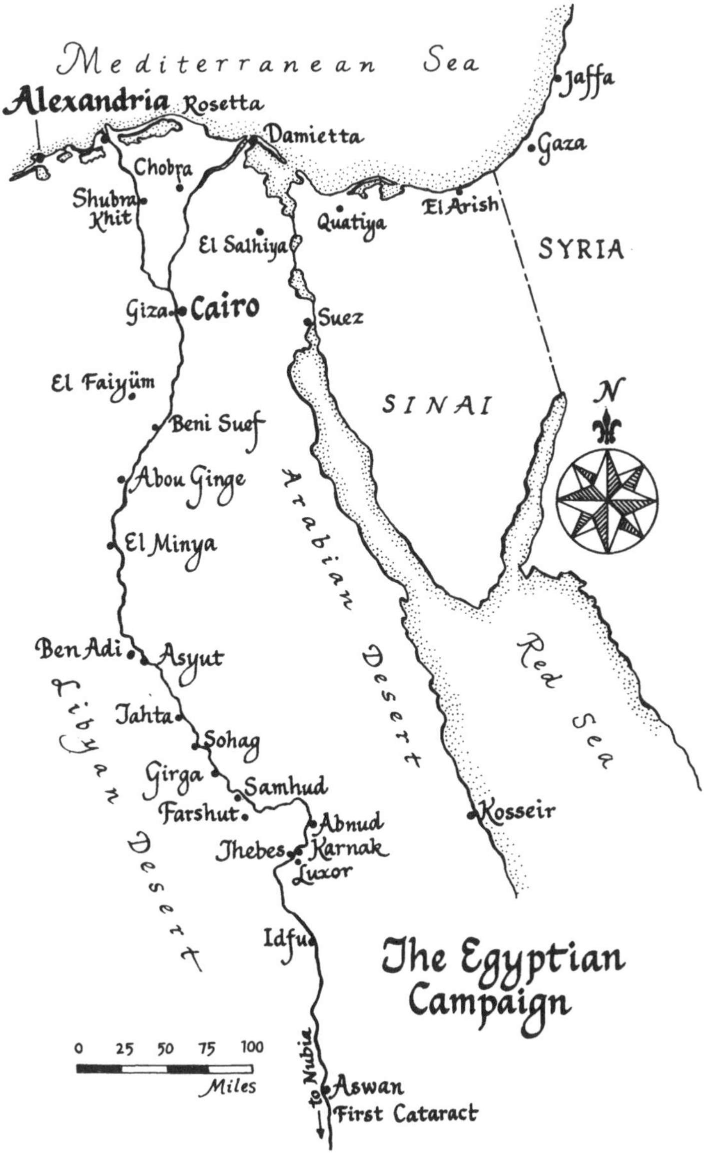

The Egyptian Campaign

Mediterranean Sea
Alexandria
Rosetta
Damietta
Jaffa
Gaza
Chobra
Shubra Khit
El Arish
Quatiya
El Salhiya
SYRIA
Giza
Cairo
Suez
El Faiyūm
SINAI
N
Beni Suef
Abou Ginge
Arabian Desert
El Minya
Ben Adi
Asyut
Red Sea
Libyan Desert
Tahta
Sohag
Girga
Samhud
Farshut
Abnud
Kosseir
Thebes
Karnak
Luxor
Idfu
0 25 50 75 100
Miles
to Nubia
Aswan
First Cataract

blew up and sank. This was the turning point. The French were encouraged and redoubled their efforts, while their enemy quickly lost all enthusiasm and withdrew. The action had scarcely slowed the French march on Cairo. Desaix's division, which had been the most advanced during the battle, continued to form the vanguard and pushed on that same day to the south.

On July 18 the army passed through Wardan, just above the fork on the Nile; and at 2:00 P.M. on the twenty-first it reached Embama within sight of the Pyramids of Giza and the assembled army of the Mamelukes. The Battle of the Pyramids as Bonaparte dramatically named it, was actually fought at some ten to fifteen miles north of those ancient monuments, though they could be seen in the distance from the battlefield. As he had done at Shubra Khit eight days earlier, Bonaparte formed his divisions into squares. Having left the wounded General Kléber at Alexandria with a garrison and having dispatched the also wounded General Jacques François Menou with a detachment to Rosetta in order to secure the mouth of the Nile, there remained only approximately twenty-five thousand men under his command. The Mamelukes had divided their army into two parts, placing the smaller on the right bank of the Nile under Ibraham Bey while the major part under Murad Bey, numbering approximately forty thousand, blocked the French advance. This figure, however, is deceiving. Only about six thousand of these were reliable and well-armed Mamelukes. The remainder of the army was made up of completely unreliable Egyptians, Arabs, and Turks, who were usually referred to in the loosest sense of the term as "infantry." [10]

The army of the Mamelukes was no match for the well-trained and disciplined French. Murad Bey knew no more than the basic necessities of tactics. When Bonaparte opened the battle by sending the divisions of Desaix and Jean-Louis Reynier forward to break the center of the Mameluke line, Murad Bey ordered his cavalry to attack them. The charge was ferocious and determined. It struck Desaix's division first but was unable to break through the square on any side. If personal bravery and good horsemanship had been the sole criteria for victory, the Mamelukes would have stood a good chance of winning the day. However, these qualities were more than equaled by the good discipline and sangfroid of the French troops, and the tactical superiority of their commander.

Murad Bey soon realized his army was helpless against the French, and turning his back to the enemy he fled with the remains of his cavalry up the Nile. That part of his army which was left behind—the infantry—was scattered or destroyed, and Bonaparte occupied Cairo without further bloodshed.

Bonaparte had hardly settled down in Cairo to reorganize the government of Lower Egypt, when Admiral Nelson returned from his futile search of the northern and central Mediterranean and destroyed the French fleet at Aboukir Bay (August 1–2). This French disaster gave the English control of the eastern Mediterranean and made communications between France and the Army of Egypt next to impossible. The expedition could receive neither reinforcements nor supplies from France, and if this defeat did not seal the doom of the isolated army—and there is still much discussion on this point—it certainly was the first good indication that all was not going well.

Bonaparte had defeated the Mameluke army at the Pyramids, but he had not destroyed it. Not only had Murad Bey fled south with a substantial force of cavalry, but Ibraham Bey, who had watched the battle from the east bank of the Nile, led his unmarred troops into the Arabian desert to fight another day. The task of pursuing Murad Bey was given to General Desaix. During the night of August 25 his division marched out of Giza in pursuit of the enemy—a pursuit which was to become legendary and which would last more than nine hectic months.

Davout had fallen ill during the early part of August and was unable to accompany Desaix during the first months of the pursuit. He had contracted dysentery, a disease which was to reoccur periodically during the two years he remained in Egypt, and which was a major cause of the depletion of French ranks during the expedition. As soon as he had recovered in Cairo, he asked to rejoin Desaix, who had not been accompanied by any cavalry because of the shortage of horses. But Bonaparte needed his services in Cairo and, not feeling that Davout had sufficiently recuperated, assigned him the task of reorganizing and mounting the cavalry. The horses that had accompanied the army from France had not held up well during the six weeks aboard ship, and their numbers were scarcely sufficient to provide for the needs of the artillery. Although the French had acquired a rather large number of horses as the result of the two battles with the Mamelukes, they seldom found their way into military service. More often they were sold by the soldiers, who quickly discovered that they brought a good price in the marketplace, or they became the personal property of the French officers and civilians who had accompanied the expedition. To remedy the army's shortage, the commanding general issued numerous orders dealing with the requisition of these animals and limiting their private use. The energetic enforcement of these orders and additional purchases enabled Davout to equip the cavalry regiments with the finest Arabian mounts to be found in Lower Egypt.[11]

Bonaparte first gave evidence of his appreciation of Davout on October 10, 1798, when the following order was issued at Cairo: "The Commanding General wishes to give to General of Brigade Davout a testimony of the satisfaction of the government for the service which he has rendered in the armies of the Republic." The order then goes on to exalt Davout's younger brother Charles and to promote him to the rank of lieutenant: "Wishing equally to reward the services of Charles Davout, his brother, who since the age of sixteen years, has served as a volunteer in the 3rd Battalion of l'Yvonne [*sic*] and the 9th hussars and has always conducted himself with zeal, morality, and intelligence, name said citizen Charles Davout second lieutenant in the 20th dragoons." [12]

With the cavalry mounted and reorganized, Davout was given menial tasks throughout the month of November. On the twenty-third he was ordered "to cross the Nile, tonight, with 300 cavalrymen; to march all night in such a manner as to be at the fork of the delta at daybreak and capture 1,500 to 1,800 camels, which are being escorted by a horde of Arabs." [13] He took with him an interpreter and several natives familiar with the country. Accompanied by several gunboats on the Nile, Davout executed these orders and drove the hostile Arab band out of the Delta where they had been causing the French much trouble. This action was followed by orders to occupy the village of Chobra (Chahab) and to bring the sheik of the village back to Cairo. He was specifically ordered "to do no harm to any of the inhabitants of the village." [14]

During the months which Davout spent in Lower Egypt, Desaix and his division, still without cavalry, had been pursuing Murad Bey to the south. Desaix's men suffered not only from the intense heat and difficult terrain, but also from a lack of supplies of every kind. In letter after letter he pleaded with Bonaparte to send him supplies and reinforcements. Finally Bonaparte, who was planning his campaign into Syria and therefore was unwilling to part unnecessarily with either men or equipment, wrote to him on December 5 that his requests were being fulfilled. "There will leave tomorrow for Upper Egypt," wrote the commanding general to his desperate lieutenant, "1,000 cavalrymen with one 3 pound and two 8 pound artillery pieces." [15] This cavalry unit was commanded by General Davout. With five gunboats and the much needed supplies he moved up the Nile and joined Desaix's ragged force on December 10 at Beni Suef. The addition of the newly arrived cavalry raised the total strength of the division to 4,000 men.

This small army, temporarily improved by the supplies it had just received, left Beni Suef on December 16 in pursuit of Murad Bey. The infantry was now able to march with lighter equipment as they were accompanied by a flotilla which carried the supplies the men did not need each day. Thus they were able to average between twenty-five to thirty miles a day, and reached Asyut on Christmas. Finding that Murad Bey had continued his flight, the French marched on to Girga, where recently received intelligence indicated the enemy would give battle. But upon their arrival in this, the chief city of Upper Egypt, they found the enemy had departed the previous day. Desaix had by this time outmarched his supplies which were traveling by water. The adverse winds and low stage of the river in December made navigation difficult and slow. Furthermore, the troops were exhausted from the long hard marches of the past two weeks. A halt was therefore called.

The three weeks which Desaix spent at Girga were not idle ones for Davout and his cavalry. On January 3, 1799, he was on a reconnaissance mission near Sohag (Souaguy) when he came upon a force of Arabs and fellahin (Egyptian foot soldiers). Despite the enemy's great superiority in numbers, Davout attacked. In a brief but lively action the French drove the Arab cavalry from the field in disorder and then descended upon the confused and bewildered fellahin. What had begun as a battle ended as a slaughter. This affair was followed by Davout's being dispatched down the Nile to make contact with the flotilla, the arrival of which was anxiously awaited by Desaix. As the French entered the town of Tahta (about halfway between Asyut and Girga) their rear guard was attacked by enemy cavalry (January 8, 1799). Repeating their performance of the previous week, the French halted the enemy attacks and sent them in disorder back into the desert. At Tahta Davout also met the flotilla. The winds were now blowing more favorably and it began to make better time. On January 19 the boats arrived at Girga, and Desaix was ready to continue the pursuit.

During the prolonged stay of the French at Girga, Murad Bey had been gathering his forces to give battle. Large numbers of Arabs had been crossing the Red Sea to join the holy war against the infidels, and the army of the Mamelukes felt numerically and morally ready to fight. Desaix thus found the enemy in full force when he advanced on the town of Samhud (January 22). The course of the battle differed little from those fought in Lower Egypt. The French infantry formed into two squares, commanded by Generals Auguste Daniel Belliard and Louis Friant (Davout's future brother-in-law), with their artillery on the flanks. Davout's cavalry was also formed into a square between Belliard and Friant. The Mameluke cavalry, two thousand strong, opened the battle with furious attacks on various sides of the French squares. Finding no weak point they withdrew to make way for the mounted Arabs (about seven thousand), most of whom were meeting the French for the first time. While Belliard and Friant slaughtered the Arabs, Davout was ordered to attack the Mamelukes. "I have never seen such a beautiful and imposing charge as that one made by our cavalry," wrote Desaix in his report to Bonaparte on the battle.[16] The impact of the two cavalry forces was shattering. The Mamelukes held their ground bravely at first, but then gradually gave way before the determination of the French. The rout became general and the pursuit persistent. Davout's men followed the enemy for four hours, leaving a bloody trail of men and horses as the Mamelukes and their army fanned out into the desert of Upper Egypt. The victory was complete; the enemy army had been dispersed with heavy casualties. The French losses were light.[17]

Murad Bey fled south, after a brief halt at Farshut to tend to his wounded, with Desaix in hot pursuit. Marching along the left bank of the Nile, the French passed the ancient ruins of Thebes and viewed to their left across the river the temples of Karnak and Luxor. On February 2 they arrived at Aswan and sent patrols as far as the first cataract. Murad, Hassan, Soliman and eight other beys withdrew from Egypt and sought refuge in Nubia (Sudan). Their forces were demoralized and depleted from ever-increasing desertions. Furthermore, the beys had fallen to quarreling among themselves. The one bright side of the picture, from their point of view, was that the flow of Arabs from across the Red Sea continued to furnish them with cannon fodder.

Desaix was now nominally, at least, in control of the Nile as far south as the first cataract. He had driven the Mameluke's army from Egypt and destroyed their flotilla just below the cataract where they had been forced to abandon it. But because of the size of his army and the hostility of the inhabitants, he had not been able to leave garrisons behind him to secure his conquests. Few towns, villages, or tribes remained loyal to the French once they had passed on. Thus the task of actually controlling the Middle and Upper Nile was just beginning. The biggest problem was preventing the Mamelukes from acquiring supplies. To this end the French were forced to undertake strenuous marches and counter marches up and down the river. Not until the Red Sea port of Kossier was captured in May of 1799 and the flow of Arabs from the east was cut off, could Desaix proclaim with any resemblance to truth that Upper Egypt was pacified.

The cataracts did not then provide the long hoped-for rest for the footweary French. On February 4, Desaix marched out of Aswan to the north leaving only the 21st Demi-brigade of Light Infantry under the command of General Belliard to keep watch on the Mamelukes. In the next fifty days he marched along the banks of the Nile some five hundred and fifty miles. Fighting was almost continuous, though seldom on a large scale. The fellahin were encouraged to resist the French; and with their ranks constantly bolstered by Arab volunteers from across the Red Sea they harassed Desaix's communication, captured and held towns and villages, and even attacked his columns.

Davout, as commander of the cavalry, took part in numerous engagements—both large and small—through the late winter and spring of 1799. On February 12 he fought a pitched battle with the superior forces of Hassan Bey near Luxor. At the head of two regiments, the 22nd Chasseurs and the 15th Dragoons, he attacked the Mamelukes on the right bank of the Nile within sight of the

Temple of Rameses II. In the melee that followed the French charge, Davout's life was saved by a cavalryman named Simon; and although Hassan Bey was wounded in the fierce fighting, he was able to escape with the remains of his army.[18] On April 2 Davout rescued the impetuous advance guard of the division after it had attacked a superior enemy force and had its commander, General Duplessis, killed.[19] Two weeks later (April 18) Davout, at the head of a substantial portion of Desaix's division which included infantry, once again engaged Hassan Bey. The Mameluke chieftain had raised the district about Beni Adi in rebellion against the conquerors. The French general divided his force into two columns and sent one against the Arab cavalry and the other into the town itself. After a brief skirmish Hassan Bey led his Mamelukes back into the desert leaving Beni Adi at the mercy of the attacking army. Resistance was stiff. In order to dislodge the enemy Davout ordered the town to be put to the torch. When the fires had burned out and fighting ended some two thousand dead Mamelukes and Arabs were counted.[20] Those who escaped from Bendi Adi descended the Nile and encourage the province to rebel. As Davout marched north in pursuit he met increased resistance. When the town of Abou Ginge, whose inhabitants believed the French had been defeated and were retreating toward the Delta, refused to provide much-needed food for Davout's tired and hungry troops, Davout ordered the town to be burned to the ground as an example to others who might follow its example.[21]

Still in command of a large portion of the division, Davout confronted Murad Bey at Beni Adi on May 1. Not only did the French drive the Mamelukes into the desert, but they inflicted heavy losses (nearly two thousand) on the fellahin. In addition to the military victory, which was complete, Captain Desvernois, who was with Davout, captured a large caravan. The caravan, made up of 897 camels, had originated in Nubia and was on its way to Alexandria. Desaix had extended to it his hospitality only a few months earlier. But Davout and Desvernois now believed that Murad Bey was about to capture it for his own use as he was in desperate need of supplies. "Captain your fortune is made," Davout is reported to have said to Desvernois. "This action of yours has ruined the projects of our enemies. . . . You will have twelve shares of the booty, your lieutenant six, and each noncommissioned officer and hussar one." [22]

No mention is made of Davout's share of the booty, and Desvernois, with a note of bitterness declared that he never received a cent from the caravan. There can be no question but that the caravan, if it had fallen into the hands of the Mamelukes, would have been a great aid to them in continuing the struggle against the French. Davout considered it his duty to prevent this from happening, while at the same time confiscation could provide reward for all who were involved.

In the last week of May 1799, Desaix ordered General Belliard, with a small detachment of men, to cross the desert between the Nile and the Red Sea and capture the port city of Kosseir. This accomplished, the flow of Arab volunteers into Egypt was virtually stopped; and the French domination of Middle and Upper Egypt was considered completed—or as complete as it could possibly be with the forces available. This pacification, however, was both relative and temporary. There continued to be revolts against the French, and from time to time the Mamelukes attacked in force; but the campaign, which had begun in late August 1798, could be considered to have ended.

While Desaix and his four thousand men were waging their frustrating campaign along the Upper Nile, events were moving in rapid succession to the north. The English victory at Aboukir Bay on August 1–2 had convinced the Turkish government of the wisdom of declaring war on France. It quickly became obvious to the Turks that Bonaparte meant to establish a French colony in Egypt despite his protests of friendship and good will. To drive the French out of Africa the Turks assembled two armies: one in Syria and the other on the island of Rhodes. Before these two forces could attack him simultaneously, Bonaparte led an army of 13,000 men into Syria. Leaving the banks of the Nile on February 6, 1799, he arrived before St. Jean d'Acre on March 17 and laid siege to the city. On April 16 he destroyed at the Battle of Mount Tabor the main Turkish army which was coming to the relief of Acre. By May his army was disease-ridden and short of supplies, while the city had received constant support from the English by sea. There were also reports coming to him from Egypt of an increased activity off Alexandria indicating that the expected landing from Rhodes would soon take place. For these reasons and others—such as the news from Europe of the renewal of hostilities—Bonaparte raised the siege of Acre on May 20 and led his sick, miserable army back to the Nile.

While Bonaparte was considering abandoning the siege of Acre, Davout marched to the aid of General Destrées at Beni Suef. The Mamelukes and Arabs had stirred up rebellions throughout the whole of Lower Egypt. Revolt against French rule had been achieved by spreading rumors that they had been defeated in battle. On his march down the Nile, Davout destroyed the rebellious village of Abou Girgeh, and a few days later defeated a combined Mameluke and Arab force under Elphi Bey on May 8. Shortly after his arrival at Beni Suef, he received orders from General Duguat, the governor of Cairo, to clear the district east of the capital of insurgent Arab war parties. Davout accomplished this and reestablished communications with Bonaparte's retreating army, which had been severed during the last weeks of May. When the commanding general entered Cairo on June 14, Davout was with him. He had written to Bonaparte earlier informing him of his recall to the Delta area and of his ensuing actions. On the same day that he entered Cairo, Bonaparte wrote Davout expressing his satisfaction with events south of the capital and added: "I approve the action which you took on your return to Cairo." [23] Two weeks later, on June 27, Davout received a letter containing the first real evidence of Bonaparte's favor.

The commanding general had not taken particular note of General of Brigade Davout during the first year they had been in Egypt. He had joined the expedition as Desaix's protégé, never having served under Bonaparte. Now, however, Bonaparte had become aware of him. In a letter dated June 27, Davout was ordered to Beni Suef as military governor of the provinces of Beni Suef, El Minya, and El Faiyüm with the commanders of these three strongholds under his orders. With the forces at his disposal—consisting of both cavalry and infantry units—he was ordered to rid this section of the Middle Nile of the Mamelukes and fellahin who had been harassing communication, attacking outposts, and causing general havoc as far north as the Delta. The most important paragraph of this letter from the standpoint of Davout's career read as follows: "You will be given, as of the 1st of messidor [June 18], the same treatment at the [conference] table as a general of division." [24] This was not, of course, a promotion in rank for Davout: but it certainly was the next best thing to it. It raised him in dignity above his fellow generals of brigade. But what was most important, it gave evidence of an increased esteem in the eyes of the future Emperor of the French.

Unfortunately, Davout was unable to carry out these instructions. He was stricken with an acute case of dysentery which almost took his life during the first week of July.[25] Thus he was still convalescing in Cairo when news arrived that the long expected Turkish invasion had begun on July 15 in the vicinity of the town of Aboukir. Bonaparte wasted no time in gathering all available forces to meet the new threat. Supported by a combined English, Turkish, and Russian fleet (the latter having recently declared war on France), between fifteen and eighteen thousand Turkish soldiers were put ashore without opposition. When the invading forces did not march on Alexandria, Bonaparte moved in and attacked them in their prepared defensive positions at Aboukir (July 25–August 2). Davout, who was not completely recovered from his recent illness, was given a secondary role during the course of the main battle. With a small detachment of cavalry and infantry—Bonaparte was outnumbered by the Turks by about two to one and could ill afford a larger force—he was assigned the task of defending the rear of the French army against the Mamelukes and Arabs who were in the vicinity intending to cooperate with the Turkish forces.[26] The position he took up also enabled him to maintain communications with General Auguste Marmont at Alexandria.

The battle itself was fought on a narrow peninsula between Lake Aboukir and the sea. Despite their numerical superiority and the aid of gunboats on their flanks, the Turkish forces were either driven into the sea or shut up in Fort Aboukir and the neighboring villages. The French immediately laid siege to the fort, which was only able to hold out a matter of days as it had not been prepared for a siege. There was neither enough food nor water for the three to four thousand men who crowded into it. Davout was placed in command of the 15th Dragoons on July 28 and took part in the siege under the command of General Menou. Two days after taking up his position he led an attack upon the town of Aboukir, and after heavy fighting which very nearly cost him his life, the town was captured. Three more days of fighting were required before the fort surrendered.[27]

The French victory was complete. Only about twelve hundred of the invading force succeeded in getting back to their ships while thousands drowned attempting to do so. The remainder were killed in battle or taken prisoner. This dealt a severe blow to the hopes of the Mamelukes and Arabs who were still resisting the French occupation, and who had been counting on the Turkish invasion to bring it to an end. Temporarily at least, their resistance slackened, and the French were in complete control. Bonaparte at once took advantage of this victory and the lull which followed it to turn over his command to General Kléber and return to France, where he reasoned quite correctly that greater opportunities were to be found. The Army of Egypt was reduced to holding out, with very little promise of aid from France, until such time as victory could be won in Europe and an advantageous peace made with England which would end the war. Its numbers had been diminishing daily since its arrival in Egypt. Sir Sidney Smith, who may have overstated his case in a letter to Lord Nelson after the Battle of Aboukir, summed up the French position as follows: "Under these untoward circumstances, we have the satisfaction of observing the enemy's losses to be such that a few more victories like this will annihilate the French army." [28]

The army, which was reduced to half of its original strength, was demoralized by the news of the departure of the commander in chief. It had placed its faith and its hopes for survival in the hands of General Bonaparte. A sense of abandonment was felt by both the officers and men who were left behind. As early as May 1799, when the siege of Acre had been raised, Kléber had given up hope that the expedition would accomplish any useful end for France or himself. Yet he now found himself in command of what he considered a doomed army.

Following the destruction of the Turkish army at Aboukir, Bonaparte had opened negotiations with Commodore Sidney Smith, commander of the English fleet off Alexandria, for the exchange of prisoners. In the course of these transactions, Smith agreed to accept letters dealing exclusively with family affairs to be forwarded to France. All such letters were opened, read, and countersigned by the English commander. One of them was from Davout to his mother. In it he spoke of himself as being in good health—which he was not at the time; of his brother Charles' promotion to second lieutenant, adding that his commander was pleased with his *bonne volonté;* and of his brother Alexandre, who was doing well and was still attached to Bonaparte's staff.[29] Other than this, he was unable to write anything of importance. That this was the only letter received by Madame Davout in well over a year, and that Davout said in the letter he had had no news from France, is an excellent testimonial of the effectiveness of the English blockade.

During the months following Bonaparte's departure (August 23, 1799) Davout took up his position as military governor of the provinces of Beni Suef, El Faiyüm, and El Minya, an area which comprised what might be called the northern half of Middle Egypt. With Desaix controlling the territory to the south, and the Delta calmed by the recent French victory, the new commander in chief seemingly ascended to a peaceful regime. But such was not the case—and General Kléber was fully aware of the fact. In a letter which he addressed to the Directors, who were no longer in office when it arrived, but was received by the new First Consul, General Bonaparte, he spelled out in detail, and slightly exaggerated terms, the untenable position of the Army of Egypt.[30]

Even before Bonaparte had departed, Kléber had been an outspoken advocate of complete evacuation. Now as commander of the army he was supported by the majority of its officers and an overwhelming majority of the men. Those officers who opposed evacuation (during the fall and early winter of 1799) were led by Davout and General Menou.[31] Desaix was some place between these two points of view—not really in favor of evacuation at the time, but realizing the hopelessness of any prolonged stay without aid from France. It may be said with respect to Davout's unpopular stand that without orders from Paris not even Kléber had the authority to enter into negotiations for evacuation so long as the country could be held by the army. Despite the advance of a large Turkish army under the command of the Grand Vizier into Syria, there was no real immediate danger of the French being driven out. Furthermore, with Bonaparte back in France the chances of reinforcements and supplies being sent to Egypt were greatly increased—at least so it seemed to those who still had faith in the former commander. The fact that Bonaparte was making no serious effort to aid the stranded army was unknown to the men along the Nile. Then too, there was the possibility of a general peace in the spring or early summer of

1800 with General Bonaparte at the head of France's armies. In this event the possession of Egypt could play an important role at the conference table.

Kléber and his supporters were familiar with these arguments in favor of staying in Egypt, but they viewed the situation in quite a different light. Now that it was obvious that the enterprise would be a failure, they felt that they had been abandoned by Bonaparte. The army could not possibly hold out twelve months—or even nine months in the opinion of some. True, General Jean Antoine Verdier with hardly a thousand men had driven back into the sea a second Turkish landing force twice his size; but the situation had not changed. Though Kléber expressed fear of the advancing Turkish army in Syria, he must have been aware that he could defeat it on the battlefield if it ever came to a showdown. However, it was not Kléber's intention to sacrifice another thousand men only to be forced to negotiate from weakness. Better, he believed, and certainly with justification, to negotiate from strength and at the same time spare the lives of those men who would die in the event of future fighting. Kléber also reasoned that even if there would be no battles—and surely there would be—his army was slowly dying of the plague. Of the fifteen thousand men in his command, between two and three thousand were on the sick or disabled list. Even without the Pyrrhic victories Smith spoke of, the French army seemed doomed.

Whether Kléber was right, as most modern historians believe, or wrong, as Bonaparte,[32] Davout, and many of his contemporaries believed, will remain an academic question. The fact is that he opened negotiations for the evacuation of Egypt on December 22, 1799, on Smith's flagship, the H.M.S. *Tigre*. Bonaparte himself had prepared the way for such negotiation in a letter he had written to the Grand Vizier on August 17, 1799.[33] In this letter he had proposed preliminary talks aimed at the restoration of Egypt to Turkey and the withdrawal of that country from the war against France. On September 17, Kléber repeated the offer. Because of the Anglo-Turkish Alliance, Sir Sidney Smith became a party of the negotiations which resulted in the controversial Convention of El Arish. The convention, which was ratified on January 28, 1800, by Kléber, provided for the evacuation of Qatiya, El Salihya, and Belbeiss by the French within ten days, and of Cairo one month later.

Kléber would withdraw all of his forces to the three seaports of Alexandria, Aboukir, and Rosetta, where they would be taken aboard Turkish transports and returned to France. The French would be allowed to leave Egypt with their arms and baggage, and the Turks would pay them two million francs for their maintenance until their departure.

While the negotiations for the evacuation were in progress, Davout was relieved of his command in Middle Egypt and dispatched to the vicinity of the Lower Nile along its Damietta (eastern) leg. By the first week of October he had established his headquarters at Mansura.[34] The Grand Vizier had been making steady, if ridiculously slow, progress with his army through Syria toward Egypt. Though formal talks had begun between the belligerents before Christmas, the Turkish army had not halted. Then on December 30 an unusual event occurred. The French garrison of El Arish mutinied, hauled down the tricolor flag and opened the gates of the town to the Turks. Rather than showing gratitude, the Turkish soldiers set about massacring the astonished French troops. Only the presence of an English officer, Major Cazal, prevented the massacre from being complete.[35] With the approach of the Turkish army Davout took up a position at Belbeiss astride the main road from El Arish to Cairo to cover the capital.[36] There Kléber joined him in mid-January. Though Kléber desperately wanted peace, he was prepared to fight if the Grand Vizier continued his advance.[37] However it was not necessary—at this point. On January 13, Desaix and Citizen Poussielgue, the two French representatives, accompanied by Sir Sidney Smith arrived at El Arish and the terms of the convention were worked out.

Throughout the negotiations Davout had remained a staunch opponent of evacuation so long as the forces available were able to maintain themselves in Egypt. He felt the massacre at El Arish demanded action, not words. At the council of war held at Salahieh on January 20 Kléber assembled nine generals in order to solicit their support for the terms of the convention which would provide for the evacuation of Egypt. Neither Desaix, who was still not a wholehearted supporter of evacuation, nor Menou, who was absolutely opposed to it, were present. Of the officers attending the council all were in agreement with their commander in chief save one. Davout voiced his opposition in no uncertain terms. But in the end he found himself a minority of one; and for the sake of unanimity, he signed the document expressing support of the actions of Kléber.[38] It should be said, to Kléber's credit, that he was not so much trying to spread the responsibility for the decision he had made—indeed every indication points to the fact that he would have gone ahead without the support of his subordinates—as he was trying to reassure himself that it was the correct one. When it became known that Bonaparte, then First Consul, was violently opposed to the Convention of El Arish, Kléber ordered that the document of support signed by the generals be burned so that it would not compromise its signatories.[39]

For all intent and purpose the Egyptian campaign seemed to have come to an end. No one in Egypt could have foreseen at the end of January that it would be more than a year and a half before the weary, homesick army would set foot on French soil. Thus a number of high ranking officers asked for, and received, permission from Kléber, Sir Sidney Smith, and the Turks to return to France as soon as possible. Among them were Davout and Desaix. Davout's request was based on his poor health. The Egyptian climate had never agreed with his European constitution. Some twelve years later he would walk many of the five hundred miles from Moscow in subfreezing temperatures and arrive in Poland in much better health than he was at the time of his departure from Egypt. Permission for his departure was granted February 12[40] and he proceeded to Aboukir to await transportation. On March 3, 1800, accompanied by his brother Alexandre he sailed for France on the *Etoile*.

On the very same day that Davout sailed from Aboukir, Desaix, aboard a Ragusan merchantman, left Alexandria. After a difficult voyage, which required both ships to put into ports on Rhodes and Sicily, they were approaching the French coast when an English frigate apprehended them. The English captain declared that the passports under which the Frenchmen were traveling were invalid unless signed by Admiral Keith, the English commander in the Mediterranean. The two ships were therefore escorted to Leghorn where the French generals were badly received by Lord Keith. He kept them in quarantine for a month at a hospital where they were treated more as prisoners of war than officers who had been given passports by an English admiral. At length they were released, but only after direct orders to that effect had been received from London. On April 29 they proceeded on their way. Again their ship was stopped on the high sea. Fortunately, this time it was not by the English, but by Tunisian pirates. The pirates proved much more respectful of the signature of the Grand Vizier than the English had of Commodore Smith's. The ship was allowed to continue on to Toulon, where it arrived on May 5.[41]

5

A Marshal's Baton

SINCE THE DEPOSITION of Louis XVI in 1792 the government of France had lacked stability. Moving to the left, the various assemblies passed from the hands of the constitutional monarchists, through those of the republican Girondists, and on to the "democratic" Jacobins. Then in the summer of 1794 the Thermidorians halted this leftward drift of the government, and the pendulum began to swing back to the right. The next five years brought little improvement in the quality of government and no change in the constant struggle for power. The Directory had to defend itself from the ever present Jacobin left and the growing influence of the royalist right. It purged itself in the late summer of 1797 in the *coup d'état* of Fructidor, reducing the royalist opposition but not destroying it. The Directors had looked with favor on the departure of General Bonaparte on his Egyptian campaign, for a popular, victorious general sitting idle about Paris could only be one more danger to the government.

By the time Bonaparte returned from Egypt in the fall of 1799, France had grown quite tired of its inefficient government. There were several plots afoot to overthrow the Directory, but support of the army was a necessary ingredient to assure success. General Bonaparte provided that necessary ingredient and the *coup d'état* of Brumaire came off, if not smoothly, at least successfully. The Constitution of the Year VIII (1799), which was basically the work of the Abbé Emmanuel Sieyès, was modified by Bonaparte just enough to make himself dictator of the French Republic with the title of First Consul. He immediately set about consolidating his political position by finding remedies for those problems which apparently had been beyond the abilities of the Directors. First came the pacification of the royalist opposition in the Vendée. This was accomplished during the winter of 1799–1800. By spring he was able to turn his full attention to the international crisis which faced France.

Nelson's victory at Aboukir Bay in the summer of 1798, combined with the French occupation of Malta and Egypt, had enabled England to form a second coalition against France. Turkey was first to join the coalition, to be followed shortly by Russia.[1] Naples was next to reach an understanding with England in December, 1798; while Austria, still smarting under the Peace of Campo Formio which she had reluctantly signed the previous year, needed little encouragement to join the coalition. The ineptness of the government of the Directory during the first year of the renewal of hostilities resulted in setbacks on all fronts. While it is true that the Republic was really no longer in danger by the time Bonaparte returned,[2] the fact remained that French armies had been driven out of Italy and Germany, nullifying all of the gains he had achieved as the result of his 1796–97 campaign.

In the spring of 1800 the First Consul accompanied the Army of Reserve[3] through Switzerland, through the Saint Bernard Pass and into the valley of the Po. In this region he conducted one of his most famous campaigns which culminated in the victory of Marengo. While Bonaparte was preparing to cross the Alps, Davout and Desaix landed at Toulon on May 5. No sooner had Davout set foot on French soil than he wrote to the First Consul and to the Minister of War, Carnot. He could not be certain of the reception he would receive from Bonaparte as he had not actually been a favorite of the former commander in chief of the Army of Egypt. General Andoche Junot, a close friend of Davout's, told his wife at the time of the latter's arrival in France: "The First Consul does not like Davoust [*sic*], because when in Egypt he associated with all those who made a point of being hostile to Bonaparte. I do not know that Davoust [*sic*] can be justly ranked among the First Consul's enemies; but it is certain that he has inspired him with an antipathy as complete as one man can entertain for another. I am the more sorry for this, inasmuch as Davoust [*sic*] is my comrade and a clever man."[4] Madame

Junot who recorded these words of her husband, went on to say: "This dislike, of which all who were with Bonaparte in Egypt might have seen proofs, had a singular source. It originated in the personal slovenliness of Davoust [*sic*], who by the way was at that time the most dirty and ill-dressed man imaginable—a fault Napoleon held in aversion, being himself always particularly neat and clean." [5] Further evidence is to be found in the *Mémoires* of Louis Antoine Bourrienne. In a conversation with Bonaparte, shortly afer Davout's return from Egypt, Bourrienne asked him: "How were you able to keep company for such a long time with a man whom you have always called a *f—— bête?"* The First Consul replied: "But I had not known him well. He is worthy of more than his reputation, you will also get over it." [6] Bonaparte did eventually "get over" this dislike of Davout, but it helps to explain why he was not brought back to France in August 1799 with the "friends" of the future Emperor.

This dislike must be balanced off against the fact that Davout had been selected to fulfill the duties and receive the honor and respect of a general of division shortly before Bonaparte left Egypt. Bonaparte had apparently begun to recognize the value of Davout's services. It must also be pointed out that Davout had been in open opposition against Kléber and his policy of evacuation, a fact which must have endeared him to the First Consul, a man who shared these same sentiments. Concerning this same problem, Desaix felt it necessary to write Bonaparte on the very day he arrived at Toulon to make excuses for his part in bringing about the Convention of El Arish, and drew in reply a reprimand from the First Consul.[7] Davout was received quite well—a fact that astonished observers such as Madame Junot. "Davoust [*sic*], however," she wrote, "on his return contrived to ingratiate himself with Napoleon, who not only extended to him his good will, but gave him, what I suspect he valued more, employment and honours." [8]

On May 14, 1800, the First Consul wrote to the other Consuls (Sieyès and Roger-Ducos) in Paris: "I wish that you would put in the official journal [*Moniteur*] that the Generals Desaix and Davout have arrived at Toulon, with several phrases which would express that these two generals had maintained, even after my departure, the reputations which they had acquired during the campaigns of Holland and the Rhine." [9] On the same day Bonaparte wrote to Davout: "I learn with pleasure, *Citoyen,* that you have arrived at

Toulon. The campaign [Second Italian] has only just begun; we are in need of men of your merits. You may believe that I have not forgotten the service that you have rendered us at Aboukir and in Upper Egypt. When your quarantine is finished, go to Paris."[10] However, only Desaix was actually invited to join the Army of Italy at this time, and so Davout proceeded to the capital. On his way to Paris he stopped at Ravières and spent a few days with his family. He arrived in the capital during the first week of July just a few days ahead of the First Consul, who was fresh from the victorious battlefield of Marengo.

Marengo became in history one of the great Napoleonic victories, but to Davout it represented the loss of a close and esteemed friend. General Desaix, who had been called by Bonaparte to join the Army of Italy as soon as his quarantine was ended, had played a major role in the victory of Marengo and paid for it with his life. During the three years these two men soldiered together Davout had come to look up to Desaix as a student does to his tutor. In the last phase of the campaign on the Rhine and throughout the Egyptian campaign Davout learned much from his commander about the art of waging war. The close personal relationship which had grown in these years, and which culminated in the difficulties they shared while returning from the ill-fated Egyptian expedition, made the death of this excellent soldier the more grievous to Davout. Bonaparte also recognized the loss of an able commander, a man he could have used well in the coming years of almost unceasing war, for he had the body of Desaix solemnly buried in the chapel of the Hospice of Saint Bernard high in the Alps looking down into Italy.[11]

The Battle of Marengo ended a campaign but did not end the war. The Austrians did not consider themselves defeated and they used the respite which was provided by an armistice signed after the battle to build up their armies in Italy and Germany. Furthermore, they had a commitment to the English not to make a separate peace with France until the beginning of 1801. They were stalling for time, and Bonaparte was anxious for peace. Marengo had given him the military victory he needed to consolidate his political position in France, but he now needed peace to take the fullest advantage of the opportunity at hand. He therefore used the lull, as the Austrians did, to regroup and supply his armies in Italy and Germany. With the likelihood that hostilities would be resumed, Davout was not destined to remain idle in Paris. On July 4, 1800, he received a letter from the minister of war, Lazare Carnot, announcing his promotion to the rank of general of division.[12] This was actually the third time Davout had been offered this rank. He had declined the promotion at the height of the Revolution because he was concerned about the responsibility of high rank and because the political situation troubled him. The grade was again offered to him by General Kléber in Egypt after Bonaparte's departure. At that time he was a divisional commander, but he again refused the promotion because he did not wish his advance to be dated from, or connected with, the Convention of El Arish to which he had been opposed. Besides, he considered the offer to be a bribe of a sort from Kléber to win him over. Now however, with the promotion coming from the First Consul after his return from Egypt, Davout was only too happy to accept. Accompanying the promotion was notification that he would be assigned to the Army of Italy. The command which he received was that of all the cavalry of Italy.

On July 11 Davout took leave of the First Consul and set out to assume his command. Passing through Dijon, the supply depot for the cavalry regiments in Italy, he arranged for shipments of vital materials to various units. Arriving in Milan, the temporary headquarters of the army, Davout found himself in an awkward situation. From the early years of the revolutionary wars, but more particularly dating from the successes of General Bonaparte during 1796–97, there had been a certain amount of jealousy between the men who had served in the armies of the Rhine and those who had served in the Army of Italy. By the end of Bonaparte's second Italian campaign there were definitely two groups, or perhaps one might better say, factions, into which the French army was divided. The men of Italy, who had served under Bonaparte, and who supported him and won his favor formed one faction. On the other hand were those officers who had served on the Rhine. Few of the men of the Rhine knew Bonaparte other than by reputation. They considered him an upstart who had been extremely lucky. They felt that they had suffered the heaviest burden of the war in the Rhine campaigns, but that he had reaped the glory in Italy. Furthermore, many of the generals of the Rhine were strongly attached to the Republic under which they had themselves risen to fame, and they were distrustful of the political ambitions of the First Consul. This is perhaps best shown by pointing out that General Moreau commanded the Army of the Rhine, General Augereau (who had served under Bonaparte in 1796–97) commanded a corps on his left flank, and General Bernadotte the Army of the West. All three were extremely jealous of Bonaparte's rapid rise to power. It would be, of course, an oversimplification to assume that all officers in the armies on the Rhine were republicans and anti-Bonaparte, or that all of those with the army in Italy supported the Consulate and were pro-Bonaparte, yet the jealousy was real enough and it is possible to make a generalization about the French Army Corps.

There can be no doubt that Davout found himself an outsider when he joined the Army of Italy—even though he had become a staunch Bonapartist. General Laboissière, a veteran of the Second Italian Campaign, commanded the cavalry. He held seniority over Davout in the rank general of division and was reluctant to give up his command. General Masséna, whom Bonaparte had left in charge of the army when he departed, sought to solve the problem by giving Davout the light cavalry and Laboissière the heavy cavalry which formed the reserve. Both generals would be directly under the orders of Masséna so that Laboissière would not feel in an inferior position to Davout. Realizing that he was considered an outsider and not wishing to create any worse feelings than already existed, Davout accepted the compromise, which also received the blessings of Bonaparte. In the months that followed, Davout prepared for the resumption of hostilities which seemed increasingly likely as negotiations failed to bring about a peace.

By the end of October 1800, the First Consul realized that Austria was stalling for time and had no intention of accepting the terms he was offering. They were virtually the same as those of Campo Formio. Therefore, on November 8, he denounced the armistice and ordered his armies to march on Vienna. Hostilities resumed on the twenty-second, and the French armies pressed forward. Unlike the campaigns of 1796–97, and the summer of 1800, the decisive action took place on the Danube rather than in Italy. On December 3 General Moreau defeated the main Austrian army in Bavaria at Hohenlinden and began an almost unopposed advance on Vienna. To the south, General Macdonald marched his small force across the Splügen Pass into northern Italy where he gave active support to General Guillaume Brune's Army of Italy. However, without the guiding hand of General Bonaparte the Army of Italy gained no spectacular victories such as it had achieved at Marengo, Rivoli, and Arcola.

Brune had been ordered to wait for the arrival of Jacques Etienne Macdonald, who would harass the Austrian right flank and rear, before pressing an attack. Thus for the first three weeks of the renewal of the war he took no action. Only after being prodded by the enemy did Brune actually begin the campaign (December 17). In the one major engagement which took place near Monzambano on December 25–26, Davout played a significant role when he personally led several regiments of cavalry in an attack which broke the Austrian center. Under General Heinrich Bellegarde the Austrian army fell back to the Adige. On January 1, 1801, Brune ordered a crossing of the river at Bussolengo. In the midst of this rather delicate maneuver General Bellegarde announced to the French that an armistice had been signed on December 25 on the Middle Danube at Steyer. When Moreau's victorious army had reached Mölk, only fifty miles from Vienna, the Austrian Emperor Francis II decided that he must negotiate in earnest and withdraw from the Second Coalition. In accordance with his instructions from Paris, Brune refused to abide by the armistice unless Bellegarde withdrew to the left bank of the Piave River (twenty miles east of Venice). As Bellegarde had no intentions of giving up the lower Po and Adige valleys without a struggle, the fighting continued. The Austrian commander felt encouraged by the news that he would receive reinforcements from the Tyrol now that the fighting had ended in the north.

The left wing of the Army of Italy was commanded by General Bon Adrien Moncey. Operating on the upper Adige he caught an Austrian force under General Laudon between himself and Macdonald who had cut off the enemy's retreat by occupying the city of Trent. But Laudon used his wits to accomplish what his guns could not. He sent an officer to Moncey to inform him that an armistice had been signed between Generals Brune and Bellegarde along the line of the one signed at Steyer two weeks earlier. Moncey agreed to cease hostilities on the condition that the Austrians evacuate the chateau of La Pietra (which dominated the position held by the Austrians before him) and Trent. Laudon was aware of that which Moncey was not—Macdonald already occupied Trent—and he was only too happy to evacuate La Pietra which he could not hold.

Moncey indeed believed that he had captured the entire Italian Tyrol without having fired a shot. But when Brune was informed that Moncey had allowed Laudon's army to escape, he relieved him of his command. Moncey's corps was immediately placed under the orders of Davout. But Davout, realizing the situation was difficult and that he would not be well received by Moncey's men, restricted himself to the command of his cavalry. In cooperation with Moncey, but without giving him or his troops orders, Davout marched through Trent to the headwaters of the Brento and down onto the right flank of the Austrians at Bassano (January 11, 1801). Moncey and Davout were on the verge of a successful turning operation when plenipotentiaries from the Emperor Francis II arrived at French headquarters. Two days later, on January 16, an armistice was signed bringing an end to the war on the Continent.

The armistice contained the desired French goals with one exception. Brune unwittingly omitted to stipulate that the fortified city of Mantua, which was in fact the key to the lower Po valley, must be evacuated. Bonaparte, in Paris, was infuriated. He denounced the armistice concluded by Brune and threatened the same for the earlier one concluded at Steyer by Moreau if the Austrians did not agree at once to evacuate Mantua. The Austrian army was not in a position to renew the struggle. On January 26, 1801, a new armistice was signed and it cleared the ground for the Treaty of Lunéville concluded between Joseph Bonaparte and the Comte de Cobenzel on February 9.

The Peace of Lunéville put an end to the Second Coalition.[13] It is true that it was not until the end of March that the last belligerent on the Continent, Naples, sued for peace, but there was never any question of the outcome of the fighting in southern Italy, and the conclusion of hostilities was regarded as an indication of a new era in international affairs. Though England remained at war with France, a great lull came over Europe. Yet there were obstacles to be removed or overcome before peace could be concluded. The presence of French troops in Egypt still posed a threat to England's possession of India; while the English occupation of Malta, which they had captured September 5, 1800, gave England a dominant position in the central Mediterranean which Bonaparte considered unacceptable. The presence of the English on Malta also had certain emotional effects on the First Consul, who had developed a personal interest in the island during his Egyptian campaign. But gradually these stumbling blocks to peace, along with others such as the continued occupation of Holland by French troops and the League of Armed Neutrality against England formed by the northern European states, were overcome. In the early fall of 1801 the Army of Egypt was evacuated by an Anglo-Turkish fleet ending that unhappy expedition and removing a major obstacle to peace. The English attack on the Danish fleet at Copenhagen (April 2, 1801) proved sufficient to convince not only the Danes but also Russia,[14] Prussia, and Sweden to follow a less hostile course toward England—at least at sea—and the League of Armed Neutrality collapsed. As for Malta and Holland, both occupiers agreed to withdraw their troops and restore control to rightful authorities. Thus was the way paved for the signing of the Treaty of Amiens, March 1802, which was welcomed with great joy and enthusiasm by war-weary people on both sides of the Channel.

The Peace of Amiens proved short-lived, and to be in fact no more than a truce. Within fifteen months France and England were again at war, this time in a fight to the death. Nevertheless, Europe was to enjoy four and a half years of comparative peace following the Treaty of Lunéville. Not until the summer of 1805 would the Third Coalition be formed against France and the invincible Grand Army march down the Danube to Austerlitz. During this interval Davout was not idle. When hostilities ended on the Continent in February 1801, Davout was assigned the task of supervising the Austrian evacuation of Mantua and the other Italian towns stipulated by the treaty. This accomplished, he set about reorganizing the cavalry under his command, and settled them in the Cisalpine Republic. He thus occupied himself into the summer of 1801 at which time he was relieved of his command.

On the first of July, General Berthier, the new minister of war, wrote Davout: "I must inform you, citizen general, that as there is not employment with the French troops in the Cisalpine Republic for the number of generals of your rank, you are authorized to retire to where it would seem best for you. . . . You will do well to inform me of your exact residence when it has been fixed." [15] Davout took advantage of the flexibility given him to return, by way of Ravières, to Paris and there to establish his residence. The capital was in fact the only place for an unemployed soldier who did not wish to end his career, and Davout did not wait long for an assignment. He had risen rapidly in the favor of the First Consul. During the recent winter campaign he had again displayed his valor and capability. He was also becoming known as a superb organizer. It was this latter talent which Bonaparte now employed. Hardly had Davout settled himself in Paris when he was appointed inspector of cavalry for the 1st, 14th, 15th, and 16th military districts. Throughout the remainder of the summer and early fall he afforded himself little leisure as he gave to his new job that same boundless energy he had displayed in battle. Yet while the summer of 1801 was primarily given to work, Louis Davout did find time to meet and win the hand of Aimée Leclerc.

The lull which followed the Peace of Lunéville afforded not only a period of reorganization for the French army but also a time of rest and relaxation for the officers and men who had been absorbed with war for nine years. Davout's unhappy marriage to Marie de Seuguenot in 1791 had ended in divorce. He had had neither the desire nor the time to repeat that error during the years of perpetual warfare on the Rhine, the Nile, and the Adige. The late summer and fall of 1801 now provided the time while Mademoiselle Leclerc provided the desire.

Louise-Aimée-Julie Leclerc was the beautiful eighteen-year-old daughter of a prominent bourgeois family from Pontoise. Her father Jean-Paul Leclerc had made a substantial fortune in grain during the year before the Revolution, while her mother, Marie-Jeanne-Louise Musquinet, came from an equally wealthy and influential bourgeois family in her own right. Aimée was the youngest of five children and was favored by her mother who continued throughout the remaining years of her life to show this preference.

Her father died while she was still a child and it was left to her brother, General Victoire Emmanuel Leclerc, to assume the duties and responsibilities of the head of the family. In 1798 he had married the sister of General Bonaparte, Marie-Pauline Bonaparte, uniting the two families. A comrade-in-arms of Bonaparte's, Leclerc had accompanied him on the Egyptian campaign and served with the Army of Italy. Aimée's second brother, Nicolas Marie, who went under the name of Leclerc Desessarts, was a cavalry officer. Her older sister, Claire, had married General Friant, a future division commander in Davout's corps, in 1798. Thus a family which had established itself in commerce under the old regime emerged as one of the prominent military families of the Empire.

In the summer of 1801 General Leclerc was preparing to lead a French expedition to the island of Haiti. Bonaparte dreamed of reestablishing a French colonial empire in the western hemisphere to compensate for the loss of Egypt and Syria. He had acquired the territory of Louisiana from Spain in secret negotiations and now planned to reaffirm French control over the western part of Haiti which had been lost during the Revolution.[16] Haiti was to be the link between Louisiana and France, and to forge this link thirty-three thousand men under the command of his brother-in-law were preparing to sail from Brest.

Before departing on this mission which could be expected to keep him out of the country for several years, General Leclerc wished to see his younger sister happily married and provided for. Being many years her senior and having had the responsibility for her upbringing and education, the relationship between this brother and sister was more like that of a father and his daughter. Earlier in the summer of 1801 the name of General Jean Lannes had been brought forth and looked on with favor by the all-powerful brother-in-law. But Aimée had quickly put an end to such thoughts by rejecting the rather uncouth young man. The next name that came to the fore was that of Louis Davout. He had the qualifications which made him acceptable to both Leclerc and Bonaparte. His noble birth was an asset—though by no means a requirement. What was more important than nobility was ability; and this Davout also had. A veteran of the Rhine, Egypt, and Italy, he had proven himself a capable general and a loyal Bonapartist.

Davout was immediately attracted to the young and lovely Aimée Leclerc. But even if he had not been, the fact that a union with her would draw him closer to the family of the First Consul could not have been overlooked lightly. Bonaparte himself not only approved of the union, he encouraged it. No man with the ambitions of Gen-

LOUISE-AIMÉE-JULIE LECLERC. Born in 1782, she married Louis N. Davout on November 9, 1801. She was the sister of General Charles Victor Emmanuel Leclerc, who was married to Pauline Bonaparte, sister of the Emperor Napoleon. She outlived her husband by forty-five years and died in 1868.—From Blocqueville, *Le Maréchal Davout prince d'Eckmühl: raconté par les siens et par lui-même*, vol. 4

eral Davout could possibly have refused the hand of the sister of the First Consul's brother-in-law. Furthermore, though the Davout family had no real financial problems, the dowry of 150,000 francs which accompanied the hand of Aimée Leclerc was not to be discounted. In truth the question was not so much would General Davout accept Mademoiselle Leclerc—but would she accept him!

Aimée was not only beautiful and wealthy, she also had received the finest and most exclusive education available in Revolutionary France. She attended the school of Madame Campan at St. Germain-en-Laye. Jeanne Louise Henriette (Genest) Campan had been *femme de chambre* to Marie-Antoinette in the last years of the old regime, and she exerted an influence on the Empire second to no other woman.[17] When the Revolution abolished crown and nobility alike, she opened a school for girls where the daughters of the wealthy bourgeoisie, and of those noble families who had not fled the shadow of the guillotine, could receive an education that would reflect the grace and politeness of the court of Versailles. Here it was that Aimée met and became the good friend of Caroline Bonaparte, the future Queen of Naples, and Hortense de Beauharnais, Bonaparte's stepdaughter and future Queen of Holland. Here also she acquired the grace and charm of the eighteenth-century aristocracy. Indeed the hand of Mademoiselle Leclerc was a prize worthy of the ex-Burgundian aristocrat.

Aimée was aware of her brother's concern for her future and that he would sail to the West Indies much relieved if that future was made reasonably secure. Though she had refused General Lannes, she found General Davout to her liking. In order that the marriage might take place before Leclerc's departure, scheduled for the month of November, the date was fixed to coincide with the the second anniversary of the *coup d'état* of Brumaire—November 9, 1801. The hand of Bonaparte was becoming increasingly evident in the life of Louis Davout. The marriage contract was signed not only by the customary Parisian notary, but also by the First Consul, his wife, and all members of his family who were in Paris at the time. Thus Davout was formally received into the family. Besides the 150,000 francs which his wife received from her brother as a dowry, her trousseau amounted to about ten thousand francs from the estate of her late father and paternal grandfather. The young general on the other hand entered the union with modest means, if unlimited potential. Davout's total wealth was estimated at about twenty thousand francs, plus the house and dependent lands of Ravières.

The Davouts had scarcely settled down on the rue Matignon when the favor of the First Consul was again expressed in the form of his appointment as general in the *Garde Consulaire,* November 28, 1801. With the new position went a fashionable apartment on the Cours de l'Orangerie just off the rue St.-Florentin, near the Place de la Concorde. Davout commanded a regiment of grenadiers in the recently created guard, which was the forerunner of the Imperial Guard. Generals Nicolas Soult, Jean Baptiste Bessières, and Nicolas Marie de Songis commanded the other three regiments. There can be no question but that Davout owed this prestigous position to the fact that he had become, in the broadest sense of the word, part of the Bonaparte family. He was not only an accepted Bonapartist; he was now in the inner circle. He had come a long way in a few years; from an obscure general of brigade on the Rhine to a commander in the First Consul's guard. His rise was envied by some and resented by others. The jealousy which had originated between the men of the Rhine and the men of Italy had become increasingly sharper and more bitter as Bonaparte's star rose, and as those he favored rose with it.

This is perhaps best seen in an exchange of letters between Davout and one General François Chasseloup in March 1802. Chasseloup was inspector general of engineers at the time and there was some question of reuniting the engineers with the artillery under one inspector. In a letter dated March 18, Chasseloup accused Davout of being Bonaparte's henchman (*séide*) and denounced the favoritism shown the officers who had served in Egypt: "You have told me that he [Bonaparte] gave much consideration to those who had been in Egypt; but is Egypt more precious to France than the departments of the Meuse, the Rhine and the North, and those who had defended them in their time of great danger, should they be considered less by the head of the French Government? Why is it that at a time when unity is desired the army is being divided into two parts, those who had been in Egypt and those who had not been there?" [18] In his reply, dated March 19, Davout denied that he was a henchman of the First Consul, defended the commands given to men of the Army of Egypt—particularly that of his brother-in-law Leclerc, and tried to reassure Chasseloup that Bonaparte was above all just, and that he did not intend to place the engineer corp under the artillery.[19]

However Davout's explanations and justifications prove weak in the face of the facts, and few observers can deny the favoritism shown the men of Italy and Egypt. Even the accusation that he was a *séide* cannot be wholly discounted. Davout was developing a strong attachment to Bonaparte, which was based not only on his admiration for the latter's military and administrative talents, but also on the firm conviction that he was acting in the best interest of France. Nor did Davout forget the ever increasing blessings Bonaparte bestowed upon him and his family in the form of positions, honors, and wealth. Yet it should be pointed out that Bonaparte's favors were in most cases bestowed upon men of ability. The combination which spelled success in Napoleonic France, though exceptions may be cited, was ability and faithful service. Even the closest members of the family were criticized, and on occasion removed from high position, because of incompetence or unfaithfulness.[20] Whether or not it was favoritism that secured General Leclerc command of the expedition of Haiti may be argumentative, but that he lost his life on that West Indian island is a matter of recorded history.

Leclerc was able to bring Santo Domingo, the western half of the island of Haiti, under his control, and with great difficulty, to maintain that control. But as had been the case with the Army of Egypt earlier, his army was slowly dying of disease. Furthermore, like the Army of Egypt, the expeditionary force to Santo Domingo was inadequately supplied from France. All went well in the early months of the expedition, but by the end of the summer, 1802, conditions had become desperate. "Sickness is making progress here," he wrote his brother-in-law, "I have already lost four aides de camp, a number of *chefs de corps,* many officers, soldiers and employees. . . . I have no money left and no hospital supplies. I have received nothing since my arrival at Santo Domingo except flour." While suffering from fever himself he wrote to Davout (September 28): "My entire army is dead or dying. Every day they die before my very eyes." [21] Of the thirty-three thousand men who had been sent to Santo Domingo, twenty-four thousand had died and an additional seven thousand lay suffering in military hospitals within one year. It was only a quêstion of time before the general himself died of yellow fever, on November 2, 1802. His wife Pauline, who had accompanied him on the expedition, returned to France with their small son Dermide and went into mourning at Montgovert in Aisne. Aimée Davout was deeply grieved by her brother's death. She felt, as did others, that if the First Consul had sent adequate supplies and reinforcements to Santo Domingo that her brother would not have been worked so hard and would have lived. This was the first, and remained the major, grievance which Madame Davout held against Napoleon; and it would begin to strain their relationship which until this time had been growing closer.

While she was still mourning the loss of her brother an even greater tragedy befell Madame Davout. On August 12, 1803, her first-born child died of convulsions. The baby boy had lived just one year. Born in mid-August of 1802, he had been named Paul after his maternal grandfather at the request of General Leclerc, the infant's godfather. This double tragedy plunged Madame Davout into a state of depression which was only relieved by the joy of the birth of her second child.

She spent most of her time at Savigny-sur-Orge. The estate, just eight miles south of Paris, was purchased by the Davouts in August 1802 from the Hamelin family for 760,000 francs. The acquisition of Savigny was an extravagant step for them, but despite the financial strain, it proved to be an everlasting source of happiness for both Davout and his wife. Madame Davout was to spend virtually every spring, summer, and fall in the country, coming to Paris only in the winter and when social etiquette and her responsibilities at court required her presence.[22]

During 1802 and the first half of 1803 Davout continued to serve the First Consul in his guard. He accompanied Bonaparte to Malmaison from time to time, though the greater part of his time was spent in Paris. He did not accompany the First Consul on his tour of Belgium and the Channel ports in the spring of 1803; but when Bonaparte made a second trip to the west Davout was by his side. Leaving Paris at the end of June, the party visited Dunkirk, Ostend, Antwerp, and returned to the capital by way of Brussels, Sedan, and Reims, arriving before mid-August.[23]

Bonaparte's two visits to the English Channel had as their main purpose the selection of ports of debarkation for the projected invasion of England. In May 1803 the Treaty of Amiens was repudiated by England. It is generally agreed that both England and France were responsible for the renewal of hostilities; but the question of who must bear the greater responsibility for the breakdown of the peace is still debatable. There is no question but that Bonaparte engaged in political aggression in Italy and Switzerland, and it is equally certain that in direct violation of the Treaty of Amiens the English refused to evacuate the island of Malta. The French troops in Holland which the English protested were of relatively little importance since Bonaparte would most likely have withdrawn them. He could have controlled the country from south of the Rhine. Thus, with the French blaming the English and the English blaming the French, both accelerated their preparations for war.

The English had no allies on the Continent when the struggle moved into this next phase. France still dominated the Continent and the English navy posed a deadly threat to any who ventured to sea. If the French could but cross the Channel all would be theirs. However, the Channel was twenty miles of water. Bonaparte was not one to be easily discouraged. Even before the peace had been completely renounced he was making plans for the invasion of the British Isles. To this end he established the main French army along the Atlantic and North Sea coasts from the Pyrenees to the Elbe. England's former continental possession, Hanover, was occupied by General Bernadotte when hostilities were resumed. His army corps formed the extreme right wing of the French army. To his left was General Marmont in Holland with his headquarters at Utrecht. Next in line moving south were three corps commanded respectively by Davout, centered at Bruges, Soult at Saint-Omer, and Ney at Montreuil. Smaller units were spread on southward to Bayonne, but the main invasion force was concentrated between the Somme and The Hague.

Davout had been informed on August 29, 1803,[24] that he was to command the camp at Bruges, which came to be known as the III

THE DAVOUT CHÂTEAU AT SAVIGNY-SUR-ORGE. Located eight miles south of Paris, it was purchased by the Davouts in August 1802. This country seat was a source of continuing pleasure for the marshal and his family. After the death of her husband, Madame Davout continued to live at the château until her own death in 1868.—*Courtesy of Donald D. Horward*

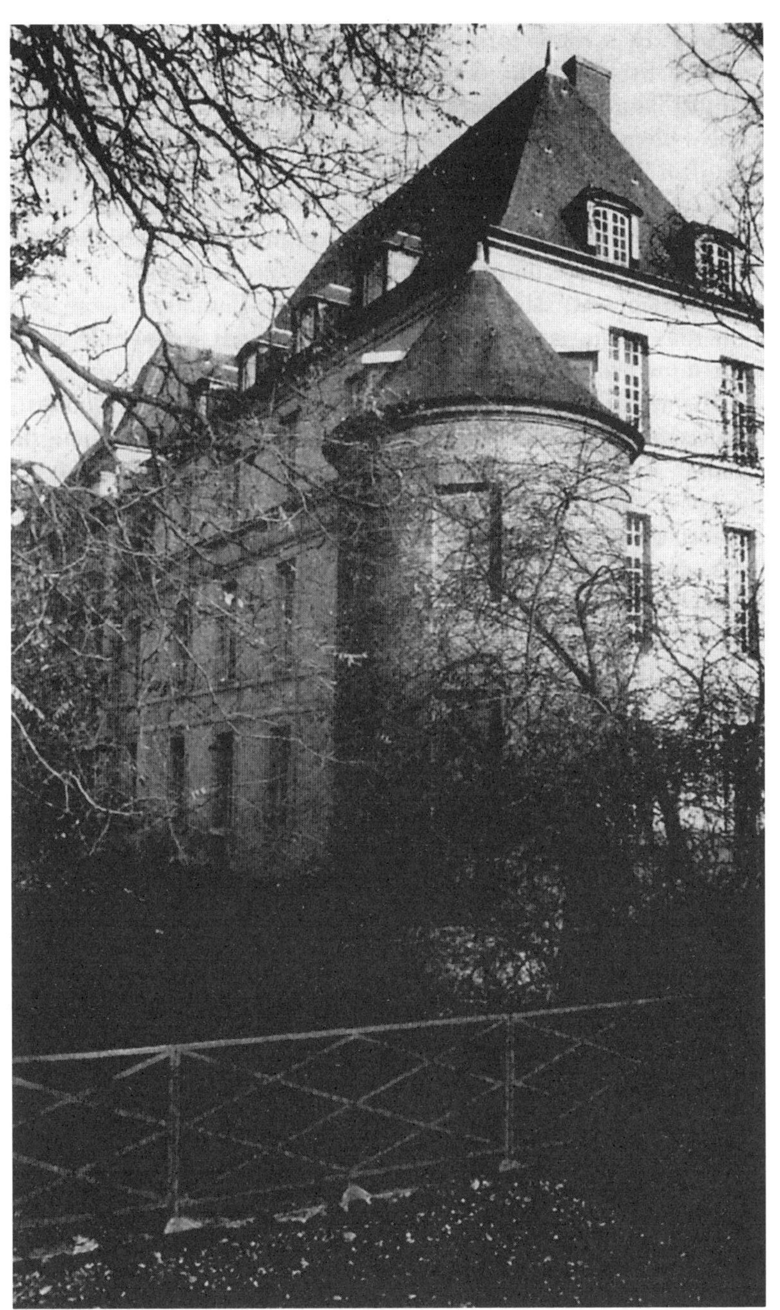

Corps of the invasion army. It was made up of three divisions commanded by Generals Oudinot, Durutte, and Friant. General Mathieu Dumas was appointed his chief of staff.[25] His command included the very important harbors of Dunkirk and Ostend, the island of Walcheren, and various other smaller islands in its immediate vicinity. Dunkirk and Ostend were to be the main centers of activities for the units under his command. The 1st and 2nd Divisions (under Oudinot and Durutte) were stationed at Ostend, while Friant's 3rd Division was encamped at Dunkirk. These were to be the staging areas from which the divisions would embark for England when the time came for the invasion.

The operation was not a feint, or a mere idle threat. Bonaparte unquestionably intended to invade England. The harbors along the Channel from Etaples to Ostend were deepened and improved.[26] Barracks and other facilities necessary for military camps were established, and boats capable of withstanding the choppy Channel were constructed to hold one hundred men each. The greater part of Davout's work during these years was of an organizational and administrative nature.

Arriving at Bruges on September 14, Davout quickly surveyed his new command, and in a lengthy letter to the First Consul gave a full account of the three main tasks confronting him: 1) "The prompt organization of the army and the construction of barracks at Ostend and Dunkirk; 2) Maritime construction [improvements of harbors]; 3) The defense of the coast and particularly Ostend." [27] The organization and quartering of his corps provided no immediate problems. The work on the improvements of the habors was slower than the First Consul would have liked, but it was completed within the time allotted. The most difficult tasks confronting Davout were the defense of the coast against English attacks, the protection of communications along the coast, and the maintenance of the health of his men in the cold wet climate of the Ostend area.

The resumption of hostilities and the concentration of French troops along the Channel were not taken idly by the English. They began to prepare for the possibility of an invasion. To prevent, or at least to delay, such an amphibious operation, the Royal Navy began to harass French communications along the coast and to blockade all ports. The commander of each French camp was responsible for the protection of coastal shipping along the coast under his control. This protection was based mainly on the positioning of artillery at strategic points to prevent the English ships from venturing too close to shore. These guns also served to prevent the enemy from making raids on the mainland to disrupt French preparation for the forthcoming invasion, or from gaining intelligence about such preparations. Supporting these coastal defense guns were horse-drawn mobile artillery and cavalry. These units were designed to come to the aid of ships in trouble which could not be protected by the larger stationary guns.

On October 6, 1803, the First Consul reprimanded Davout for the loss of a sloop northeast of Dunkirk. "Citizen General Davout," wrote Bonaparte, "a French sloop has been captured between Nieuport and Dunkirk by the English. . . . This sloop had run aground; but there were only three gendarmes and two men of the 108th there to defend it, the English forced them away and took the sloop. You have not, as had been ordered, stationed cavalry and mobile artillery at all points necessary for the support [of shipping]. If these patrols and mobile artillery are not properly organized, give the necessary orders without delay." [28] Three days later, October 9, Davout answered: "My General, I have the honor of assuring you that the two companies of *artillerie légère* which exist in this military district are organized into mobile batteries; one is at the disposition of Adjutant General [Maximilien] Foy at Dunkirk, and the other is in the vicinity of Ostend at the disposition of Vice-Admiral Emeriau. . . . This latter company did not receive any horses until after the capture of the sloop to which you made reference in your letter of the 13th [13 Vendémiaire—October 6]." [29]

The lack of supplies, such as horses, filled Davout's correspondence to Bonaparte through the fall of 1803. As early as September 15 Davout had pointed out that he had but two companies of feeble foot artillery to defend Ostend. On September 24 he wrote that while six pieces of artillery had arrived, the ammunition which was to accompany them had not, and there was a great shortage. This same letter included an itemized list of supplies deemed necessary for the defense of the coast.[30] As the season advanced the question of some eight thousand blankets for the troops was raised. Davout wrote on October 29 that they existed on paper only.[31] Yet, comparatively speaking, the camp at Bruges was fairly well supplied by the time winter set in, and defenses along the coast were giving adequate protection to the limited shipping which dared the guns of the Royal Navy.

The fall of 1803 witnessed also the capture of Baron Friedrich Wilhelm Bülow and his execution as a spy. The baron arrived at Ostend on November 13. On that same day, he entered the military barracks and began to question the soldiers about reinforcements they had received, their life at Ostend, and their pay. Bülow was immediately arrested and imprisoned by order of the commanding general. In his possessions were discovered a sword, two English pistols, 500 louis in gold, and a letter from his wife indicating that she knew of his dangerous mission which would result in a large financial reward. Furthermore, his servant who accompanied him declared that his master was in the service of the English.[32] Duly informed of these events, the First Consul wrote Davout on November 23, "name a commission of five officers to judge him [Bülow] within twenty-four hours for espionage, and have him shot. This example is necessary; our coasts are inundated with these miserable ones." [33] The Baron Bülow was tried, convicted, and on December 6 shot by a firing squad in the presence of a large number of inhabitants of Ostend.[34]

The French army encamped along the English Channel seldom saw the enemy except at a respectable distance, from which the Royal Navy kept watch on the French preparations. There were occasional skirmishes but scarcely anything that might be called a battle. Life in the various camps was dull and the real enemy was not the English but the fever which was the major cause of disablement and death. Bonaparte was very much aware of this fact and concerned himself constantly with the health of his army. The health of the troops, he wrote to Davout in September of 1803, is "the first of all military considerations." [35] To be killed on the field of battle was a glorious death in the eyes of Napoleon, but to die in camp of disease was a deplorable waste of human life. In the low-lying lands about Ostend and on the islands of Zeeland, which were occupied by Davout's troops, yellow fever was the chief foe. Militarily the island of Walcheren was deemed strategically important and had to be defended. The neighboring island, Cadzandt, of less importance itself, served as a necessary link in the entire Zeeland district. In accordance with his orders Davout had garrisoned both.[36]

Two weeks after reporting this action he received a dispatch from the First Consul ordering the withdrawal of the Cadzandt garrison due to the poor health of the troops. Cadzandt, he went on to say, could be reoccupied in the event the English attacked Walcheren.[37] The demi-brigade which had been stationed on the island was withdrawn and only 250 men were left; and they were rotated frequently.

In almost every letter that Davout wrote to the First Consul or to the minister of war he commented the health of the troops. Early in October he reported that there were not as many sick as had been expected. By the middle of the month he had established a house in each camp to take care of soldiers when they first came down with fever. Not only did this render quick first aid to the sick, but it also prevented those who recovered quickly from being absent from their units for a prolonged time. At the end of October he wrote that few were sick and the morale of the troops was high. By the second week of November there was only one hospital in use at Ostend, and on the twenty-first Davout reported that only 1,106 men were in hospitals and of this number 400 were in regimental hospitals and not very ill.[38] By December the worst of the yellow fever season had passed and the subject is no longer mentioned in his correspondence.

The fall of 1804, however, witnessed a return of the fever in even greater proportions than the previous year. In preparation for the expected epidemic Davout established a commission in each division which consisted of three officers—a line officer, a medical officer, and a special service officer—who were charged with the responsibility of assuring the best possible conditions for the maintenance of good health. They inspected meat and fruit and kept a constant check of the water the men drank. Then a special order of the day, September 13, forbade the eating of green fruit and required that only cooked fruit could be served the men. Orders were also issued for the proper ventilation of barracks.[39] In his letter to Napoleon on September 5, Davout had stated that his army corps was suffering greatly from yellow fever. The division at Dunkirk had one-third of its men on the sick list. In some units the figure ran higher. On September 21, 1804, he wrote: "I have the honor to inform you, Sire, that I have sent the 111th Line into cantonnement; it has one-half of its men in the hospital." [40] At Ostend he ordered the barracks to be raised seven or eight inches off the ground in order to diminish the dampness. But despite this and other measures taken he found it necessary to rotate the troops of the two divisions at Ostend so that they spent every other twenty days in convalescent camps which were set up in healthier areas inland.[41] Additional hospitals were established to accommodate the sick, and in some cases entire positions were evacuated, such as the military installations at Nieuport, Gravelines, Furnes, and l'Ecluse.[42] But despite all care and precautions the fever ran its course and continued to ravish the army until the cold weather set in. While the measures taken did improve the overall sanitation of the army, and certainly the evacuation of the most unhealthy camps reduced the numbers affected by the fever, the fact remained that the cause of yellow fever was unknown and there was no real cure for the disease. As October wore on and the weather turned cold, the numbers in the hospitals declined and life began to return to normal. Nevertheless, the death rate had been awesome. During the height of the fever Davout reported that fifty men had died each day in the hospitals.[43]

The relationship between Davout and Napoleon continued to improve during the two years which he commanded the camp at Bruges (September 1803–August 1805). In December, 1803, he became one of the first members of the *Légion d'honneur*. This honor he owed to a combination of factors—his relationship to the Bonaparte family, his past military service, and his present position as commander of the camp at Bruges—but they could all be condensed into a simple formula: the good will of the First Consul. Their cordial relationship can also be seen in Napoleon's correspondence to Davout during these years. He continually expressed satisfaction—though not without occasional criticism—with the manner in which the camp at Bruges was being operated. It should, of course, be pointed out that Davout did everything within his power to satisfy his superior and court his favor. The degree to which he succeeded is perhaps best illustrated in his being named Marshal of the Empire with the original eighteen.

The creation of the Marshals of the Empire was directly connected to the establishment of the Empire itself. Napoleon Bonaparte had become Consul for life in 1802 with the right of nominating his successor. But the plots against his life—real or fictitious

—aroused many Frenchmen to concern over the possibility of Bonaparte being removed from the political scene. Whether by an assassin's bullet while he slept, or a cannon ball while in battle, or simply by more natural causes, the question of what would follow seemed to them a real one. Would France lapse back into the turmoil of the 1790s from which, many felt, Bonaparte had lifted it. Or, and what was equally feared by the majority, would his death lead to a restoration of the Bourbons and the old regime. Bonaparte had become complete master of the state when the Constitution of the Year VIII had become the law of the land. The change from Consulate to Empire did not affect the basic structure of government; rather it was merely a question of changing the terminology. The one advantage to be gained was the establishment of the Bonaparte dynasty to assure a continuation of those gains of the Revolution which had been consolidated by their incorporation into the Napoleonic regime. While it was true that the new Emperor did not have any children at the time, he did have four brothers who might succeed him and establish the succession.

Davout first heard rumors that an Empire was in the offing during the spring of 1804. On April 21 his good friend Michel Duroc wrote to him from Paris: "Everyone here is speaking of an emperor, heredity, and succession; it is the subject of every story which has been invented since the last action of the Senate. The fact is that we are not absolutely positive of anything; it can only be said that there is intrigue on every side."[44] Such news was not unwelcome to Davout's ears. With his future firmly attached to Bonaparte, he could anticipate only personal gain from the establishment of an Empire. On the first of May he gave his wholehearted approval: "Citizen First Consul," he wrote, "I have the honor of addressing to you the spontaneous expression of the generals, officers, soldiers, inspectors of the services and the administrators of the camp of Bruges. They demand, along with all Frenchmen, to be assured, by an order of unvarying succession in your family, of the heredity of the supreme Magistracy. The army also desires for you to take the title of Emperor of the French [*empereur des Gaules*]. This is less an honor for you than a guarantee of our happiness to come. Your name alone surpasses all the titles which are given to those who govern. But as you command a grand and brave nation, you must take a title as is assigned to sovereigns of the most powerful nations. . . . You will remove all hope of the Bourbons who are without virtue or glory."[45]

Assurance of support from the army[46] such as that received from Davout removed the last traces of doubt and hesitation, if indeed there had been either doubt or hesitation in the mind of Bonaparte, and on May 18, 1804, the Empire became a reality. The final decision was presented to the electorate in the form of a referendum as the establishment of the Consulate had been in 1799 and the appointment as Consul for life in 1802; and, as in the two previous plebiscites, the French people voted their overwhelming approval. The founding of the Empire brought about numerous changes from the revolutionary Republic of the 1790s. Such terms as *citizen* gave way to *subject,* and the necessity of reestablishing the old social hierarchy which the Revolution had destroyed became apparent as an Emperor must have a court, complete with the ceremonies and habits of an eighteenth-century monarchy. The Emperor's older brother Joseph was given the title of Grand Elector as he was the heir apparent to the throne. Other members of the imperial family also received titles as did the high officials of the government. In keeping with this trend eighteen generals of the army were raised to the dignity of Marshal of the Empire.[47]

The eighteen men singled out by the new Emperor in the decree dated May 19, 1804, were chosen for a variety of reasons. Four were "honorary" (Kellermann, Lefebvre, Pérignon, and Serurier) and their nominations were based on services rendered to the Republic. They were not expected to command army units in time of war, but rather were meant to signify the continuity between the Republic and the Empire. The selection of the fourteen "active" marshals was based on a more complicated formula.[48]

The selection of the marshals was based not only on the criteria of faithful service and personal loyalty but also on the necessity of winning over the opposition. Men like Berthier, Ney, Murat, and Davout were attached personally to the Emperor and their appointments surprised few. But others, such as Augereau and Bernadotte—outspoken opponents of the Consulate—need more of an explanation. In their cases (which also included Jourdan and Masséna) Napoleon hoped to win them over to his side by making them a part of the new order. If they held high positions under the Empire which were accompanied by equally high financial status, they would have a vested interest in the Empire and would be less likely to plot against it or to grumble of the even more honored position of their once equal Emperor. The number of marshals did not remain fixed throughout the Empire. With endless war, petty jealousies and rivalries, the number rose to twenty-two by 1814.[49] In all there were twenty-six men named Marshal of the Empire. Eighteen were named in May 1804: Pierre François Augereau, Jean Baptiste Bernadotte, Louis-Alexandre Berthier, Jean Baptiste Bessières, Guillaume-Marie Brune, Louis Nicolas Davout, Jean Baptiste Jourdan, François Christophe Kellermann, Jean Lannes, François Joseph Lefebvre, André Masséna, Bon Adrien Jeannot Moncey, Edouard Adolphe Mortier, Joachim Murat, Michel Ney, Dominique Catherine Pérignon, Jean Mathieu Serurier, and Nicolas Jean de Dieu Soult. Those marshals appointed during the Empire were: Claude Perrin Victor (1807), Jacques Etienne Macdonald (1809), Auguste Frédéric Marmont (1809), Nicolas Charles Oudinot (1809), Louis Gabriel Suchet (1811), Laurent Gouvion St.-Cyr (1812), Joseph Anthony Poniatowski (1813), and Emmanuel Grouchy (1815). These were Davout's peers, colleagues, and enemies.

Davout owed his own promotion to the dignity of Marshal directly to Napoleon. There were other generals in the French army in 1804 with more impressive military records. He had not, in fact, commanded an army in combat. His years with the armies of the Rhine and in Egypt were spent below the rank of divisional commander, and in the final phases of the Second Italian Campaign he served under General Brune. His first major command was the camp of Bruges. He was known only in limited circles in the army as a whole. This is not to say that he did not have a good war record; but the reasons behind his elevation must in the main be sought elsewhere, for France at this time had perhaps a surplus of generals with good war records, and this was actually a minimum requirement. Davout had literally attached himself to Bonaparte. He had become one of the "men of Egypt," one of the *"sans culottes"* of the Army of Italy. In Egypt he had opposed Kléber and evacuation, a position which endeared him to the First Consul. He had been the close friend and protégé of Desaix, whom Napoleon had held in high esteem. With the death of this capable and talented soldier Bonaparte seemed to have shifted his affection to Davout, and perhaps even to have heaped upon him the honor which Desaix would certainly have received had he lived. Still one additional consideration must be included in this explanation of Davout's marshalcy. It is his marriage to Aimée Leclerc. By this union he was drawn into the "greater" Bonaparte family. He was the brother-in-law of the Emperor's deceased brother-in-law. Had General Leclerc lived he surely would have been named Marshal in 1804 and perhaps in time even a king. The Emperor's brother-in-law Murat was to follow this path to the Kingdom of Naples. Thus it may have been that the Leclerc baton was given to his sister's husband.

To suggest that Davout's rapid rise during the Napoleonic era was "blood money" would be stretching the imagination and misunderstanding the Emperor; but the Marshal's close connections with both Leclerc and Desaix cannot be passed over lightly. It may appear that Davout's own talents and merits have been slighted in this search for an adequate explanation of his appointment; yet the fact remains that while he would prove to be one of the most capable commanders and administrators of the Empire, these talents had not, by 1804, had sufficient opportunity to be shown. Bonapartists have, in retrospect, used Davout's promotion to indicate the Emperor's good judgment in the selection of men to serve him. In this instance they indeed have one of their strongest cases.

Davout's marriage to Aimée Leclerc was a successful one when the general qualifications of success are applied. In the five volumes of correspondence and comments edited by his daughter, the Marquise de Blocqueville,[50] he gives unquestionable testimony of his love and affection for his *petite Aimée*. Although few of her letters to him have survived, those which have, coupled with her absolute faithfulness, bear witness to her own devotion to her husband. On only one occasion is he accused of infidelity—during his command in Poland.[51] This "romance" was in fact little more than a passing fancy. Davout was known to both his friends and enemies alike as a man of high personal morals.

During the first fourteen years of their marriage[52] France was at war for all but eighteen months. Davout was able to spend very little of his time with his wife and family. Even when he was not actually on campaign he was stationed outside of France as military governor or commander of a military district. His marriage was thus saddened by prolonged absences and the anxiety of numerous battles, any one of which could have made Mme. Davout a young widow. As a general, and then as a marshal, Davout was able to visit Paris and Savigny on personal, as well as official, business more frequently and for longer periods of time than lesser officers; yet still there were long periods—some more than a year—when he did not see his wife or children. She never accompanied him on campaign for Napoleon would not allow it. However, during lulls in the fighting while he commanded in the Germanies and Poland she would visit him for periods of up to several months.

Under normal circumstances the prolonged absences of Davout could have been endured by his wife. The Napoleonic period was, after all, marked by the long departure of the men at war, and it would have been more unusual had her husband been home during these years. But all was not normal in the Davout household. Their first two children died within a year of their births. These tragedies, preceded by the death of her brother, kept Mme. Davout in an almost constant state of depression for more than four years. Without her husband to support and comfort her, except during brief visits and in his letters, she spent the greater part of this time in mourning and in poor health. The birth of their third child (named Josephine) in the summer of 1805 brought her some relief; and as the family grew in the years that followed, life became more pleasant. After his return from Hamburg in the early summer of 1814 the family remained together, except for a brief period after the Hundred Days, until his death in 1823.

Davout's first prolonged separation from his wife began in late August 1803 when he took command of the camp at Bruges. It was also at this time that he began the voluminous correspondence which provides an excellent insight into the man. During the winter of 1803–4 he suffered from the fever which was so common among the men in the unhealthy regions along the Channel. In December his wife who was then four months pregnant, joined him at Bruges and remained with him until the end of January. During this period she cared for him as best she could, but as he would not rest in bed the fever remained with him for more than six weeks. Sick though he was he insisted upon continuing in personal command of his army.

Madame Davout gave birth to her second child—a daughter—in May of 1804. As Madame Bonaparte was chosen to be the child's godmother, she was appropriately named Josephine. The baby quickly became a source of joy for her mother, and the memory of the loss of her firstborn seemed to be crowded out of her thoughts. In the weeks preceding this joyous event there had been much anxiety at Savigny and Bruges. Davout had requested a leave of absence, but had received no reply. The expectant mother tended to grow resentful at his continual absences [53] and he found it necessary to explain and justify his remaining with his army. In his letter of March 18, 1804, he wrote: "The First Consul has judged it appropriate to give me employment which forces me to be away from you: the gratitude which I owe him, the honor, and my unlimited devotion toward him, impose on me the obligation to do that which is required of me to fulfill his intentions and merit his confidence. These same motives obligate me to be separated momentarily from my *petite Aimée.*" [54] One week later, when it was still uncertain as to whether he would be home for the coming event, he again defended Bonaparte's judgment: "If the First Consul does not give me this permission [to leave his army], it is because he will have judged my presence here necessary for the good of the army, and this reason is law for me." [55] Permission was then granted and Davout was able to spend nearly a week near his wife and new daughter.

Despite the birth and good health of the infant Josephine, Madame Davout lapsed into periods of melancholy. She did not enjoy Paris society, prefering the quiet of Savigny to which she invited only a few close friends and family. She dearly missed her husband and complained in her letters that he did not visit Paris as often as other generals, and that he should write more often, like M. Cafarelli, who wrote sometimes three times a day.[56] In reply to such charges Davout countered: "You cite me the example of Cafarelli who writes sometimes three times in the same day; but Cafarelli stays with Mme. Bonaparte all of the time [this referring to the Bonapartes' visit to the army in August 1804], whereas I am always with the Consul. Bessières and Duroc are in the same situation as I am. Find out which of the three of us writes most often to his wife." Besides, he went on: "I have a better right to complain of the rarity of your letters." [57]

As winter settled over the French army along the Channel the marshals of the newly created Empire were summoned to Paris for the coronation of Napoleon I as Emperor of the French. In late November Davout turned over command of the camp of Bruges to the senior officer and, accompanied by his three lieutenant generals, Oudinot, Charles Etienne Gudin, and Friant, and three brigadier generals, he left for the capital. The coronation took place on December 2, 1804, but the round of parties and entertainment lasted well into the new year. At last, at the Emperor's bidding, the minister of war issued the following instructions: "Give orders to Marshals Soult, Davout, Jourdan, Bernadotte, Augereau and General Marmont to rejoin their armies before the 1st of Ventôse [February 26, 1805]."[58]

With the creation of the Empire, the royal family, the line of succession, and the marshals, it followed quite naturally that all of the trappings of a monarchy, which had been abolished by the Revolution, would gradually be restored. The title of marshal was not meant to be a military rank or distinction but a political one. Napoleon made it clear that on campaigns the marshals were no more than generals, and that the mere possession of a baton did not raise one general above any other. The honors and distinctions which the marshalcy carried were to be found at court and in the social hierarchy of the Empire, as were also their duties and obligations. Davout, for example, became the president of the College of Electors of Yonne, a position which was purely political.

In carrying out the restoration of the monarchy the wives of the newly created imperial dignitaries bore their husband's titles—thus Madame Davout became *la Maréchale*—and were assigned to household duties with the imperial family as ladies in waiting. In the spring of 1805 Madame Davout was attached to the household of Madame Mère, the Emperor's mother. The assignment was not at all to her liking, and she immediately wrote her husband that she intended to refuse the position. She believed that she had ample reason in that she was once again pregnant and her general health was poor; in fact her health had not been good for the past several years. However, there was more to her refusal than her health. She was disappointed at not being attached to the household of the Empress, which would have been a higher honor even if turned down for reasons of health. In her *Mémoires* Madame Junot wrote the following: "The Marechale Davoust [*sic*] formed a member of the court of Madame Mère. But her pretensions were more elevated, and she was disappointed in not having been named a lady of honour to the Empress. She professed ill health, and gave in her resignation before my arrival at Paris." [59] There was no friendship between Madame Davout and Madame Junot, whose husband never received a marshal's baton and who was considerably beneath the Princess of Eckmühl in the social structure at the time she wrote. But there was undoubtedly truth in her words. What Madame Junot did not see fit to mention, although it was rapidly becoming common knowledge, was that Madame Davout had lost most of the affection for the Bonaparte family which she had once had and did not wish to be a lady in waiting to any member of the royal family. Such service would require her to spend long periods of time at court which she wished to avoid as much as possible.

When informed by his wife that she intended to refuse the Emperor's appointment, Davout immediately wrote: "We have had kindness and favors heaped on us by the Emperor, thus to show our gratitude, it is necessary to do what he wishes, and to do so with grace so that he may never know how much it vexes us. . . . Finally, I will terminate with a reflection: It would be selfish to refuse a duty because it involves duties when one takes from the same person on the other hand high honors and financial rewards; and neither you nor I are selfish." [60] Then four days later he again urged his wife to accept the position offered her and added: "We owe so much to the Emperor and Empress, because it was they who made possible our marriage, that it seems to me that we should accept all with gratitude; . . . I know well that your health, your preferences and my own, are in opposition; but, *ma petite Aimée,* these are reasons dictated by selfishness; we owe everything to our Majesties." [61] Still Madame Davout hesitated. Finally on March 31 he wrote: "In my letters of the 4th and 6th [of Germinal] I have tried to prove to you that not only should you have accepted, but that it was necessary to do so with grace and gratitude. The kindness which I have received from the Emperor imposes the obligation of that which he desires." Yet he concluded by telling her to make the final decision. "Do what you must, and I swear to you that I will never reproach you." [62] Thus despite the strong urging of her husband Madame Davout requested, and received, permission to be detached from the household of the Emperor's mother on grounds of her poor health. But neither

her health nor her advanced stage of pregnancy prevented her from accompanying her husband to Auxerre late in April.

As President of the Electoral College of Yonne the Marshal was required to preside over sessions of that body beginning April 26, 1805. The occasion was used for a reunion with his wife. After spending three days at Savigny, they made the journey to Auxerre together arriving the day before the opening session.[63] In addition to fulfilling his political duties, Davout sought out his old teacher Dom Laporte, who had contributed so much to his student days. The school itself had been closed as anticlericalism had gained ground during the Revolution and was then reopened as a secular military academy in the former abbey Saint-Germain—the monks having been turned out. Its title was changed first to *Ecole centrale,* and then to *Ecole secondaire,* but the school had not flourished despite capable leadership. The Benedictines who had run it before the Revolution had been scattered; Dom Laporte had found asylum in the hamlet of Augy not far from Auxerre.[64] Davout requested that he be brought to the *préfecture* where he was staying. The elderly cleric was not received well by the local officials when he arrived, but when they saw the Marshal embrace him as a long-lost friend and show him the greatest respect, they quickly followed suit. As the direct result of the wishes of the Marshal the school was reopened on January 1, 1806, in its former location with Dom Laporte as its principal.[65]

The pleasant weeks which the Davouts spent together during April and May were quickly followed by tragedy and sorrow. The death of their second child (Josephine) who was not yet one year of age, left Madame Devout inconsolable. The Marshal again left his army at Bruges to be with her, but the relief was only temporary as he had to rejoin his command in less than a week. The long awaited invasion of England was drawing close, and it was absolutely essential that he be with his troops.

The Bonapartes were in Milan when they heard of this tragedy. On the first of June the Empress wrote to Madame Davout: "I take, Madame, a very real part in the great sadness which is testing you, and the interest which your daughter had inspired in me makes me even more sensitive to your pain and her loss. If I were not so far from you it would be with true feeling that I would endeavor to aid you to support this painful blow. It comforts me to know that my daughter [Hortense de Beauharnais Bonaparte] takes my place, and I hope that her affection for you will cause you to recall that assurance which I renew here." [66]

Throughout the summer of 1805 Davout did all he could to console his remorseful wife but with little success. He advised her not to spend the summer at Savigny alone but go to Paris where she could take a more active part in social events which would occupy her mind. If she insisted upon remaining in the country, then she should invite friends, such as her sister-in-law, Madame Soult, and Madame Dumas.[67] Despite all efforts she remained in mourning even as the time approached for her to give birth to a third child. Finally on August 4 the Marshal wrote a rather sharp letter to her telling her that she should take better care of her health and be more concerned with her unborn child than with the one which was dead.[68]

The constant realization that her husband might not be at her side when her time would come was still another thorn in the side of the already depressed expectant mother. Davout's pressing responsibilities on the Channel during the summer months, when an invasion of England could take place, left only a remote possibility that he would be free to return to Paris, even for such an important event. And so it was that Madame Davout gave birth to a baby girl without the support of her husband, which she so desperately needed. Their new daughter was named Josephine after the Empress and in memory of the child they had just lost.[69]

6

The Austerlitz Campaign

THE POSSIBILITY of the renewal of hostilities on the Continent had been an ever present danger since the rupture of the peace of Amiens in May of 1803. Although Napoleon's armies were on the Channel facing England, he was constantly looking over his shoulder across the Rhine and the Alps. Austria was still basically discontented with the Treaty of Lunéville which she had been forced to accept following the victorious campaigns that broke up the Second Coalition. Furthermore, Napoleon used his dominent position in western Europe to reorganize not only Italy but Germany as well.

The Imperial Recess of 1803 strengthened French influence in Germany at the expense of Austria. This settlement not only recognized France's annexation of the Left Bank of the Rhine, but enlarged the south German states of Bavaria, Baden, and Württemberg. It also increased the size of Prussia by adding to it some half million souls. These gains were made at the expense of the ecclesiastical states and free cities of the defunct Holy Roman Empire, which had existed only on paper and in the minds of the Hapsburg emperors for the past hundred and fifty years. This Imperial Recess served the dual purpose of winning over the south German states as French allies and preventing Prussia, at least temporarily, from aligning herself with England and Russia.

Russia had accepted the Recess, which directly benefited the relatives of Alexander I (1801–25) on the thrones of Baden and Württemberg, but relations with France had grown cooler with the ascent of the new Tsar. Not only were Alexander and his advisers Anglophiles, but the Tsar suspected and distrusted Napoleon's intense interest in the Ottoman Empire and the east. His objections to the French occupation of the seaports of the kingdom of Naples stemmed more from this fear of French expansion toward the Balkans and Constantinople than from the fact that Russia had a treaty of alliance with the King of Naples. Shortly after Pitt returned to power in May of 1804 Russia began negotiations with both England and Austria to form a coalition against France.

Napoleon did not want a war on the Continent in 1805. He was absorbed with his plans for the invasion of England, and to carry out this operation it was necessary for Prussia and Austria to remain neutral. Yet the French Emperor had done nothing to gain the friendship of Austria and, it would seem, much to antagonize that already potential enemy. Austria was rapidly drifting toward a state of war psychology in 1804 and needed little encouragement from either Russia or England. The Emperor Francis II held back only because his army was not yet ready to march against the powerful war machine which Napoleon had built. Already vexed by her loss of influence and prestige in Italy and Germany, Austria was to become even more unhappy as the months passed. The creation of the French Empire, the *Te Deum* sung at Aix-la-Chapelle in the presence of the relics of Charlemagne (September 1804), the assumption of the iron crown of the Lombards (May 1805), and the kidnapping and execution of the Duke of Enghien [1] (which also provoked the Russian court and Europe in general) all served to bring about Austria's entrance into the coalition.

The first overt act in the formation of the Third Coalition was the signing of an Anglo-Russian alliance on April 11, 1805.[2] But before operations could begin on the Continent Austria had to become a party of the Coalition. During the summer of 1805 the Austrians redoubled their efforts to bring their military forces up to a state of readiness. They reinforced their garrisons in the Tyrol and in Italy. Napoleon was not ignorant of these movements nor of the general attitude at the Austrian court. What he did not know, but did suspect, was that Austria formally joined with England and Russia in a coalition against him late in the summer. As early as the third week in July the French emperor had requested that Austria make clear her position. When he received no satisfaction he demanded that the Austrian emperor declare openly his position of neutrality. By this time, August 12, Francis II had already made his decision—war was inevitable.

Although the clouds of war were gathering in central Europe throughout the summer of 1805, Napoleon's principal focus remained in the west. The invasion of England, for which such elaborate preparations had been made, would require complete control of the English Channel during the critical period of the amphibious operation. The Emperor's estimate of the length of time his navy would have to control the waters between France and England tended to decrease as the tentative date for the operation approached. From an original estimate of two weeks he had narrowed it down to three days. Less than this would more than likely lead to disaster; more time would assure success. The army was ready by mid-summer 1805. It had the necessary small boats for the shore-to-shore operation and had been trained for the amphibious maneuver. Furthermore, Spain had become involved in the war with England, and Napoleon could count on the support of the Spanish navy to assist in gaining control of the Channel waters. It was only necessary to eliminate all possibility of Lord Nelson's powerful fleet being in home waters during the crucial days of the invasion.

To meet Nelson in pitched battle was not Napoleon's intention. Even should the combined Franco-Spanish squadron emerge victorious—which was highly questionable even in French quarters—it would be weakened to such an extent as to be of little use in the Channel. Therefore, Nelson had to be eliminated by some ruse of war. The plan settled upon was for the French and Spanish, under the command of Admiral Pierre Charles de Villeneuve, to sail to the West Indies under the pretext of menacing the English colonies there and thus lure Nelson out of European waters. Then Villeneuve would return without Nelson's knowledge and, with the support of the French squadron at Brest, dominate the Channel long enough for the army to be transported to England.

All went well up to the final phase of the plan. Nelson followed Villeneuve to the West Indies, and the French started back east without being detected. When the British admiral realized that Villeneuve had sailed east he sent a fast brig ahead which overtook the French fleet, noted its course, and reaching England first,

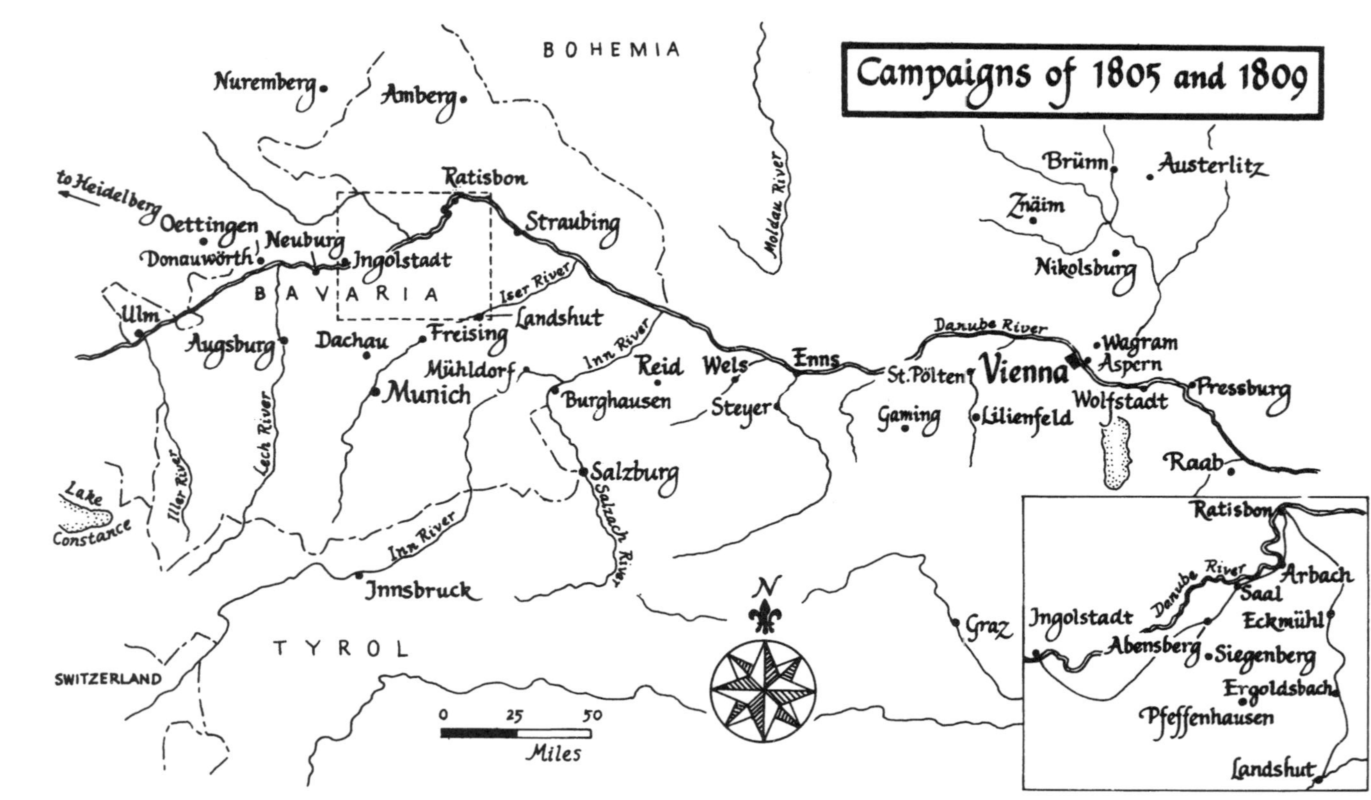
Campaigns of 1805 and 1809
BOHEMIA
Nuremberg
Amberg
to Heidelberg
Ratisbon
Oettingen
Neuburg
Straubing
Donauwörth
Ingolstadt
BAVARIA
Iser River
Ulm
Landshut
Augsburg
Dachau
Freising
Mühldorf
Inn River
Reid
Wels
Enns
Munich
Burghausen
Steyer
Lech River
Iller River
Lake Constance
Salzburg
Salzach River
Inn River
Innsbruck
TYROL
SWITZERLAND
0
25
50
Miles
N
Moldau River
Danube River
St. Pölten
Vienna
Gaming
Lilienfeld
Wagram
Aspern
Wolfstadt
Pressburg
Raab
Brünn
Austerlitz
Znäim
Nikolsburg
Graz
Ratisbon
Danube River
Arbach
Saal
Ingolstadt
Eckmühl
Abensberg
Siegenberg
Ergoldsbach
Pfeffenhausen
Landshut

sounded the alarm. Thus when Villeneuve arrived back in home waters he was faced with a hastily gathered English squadron. Rather than forcing the issue by engaging the enemy in battle, he sailed south to Cadiz (August 15) where Nelson found him upon his return.

Napoleon blamed Villeneuve for the failure of the invasion plans and he made a veritable whipping boy of him. Then the Emperor sent implicit orders to the admiral to break out of the blockade at Cadiz and sail into the Mediterranean. This played right into the hand of Nelson who was trying to find a way of tempting the enemy into the open sea to destroy him. Against his better judgment Villeneuve put to sea on October 21, 1805, and was engaged by the English squadron off Cape Trafalgar. The results were disastrous for the combined French and Spanish fleets. Though he lost his own life during the course of the battle, Lord Nelson won the greatest naval victory of the century. He sank or captured more than half of the enemy ships, thirty-three in all, in six hours, and captured four more in the pursuit which followed. All doubt was now gone, if indeed there had ever been any serious doubt, as to who was master of the seas. Napoleon did not again seriously contemplate an invasion of England, and it appeared that the initiative was slipping from his hands.

England now put into operation plans which would threaten Napoleon on the Continent. Using the armies of Austria and Russia, which were heavily supported by English gold, France's supremacy in central Europe was to be challenged in both Germany and Italy. The question of which of these traditional theaters of war should be dominant was one upon which the Allies had great difficulty agreeing. England desired the major effort to be made in Germany in order to draw the French army away from the Channel to the Rhine. On the other hand, Austria considered the expulsion of French influence from Italy of greater importance. The result was a division of Allied strength. Francis II sent his best troops under his most able commander, the Archduke Charles, to Italy and a smaller army commanded by the not so capable General Karl Mack up the Danube. Mack's army, actually under the command of the Archduke Ferdinand but directed by the general, was to be supported by a Russian army which was moving west toward the upper Danube. The Archduke Charles would conquer Italy and threaten southern France while Mack and his Russian ally would strike through southern Germany to Strasbourg. The plan was not a bad one, it simply was not carried out well in the north; and Napoleon was quick to take full advantage of errors.

Napoleonic strategy called for a reversal of the Austrian concept of importance with respect to the two traditional theaters of operation. The fact that his army was encamped along the English Channel and the North Sea dictated to Napoleon the necessity of making Germany, not Italy, the principal battlefield in the rapidly approaching struggle. The French emperor thus planned to march his army across the Rhine to the upper Danube and down the river to Vienna. As for Italy, Marshal Masséna, with an army half that of Charles's, was to contain the Archduke while General St.-Cyr's corps protected his right flank from a possible attack by a Neapolitan army supported by the English and Russians.[3]

The French forces on the Channel had been reorganized in June of 1805, and the terminology changed. Davout became the commander of the corps of the right of the *Armée des côtes de l'Océan,* and the term *camp de Bruges* was no longer used.[4] Marshal Soult commanded the center, Ney the left, and Lannes the advance guard. Then in August, when the *Armée des côtes de l'Océan* prepared to turn its back on the sea and march against the Austrians, it became known as the *Grande Armée*. The Grand Army was composed of seven corps, a cavalry reserve and the Imperial Guard. The seven army corps were commanded, respectively, by: Bernadotte, I; Marmont, II; Davout, III; Soult, IV; Ney, V; Lannes, VI; and Augereau, VII.

On August 27 this army broke camp and began its march to the Rhine. Davout's III Corps was made up of three infantry divisions commanded by Generals Bisson, Friant, and Gudin,[5] and one light cavalry division under the orders of General Vialannes. In all it comprised some twenty-six thousand five hundred men.[6] His orders were to begin his march on August 29 and to proceed to the Rhenish city of Mannheim where he was to be in position by September 26, establishing there temporary headquarters. On his left flank was Marmont's II Corps marching on Mainz, while his right flank rested on Soult's IV Corps moving on Bruchsal. The VI Corps of Marshal Ney approached the Rhine at Seltz as Lannes's V Corps prepared to cross the river at Strasbourg.[7] Bernadotte's I Corps, which was already east of the Rhine, marched south from Hanover, where it had been encamped, to Würzburg on the Main.

Napoleon arrived at Strasbourg on September 26 and, despite some confusion in the supply system, ordered the army forward. Between the twenty-sixth and the thirtieth the French crossed the Rhine—though not without difficulties. The pontoon bridges which were to be used by Ney, Soult, and Davout were not ready on the twenty-sixth when these corps were ordered to start their crossing. Davout was forced to gather ferryboats and various other types of small craft in order to begin the operation on the scheduled day. As Ney and Soult waited for the bridging pontoons, Davout completed his crossing a full twenty-four hours ahead of the IV and VI Corps.[8]

Reliable information was filtering into imperial headquarters that the Austrian army had advanced into Germany to the Iller River and had taken up a strong position south of the Danube with its center in the vicinity of Ulm. Napoleon ordered part of Murat's cavalry to maneuver in the Black Forest so as to give the enemy the impression that the French army was preparing to cross the Rhine about Strasbourg, traverse the Forest and appear on the upper Danube. With the Austrians thus misled, the Grand Army actually moved much further to the north, by-passing Ulm, and arrived on the middle Danube east of the main enemy positions. Davout's line of march followed the Neckar through Heidelberg to Neckarelz (September 29), then southeast to Mosbach (October 2), Oettingen (October 6), and Neuburg on the Danube. Crossing the river he pushed on south to Aichach and Dachau. At Dachau he took up a strong position astride the Ammer river in support of Bernadotte's I Corps, which had occupied Munich.

While Davout and Bernadotte faced east the other corps of the Grand Army swung to the west after crossing the Danube, completing the encircling movement which trapped General Mack at Ulm. Although isolated Austrian units initially escaped the trap—the Archduke Ferdinand made his way north with remnants of General Werneck's division and reached safety in Bohemia, and General Jellacic made his way south toward Switzerland with some five thousand men, who were eventually rounded up by Augereau's VII Corps—the major portion of Mack's force, some twenty-seven thousand men strong, surrendered at Ulm on the twentieth of October.

Davout's march from the Rhine to Dachau was relatively uneventful. There was no enemy resistance. The Austrians had been caught completely unaware of the French troop movements. The most pressing issue was that of feeding the men and animals. Despite the preparations and the efficiency of the corps commander, his letters to the Emperor and the minister of war continually referred to this matter. The other problem which occupied much of Davout's time was preventing the numerous columns from colliding with or crossing in front of one another. As Davout approached the Danube he came into close contact with the corps of Soult and Marmont. Both he and Marmont crossed the river at Neuburg and marched one behind the other along the Neuburg-Augsburg road. But considering the vast expanse and large numbers of men in motion at the same time there were amazingly few delays due to corps becoming entangled with one another.

The remnants of Mack's right flank, under General Michael Kienmaier, fell back on Munich under pressure from the advancing columns of Davout and Bernadotte. Crossing the Iser the Austrian general continued his retreat to the Inn where he was joined by a Russian army under General Mikhail Kutusov. The Russians had advanced at a leisurely pace from Poland through Silesia and Moravia to the Danube. Kutusov commanded the most advanced of three armies. Marching behind him, at two hundred mile intervals, were the armies of Buxhöwden and Bennigsen. The entire force numbered some one hundred thousand men in all. But as Kutusov had with him only forty thousand men and Kienmaier sixteen thousand men, they fell back before the numerical superiority of the advancing French. Napoleon now marched on Vienna with one hundred thousand men while the Austrian emperor looked on helplessly. The Archdukes Charles and John, the latter having been in the Tyrol to maintain communications between the two principal Austrian armies, were able to unite their forces as they fell back into Carinthia. But Ney, advancing into the Tyrol from Bavaria, and Masséna, whose Army of Italy was marching through Venetia, maintained sufficient pressure on the Austrians to prevent them from posing a threat to the right flank of the main French force. As Napoleon approached Vienna he ordered Marmont to move south with his II Corps to Leoben in order to prevent Charles and John from falling back on the Austrian capital. As Kutusov retreated eastward toward Vienna he began to fear that he might be separated from the rest of the Russian army which was still advancing through Moravia. He therefore declined to defend the Austrian capital, and crossing to the north bank of the Danube, fell back on Brünn where he was joined by the other two Russian armies and the Tsar.

Davout crossed the Iser at Freising on October 26 after having remained inactive for two weeks along that river. The Russian army withdrew rapidly before the advancing French, leaving only bad roads and inclement weather to slow their enemies' advance. The III Corps's line of march took it through Mühldorf, Burghausen, Steyer, and Gaming, to Lilienfeld. South of Lilienfeld, on November 8, Davout's advance guard came upon the Austrian corps commanded by General Meerfeldt. Meerfeldt was retiring before Marmont's II Corps in an attempt to reach Vienna when he found Davout blocking his way. The engagement which followed was very much one-sided. The Austrians (about ten thousand strong) had no intention of fighting a major battle. To get from between the two French armies was Meerfeldt's only concern. However, before he was able to break off the action his army corps was nearly destroyed.[9] Davout's advance continued, and he entered the Austrian capital on November 15. His army corps, less the division of General Louis Marie Caffarelli (who had replaced P. F. J. G. Bisson) which was ordered north with the main French force, took up a position between Vienna and Pressburg with advance patrols to the north along the March river.[10] The division of General Friant was stationed in the capital itself, while General Gudin's division was encamped on the Hungarian frontier at Pressburg. These two divisions had taken up their respective positions by November 16 and remained stationary for nearly two weeks while the decisive battle was shaping up some seventy miles to the north.

Caffarelli's division, which was temporarily detached from the III Corps, joined the corps of Marshals Bernadotte, Lannes, and Soult, which were also supported by the cavalry reserve under Murat and the Imperial Guard. This force, under the skillful eyes of the Emperor, pursued the retreating Kutusov into Moravia where the Russian Tsar was joined by the Austrian emperor. The French army had been on the march almost continuously since it had broken camp on the English Channel. It had been a long, hard, and hungry trek since the supply trains had seldom been able to keep pace with the marching troops. Their equipment and clothing—particularly their shoes—were in poor shape and in need of repair and replacement. Furthermore, the enemy had proven to be so elusive that there was no assurance that further pursuit would bring about the desired battle. As if these were not sufficient reasons to call a halt to his advance into central Europe, Napoleon had been receiving intelligence of growing unfriendliness on the part of Prussia. That kingdom had in fact—though quite unknown to Napoleon at this time—come to an understanding with England and Russia that it would enter the struggle on the side of the Allies. It was just a matter of time before the French lines of communication would be attacked by what was still considered one of the finest armies in Europe.

On November 20 Napoleon called a halt to the campaign and began to make preparations for the army to go into winter quarters.[11] His adversary however had other thoughts. Buxhöwden, accompanied by the Tsar, had joined Kutusov at Olmütz. An Austrian corps under Lichtenstein had also rendezvoused with the Russians in Moravia bringing their combined strength to eighty-five thousand seven hundred men.[12] Seeing that they had a numerical superiority over the French—Napoleon commanded only sixty-six thousand men [13] until Davout arrived on the scene the day of the battle—the Tsar Alexander and the Emperor Francis decided to march against their enemy and destroy him. As the predominately Russian force advanced southwestwardly toward the small Moravian town of Austerlitz, it became obvious to the French emperor that they meant to give battle. He could scarcely contain his joy. Only the possibility that Alexander might change his mind and retreat prevented him from celebrating before the battle was even fought.

As early as November 28 Napoleon began issuing orders in preparation for the battle.[14] He ordered Berthier to write the following to Davout that morning: "It appears certain, Monsieur Marshal, that we will have a major battle tomorrow or the next day in the vicinity of Brünn. His Majesty orders that you should leave immediately with your two divisions and by forced marches arrive at Brünn as quickly as possible." [15] Davout was not at his headquarters (Vienna) when the dispatch arrived at three o'clock that same afternoon. In the absence of the Marshal, who was at Pressburg by previous orders of the Emperor, his chief of staff, General Daultanne, sent copies of the dispatch to the divisional commanders, Generals Friant and

Gudin. Friant received the order at eight o'clock on the evening of November 29, and his division was on the march within one hour and a half. Marching all night and the next day they arrived at Nikolsburg in the evening of the thirtieth. The men had covered a distance of forty-five miles. After a night's rest they continued on to the abbey of Raigern where they arrived at 7:00 P.M., December 1. In all the division had covered a distance of seventy miles.[16] It did not match the Spartan's march to the Battle of Marathon (one hundred and fifty miles in three days), but then the French fought the entire next day against tremendous odds, whereas the Greeks arrived after the battle had been won. Gudin's division did not arrive in time for the battle as it had been at Pressburg—some forty miles further from Austerlitz than Friant who had been at Vienna. Davout, therefore, had only one of his three infantry divisions, for Caffarelli's division, which also took part in the battle, was under the command of Marshal Lannes.

The two armies moved into position on the evening of December 1. Napoleon had selected a defensive position along Goldbach Brook. Lannes's V Corps, plus Caffarelli, formed his left flank. Bernadotte, less Karl Philipp von Wrede's division, was behind Lannes, but moved up on his right early on the morning of the battle. Soult's IV Corps formed the center with one of his divisions, that of General Claude-Juste-Alexandre Legrand, overextended to form the right flank until such time as Davout could move into line on the right. The Austro-Russian army took up its position in front of Austerlitz. General Peter Bagration's infantry formed the right flank and straddled the Brünn-Olmütz road opposite Lannes. The left was commanded by Buxhöwden. It rested on Satschan pond and extended to the north to the heights of Pratzen—which would, in fact, be the center of the battle line. The Allied center under John Charles Kollowart was behind the Pratzen heights.

The Allied strategy was simple and sound—so much so that Napoleon had figured it out the day before the battle was even fought. Buxhöwden's left flank, comprising fully half of Alexander's army, would turn the French right, cut the Brünn-Vienna road, and force the defeated invaders back to the northwest away from their supply and communication lines and reinforcements. To counter this movement Napoleon ordered Davout to take up a defensive position behind Goldback Brook on the extreme right and hold. When the enemy had committed his forces to a turning action, he would attack in the center of the line. Thus the key to the entire battle rested on the French right. If it held firm against the overwhelming odds which the Russians would throw forward, the battle would go as Napoleon planned. If on the other hand it broke, or was forced back too rapidly under the merciless pressure, the entire French army would be enveloped and the battle lost.

At five o'clock on the morning of December 2—the first anniversary of Napoleon's coronation—Friant's division broke camp at the abbey of Raigern and began to march north to take up its position at Turas. These were the orders Davout had received the night before when he arrived at Raigern. Napoleon believed on December 1 that the Allied left would attack through the vicinity of Kobelnitz (directly in front of Pratzen) and had, therefore, ordered the III Corps to Turas so as to take them on their flank. But the noise of the Russian and Austrian troops moving south of Pratzen during the night caused him to change his battle tactics. Through some confusion Davout did not receive the change of orders until Friant's division was in full march toward Turas. With the battle shaping up further south Davout was ordered to move into line between the villages of Tellnitz and Sokolnitz. He thus became the right flank of the French army, commanding not only Friant's infantry and Bourcier's cavalry divisions, but also the greater part of Soult's cavalry. In all he commanded about ten thousand five hundred men on that fateful day while his opponent, Buxhöwden, had fully four times that number marching against him.[17]

This was the first time that the Marshal had fought under the direct command of Napoleon since they were together in Egypt. But in Egypt he had been only a general of brigade commanding Desaix's cavalry. Now he commanded a corps and was entrusted with the most difficult work of the battle. It was his first opportunity to prove to the Emperor that he had been right in selecting him for a marshalate and giving him command of the III Corps of the Grand Army. It was, in fact, the first real test of Davout's ability to command a large unit in battle. Since his promotion to general of division there had been little real fighting on the Continent—only the final phase of Austria's defeat in the war of the Second Coalition, and he had played but a minor role in Italy. The years preceding the formation of the Third Coalition had given him an opportunity to demonstrate his ability as an organizer and administrator. His superb work at Bruges had bred confidence in Paris. On the long march into central Europe he had handled the divisions of his army corps

The battlefield of Austerlitz. On December 2, 1805, Marshal Davout commanded the right wing of the French army which defeated the combined forces of Russia and Austria.—*Courtesy of Donald D. Horward*

like a born leader. Now he was to display that talent which singled him out, perhaps as the most capable of Napoleon's lieutenants.

The battlefield was dominated by Pratzen Plateau, which the French had evacuated to encourage the Allies to turn their flank. The ground sloped away gradually to the west toward Goldbach Brook behind which the French had taken up their positions. A slight thaw had occurred, just enough to make roads muddy and slippery but not so much as to affect the lakes to the south, which remained frozen. A heavy mist which had settled over the valley served the dual purpose of hiding the concentration of Soult's IV Corps before Pratzen and of concealing the arrival of Davout during the early twilight hours of the morning. The sun did not rise over Austerlitz until 8:00 A.M. on December 2.

The Allied left opened the battle with an attack on the village of Tellnitz, which was held by a regiment of General Legrand's divi-

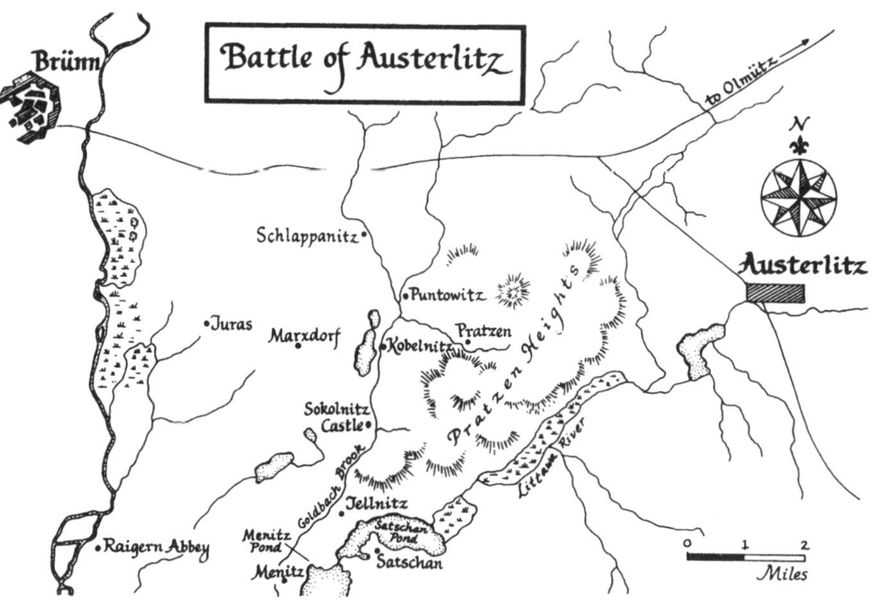

sion. The fighting was sharp and despite cavalry support the French were driven from the village by 8:30 A.M. Before the Russians could consolidate their gain Friant's first brigade, under the command of General Etienne Heudelet, arrived on the battlefield. Friant's division was composed of three brigades commanded by Generals Heudelet, Kister, and Lochet. Heudelet immediately launched his entire command against the enemy in Tellnitz. He was on the point of capturing a large number of Russians, who were retreating in great disorder, when Legrand's 26th Line, which had been sent to Tellnitz to support the extreme right, opened fire on him from the rear. In the confusion of the battle Heudelet's men had been mistaken for Russians as they were in possession of Tellnitz which Legrand believed to have been lost to the enemy. By the time the mistaken identity had been realized, Heudelet's brigade had suffered heavy losses and had been thrown into a state of confusion. At the same time the Russians had been given a much needed break, and had been able to regroup their shaken troops and bring up reinforcements. Advancing, they easily ejected Heudelet and once again occupied Tellnitz.[18]

At this point the Russian commander made a major error. He held up his victorious troops at Tellnitz to await the capture of the village of Sokolnitz and its castle, which were about a mile and a half to the north along Goldbach Brook. As Buxhöwden's right wing overran elements of Legrand's division and occupied both village and castle by about 9:00 A.M., Davout realized at once that the enemy was driving a wedge between the III Corps and Soult's IV Corps. He, therefore, left the reorganized 1st Brigade (Heudelet), and Bourcier's cavalry to contain the Russian bridgehead at Tellnitz and marched north with Kister's 2nd Brigade and Lochet's 3rd Brigade. The Russians had been hampered in their crossing of the Goldbach at Sokolnitz by much confusion. Thus their full strength could not be employed at 10:00 A.M. when Davout launched a determined attack against them. The fighting was fierce; but despite the enemy's superiority in numbers Davout's infantry, supported by Legrand's 36th Line, not only drove them out of both village and castle but held on to the entire west bank of the Goldbach while the victory was decided on the plains of Pratzen.[19]

The decisive action on that cold December day occurred in the center. Kutusov, who commanded the Allied army, continued to reinforce his left throughout the early hours of the battle. In doing so he withdrew Generald Prschibitscheski's division from Pratzen to attack Sokolnitz and ordered Kollowrat's army corps, which made up the Allied center, to file off to the left to support a flanking action against Davout. When Napoleon saw that Kutusov was fully committed to his plan of battle, and believing that the Pratzen Plains were virtually evacuated, he ordered Soults' corps, less Legrand, to storm and capture the heights. The divisions of Generals St. Hilaire and Vandamme did their work well. Despite the fact that Kollowrat's two divisions had not yet completed their evacuation of the heights—they were in the process of marching parallel to the front in two columns—the French were successful.[20] Kollowrat's corps fell back toward Austerlitz in disorder. Soult then pivoted to his right on Legrand's division, thus taking Buxhöwden's in the rear.

By two o'clock in the afternoon not only had the battle been won, but the entire Allied left wing was completely severed from the rest of the army, pinned against Satschan Pond, and on the verge of annihilation. As Soult, supported by Oudinot's division (reserves) and the Imperial Guard under Bessières, descended from the Pratzen heights on Buxhöwden's rear, Davout and Legrand drove across Goldbach Brook. The retreat quickly became a rout as the predominately Russian corps attempted to pass between Menitz and Satschan ponds on a narrow strip of land. Some attempted to cross the ponds which were frozen solid. But the weight of so many men, horses, and guns caused the ice to give way in places and forced the fleeing men to jam the only firm exit between the ponds. There has been much discussion about the use the Russians made of the ice on the ponds and just how many men and guns found a cold watery grave. Virtually every eyewitness account speaks of great numbers having drowned in the ponds, and many historians have taken their words as truth, debating only about the numbers. But when the ponds were drained some years after the battle in order to recover the pieces of artillery, only a few bodies were found.[21] We can only be certain that the Allied left flank suffered enormous losses during the final rout.

On the other side of the battlefield the French left (under Lannes) and the Allied right (under Bagration) sparred lightly throughout most of the morning. Both sides were aware that the major action was to take place to the south. Then shortly after Napoleon sent Soult's corps up the Pratzen slopes he ordered Lannes, supported on his right by Murat's cavalry, to attack the enemy before him. Despite support from Lichtenstein's cavalry and the Russian Imperial Guard, commanded by the Crown Prince Constantine in person, the Allies were unable to sustain the French onslaught. Bagration's corps retreated along the Brünn-Olmütz road with Murat's cavalry in hot pursuit. Constantine and Lichtenstein fell back through Austerlitz in considerable disorder. Marshal Bernadotte's I Corps had filled the gap in the French line between Lannes and Soult as the latter turned to the right to destroy the Allied flank.

The battle was a textbook example of how to annihilate an enemy who attacks with superior forces. Austerlitz went exactly as Napoleon planned it—as if he had written the script himself in advance. Throughout the remainder of his life he always considered it his greatest victory. In the years to come the Emperor would give to his marshals titles of nobility commemorating battles in which they had distinguished themselves. Davout thus became the Duke of Auerstädt and later the Prince of Eckmühl and Marshal Ney the Prince of the Moskova (which commemorated the Battle of Borodino), but despite Soult's bitter disappointment Napoleon kept Austerlitz for himself.

The night of December 2 found Davout's weary troops in the vicinity of Menitz. Darkness had come early on this short winter day, a factor which greatly aided the defeated Austro-Russian troops in escaping the disaster which surely would have followed had the battle been fought during the summer. That Friant's exhausted division could have engaged in a pursuit was, of course, out of the question, but other units of the army had not made such a strenuous march prior to the battle nor had they borne so heavy a burden of the fighting.

In his reports on the Battle of Austerlitz Davout's praise for his officers and men knew no bounds.[22] "I render, with great pleasure," he wrote, "to the brave men of Friant's division, the honor of saying that they did not count the enemy on the glorious day of Austerlitz." [23] He singles out General Friant particularly for bravery in exposing himself to enemy fire. Four times the general had his horse shot out from under him.[24] His three generals of brigade Kister, Heudelet, and Lochet also lost horses while in the saddle. The losses suffered by the division reflected the heavy fighting of the day. The fourteen hundred casualties which Friant's battalions sustained represented about thirty-three percent of their total strength. General Bourcier's cavalry suffered relatively slight casualties—only seventy-six killed and wounded.

The Russian army was in complete disorder and full retreat when darkness and a heavy snowfall forced the French to terminate the pursuit. Allied losses, which were predominately Russian, stood at fifteen thousand killed and wounded, and eleven thousand taken prisoner. As Alexander accompanied his fleeing men to the east with tears streaming down his cheeks, the Austrian emperor made plans to meet his conqueror and put an end to the futile bloodshed. To continue the struggle without active Russian support, when it could not even be won with that aid, would be absurd. The only Austrian army which had not yet been destroyed in battle was commanded by the Archduke Charles; and alone it could not hope to withstand the onslaught of the victorious French. Nevertheless, it was several days before victor and vanquished met formally to sign an armistice. In the interlude the French army undertook the pursuit of the fleeing enemy.

Davout was joined on December 3 by Gudin's division which had been unable to reach Austerlitz in time to take part in the battle. Friant's weary men received only a "good" night's rest after the battle before they too joined in the pursuit of the remnants of the Allied left flank. On December 4 the III Corps, supported by Dominique Louis Antoine Klein's cavalry, overtook the enemy at Josephdorf.[25] The Russians overestimated Davout's strength, which was, in fact, inferior to their own. But even had they known the truth it is unlikely they would have ventured to give battle, for their own troops were disorganized and demoralized. They, therefore, resorted to deception in order to save what was left of the army. General Meerfeldt sent the Count of Walmoden to Davout to announce that a twenty-four hour armistice had been signed and that the Austrian emperor was to have an interview with Napoleon to arrange a permanent cease-fire. Davout met with Meerfeldt and told him that he was not convinced an armistice had really been signed. He reminded Meerfeldt of the trick played on General Moncey in Italy to save an Austrian army in January 1801,[26] and demanded a written statement from the Tsar Alexander stating that such an armistice had been signed. Davout had had no word from Imperial headquarters of an armistice and did not wish to be taken in by a *ruse de guerre* and run the risk of falling out of favor as Moncey had five years earlier. Meerfeldt departed proclaiming that verification of the armistice would soon reach the Marshal.[27]

The first word Davout received was from General Kutusov. The commander of the Allied army wrote the following to him:

> MONSIEUR MARSHAL, His Majesty the Emperor, my august master, not being present, I will request from him at once assurance in writing that a truce is being arranged between the French army and the one which I command. In the meantime *I give you my word of honor that an armistice has been concluded for twenty-four hours* beginning at six o'clock this morning, and that the German Emperor, after having spoken with my august master, has gone to Austerlitz to meet with

your Emperor. I, therefore, request that your Excellency suspend hostilities until the terms of the armistice are fixed. I offer you the same assurance on my part. [Italics mine.]

The commander in chief of the combined armies of their Imperial Majesties of Russia and Germany.

KUTUSOV.

P.S.—I take it upon myself to transmit to you, within two and a half hours, the assurance of my august master.

KUTUSOV.[28]

Davout waited, and shortly the Count of Walmoden returned with a brief note written in pencil on a blank page torn from a book. It was in the hand of the Tsar Alexander and read as follows:

FOR MARSHAL DAVOUT
Commander of the III Corps of the French army.

General Merfeld [Meerfeldt] is authorized to say to Marshal Davout on my behalf, that an armistice of twenty-four hours has been concluded in order for the two supreme rulers to meet today at Utchetz.

ALEXANDRE.[29]

The Marshal could hardly refuse to accept the word of so high a dignitary as the Russian tsar. He, therefore, informed Kutusov that he would suspend hostilities until six o'clock the following morning (December 5) and informed Napoleon of all that had taken place.[30]

When Napoleon received Davout's aide-de-camp with news of what had transpired at Josephdorf, he declared that there was no truth whatsoever in the words of the Tsar. Davout had indeed been deceived by the Russians. It was a *ruse de guerre* designed to save the remnants of the Allied army—and it had worked. Had Davout attacked the force before him, as he most certainly planned to do, he might very well have taken the Russian Tsar prisoner. As it was, the Russians were able to withdraw unmolested. Napoleon did not scold his Marshal for his actions as the campaign had been won two days earlier. Had it not been so, Davout would surely have felt the wrath of the Emperor for allowing the enemy to escape. Instead, Napoleon sent the Marshal's aide back to him saying that he had done that which honor had dictated under the circumstances in accepting the word of Alexander I.[31] Fortunately for the Marshal's career the deception of the Russians had no serious consequences. But this experience, coupled with that of General Moncey's, had engraved itself upon his memory. He would not be so easily duped in the future.

Davout had been deceived. He had been cheated of an opportunity to destroy the remnants of the Allied army and capture the Russian tsar. But the deception was not so complete as it would appear at first glance. Napoleon did, in fact, meet with the Austrian emperor late on December 4, and they did agree upon an armistice which went into effect the following day, December 5. Furthermore, the French emperor agreed to allow the Russian army to withdraw unmolested east of its own frontier. Alexander was undoubtedly aware of the fact that these negotiations would take place on the fourth. However, he must have been equally aware that the armistice had not yet been signed and was therefore not in operation at the time he gave his royal word to Davout that it was in force.

The terms of the armistice provided for the French occupation of Austria while the peace talks were taking place at Pressburg. Davout deployed his III Corps along the river March.[32] During the third week of December he was ordered to take up a more permanent position along the Hungarian frontier with his headquarters at Pressburg.[33] On December 27 the Franco-Austrian representatives concluded a peace at Pressburg. Its terms provided for the expulsion of Austria from Italy as well as Germany.[34] Furthermore, Austria was required to give to France the Dalmatian coast. Also in accordance with the terms of the treaty the French army would be withdrawn from Austrian territory as the Austrians evacuated those provinces required by the Pressburg agreement. All might have gone smoothly for the French had not the Russians interfered. Fearing French expansion into the Balkan peninsula, Russia occupied the mouth of the Cattaro river in southern Dalmatia. This led to a slowdown of the French evacuation of Austrian territory.

In the first phase of the withdrawal the French army pulled back to the Enns. General Caffarelli's division was reunited to the III Corps,[35] which was then ordered to march along the right bank of the Danube to the Enns. From the Enns, Davout withdrew through Wels (January 28, 1806) to Ried (February 8). During the second phase of the evacuation he recrossed the Inn and established his headquarters at Munich, which he reached at the end of February.[36] As the Russians had not evacuated Cattaro, Napoléon refused to withdraw his armies from southern Germany. The various corps were ordered into winter quarters between the Rhine and Inn. In a letter to Marshal Berthier dated March 14, the Emperor, who was himself back in Paris, wrote the following with respect to the III Corps:

"Marshal Davout will retire, with his army corps, to Oettingen, and quarter his troops in that principality, which is quite large, having a population of 70,000 inhabitants, without any discomfort to Bavaria. He will send one of his divisions to occupy the *seigneurie* of Limburg [misspelling of Limpurg], and another to the principality of Hohenlohe. If his stay is prolonged for longer than I expect at present, it will have to be extended into Mergentheim. The principalities of Oettingen, Limburg [*sic*] and Hohenlohe have more than 100,000 inhabitants; his army can live there in comfort without exhausting any of my allies." [37]

7

Military Glory

THE CRUSHING DEFEAT at Austerlitz not only put an end to the Third Coalition, it also consolidated the Napoleonic Empire in the west. While the Russian army limped back into Poland, Sir William Pitt, the Prime Minister of England, was reported to have exclaimed: "Roll up the map of Europe, we won't be needing it for the next ten years." Pitt's death in January 1806 led to the appointment of Charles James Fox as Secretary of State for Foreign Affairs. Without the possibility of an active ally on the Continent, Fox came to the conclusion that it was in the best interest of his nation to conclude peace with France—even if it would be in effect no more than a truce, such as the Treaty of Amiens. With her domination of the sea confirmed by Nelson's impressive naval victory at Trafalgar, England need no longer fear a French invasion. Napoleon's position on the Continent was now equally strong. Thus the continuation of the struggle seemed pointless. Nevertheless, Europe was not destined to achieve the peace which it so desperately desired.

The negotiations between Fox and Napoleon might have led to an end of hostilities had either—or both—sides been willing to make meaningful concessions. But both had scored major military victories within six weeks of one another; and each felt that it was bargaining from strength. Yet while it was true that Napoleon had never been stronger on the Continent, the fact remained that Russia had not made peace with him, and Prussia was growing progressively less friendly through the spring and summer of 1806.

7 / Military Glory

The news of Austerlitz had been received in Berlin like an unhappy clap of thunder. Prussia had entered into the Agreement of Potsdam on November 3, 1805, which had pledged her to join the Third Coalition if Napoleon refused to accept armed mediation. Her armies had been preparing to march against the French lines of communication, which ran through southern Germany to the Rhine. Austerlitz changed all of this, and a Prussian envoy, Christian von Haugwitz, had hurried south to Schönbrunn to make the best terms possible with the victor. All thoughts of war had vanished in Berlin, where the peace-loving Frederick William III had not been anxious to take up arms in the first place. The history of Franco-Prussian relations had been, with but a few brief periods such as the Seven Years' War and the early war of the French Revolution, amiable. The common foe had always been Austria. Moreover, Napoleon had made sincere efforts to prevent Prussia from drifting toward the Anglo-Austrian camp. In September 1803, when he had reorganized western and southern Germany, he had seen to it that Prussia had annexed a sufficient amount of territory to assure her friendship.[1]

At Schönbrunn, on December 15, 1805, Haugwitz signed the preliminaries of a treaty which would allow Prussia to keep Hanover—which she had already occupied. The agreement also provided for an offensive-defensive alliance with France as the occupation of Hanover was expected to meet with open English criticism. Despite a counter-offer from England, which came at the same time, to give Hanover to Prussia in return for her making war on France, the King ratified the Schönbrunn agreement which had been slightly altered (Treaty of Paris, February 1806). Frederick William had no desire to send his armies against the victorious veterans of Austerlitz. He genuinely desired peace for his nation. Nevertheless, relations between Paris and Berlin began to deteriorate almost before the ink was dry on the treaty. Prussia had negotiated out of fear and indecision. The treaty proved damaging to her overseas commerce, which had become a principal source of the nation's recent economic prosperity. Nor was the pro-French orientation popular with the Prussian people as a whole; and Napoleon only worsened relations by treating the proud Prussians as a second-rate power, rather than as an equal.

During the spring of 1806 Napoleon learned of the Potsdam

agreement of November 1805, and Prussia learned of negotiations between England and France for the return of Hanover to England as a prerequisite for peace. French troops remained in southern Germany, and Prussia became more and more suspicious of Napoleon's motives. These strained relations reached a breaking point in mid-July when Napoleon announced the formation of the Confederation of the Rhine.[2] Including most of the states in southern and western Germany, the Confederation was tied firmly to the coattails of its creator by an alliance which guaranteed him sixty-three thousand men in time of war. Its creation was indeed the deathblow to the Holy Roman Empire which had been established by Otto the Great in the tenth century.[3] On August 9, orders were issued for the mobilization of the Prussian army.

Through the spring and summer of 1806 hostility against France had been building up in court circles and throughout Prussia in general. The Circle about the Prussian Queen, Louise, openly denounced Napoleon and his German policy. Other influential members of the court, such as Prince Louis-Ferdinand, Baron Karl von Stein, and the King's military advisors, were clamoring for war. The German press began to speak of "the enslavement of Prussia and the catastrophe of the Holy [Roman] Empire." [4] General Marbot, who was in Berlin at this time, wrote in his *Mémoires:* "The [Prussian] officers whom I knew no longer dared to speak to me or even to greet me." [5] Undecided Prussia, who had missed her golden opportunity to tip the balance of power in favor of the Allies in the fall of 1805, had at last come to a decision—she would have war in the fall of 1806.

Davout had not had leave since before the army broke camp on the Channel late in the summer of 1805. Although the III Corps had settled in southern Germany during the spring of the following year, its stay was thought to be only temporary; and Napoleon continued to speak of bringing it back to France. Then on September 4, 1806, the Emperor wrote to Marshal Berthier at Munich: "You may grant to Marshal Davout a leave of absence for twenty days for the same reasons [as Marshal Ney] and on the same conditions—if he wishes to take advantage of it." [6] The pretense for both Ney and Davout was that their wives had given birth to children. Madame Davout had had a baby girl in 1805, and the Marshal had not yet seen his new daughter. She had been named Josephine,[7] after the Empress. Remembering the early deaths of the Davout's first two children, their physician suggested that they rent a farm in the country for the mother and child. This was done; and under the strict surveillance of Madame Petit, whose husband, the General, was serving under Davout, both Josephine and her mother grew stronger with each passing week through the summer of 1806.

Davout arrived in Paris on September 15 much to the surprise and joy of his wife.[8] Unfortunately his leave was cut short by the gathering clouds of war. The very day on which he arrived in the capital he wrote to his brother-in-law, General Friant, whom, as the senior officer, he had left in command of his army corps, that he might be on his way back within a few days. "Everything here is of war," he wrote, "a portion of the guard has departed this morning."[9]

On the sixteenth the Davouts left Paris for Savigny where the Marshal held his new daughter for the first time. But as he had written Friant, the happy days at Savigny were few. On September 19 the Emperor wrote to General Jean François Aimé Dejean, minister of war: "You will give orders to Marshals Davout and Ney, who have returned to Paris, to return to their army corps by September 28."[10] By this time Napoleon, who had desired peace in Europe to enable him to consolidate the fruits of Austerlitz and Pressburg, had come to realize that war with Prussia could not be avoided.

The III Corps of the French army was still camped in Württemberg. It was made up of three infantry divisions and three regiments of cavalry. The 1st Division was commanded by General Charles Antoine Louis Morand, the 2nd by General Friant, and the 3rd by General Gudin. Morand had joined Davout's corps in February 1806, after having been promoted to the rank of general of division on December 24 in recognition of his outstanding services at Austerlitz, where he had been seriously wounded on the Plains of Pratzen. The son of an influential member of the middle class, he had studied at the *Ecole de Droit* at Besançon and had been admitted to the bar in 1791. Despite the prospects of a bright future in law he had entered the army as a volunteer. Elected to the rank of captain shortly after, he began a brilliant career during which he served on the Rhine, in Italy, in Egypt, and on all of the major campaigns of the Empire.[11] Upon his joining the III Corps the powerful

LOUIS FRIANT, Count of the Empire. Born at Villers-Morlancourt in 1758, he served in the army during the wars of the Revolution and rose to the rank of general of division. Friant, who was married to Davout's sister, served under the marshal as commander of the 2nd Division from 1804 to 1813. He took part in all of the major battles in which Davout fought. He died in 1829. *—Courtesy of Bibliothèque nationale*

trilogy of Friant, Gudin, and Morand was completed. They would serve together under Davout until the death of Gudin (August 1812) and the disastrous retreat from Moscow put an end to the Corps.[12]

The strength of the III Corps stood at 28,874 men[13] when the campaign opened. Morand commanded the 1st Division (10,339 men), Friant the 2nd (7,884 men), and Gudin the 3rd (8,595 men). The cavalry, under General Vialannes, was composed of 1,420 well-mounted chasseurs. When the Jena campaign began, Morand was at Nördlingen, Friant at Halle, Gudin at Oettingen, and Vialannes at Mergentheim.

Davout was still with his family at Savigny when the orders were issued for the Grand Army to concentrate on the Saxon frontier.[14] The III Corps was directed to unite at Oettingen and to proceed

7 / Military Glory

[LEFT] CHARLES ETIENNE CÉSAR GUDIN. Born at Montargis in 1768, he rose to the rank of general of division after distinguished service in the wars of the Revolution. He commanded a division under Marshal Davout at Auerstädt, Eylau, Eckmühl, and Wagram and was killed in action in Russia on August 19, 1812, at the Battle of Valutino (Lubino).—*Courtesy of Bibliothèque nationale*

[RIGHT] LOUIS CHARLES ANTOINE ALEXIS MORAND, Count of the Empire. Born at Pontarlier in 1771, he entered the army in the early years of the Revolution and rose rapidly in rank to general of division. He commanded a division under Marshal Davout at the battles of Auerstädt, Eylau, Wagram, and Borodino and served as an aide de camp to Napoleon at the Battle of Waterloo. He died in 1835.—*Courtesy of Bibliothèque nationale*

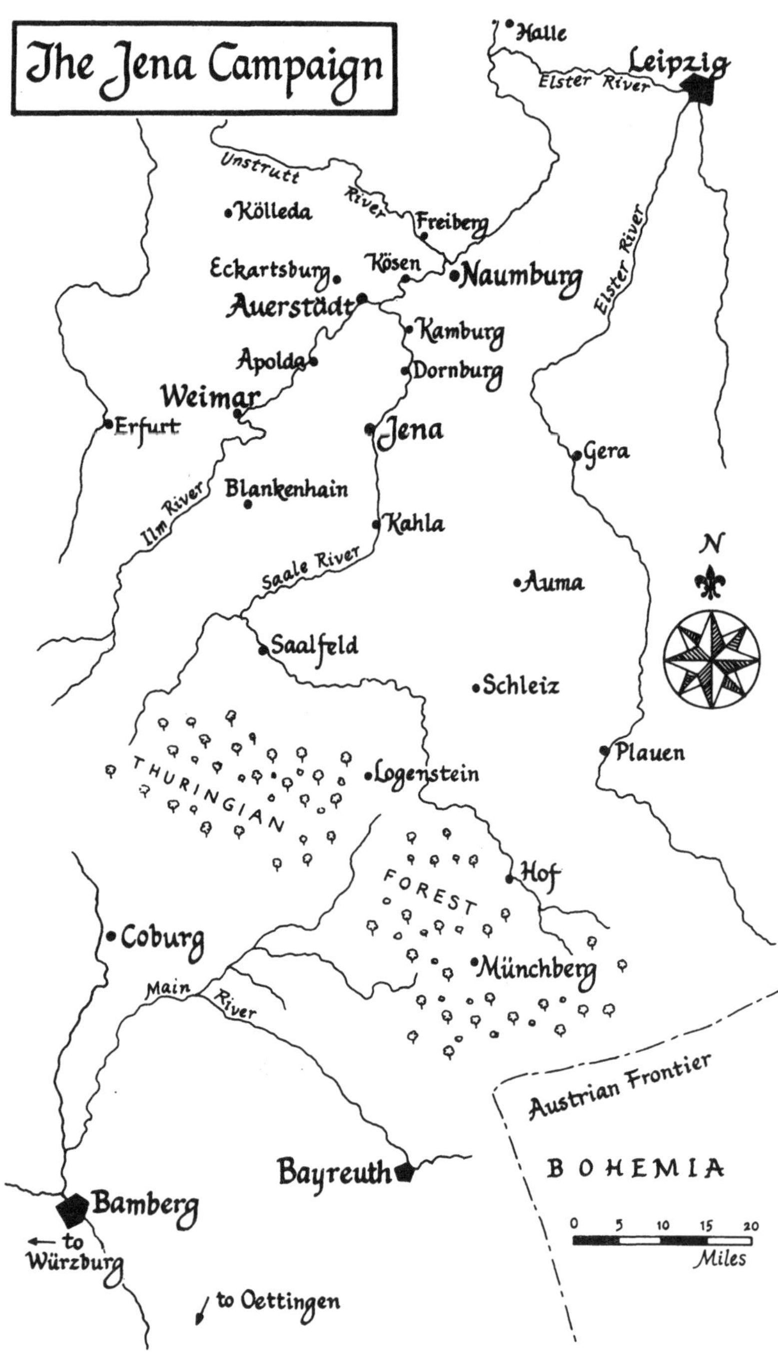
The Jena Campaign
Halle
Leipzig
Elster River
Unstrutt River
Kölleda
Freiberg
Eckartsburg
Kösen
Naumburg
Auerstädt
Kamburg
Apolda
Dornburg
Weimar
Erfurt
Jena
Gera
Ilm River
Blankenhain
Kahla
Elster River
N
Saale River
Auma
Saalfeld
Schleiz
Plauen
THURINGIAN
Logenstein
FOREST
Hof
Coburg
Münchberg
Main River
Austrian Frontier
BOHEMIA
Bayreuth
Bamberg
0 5 10 15 20
Miles
to Würzburg
to Oettingen

to Bamberg, where it was to be encamped by October 3. On September 26 the various divisions broke camp and the campaign was underway. The Marshal joined them on the twenty-eighth, and by the evening of October 2 they took up a position about Bamberg and along the Nuremberg road.[15] On the third Davout reviewed his men and reported to Berthier: "In general the troops are profiting from this moment of rest to prepare to enter the campaign; and, I might add, that the solicitude of the generals and officers has had an excellent effect. The equipment is in very good condition. There was lacking only about fifteen to twenty bayonets, which were replaced within a few hours. Clothing had been received and distributed to all of the regiments; the troops are dressed as well as they would have been if the Emperor had been reviewing them in Paris. The infantry is as the Emperor has instructed; each soldier has two pairs of shoes in his sack and one on his feet; . . . The artillery is lacking nothing."[16]

Napoleon had been slow to believe that Prussia would be so foolish as to make war on him without substantial support from Russia or Austria; however, by the end of September there was no longer room for doubt, and he became completely absorbed with preparations for the forthcoming struggle. In a flood of dispatches written on September 30 the Emperor laid the groundwork for the opening of the campaign. A cavalry screen was extended from the Rhine to the Bohemian frontier to conceal the French army's concentration about Bamberg. With the Prussian army moving south toward Würzburg, Napoleon would seize the initiative by striking directly at the heart of his enemy in a series of marches on Gera and Leipzig. He did not formulate a more exacting plan. His strategy would depend upon the enemy's reaction once he had entered his territory.

The Prussian army which took the field during the late summer of 1806 was a sad descendant of the army that had so thoroughly defeated the French at Rossbach some fifty years earlier. Overtrained in parade-ground tactics, it had not kept pace with the changes in warfare introduced during the thirteen years of Revolutionary and Napoleonic wars. Its armament, with few exceptions, was outdated; its soldiers were poorly fed and poorly clothed; its officer corps was overage for the ranks held; and the general spirit of the troops, though by no means poor, could not compare with that of the French who could still smell the gunpowder of Austerlitz.[17] Nor was the situation improved by the halfhearted attitudes of Frederick William III and the supreme military commander, the Duke of Brunswick, neither of whom had truly desired war with France.

The Prussian army suffered from still another disadvantage. Though in theory it was commanded by the Duke of Brunswick, who was appointed by the King, the ultimate supreme commander of all Prussian forces, it was in fact divided into three armies: Brunswick commanded the main army (sixty thousand seven hundred men), Prince Friedrich Ludwig Hohenlohe a second army of forty-two thousand men, and General Ernst Friedrich Rüchel a third of twenty-eight thousand five hundred men.[18] Neither Hohenlohe nor Rüchel liked Brunswick, and both tended to act in as independent a manner as possible. Thus in practice unity of command was non-existent.

The formulation of Prussian strategy also proved to be a factor which weakened the effectiveness of the army. Frederick William was not himself militarily inclined, and the Duke of Brunswick was sadly lacking in self-confidence. Thus councils of war were frequent, long, and often undecisive.[19] The initial Prussian plan for the opening of the campaign was offensive in nature. It called for a bold advance against the enemy encamped in southern Germany in order to drive him back across the Rhine. However, even before actual contact was made with the French, the plan was changed to one which was basically defensive.

Meanwhile, the French army, moving in three columns, crossed the Saxon frontier into Thuringia on October 8. The main column, led by Murat's cavalry and Bernadotte's I Corps, and followed by Davout's III Corps, marched along the Saalburg-Schleiz-Auma road. On its right Soult (IV Corps) followed by Ney (VI Corps) advanced on the Hof-Plauen road. On its left Lannes (V Corps) and Augereau (VII Corps) moved on Saalfeld. The Emperor marched with the Guard behind Davout. In this quadrangular formation the French army would be able to face front or flank, wherever the enemy might appear in strength, and concentrate its full might in twenty-four to forty-eight hours.

Leaving Kronach on October 9, the III Corps marched northward into Saxony through Lobenstein and Schleiz on the tenth, Auma on the eleventh, and arrived at Naumburg on the twelfth. On the thirteenth the Corps's three divisions were able to rest most of the day while taking up a position on the east bank of the Saale astride the main Erfurt-Leipzig road.[20] Upon reaching Naumburg Davout's III Corps formed the northwest arch of the French army's circular formation. Murat and Bernadotte, facing Leipzig, formed its northeast arch; Soult and Ney the southeast arch; and Lannes and Augereau the southwest arch. At this point (October 13) the location of the Prussian army was determined to be between Erfurt and Jena. The various corps which had been facing north at once turned to their left, and Davout became the right wing of the army with Bernadotte to his left rear. Augereau, who had been marching behind Lannes, continued to form the left; while Lannes himself, at Jena, became the center with the Guard, Soult, and Ney moving up to support him. On the night of October 13 the French army faced west with its front extending along the Saale from Kösen south through Jena to the Kahla vicinity.

During these critical days of the opening of the campaign the Prussian army displayed none of the talents which had led to the impressive victories during the Seven Years' War. Lacking intelligence on the location of the French army, the Duke of Brunswick abandoned the idea of an offensive and ordered a concentration in the general vicinity of Blankenhain.[21] On the eighth the Duke of Saxe-Weimar was sent south from Eisenach to attack French lines of communication at Würzburg, as Hohenlohe's advance units began to fall back on the Saale. On the tenth Marshal Lannes fell upon the division of Prince Louis at Saalfeld. The outnumbered Prussians, in a poor defensive position, were routed and thrown back with heavy losses; and the Prince himself was killed in the heavy fighting. By the eleventh Hohenlohe's army was in a state of confusion and only by the utmost effort on his part was order restored before nightfall.

As the French offensive gained momentum, Brunswick lost his nerve. Never completely convinced of the merits of attacking the enemy, he held another council of war. After much bickering and even more indecision, the Duke decided not to accept battle on the Saale, but rather to retire on Leipzig and Magdeburg to protect his lines of communication which were being threatened by the swift advance of Murat, Bernadotte and Davout. Saxe-Weimar was recalled from Franconia, and General Rüchel was ordered to hold Weimar.[22] Hohenlohe took up a defensive position on the left bank of the Saale, in order to cover the main army which would file off to its left along the west bank of the river. Thus on October 13 Brunswick marched toward Auerstädt with the intention of avoiding battle, while Hohenlohe, either through a misunderstanding of his orders or in direct violation of them, prepared for battle at Jena.

Napoleon believed that he had before him on the plains behind Jena one hundred thousand Prussians—virtually their entire army. Accordingly he issued orders during the night of October 13–14 for battle. Ney and Soult were to hasten to Jena; Murat was also called back from the vicinity of Naumburg; and Augereau was instructed to close in on Lannes's left. At 10:00 P.M. Napoleon wrote to Davout at Naumburg that he would attack the Prussian army on the plains between Jena and Weimar in the morning; and he ordered him to march his III Corps to Apolda so as to be able to take the enemy in the rear or left flank—depending upon its position as the battle developed. To this order of the Emperor's, Berthier added: "If Marshal Bernadotte [Prince of Ponte-Corvo] is with you, you may both march together, but the Emperor hopes that he will be in the position which had been indicated at Dornburg." [23]

Davout received this order at 3:00 A.M. on the fourteenth. He immediately summoned his divisional commanders and informed them of his intention to march at once on Apolda. He then went in person to the headquarters of Marshal Bernadotte, whose I Corps had arrived at Naumburg that night, the thirteenth, and passed on to him in writing the orders he had received from the Emperor. He then informed Bernadotte that he was marching at once to Apolda, and the latter told Davout that he would depart in the morning for Camburg (about halfway between Naumburg and Dornburg).[24]

The III Corps was set in motion on the morning of October 14 along the Naumburg-Weimar road. Gudin's 3rd Division, eight thousand strong, led the corps. It was followed at about an hour and a half's march by Friant's 2nd Division, seven thousand men, and another hour's march by Morand's 1st Division, ten thousand men strong. Together with General Vialannes' cavalry (about one thousand men) the corp's fighting strength was twenty-six thousand men.[25] Davout's advance guard had made contact with the enemy on the thirteenth, but as Napoleon stated that the Prussian army was before him at Jena, it was believed that this contact was merely with Prussian patrols. Heavy fog reduced visibility during the early hours of the morning, so that effective reconnaissance was impossible. Thus both the French, who were completely unaware of the presence of the Prussian army, and the Prussians, who thought that Davout was in the Naumburg-Kösen area, were somewhat startled when they ran onto one another's advance guards at Hassenhausen.

Brunswick's command was divided into five divisions plus cavalry, and numbered sixty-three thousand men[26] in all. General Gebhard Blücher commanded the Prussian advance guard. His leading squadron, marching in a careless manner, was roughly handled by Davout's advance guard and thrown back behind Hassenhausen. Blücher reacted quickly. Moving his cavalry forward he attacked Gudin's leading regiment (the 25th). The French infantry formed a square, and aided by the misdirection of a battery of Prussian artillery,[27] beat off the enemy attack. Then supported by the 85th line, they occupied Hassenhausen. Davout now moved Gudin's entire division into a defensive position with the newly captured hamlet in its center, and sent word to Friant and Morand to come forward on the double. General Friedrich Wilhelm Karl von Schmettau, who commanded the leading Prussian division, drew up his regiments in parade ground formations and began to fire ineffective volleys into Hassenhausen while he awaited the arrival of the division of the Prince of Orange. The fog began to lift by eight o'clock and Gudin could see a portion of Orange's division moving into position on Schmettau's left, and the leading regiment of still a third Prussian division (Wartensleben) moving against his left. Only the timely arrival of Friant enabled Gudin's hard-pressed regiments to hold their ground. Davout launched Friant straightaway against Orange's brigades, which were threatening to engulf Gudin's right, and drove them back beyond Spielberg. At 9:00 A.M. Davout's cavalry arrived on the battlefield and was placed on the extreme right to support Friant and to prevent the enemy from maneuvering against this vulnerable flank.

Three Prussian divisions now faced two of Davout's. The Duke of Brunswick, who realized that his army was numerically superior to that of the French, ordered Wartensleben's division, supported by Schmettau, to turn the enemy's left flank and gain control of the main road leading to Kösen—a maneuver which if successful would have cut off Davout's line of retreat. Schmettau's attack on Hassenhausen was met by fierce resistance on the part of Gudin's already hard-pressed men. Nevertheless the French left was driven back and badly shaken. At this decisive moment Morand's 1st Division began to arrive on the battlefield. Davout ordered these fresh troops into action on the double. They not only steadied Gudin's wavering left, but absorbed the shock of Wartensleben's attack which would easily have been decisive in their absence. Both Schmettau and Brunswick were mortally wounded in the attack on Hassenhausen. The Duke's removal from the field of battle (he died several days later) resulted in some confusion, for neither the King, who was present on the field of battle with Wartensleben's division at the time, nor Scharnhorst, Brunswick's chief of staff who was with Orange on the left flank, were immediately informed that the supreme commander had been wounded. When it became known, Frederick William assumed command of the army in person.

As the battle reached its climax at noon, the King called up fresh troops. Blücher's infantry, part of Kuhnheim's division which was in reserve, and the infantry of the Prussian Guard were launched against Morand's division in a desperate attempt to turn the French left and cut off their line of retreat toward Kösen. But with Davout himself encouraging and rallying his men, the attack was beaten off and Prince William of Prussia was seriously wounded. This was the last major effort made on the part of the Prussian army. Davout now seized the offensive and ordered Morand on his left and Friant on the right to move to the attack. Pivoting on Gudin, the 1st and 2nd Divisions moved forward until they brought the enemy under an interlocking cross fire that swept the entire Prussian line. In desperation the King ordered Kuhnheim's division and the remaining brigades of von Arnim's division into the line to check Friant's threatening advance. However, these fresh troops were caught in the murderous cross fire of Morand and Friant who occupied the high ground on both flanks, and the Prussians were forced to fall back and take refuge behind Gernstadt.

The Prussian army was now retreating from Hassenhausen with three of its divisions in disorder. Seeing this Davout ordered Gudin's division forward, and the entire III Corps advanced on Auerstädt and Eckartsberg. Heavy fighting now took place for the village of Gernstadt, which was stubbornly defended by the divisions of Kuhnheim and von Arnim under the command of Count Friedrich Adolf von Kalkreuth. Morand was also harassed on his left by Blücher, who had gathered what cavalry he could find in support of

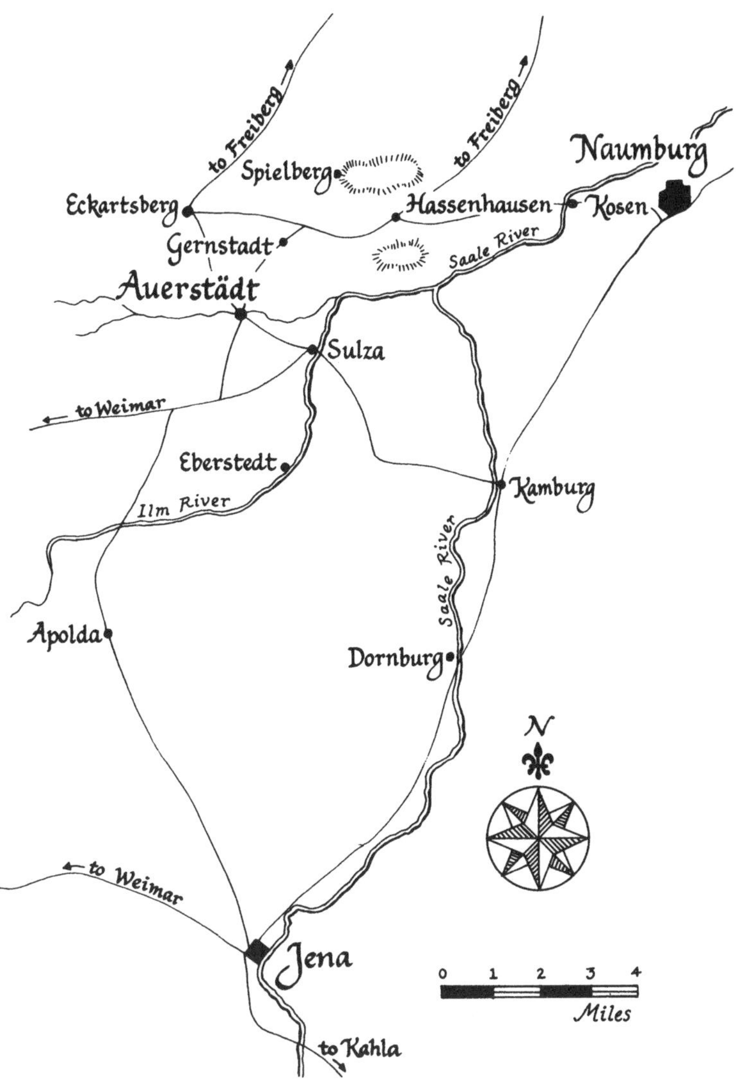

The Battle of Jena-Auerstädt

Kalkreuth. Not only did Morand beat off the Prussian cavalry, but he moved his artillery into position before Emse's mill and swept Kalkreuth's position with a deadly fire. At the same time Friant turned the Count's left and brought his artillery to bear on the unfortunate Prussian lines. Attacked on both flanks and in the front, Kalkreuth fell back from Gernstadt in relatively good order and took up a new position before Eckartsberg. His defense of Gernstadt had enabled the broken divisions of Orange, Wartensleben, and Schmettau to escape the onrushing enemy. But the Count was unable to defend his new position under the thundering attack of the victorious French.

While Kalkreuth delayed Davout at Gernstadt, Eckartsberg, and Auerstädt during the midafternoon, some order was restored in the other three divisions. Yet despite urging on the part of some of his advisors to continue the struggle, Frederick William decided that prudence was the better part of valor. He ordered a general retreat in the direction of Weimar. Assuming that Hohenlohe and Rüchel were in good order and controlling the ground behind him, for he had received no news of the events of the battle at Jena, the Prussian army began to retrace its steps toward Weimar.[28]

As the last rays of the sun faded on the western horizon the Prussian King led his defeated troops from the battlefield. The weary but triumphant soldiers of the III Corps turned to the task of rounding up prisoners and caring for their wounded before taking a well-deserved rest. Davout was unable to undertake a vigorous pursuit as his men were exhausted and his divisions reduced in strength and in need of reorganization. The day had been the most glorious in the annals of any single French corps in centuries. The III Corps had engaged a well-trained enemy more than twice its own numbers and defeated it. Auerstädt was also Davout's finest hour. He had fought well at Austerlitz; he would cover himself again with glory at Eckmühl (1809); he would withstand the assault of the superior forces of Bagration at Mogilev (1812); and his defense of Hamburg

LOUIS N. DAVOUT, Duke of Auerstädt, Prince of Eckmühl (1770–1823). He commanded the 3rd Corps of the Grand Army at the battles of Austerlitz, Eylau, Eckmühl, and Wagram and the 1st Corps during the Russian campaign of 1812. He was minister of war during the Hundred Days and was named a Peer of France in 1818 by Louis XVIII.—*Courtesy of Musée de l'armée, Service photographique*

would be a military triumph. However, none of these would compare with the brilliant display of arms at Auerstädt. If his marshal's baton had been granted because of family ties and personal attachment to the new Emperor, Auerstädt justified Napoleon's judgment of the man. He did not win his baton on the battlefield, as would Oudinot at Wagram (1809), rather he proved beyond all doubt his worthiness to bear the title in a manner which was universally acknowledged.

While Davout was driving the main Prussian army from the field at Auerstädt, Napoleon was defeating Hohenlohe on the plains between Jena and Weimar. The outcome of this engagement was never really in question. By the time the battle had reached its climax, Napoleon had mustered more than ninety-thousand men under his direct command; whereas Hohenlohe fought the greater part of the day with only forty thousand men. Nor did the arrival of Rüchel's thirteen thousand men in the middle of the afternoon appreciably change the situation. Even had the numbers been equal, Hohenlohe was no match for Napoleon; and while the Prussian soldiers fought and died bravely, they were pitted against the finest and most experienced troops on the Continent. The French victory was complete, and the entire Prussian army was in disorder and retreat by nightfall.

When darkness and exhaustion interceded on behalf of the fleeing Prussian troops, the III Corps camped on the field of battle (between Eckartsberg and Auerstädt). Davout then wrote to the Emperor, dated at Eckartsberg, October 14,[29] announcing that he had fought the Prussian army of the Duke of Brunswick accompanied by the King; and that he had driven them back upon Weimar in confusion. Napoleon at first doubted the report, which Colonel Falcon [30] brought him in the early hours of the fifteenth, and he is reported to have remarked, in reference to the fact that Davout wore glasses, "your Marshal is seeing double." [31] However, as additional reports poured into headquarters throughout the morning, it gradually became clear that the battle which had taken place at Jena had not involved the entire Prussian army, nor even the major portion of the enemy's forces. The fact was that it had been Davout's III Corps which had stopped the main enemy army, and that the Emperor would have to share his victory with one of his subordinates, which he had never done in the past, was becoming painfully clear.

Napoleon was fully aware that his throne, his position in Europe, and his popularity with the French people was based largely upon his military reputation. This reputation must, therefore, be guarded and enhanced. France must believe that only the Emperor could win great victories, and bring glory and peace to the Continent. He did not intend to share this great victory over the renowned Prussian army with one of his lieutenants. This is not to say that he did not heap praise, honors, and reward upon the future Duke of Auerstädt. "My cousin," he wrote Davout on October 16, "I send you my compliments with all my heart on your fine conduct. I regret the loss of your brave men; but they have died on the field of honor. Extend to all of your corps and your generals my satisfaction. They have acquired an everlasting right to my esteem and recognition." [32] And to Murat he wrote: "Marshal Davout has had a superb affair; he alone has battled 60,000 Prussians." [33] While to Talleyrand he wrote: "He [Davout] has fought the entire day and has put to flight more than 60,000 men commanded by Moellendorf, Kalkreuth and the King in Person. This army corps has covered itself with glory." [34]

Yet Napoleon considered the two engagements to have been one battle—Jena—and Davout to have formed the right flank of that battle, as he had at Austerlitz and would at Wagram. Neither the name of Auerstädt nor Eckartsberg appeared in the "5th Bulletin of the Grand Army." In one short paragraph of the Bulletin which ran six and a half pages, the Emperor summed up the achievements of Davout's Corps "at our right." [35] Furthermore, in the official account of the action which appeared in the *Moniteur* and which was referred to as the "Battle of Jena," only eight lines of the eight-page article pertained to the fighting of the III Corps. It was thus left to history to rectify this deliberate error by the use of the double title of Jena-Auerstädt. This terminology was adopted by the Prussians from the outset. In fact, they quite correctly saw in the action at Auerstädt a much more serious defeat than that at Jena. Had the Duke of Brunswick been victorious and thrown Davout back into the Saale, it would have offset the defeat of Hohenlohe and left the Prussians in the field with a substantial army—reinforced by Württenberg—behind which the shattered forces of Hohenlohe and Rüchel could have rallied. In this manner the campaign would have continued and moved into a second phase, rather than becoming a contest between an army on the one hand and a mass of fleeing soldiers on the other.

The lingering impression of Auerstädt was brought out most clearly in 1867 when the Prussian King William paid a visit to the Napoleonic collection in the Invalides during his stay in Paris. As Marshal Canrobert was showing his royal guest the portraits of the Marshals of the Empire, the King stopped at one and asked who he was. When Canrobert replied that it was Marshal Davout, the Prince of Eckmühl, the King exclaimed: "Marshal, you have not named all of Marshal Davout's titles; he was also called the Duke of Auerstädt. Prussia has not forgotten!" [36]

One last matter must be mentioned before passing from the combined battles of Jena and Auerstädt to the pursuit of the broken enemy armies. The role of Marshal Bernadotte on October 14 was a source of embarrassment for the future King of Sweden for many years thereafter. His I Corps was at Naumburg during the night of October 13–14. When Davout received his instructions from Berthier at 3:00 A.M. on the fourteenth, he went to Bernadotte's headquarters, informed the Marshal that he would march at once by Kösen to Apolda to attack the enemy in the rear, and gave to him in writing the following statement which had been added by Berthier to his orders: "If Marshal Bernadotte is with you, you may march together, but the Emperor hopes that he will be in position at Dornburg which he had indicated earlier." [37] As Davout did not anticipate any difficulty on his march to Apolda—Napoleon had informed him that the Prussian army was at Jena—he apparently approved of Bernadotte's decision to march toward Dornburg at dawn. Thus on the morning of the fourteenth, while Napleon was fighting on the plains of Jena and Davout before Hassenhausen, the I Corps, whose progress toward Dornburg was blocked by part of Murat's cavalry from crossing the Saale, sat idle.

Bernadotte was severely reprimanded by the Emperor for having reached neither the plains of Jena, nor having attempted to aid Davout; [38] and he is reported to have said at the time: "I should have had him shot! I should have turned him over to a council of war which would have condemned him to death, but preferred to deliver him to his own conscience and the scorn of the army!" [39] And indeed the army was quick to accept the judgment of the Emperor. In memoir after memoir Bernadotte is accused of having deserted Davout, of having refused to aid him even when that hard-pressed Marshal asked for help, and of having made no real attempt to arrive at Jena in time for the battle. Davout himself, despite the fact that his hatred of Bernadotte stemmed from this day, did not criticize the actions of his comrade-in-arms either in his official correspondence, his *Operation du 3e Corps,* or in his private correspondence. While it is true that the I Corps could clearly hear the guns of Auerstädt, its commander had received no orders from the Emperor to support Davout. The gravest charge that can be leveled against him is that he should have marched to the sounds of the guns and aided Davout. Had the III Corps been defeated and destroyed by the Prussian army, Napoleon would undoubtedly have relieved him of his command, his military reputation would have been seriously jeopardized, and the present Swedish royal family descended from another French general![40] The most damaging evidence against Bernadotte appears in the form of a letter which General Trobriand declared he sent to Davout at the time. In this letter Captain Trobriand, at the time aide-de-camp to Davout, reported that Bernadotte refused to assist Davout when he was asked to do so; that he dismissed him with the following words: "Return to your marshal and tell him that I am here and that he need not fear. Go!"[41]

During the morning of October 15 Napoleon was unsure of the movements of the Prussian army. He did not at first believe the report which Davout sent him; and it was only as the day wore on that the disastrous condition of the enemy became clear. Early the following morning he issued orders to the various corps commanders, and the legendary pursuit began. It was believed that the enemy would fall back behind the Elbe. Magdeburg therefore became the key target. Murat's cavalry, supported by Ney's Corps and Soult's IV Corps, pursued the fleeing Prussian army which had broken up into small units and, in fact, no longer formed an army. Hohenlohe, commanding the largest unit, fifteen thousand men, retired on Magdeburg, where he hoped to at least slow up the French advance; but on the twenty-first he realized that his position was untenable and, leaving a strong garrison, he marched out of the doomed city with an accumulation of forty thousand demoralized and disorganized men.

The III Corps, after a well-deserved rest, joined in the pursuit of the Prussian army. It advanced on Leipzig, which although well garrisoned offered no resistance. Passing through the city on October 18, the corps, now forming the right flank of the French army, occupied Duben on the Mulde on the nineteenth and reached the Elbe at Wittenberg on the twentieth. Three days earlier, on the seventeenth, Bernadotte had overtaken the Prince of Württenburg at Halle and engaged in battle with the only segment of the Prussian army still fit for combat. Although the outcome of the campaign had already been decided, his victory did much to lessen the Emperor's displeasure caused by his lack of initiative on October 14. Württenburg's defeat only served to hasten the retreat of the scattered Prussian units. When Davout's advance guard reached Wittenberg the enemy troops on the right bank of the Elbe made no serious effort to prevent the French from crossing the river. They did set fire to the bridge, but with the help of the inhabitants the French soldiers were able to extinguish the blaze before any extensive damage had taken place. Within two hours the bridge had been repaired and the III Corps began crossing the last natural barrier before Berlin.[42]

Davout reported to the Emperor on October 21 that two of his divisions had crossed the Elbe and had taken up a position on the right bank of the river while the third remained in reserve on the left bank. The Prussians had retreated in such haste that they had not destroyed the large quantities of supplies, particularly powder, which filled the warehouses of Wittenberg.[43] After a brief rest the III Corps once again moved toward Berlin. On the night of the twenty-fourth Davout camped just south of the city. In recognition of his contribution to the victory of Jena-Auerstädt, Napoleon granted to him the privilege of being the first to enter the Prussian capital at the head of his army corps.

The morning of October 25 was a memorable one not only for the men of Davout's III Corps but also for the inhabitants of Berlin. The Marshal, with his entire staff, rode at the head of Friant's division toward the Dresden gate. At a "cannon shot's distance" he was greeted by the magistrates and important dignitaries of the capital, who brought with them the key to the city. Davout prudently refused the key and told the city fathers that "they need pay homage only to the Emperor,"[44] who would arrive the following day. He then entered the city and marched his army corps through its center and out its east gate to bivouac on its outskirts along the road to Frankfort-on-the-Oder. His orders had been that he would leave only one regiment in the city to garrison it, and that the rest of his corps, including officers, would spend the night under canvas.[45] The population was amazed at the discipline displayed by the French. There was no disorder, no looting, not a man broke ranks as the three divisions filed through the city.

On the following morning Napoleon entered the Prussian capital and took up his quarters at the Charlottenburg Palace, which Davout had prepared for him. The III Corps remained encamped just east of the city, where, for the first time since the opening of the campaign, it received a somewhat prolonged rest (five days). Then on the twenty-eighth the Emperor came out to the Plains of Biesdorf and reviewed the corps. After the review he made numerous promotions to fill the vacancies left by the Battle of Auerstädt. He also distributed five hundred decorations of the *Legion d'honneur* to officers, noncommissioned officers, and men. This accomplished, he gathered about himself the officers and noncommissioned officers and said:

> Generals, officers and non-commissioned officers of the III Corps, I have gathered you here together to tell you in person that I am satisfied with your splendid conduct at the battle on October 14. I have lost brave men; I regret their loss as if they were my own children, but they died on the field of honor as true soldiers. You have rendered to me a great service in this particular circumstance; it has been particularly the brilliant conduct of the III Corps of the army which has produced the results you now see. Tell your men that I have been satisfied with their courage.
>
> Generals, officers, non-commissioned officers, you have acquired an everlasting right to my gratitude and favor.[46]

Moved by these touching remarks Davout replied that "the III Corps would always be worthy of the confidence of their sovereign and that it would be for him, in every circumstance, that which the X legion had been for Caesar."[47]

While the III Corps remained camped near Berlin General Vialannes took a small portion of his cavalry and advanced toward Frankfort-on-the-Oder. He entered the city, which made no attempt to resist, on the twenty-sixth; but as the bridges had been burned, another twenty-four hours passed before his chasseurs were able to cross to the river's right bank. Thus by October 27 a bridgehead had been established on the east bank of the Oder. The Vistula now remained the last natural obstacle to the complete occupation of the Prussian state. Two days later, on the twenty-ninth, General Antoine Charles Louis Lasalle accepted the surrender of Stettin, and Lannes's V Corps quickly dominated the lower Oder. As the various remnants of the Prussian army laid down their arms—Hohenlohe's command on October 28, and Blücher's at Lübeck on November 6–7 —Napoleon prepared to march east.

In three short weeks the once famed Prussian army, one of the principal legacies of Frederick the Great, had been destroyed. Some units of the army which had remained in East Prussia continued to bear arms, but one hundred and forty thousand prisoners had been taken with two hundred and fifty flags and eight hundred pieces of artillery. Unable even to slow down the French advance, Frederick William fled to East Prussia and the protection of an advancing Russian army.

The victory over the Prussian army did not bring an end to the war. Frederick William refused to make peace with the French emperor on the victor's terms. Thus the campaign entered a second phase—often referred to as the "Polish Campaign," or as Napoleon preferred to refer to it, the "Polish War of Liberation."[48] This phase pitted the Grand Army against the forces of Alexander I, supported by those units of the Prussian army which had not taken part in the Jena-Auerstädt disaster. As a result of the slow Russian mobilization and the news of the defeat of the Prussian army, Alexander's forces had not reached the Vistula until mid-November. The winter campaign of 1806–7 and the short summer campaign of June 1807 were therefore fought between the Vistula and the Niemen.

Napoleon was not slow to perceive the prolongation of the war. Before the end of October he was preparing to push east and occupy as much Prussian territory as possible. He would then bring the Russian army to bay and destroy it as he had done at Austerlitz. If this were not possible before the rigorous winter set in, he would go into winter quarters and make ready his forces for the renewal of the struggle when the snow, cold, and mud had vanished.

The III Corps, which had formed the army's right wing during the advance north, now became the lead corps as Napoleon faced east. Breaking camp on October 30, Davout marched toward the Oder. The following evening Morand and Friant reached Frankfort and Gudin bivouacked before Küstrin. Thanks mainly to the efforts of General Petit, Davout's aide-de-camp, the garrison of Küstrin—four thousand men strong—surrendered to the 21st Regiment on November 1.[49] While his three infantry divisions remained on the Oder until the sixth, the Marshal sent his cavalry east to attempt to locate, or gain information of, the Russian army. On the fourth the 2nd Regiment of chasseurs was warmly greeted by the inhabitants of the Polish city of Posen. The infantry resumed its advance early on the seventh and the Marshal, at the head of Friant's division, entered Posen amid much joy and celebration on November 9.[50]

At Posen the III Corps was strengthened by the arrival of a division of dragoons under General Marc-Antoine Beaumont and a division of light infantry under General Edouard Jean Baptiste Milhaud on November 11. Both divisions were temporarily placed under Davout's direct orders. His advance was held up at Posen through the fifteenth while other army corps moved forward on his flanks and behind him. Prince Jérôme Bonaparte (IX Corps) was advancing on his right through Silesia to Kalisz. Lannes and Augereau on his left were converging on Schneidemühl, with instructions to cut the lower Vistula below Thorn. Ney and Soult were following the earlier line of march of the III Corps through Berlin and on to the Oder. Then at dawn on November 16 Davout pushed east. As the Emperor remained in Berlin to organize the occupation of Prussia and direct the overall operation, Marshal Murat was placed in command of all troops east of the Oder; Davout continued along the main road to Warsaw. Detachments were sent south to capture key cities, such as Kalisz, Czestochowa, and Lenczycz, and north to observe enemy movements on the right bank of the Vistula; but the III Corps's principal objective was the capital of the former Polish kingdom.

Murat, who now led the advanced cavalry units in person, entered Warsaw on November 28, following its evacuation by the Russians. General Bennigsen, at the head of sixty-two thousand Russian troops, had reached the Polish capital in the middle of the month, and even pushed a cavalry regiment west of the Vistula as far as Sochaczew. But as the second Russian army, under General Buxhöwden (fifty thousand men), had not yet crossed the Niemen, Bennigsen pulled back behind the Narew. Davout moved through Warsaw (December 1–2) and prepared to force a passage of the Narew river [51] in the face of the enemy.

The shore-to-shore operation began on December 10 and was met by stubborn Russian resistance. The point chosen for the crossing was at Okunin; and despite feints above and below the village the enemy was not caught completely off guard. Floating ice in the river further complicated the maneuver. Only the determination of the troops and the skill of their officers enabled the French to gain a foothold on the right bank and hold. On the eleventh Davout strengthened his bridgehead as Bennigsen launched a determined counterattack to drive him back into the icy waters of the river. The encounter was lively, but the French held on; by nightfall the Marshal was able to inform Murat that the operation had been successful.[52]

During the second two weeks of December the Grand Army moved across the Vistula between Thorn and Warsaw to attack the new Russian line which ran north from the Narew along the Wkra river. Marshal Kamenski had been given supreme command of the allied forces (including General Lestocq's Prussian corps of 15,000 men); and as Buxhöwden neared the theater of operations, he made preparations for an offensive. But before the Russians were ready to attack, Napoleon ordered Davout, supported by Murat and Lannes, to force a passage of the Wkra and dislodge the enemy from his prepared positions.

The attack was spearheaded by Morand's 1st Division on December 23. Crossing the river a few miles north of its junction with the Narew under protection of artillery on the heights behind Pomichowo, Morand gained a foothold on the east bank while the French engineers bridged the river.[53] Once the Wkra had successfully been passed Davout ordered the 1st Division to storm Czarnowo. The struggle which ensued was fierce and lasted well into the night. The 1st Division overran the Russian defenses and drove the enemy to the north; but the enemy did not break off the action. Several determined counterattacks failed to dislodge Morand, and as the sun rose on the morning of the twenty-fourth the exhausted men of the 1st Division still occupied the disputed town.

The Emperor, who was not present in person on the battlefield, now ordered Davout to take the heights behind Czarnowo. As Morand's weary division could not be asked to undertake this major attack, the Marshal brought forward Friant's 2nd Division. Placing himself at its head, Davout stormed the center of Bennigsen's position. Again the Russians contested every foot of ground, and again the French forced their withdrawal. By nightfall Bennigsen's center had been breached, and he retired upon Pultusk with the French in full pursuit.

On December 26 two separate battles took place. Lannes, supported by Davout's 3rd Division, which was temporarily commanded by General Daultanne (Gudin's chief of staff), attacked Bennigsen in a strongly defended position at Pultusk. Though he was unable to dislodge the enemy during the course of the heavy fighting, his position was favorable by nightfall and the Russians withdrew. At the same time Augereau and Murat fell upon part of Buxhöwden's army corps under D. C. Docturov at Golymin (fifteen miles northwest of Pultusk). Here again the French were unable to rout the superior Russian forces. Davout arrived at Golymin in the middle of the afternoon with Morand's infantry and a cavalry division commanded by General Jean Rapp, which had been attached to the III Corps. These units took an active part in the fighting during the late afternoon. Friant's division did not arrive until after dark primarily because of the thaw which had turned the roads into rivers of mud. This same mud also prevented Morand's artillery from taking part in the battle—a factor which diminished his division's effectiveness and increased its casualties.[54] Under cover of darkness Docturov led his roughly handled, but undefeated, corps from the battlefield. On December 28 the Russian army was in full retreat. Kamenski resigned as supreme commander. Bennigsen and Buxhöwden withdrew to the north to protect the bases of supply at Köngsberg and on the Niemen.

The French army was by now in wretched condition. It had had little rest since the campaign had opened early in October. Supplies of every kind had dwindled to a dangerous low, and the men were exhausted from prolonged marches over miserable roads in cold and rain. Food had become scarce after crossing the Oder, and east of the Vistula it became all but impossible for the troops to sustain themselves off the land.[55] The III Corps was in no better condition than the rest of the army despite the methodical staff work under the skillful eyes of its commander. It had been called upon to do the heaviest fighting of any of the corps and had suffered the heaviest casualties. In the days of fighting between December 23 and 26 it had lost more than fifteen hundred men. Sickness also reduced the effective strength of the corps—as well as of the entire army. These considerations, coupled with the enemy's genral retreat, caused Napoleon to declare the campaign ended. As the new year began the army was ordered into winter quarters, and Napoleon began to make preparations for the renewal of the war in the late spring.

Davout's three divisions were assigned the district between the rivers Bug and Narew and the right bank of Narew from the junction of the two rivers to Rozan. His headquarters were established at Pultusk, which also served as the corps's assembly area.[56] The rest of the army took up quarters between Warsaw and the Baltic Sea. But the respite was brief, as the Russians did not agree that the campaign had ended.

Bennigsen, who replaced Kamenski as commander of the Allied Army, launched an offensive aimed at driving Ney and Bernadotte out of the district of the lower Vistula and the Passarge. With Königsberg at his back to supply him, he was determined to relieve Danzig and go into winter quarters in East Prussia. To achieve this goal he struck at Ney's overextended corps on January 18 and drove it south. This move threatened to cut off Bernadotte from the rest of the army in Poland; therefore, he at once began to retire upon Strasburg (on the Drevenz). Not until the twenty-seventh did Napoleon decide that the enemy had actually taken the initiative and that this was a full-scale attack rather than a harassing action. The army, which had merely been alerted earlier, was at once assembled.

The Emperor's plan was to strike straight north from Warsaw toward Königsberg. If Bennigsen persisted in his westward offensive he would soon find the French army between himself and his line of retreat—and forced to fight a major engagement. Realizing quickly what Napoleon intended to do, the Russian commander began to pull back on February 3 to cover his supply bases. Hotly pursued by Murat's cavalry, supported by several army corps, Bennigsen was brought to bay at Eylau on the eighth.

As the French army approached Preussisch-Eylau it was spearheaded by Murat with the corps of Marshals Soult (IV) and Augereau (VII) in support. Ney had been dispatched northward with orders to pursue General Lestocq's Prussian corps and to prevent it from linking up with Bennigsen. He thus formed the army's extreme left flank. To the south of the main body Davout formed the right flank. Marching by way of Spiegelberg and Guttstadt, the III Corps had found a strong Russian force defending Heilsberg (February 5). As the two leading divisions (Morand and Friant) came forward, they were deployed for battle. The enemy, overwhelmed by numbers and firepower, continued his retreat. On the morning of February 7 Davout changed his direction of march to the north. At first he advanced toward Landsberg—in accordance with orders which had been written during the night of 5–6—but when it became clear that the battle would take place at Eylau, Davout was ordered to march on Serpallen (immediately southeast of Eylau) by the Heilsberg-Eylau road.[57]

The Russian artillery opened the battle at daybreak (about 8:00 A.M.) with a cannonade to which the French artillerymen promptly replied. Bennigsen had not chosen a particularly good position, nor was his army (sixty-seven thousand men strong)[58] well deployed. His strong center was on the high ground one thousand to fifteen hundred yards behind (east of) Eylau and would prove a formidable obstacle. But both of his flanks hung in mid-air! The right, extending toward Althof, had neither town, nor woods, nor river to prevent its being turned. The left reached south to the hamlet of Serpallen; however as there was open country to the south of the town and to its rear, it was an inadequate anchor and could be easily turned. Bennigsen seemed to have hoped to lure Napoleon into an attack upon his center—as the Emperor had done at Austerlitz—and thereby destroy the French army with his superior numbers.

The center of the French line lay just south of Eylau, which had been taken from the enemy during the previous night. Soult's three divisions actually formed the main line. Augereau's entire corps was massed behind high ground opposite the enemy's left flank, as was Murat's cavalry reserve. Napoleon had only forty-four thousand five hundred men[59] under his command when the battle opened. He was counting on Davout to arrive with the III Corps

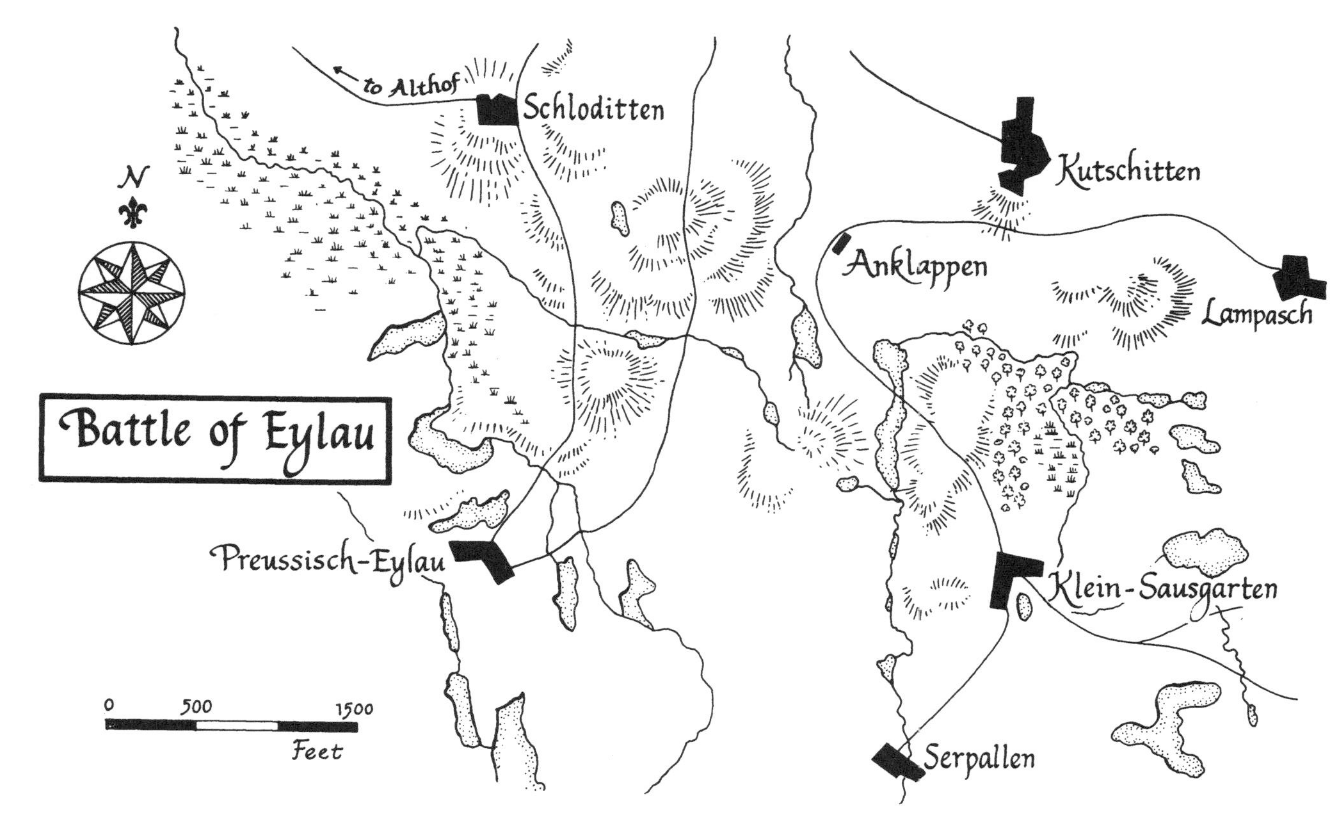
Battle of Eylau
N
to Althof
Schloditten
Kutschitten
Anklappen
Lampasch
Preussisch-Eylau
Klein-Sausgarten
Serpallen
0
500
1500
Feet

(fifteen thousand one hundred men)[60] and hoped that Ney's IV Corps, ten thousand strong, would also take part in the battle.[61] The Emperor planned to launch Augereau and Murat against the Russian left as Davout outflanked it, and drive the enemy north against the sea.

Breaking camp two hours before dawn, the III Corps hastened to join the main army. Friant's 2nd Division led the way, with Morand close behind him. Gudin's 3rd Division was several hours march behind and did not arrive on the battlefield until afternoon. Just before dawn the corps's light cavalry and Friant's advanced guard startled the Cossacks who formed the enemy's extreme left. As the sky brightened from east to west a scout in the top of the church tower at Eylau could see Davout's men forming on the high ground south of Serpallen and preparing to attack Bennigsen's exposed flank.[62]

By nine o'clock Davout had launched Friant against Serpallen with the successful results to which that hardy General had become accustomed. As Friant drove the Russians back upon Klein-Sausgarten, Morand's division began to form on his left rear and quickly moved into the line between the 2nd Division and General St. Hilaire's division (IV Corps) which had formed Napoleon's right flank. Davout's attack gathered momentum, despite Bennigsen's attempts to halt it by committing a portion of his reserves. Napoleon now ordered Augereau's VII Corps forward. Two divisions moved out over the frozen marshes and lakes toward the enemy lines. But they had hardly advanced a third of the distance when the light snow which had already begun to fall turned into a full-scale blizzard. The attack slowed, and strayed to the left. The murderous fire from the Russian guns, to which the French now presented their flank, took a ghastly toll. Furthermore, as they moved to their left they came under the fire of their own guns, which kept up a blind barrage in support of the attack. When the storm suddenly lifted the plight of the VII Corps became apparent to all. Bennigsen ordered his reserve cavalry, with infantry support, to fall on the disorganized French lines. Napoleon responded by sending Murat, at the head of two cavalry divisions, supported by the Guard cavalry, to Augereau's aid. Not only were the Russian horses driven off in disorder, but the French broke through the enemy's center. At this point the Russian infantry displayed the steel of which it was made. Reforming their broken lines they forced General Emmanuel Grouchy's cavalry to turn about and fight their way back to their own lines.

The attack had been a failure. Augereau's Corps had virtually been eliminated from the battle. The Marshal and every general and colonel in the VII Corps had been wounded or killed. Of the fifteen thousand men who had formed the corps on the morning of the battle, only three thousand were still with their colors (under Lieutenant Colonel Massy) when darkness silenced the guns.[63] Yet it had not all been in vain. The Russian center had been battered, Russian reserves committed to the fight, and the Russian commander's nerves a bit shaken. Furthermore, it had prevented Bennigsen from sending needed assistance to his hard-pressed left where Davout continued his advance.

With Gudin's arrival on the battlefield the III Corps, now supported by Milhaud's division of heavy cavalry, dominated events. Gudin took his position between Morand and Friant and drove the enemy out of Anklappen while the latter captured Kutschitten. By four o'clock in the afternoon victory seemed to be within reach. Caesar's X Legion had arrived and was rolling back the enemy's flank. But the "sun of Austerlitz" was unable to penetrate the frigid Baltic cloud mass, and the pendulum began to swing back in favor of the Russians.

Shortly before darkness engulfed the bloody battlefield, Lestocq's Prussian corps, seven thousand strong, struck Davout's right flank. The Prussians, pursued by Ney, had arrived at Althof (several miles northwest of Eylau) about two in the afternoon, following a strenuous march during which they had lost their rear guard and one of their flanking guards to Ney's eager troops. However Lestocq had managed to save the bulk of his corps, and after a brief rest was committed to the battle. Striking Friant's weary division—it had borne the brunt of the fighting since the battle had begun—the Prussian soldiers seemed to be fighting as though they were avenging Auerstädt. Kutschitten was recaptured after a stubborn defense and heavy losses by the 51st and 108th Lines. As Friant was driven back into the woods before Klein-Sausgarten, Gudin was forced to evacuate Anklappen; for the Russians, seeing Friant's men retreating, took heart and rallied to the attack.

The battle now reached its critical point for the III Corps. The enemy's entire left, heavily reinforced, was threatening the very existence of two of Davout's divisions. Grasping the gravity of the situation, the Marshal rode forward to rally his weary and disheartened troops. Displaying great personal courage under direct enemy fire Davout consolidated his position before Klein-Sausgarten. Riding along the hastily formed lines he exhorted his men to stand and fight: "The brave will find a glorious death here, the cowards will visit the deserts of Siberia." [64] With its artillery well placed and its infantry determined not to visit Siberia, the III Corps met attack after attack of the enemy. Despite their numerical superiority the Prussian and Russian troops were unable to penetrate the French line. Nor did darkness put an end to the fighting. For nearly five more hours the battle continued to rage.

Bennigsen had committed the last of his reserves, and although he outnumbered his enemy he had been unable to wrest the initiative from his opponent. In fact, he had barely prevented his flanks from being turned and his entire army from being routed. He was also aware that if he were to renew the battle the following morning that Ney's VI Corps, and possibly Bernadotte's I Corps, would give the French a superiority in numbers. He, therefore, wisely ordered a withdrawal, which began about midnight.

Both sides proclaimed victory. But, in fact, the Battle of Eylau had been a stalemate. The Russians left the battlefield in the hands of the French, which, in theory at least, gave them the right to claim victory. However, the Russian army had still maintained a solid unbroken front when the last shot was fired. The French had had the best of the fight and their foe was unable to renew the struggle the following day—yet Eylau was no Marengo, Austerlitz, or Jena-Auerstädt. It had not destroyed the enemy's army, nor brought Alexander I to the conference table.

Napoleon had not wished to continue the campaign through the bitter winter months. He preferred, as was indicated by sending his army into winter quarters early in January, to wait until spring to renew the war. The Russians had forced his hand by their attempted offensive; but now that their army had been roughly handled and forced to withdraw to Königsberg, Napoleon slowly pulled back and again took up winter quarters. This time Bennigsen followed the example and the campaign came to a close. This was somewhat of a setback in morale for the French emperor, who had become accustomed to concluding his campaigns with a spectacular victory and dictated peace.

The III Corps suffered heavy casualties during the battle. Its effective strength was reduced by 5,007 men[65]—one third of its total number. Yet its divisions were in good order at the end of the day and camped on the battlefield the night of the eighth. The Emperor reviewed his "X Legion" the day following the battle and expressed his satisfaction with their conduct in the face of the enemy. On the tenth, Friant and Gudin advanced eastward to Domnau, half the distance from Eylau to Friedland, but it quickly became apparent that the enemy had no intention of renewing the fighting. Thus on February 16 Napoleon ordered the *Grande Armée* to fall back toward the Vistula and take up winter quarters.[66]

Davout did not return to his January quarters between the Narew and the Bug; instead he remained in East Prussia, as did virtually the entire army. Between February 21 and 27 the III Corps settled into a triangle formed by Hohenstein-Allenstein-Deppen. On his left was Ney's VI Corps, while his right was only loosely tied to Masséna's V Corps (at Willenberg) by Joseph Zajonczek's newly formed Polish division. Here the Corps recuperated from its many wounds from the most bloody and strenuous campaign it had undertaken since its formation on the Channel. Supplies and replacements began to arrive, and Davout once again assumed the role of organizer which he filled so well. The dissolution of the VII Corps after the Battle of Eylau resulted in the distribution of its survivors throughout the various other corps. Large numbers of recruits also arrived from France. In this manner the various army corps were brought up to full strength. When the Friedland campaign opened in the first week of June, the III Corps stood at 28,891 men.[67] They were rested, well equipped, and supplied. Davout's boundless energy, his unusually keen organizational ability, and his strict sense of duty combined to bring his corps once again to a peak of military efficiency and readiness.

The French emperor remained with the army in Poland through the spring of 1807. Disappointed with the outcome of the Polish campaign, he diligently prepared for the renewal of hostilities. He planned to move against Bennigsen on June 10, but his adversary struck first. On the fifth Bennigsen sent Lestocq's corps against

Bernadotte on the lower Passarge while he attacked Ney's exposed VI Corps with six separate columns. His primary objective was to cut off Ney from Soult (on his left rear) and Davout (on his right rear). The French army was ordered to arms without delay, but it was clear that the Russians had gained the element of surprise which they had desired. There was little that could be done by either Davout or Soult to alleviate Ney's critical position. The VI Corps fell back fighting, and Ney displayed that talent for conducting a rearguard action for which he was to become famous in the Portuguese and Russian campaigns.

Preempting Napoleon's orders, Davout began the concentration of the III Corps as soon as he received news of the attack upon Ney. Not only did he receive news of Ney's plight, but also that enemy cavalry crossed the Alle and fell upon a company of his 1st Division and routed it.[68] Assembling his Corps between the Alt-Ramten and the Alle he posed a threat to Bennigsen's left flank as Ney fell back behind the Deppen. Unable to move against the enemy on June 6—having started late on the fifth the corps was not yet assembled—Davout dispatched a message to Ney stating that he was marching at once with forty thousand men on the enemy's rear. The officer entrusted with the message was directed to take such a road as to ensure his being captured by the Russians. The note found its way to Bennigsen's headquarters and produced the desired effect. The victor of Auerstädt at the head of that same tough III Corps could neither be ignored nor taken lightly. The Russian offensive came to a dead halt! By the morning of the seventh Bennigsen not only had confirmation of Davout's movements on his flank, but also that the entire French army was on the march. Lestocq's attack on Bernadotte—now replaced by General Victor—had not materialized. The Russian commander, his confidence shaken, sounded the retreat.

The French army now assumed the offensive and Bennigsen fell back upon the prepared camp at Heilsberg, where he intended to make a stand. He did not, however, call Lestocq's corps to join him. The Prussians retired to Königsberg to protect that major base of supplies. Then as Napoleon advanced on Heilsberg, Bennigsen again decided upon retreat rather than battle. But as he marched down the Alle it became increasingly obvious that he would either have to abandon Königsberg—and Lestocq—or fight a general battle. Heartened by his near success at Eylau, Bennigsen chose to fight.

The III Corps did not take part in the annihilation of the Russian army at Friedland (June 14). It had been directed to the north to support Soult's IV Corps and Murat's cavalry in their advance against Königsberg. By June 14, troops of the III Corps had reached the outer defenses of that fortified city, but they had been instructed not to attack it. As the battle shaped up some twenty-five miles to the south, Davout and Murat received orders to march on Friedland in all haste.[69] The III Corps was on the Friedland road by 11:00 A.M. and marched until after dark with only one two-hour break. But by the time it arrived the battle had ended, and there only remained the pursuit of the fleeing Russian army.

Friedland had not been a repeat of Eylau—it was another Austerlitz. The Russian army had been badly mangled; and Bennigsen, stripped of all self-confidence, advised the Tsar Alexander to ask for an armistice. This the Russian tsar did, and on June 19 Murat received his plenpotentiaries as he approached Tilsit. Napoleon, who was exceedingly pleased at the opportunity of ending the campaign without crossing the Niemen, entered eagerly into negotiations; and an armistice was confirmed on the twenty-third.

8

The Administrator

BENNIGSEN'S DEFEATED ARMY had fallen back across the Niemen in great disorder from Friedland. Yet no French soldier had set foot on Russian soil, nor had the Russian army been destroyed. Alexander I's position did not parallel that of the Austrian emperor's after Austerlitz, or the Prussian king's after Jena-Auerstädt. He could have continued the war had he so desired. But Alexander was disappointed by Austria's continued neutrality, Sweden's inability to render support, and England's lack of aid. Furthermore, while his military situation was not hopeless, neither was it comforting. The thirty thousand troops (Labanoff's corps) which joined Bennigsen on the Niemen were mostly untrained recruits who were poorly equipped. They were hardly a match for the French veterans who could still smell the smoke of the victorious battlefields of Prussia and Poland. If an honorable peace could be obtained, Alexander was ready to accept it as the better part of valor.

Napoleon, on his part, was no more anxious to continue this struggle, which he had not wanted in the first place. Now that Friedland had reestablished his military supremacy which Eylau had questioned, he was more than willing to cease hostilities. He had no desire to cross the Niemen, and indeed he was not at all prepared for a campaign which would overextend his already strained lines of communication and supply. He was ready to offer Alexander a face-saving settlement which would turn an enemy into an ally.

With both Emperors eager for peace, negotiations opened on June 25, 1807, on a raft moored in the middle of the Niemen and then moved ashore into the town of Tilsit. Napoleon, though he spoke in vague and general terms, seemed to give his consent to Russian expansion toward the north (Finland) and south (Bessarabia). Alexander, on his part, was willing to recognize those changes the French emperor had already made in western Europe, as well as those he was contemplating. For Alexander this represented little more than the acceptance of the *status quo,* with one exception. This exception was the creation of the Grand Duchy of Warsaw.

The Russian emperor feared that the reestablishment of an independent Polish state would lead to unrest among the Polish-Lithuanian population which comprised his western provinces. These provinces had formed a major part of the old Polish kingdom before the partitions of the late eighteenth century. Much of this fear was alleviated when Napoleon agreed to create the Duchy from Prussian-held territory, and, rather than giving it an independent status, to place it under the sovereignty of the King of Saxony. This satisfied Alexander, who hoped he would be able to control the Saxon king, and through him the Duchy.

One last significant aspect of this treaty signed at Tilsit was Alexander's pledge to use his influence to bring England to the conference table. If his former ally should refuse, he would close all Russian ports to English goods and make common cause with the French. Russia was thus brought into the framework of the famed—or perhaps more correctly, ill-famed—Continental System which Napoleon was bringing into existence (1806–7). All British goods would be barred from the continent of Europe as one by one the various nations were pressed into the system. In this manner Napoleon hoped to put sufficient economic pressure on the "nation of shopkeepers" to force it to make peace.

The humiliating peace which the Prussian king was required to sign—Alexander made little more than a pretext of securing lenient terms for his unfortunate ally—not only stripped Prussia of her western provinces and closed her ports to British shipping, but took most of her Polish population in the east to create the Duchy of Warsaw. Thus the once proud and powerful Hohenzollern state was reduced to a second-rate power.

The III Corps had advanced on Tilsit with the bulk of the French army and camped in the vicinity during the peace negotiations. Davout took up residence in the unpaved provincial town itself. The limited distractions of Tilsit rendered the celebration of the victorious campaign somewhat difficult. During the three weeks he remained on the banks of the Niemen, he dined frequently with General Oudinot and other generals and marshals, talking and drinking long into the night. On one occasion they were reprimanded for damaging an inn when they put out the candles at the end of the evening with their pistols.[1]

On July 12, 1807, Davout received orders to proceed with the III Corps to the newly created Duchy of Warsaw, where he was appointed military commander. Breaking camp on July 20, the divisions of Morand, Friant, and Gudin marched on the twenty-fifth via Thorn to the vicinity of Warsaw. During the month of August the corps took up strategic positions in the Duchy. Morand's 1st Division occupied the capital itself. Friant's 2nd Division camped at Sochaczew, and Gudin occupied the vicinity of Thorn with his 3rd Division. The two cavalry divisions attached to the III Corps were assigned the districts of Sieradz and Uniejow on the Warthe, and on the Pilica between Rawa and the districts of Lelow and Siewierz.[2] Deployed in this manner Davout's command could be quickly assembled in the Warsaw area to form an advance guard in the event of a renewal of hostilities with Russia, or a flanking force if war broke out with either Austria or Prussia.

Davout spent the months of August and September caring for the needs of his troops. The campaigns of 1806 and 1807, particularly during the winter months, had been exceedingly strenuous. Yet the restoration of peace had not resulted in the corps's return to France, much to the disappointment of the troops. The Marshal busied himself with the preparation of winter quarters so that his command might take advantage of the lull for reorganization, recreation, and training of replacements. The care of the men under his orders was always of primary importance to Davout. His army corps was consistently one of the best equipped, best supplied, and best disciplined in the French army except for the Imperial Guard. While Davout the administrator worked out the details of reorganization, Davout the disciplinarian took in hand the training. More interested in being respected than loved, he saw himself as a father to his men. He assumed the responsibility of preparing them for battle with dead seriousness, and demanded in return strict obedience. Without discipline an army becomes a mob, and while the Marshal is frequently criticized for having been too severe, he is even more frequently praised for the high quality of the troops he led into battle. However, life for him was not to be so simple as merely the care of his III Corps.

Napoleon envisaged Davout as more than just the military commander of French troops in the Duchy of Warsaw. He was in fact to be the eyes, the ears, and the strong right arm of the master of Europe. He made regular reports to Paris regarding the military and political activities in Russia and Austria,[3] and became preoccupied with Polish political affairs. His correspondence with the Emperor is filled with the intrigues of the various factions in the Duchy.

The creation of the Duchy of Warsaw was, in many respects, the logical outgrowth of the campaign which reduced Prussia to impotency. Napoleon called it—and in a sense it was—the War of Polish Liberation, and the Polish people had been encouraged to rise up and drive out the Prussians and Russians. The restoration of their independence had been held before them, and many had answered the call.[4] During the III Corps's eastward advance in November and December of 1806, Poland had responded enthusiastically and the nucleus of a Polish army had taken shape. But once liberation had been achieved, Napoleon began to have second thoughts—if indeed he had ever really been sincere—about recreating an independent Polish state. At Tilsit he apparently had assured Alexander I that he would not establish a sovereign Polish kingdom, and the formula agreed upon was the creation of a Grand Duchy, exclusively from former Prussian territory, which would be ruled over by the King of Saxony.[5] When Napoleon left Tilsit in July 1807, he pointedly avoided passing through Warsaw, but went instead to Dresden. Here, in the ancient Saxon capital, he proclaimed the *statut constitutionnel* of the Grand Duchy of Warsaw.[6]

In the eight short months between the liberation of the Duchy and the arrival of the newly appointed military commander, many of the old petty rivalries and factions which had characterized the former Polish kingdom reappeared. Davout had been enthusiastic in his praise of the Polish people and of their friendship toward the French during his march on Warsaw in the winter of 1806.[7] He wrote to his wife on November 8: "The Poles are receiving us as liberators . . . they give themselves up to it with enthusiasm." [8] But his arrival in Warsaw the following summer led to an involvement in Polish domestic affairs and a more realistic understanding of the Polish nation. Its dream of independence was being thwarted, and disenchantment with the "liberators" of 1806 had set in in many quarters.

"There exist in Poland two pronounced parties," Davout wrote on October 9, 1807, "which divide the entire nation. The one is composed of the majority of the upper nobility and their supporters. They are those who have lost their lands by their division [a reference to eastern Poland, which remained under Russian control] devoid of any true patriotic sentiment . . . these men, I assure you are neither friends of the Emperor nor of France. . . . The Russians alone can claim their affection, because Russia had reaffirmed feudal institutions and has assured them their prerogatives of which they are so jealous." The other party was composed of the "lesser nobility," he went on to say, "who have nothing to lose by the change and who stand to gain influence and wealth, [and] the bourgeoisie who await the benefits of the French changes rather than patrician generosity. . . . This class is the only instrument which serves the designs of France." [9] It was this latter class which formed the backbone of Polish resistance during the 1790s, Davout added, and which filled the ranks of the existing Polish army.[10] In letter after letter he advised Napoleon to work with and to support this middle class, while at the same time he pointed out plots and intrigues involving the upper nobility.[11]

A majority of the Polish nobility unquestionably did not welcome French domination and influence. They desired the restoration of the old Kingdom, with its weak monarch, feudal privileges, and personal independence. The Duchy of Warsaw, on the other hand, represented a negation of the old régime, which they had dominated, and the introduction of those principles and ideas of the French Revolution which had been carried over into the Empire. Davout, who was in complete accord with the new revolutionary Empire, still had a dislike of the old nobility of birth—despite his own ancestors and his noble birth. Authority, privilege, wealth, and power, he believed, should be based upon merit, not inheritance.

These bourgeois characteristics were tempered by his authoritarian nature, his hatred of disorder, and his devotion to the Emperor. Yet the Marshal, though no equalitarian, was still in many respects bourgeois at heart, and championed those ideas for which he had fought as a young officer in the Revolutionary army.

The Treaty of Tilsit marked the apex of the French Empire.[12] Napoleon, who had imposed his will upon the greater part of Europe following the victories of 1805–7, now sought legitimacy for that which he had attained by force. To this end his Polish policy called for the courtship of the nobility of the Duchy rather than that of the bourgeoisie. He was convinced that the nobility was still the most powerful and influential class in Poland, and that control of the Duchy depended upon their support. At the same time he was astute enough to realize that any policy would also depend upon support of the bourgeoisie. Thus his instructions to Davout were to walk that thin line between these two strata of Polish society.[13]

Davout's sympathies rested squarely with the Polish "middle" class, and his mistrust of the upper nobility grew stronger with the passage of time. Yet the goals of the "middle" class were not infrequently those of self-interest, and not at all necessarily synonymous with the interests of France. Thus the Marshal did not always find himself in complete agreement with his staunchest supporters. Nor, for that matter, did he always agree with Napoleon's interpretation of what was in the best interest of France. Whereas the Emperor grew progressively less enthusiastic about Polish independence, Davout continued to champion the cause. But to no avail did he insist that "an ally is of more value than a slave."[14] Napoleon merely parried his recommendations designed to lead to the establishment of a sovereign Polish nation.

Destined to remain under French control—at least for the present—the Poles began to make the best of what they hoped to be a temporary situation. This is not to imply that the spirited Polish people intended simply to submit passively to French domination. If they did not actively agitate for complete independence, it was because they felt that the timing was not right. They therefore settled for accepting those aspects of French reform which suited them and placing every obstacle in the way of those which did not. The Constitution which Napoleon granted the Duchy in July 1807 was of a liberal French nature.[15] The document was unacceptable to the upper nobility, and they did all within their power to prevent it from functioning smoothly during the year following its proclamation. Then in the spring of 1808, the Napoleonic Code was introduced into the Duchy. This was also resisted by various segments of the population for different reasons. The upper classes objected to its liberal characteristics, while the lower classes resisted it primarily on religious grounds. Davout, who saw in the Constitution and the Code tremendous strides forward for Poland, found it difficult to comprehend how any sincere person could oppose the introduction of these benefits. In his correspondence he complained to the Emperor of the delaying tactics of the gentry, and declared that he was using every means at his disposal to ensure the speedy implementation of the laws.[16]

Davout's principal contact with the Polish administration was through its minister of war, Prince Joseph Poniatowski.[17] The nephew of Poland's last king (Stanislas Augustus Poniatowski), Poniatowski had gained a considerable reputation as a soldier during the decade preceding the last partition. He had been appointed commander in chief of the Polish army in May 1791. Following the final dissolution of the Polish state in 1795, he went into retirement. The expulsion of the Prussians brought him back into the service of his country—first as commander of the National Guard and then as minister of war. It was virtually a foregone conclusion that this proud, energetic, and patriotic Pole would clash with the loyal, methodical disciplinarian who came to command *all* military forces in the Duchy.

Posing as the liberator of Poland, Napoleon had called upon the Poles to aid in driving out their oppressors, and during the closing months of the 1806–7 campaign four Polish Legions (brigades) were formed. After Tilsit these Legions were placed under the *suprême* command of Marshal Davout. However, the chain of command passed through Poniatowski, who was directly responsible for the Polish units. The principal conflict of interest arose out of the increasing demands made by Napoleon to raise the numbers and improve the effectiveness of the Polish Legions, and the desire on the part of the minister of war to pursue policies which he believed to be in the best interest of Poland. The creation of the Duchy of Warsaw, under the King of Saxony, rather than an independent kingdom of Poland also caused much disillusionment. Poniatowski, and the influential circle which looked to him for leadership, strongly suspected that the Polish Legions existed in the mind of the French emperor to strengthen his Empire rather than to form the nucleus of an independent Polish army. Napoleon continued to give lip service to Polish independence, but his actions fell far short of his words and the desires of the Polish people. Thus the Minister of War strove to maintain a maximum of control over all Polish troops, and to see that these troops were employed in the best interest of the Polish cause—independence. This inevitably led to strained relations between Davout, who was bent upon carrying out the wishes of his Emperor, and Poniatowski, who was equally bent on resisting those wishes when they did not coincide with Polish national aspirations.

During the first year of his residence in Poland, Davout neither understood nor trusted Poniatowski. The Prince, he warned Napoleon (October 1807), was a questionable man of dubious character, who was guided by a woman who disliked France.[18] With reference to Poniatowski's position as minister of war, Davout wrote: "He will profit from his influence to place his supporters in all of the important posts. The government will no longer form a national force, but rather that of a single party, and I repeat, this party is not the pro-French party." [19] Throughout the winter of 1807–8 Davout continually complained to the Emperor of the lack of co-operation on the part of Poniatowski. On November 14 he wrote that the minister of war's house was a center of intrigue, that the known *émigrée* and conspiratress Madame Vaubon frequented his home, and that the Prince was neither a friend of France nor of the Emperor.[20]

In March of 1808 Davout was still finding fault with the Polish prince, but his tone was changing as the two men worked out some of their differences and gained a better understanding of each other.[21] By midsummer the two former antagonists had acquired a certain degree of mutual respect. "I have continually studied Prince Poniatowski," Davout wrote to the Emperor on June 22. "It is possible that a cannon shot would change him; up until now his conduct has been that of a man lacking sincerity. . . . It would seem to me that in the event of a war with Austria he would not inspire in me distrust." [22] During the remaining weeks of the summer this lack of distrust was gradually replaced by confidence. When the Marshal received orders to move his headquarters from Warsaw to Breslau (August 25, 1808), he appointed Poniatowski commander of the troops in the Polish capital. "I have studied him for quite some time now and perhaps because of my own suspicious nature I continued to suspect him; but since affairs appear to be getting serious, his conduct has taken on a frankness which inspires in me much confidence and persuades me that he will serve Your Majesty with fidelity. . . . He is both honest and honorable. I have given him command of the troops which remain in the vicinity of Warsaw, that is to say of 12 to 15,000 men." [23] Then, as he was leaving Warsaw in September, the Marshal reassured the Emperor of the wisdom of his choice: "Everything makes me believe that he will justify the confidence which I have placed in him." [24]

The pendulum which swung from animosity to trust continued in the same direction during the years which followed. Poniatowski came to consider himself a disciple of Davout's,[25] and the Marshal respected the administrative and military abilities of the Polish prince.

As Military Commander of the Duchy of Warsaw, Davout was charged with the organization and training of the Polish army as well as his own III Corps. To this task he applied the same energy and superb talents which had characterized the formation of the III Corps during 1802–4 and made it the pride of the Grand Army during the Prussian campaign. Organized into four legions, the Polish army was instructed in French infantry tactics. Its artillery, under the watchful eyes of General Pelletier, was modeled after the French. Only the Polish cavalry, which had shown considerable effectiveness during the last years of the Commonwealth, remained virtually unchanged, and continued to carry their lances. Davout strove to improve the lot of the common Polish soldier, but was able to achieve only moderate success. He complained to Napoleon that the Polish troops under his command in Polish units received less pay and lived under poorer conditions than those Poles in French army units.[26] In March 1808 he had written that the Polish troops were absolutely without shoes; and that while the government did manage to pay the troops, their living conditions and their equipment, already bad, were rapidly becoming worse.[27] By July the effects of the Spanish "diversion" were beginning to be felt in the east. "There are not the necessary arms," wrote Davout, "to equip the new recruits for the Polish regiments." [28]

Napoleon's preoccupation with affairs on the Iberian Peninsula in 1808 had a dual effect on the Duchy of Warsaw. On the one hand, military supplies tended to move to the south where a campaign plan was developing—even though it was not thought at first that it would be of a serious nature. On the other hand, Napoleon relieved the financially hard-pressed Polish government of the support of eight thousand men. He had never intended for the Polish people to pay the cost of the French troops stationed in the Duchy,[29] and indeed they did not, but he did expect them to maintain the thirty thousand Poles under arms who were stationed at home.[30] But the unstable financial conditions of the new Duchy were so aggravated by the rigid enforcement of the Continental System that Davout wrote to the Emperor on March 30, 1808, that either he or the King of Saxony would have to come to the aid of the Duchy: "I believe that with 300,000 fr. a month the services which are lacking could be provided." [31]

In order to help alleviate, at least in part, the economic difficulties which beset the Duchy, but even more important to bolster the ranks of his own forces being sent to Spain, Napoleon offered to assume complete support and control of three Polish regiments, eight thousand men. The army corps would be returned to Poland in the event of war in eastern Europe, but until such time it would serve directly under the orders of the French emperor.[32] The King of Saxony and Prince Poniatowski agreed to this arrangement, and Davout undertook the necessary details. By the end of the summer of 1808 a fully equipped and well-organized army corps moved westward from the Vistula, destined to serve for the next four years in Spain. However, the departure of the corps had little effect on the unhappy status of the Duchy's financial problems.

The principal difficulties of the Polish state were grounded in its economic structure and the malfunctionings of its disorganized government. Davout had no more than an average understanding of the fundamental economic structure of a state, but he was an acute student of practical politics and a superb administrator. His criticism of the Duchy's "inept administration" [33] reached its height during the summer of 1808. "I will do all that I can to keep my patience and remain level headed for the good of your service," he wrote the Emperor in mid-June. "I realize that, although difficult, this is very necessary; in a country where nothing was organized and where nothing is being organized."[34] He considered the absence of the King of Saxony to be one of the fundamental problems of the administration. Frederick Augustus was desirous of good government in the Duchy, but, as the Marshal stressed, "it was organization that was lacking."[35] When the King came to Warsaw in October 1808, the Marshal expressed the hope that he would bring order to the chaotic government of Poland; and, in fact, he reported to Paris during the fall that the administration, which had been woefully inactive, had greatly improved. But the departure of the King on December 27, left a vacuum which his ministers—who were not necessarily of his own choosing—never filled.[36] Conditions did not substantially improve during 1809, and in some instances they even worsened.

The judicial system was one example of an institution in which time did not bring improvement. There was the greatest disorder in the courts, Davout reported in June of 1808. There was no solid basis upon which to judge many of the problems plaguing the new relationship between peasants and their *seigneurs* and nothing was being done to improve the situation.[37] This confusion was largely the result of hostility in many quarters to the introduction of the Napoleonic Code. The old entrenched nobility, who formed the upper layer of the stratified society, exerted their still-powerful influence to hamper the enforcement of the Code when they could no longer prevent it from becoming the law of the land. Davout complained in July that no preparation had been made for the enforcement of the Code at the time of its enactment.[38] The translation of the Code into Polish, he further noted, was extremely poor and led to what he believed was intentional confusion. In addition to deliberate barriers, the new legislation was not popular with the masses of the people.[39] While it was no accident that they did not understand those aspects of the Code which were designed to improve their conditions with respect to their lords, neither was it an accident that those sections of the law which legalized divorce were most explicitly clear. This generated a sincere hostility on the part of the predominantly Catholic population.

Davout had little genuine sympathy with the religious convictions of the masses of the Polish people, who were still firmly attached to Roman Catholicism and the Papacy. He was not an anticleric, but he had availed himself of the civil law passed by the revolutionary regime to divorce his first wife. Though she had died before he remarried in 1801, it is unlikely, judging from his attitude toward religion, that had she lived he would have remained single. Mademoiselle Leclerc, however, may well have had second thoughts about marrying a divorced man whose wife was still alive. She had been raised a devout Catholic and remained so throughout her life. The breakdown of harmonious relations between Napoleon and Pope Pius VII in the years following the creation of the Empire saw Davout follow the Emperor's "official" religious line. The Marshal did not concern himself with church doctrine as long as it did not interfere with affairs of state, but when certain religious orders began to pursue anti-French policies he took stern action.

The Redemptorist fathers had set a fixed course in opposition to the Frenchification of the Duchy. The order had already been expelled from various states which had come under the control of France—the most recent of which had been Switzerland and Bavaria during the early months of 1808. In Poland the order led the attack against the introduction of the Napoleonic Code because of its secular characteristics, primarily the sanctioning of civil marriage and divorce. Davout first mentions the Redemptorists in April 1808, in a lengthy discussion of intrigue.[40] Then on May 25, Napoleon wrote him that he was instructing the King of Saxony to expel the order as they had already been expelled from France and Italy.[41] The decree was promulgated during the first weeks of June, and Davout, who considered the Redemptorists a "real danger," particularly among the lower classes where their influence was strongest, gave them three days to put their affairs in order and leave the country. Amid the tears of the pious Polish women, the Redemptorists made their hasty departure.[42]

As the eyes and ears of the Emperor in east-central Europe, Davout was not solely concerned with domestic affairs in the Duchy of Warsaw. Almost weekly the Marshal included in his dispatches news of Austrian, Russian, and Prussian affairs. Prussia no longer posed a major threat to Napoleon. Her major fortresses were occupied by French troops, her army was limited in size, and the country was surrounded by the French army. Yet Davout found occasion to complain to the Emperor that Prussian agents were active in their former Polish provinces sowing seeds of discontent and stirring up anti-French sentiment whenever the occasion presented itself.[43]

Russia provided a more interesting, active, and potentially dangerous subject. Davout gathered military intelligence from every possible source concerning Russian army units along the Niemen, and any other information he deemed of use to the Emperor. During the months following the Treaty of Tilsit he gained much knowledge from returning French prisoners of war.[44] When this source dried up he sent French spies into Russia to gain the desired information.[45] But although the vigilant Marshal kept close watch on Prussia and Russia, his primary concern was with the military preparations being undertaken by the Austrian empire.

Austria was still considered France's long-established rival and potential enemy. Furthermore, whereas Prussia had been rendered militarily impotent and Russia posed no direct threat to French soil, Austria had been using the years since her defeat at Austerlitz (1805) to reorganize and rebuild her military forces. Davout was convinced as early as August 1808 that war with Austria was inevitable. This belief was based upon the military activity within the state as well as upon the diplomatic intrigues being undertaken by the court at Vienna. "The Austrians . . . are the worst neighbors," [46] he wrote on June 15, 1808, and a few days later he informed the Emperor that they were massing troops in the vicinity of Cracow.[47] During July his anxiety grew, and in August he wrote that "all the measures being taken by the Austrians cause me to believe that . . . they are preparing for war, either because they want war, or because they fear it." [48]

Napoleon took Davout's warnings lightly and expressed an optimistic view of conditions in eastern Europe. He continued to reassure his conscientious Marshal that while he was aware of Austrian preparations, they were the result of fear. He did not believe that they would undertake a war without the assistance of a major continental power, and that was out of the question in the immediate future.[49] On August 23, 1808, he summed up his sentiments in the following manner: "The Austrians are arming, but they arm out of fear; our relations are good with this power; but nevertheless they are arming and I have begun by demanding an explanation from them. I am sure of Russia, and it is this that causes me not to fear Austria." [50] In fact, Napoleon was preoccupied with affairs in Spain and Portugal throughout 1808.

During the years immediately following Tilsit the harmonious relationship between Davout and Napoleon reached its highest peak. Everything seemed to be going as the Emperor planned despite the fact that England could not be forced into line, nor the Pope made to acquiesce. Still he had high hopes that the Continental System would force the "shopkeepers" of London to seek the peace which his military might was unable to impose. His other problems could then be handled in the course of time. Davout had served him well since Egypt. He had completely justified his promotion to the rank of Marshal at Austerlitz and Auerstädt, and now in Poland he was displaying his administrative talents. At no time had Napoleon ever had cause to doubt either Davout's ability or his loyalty. It is not then surprising that the Marshal reaped substantial rewards from his services.

In August 1807 Napoleon bestowed upon Davout the Duchy of Lowicz. The Emperor estimated the income from this land at between two hundred and fifty and three hundred thousand francs a year—depending upon how well it was managed.[51] In December of the same year the shrewd Marshal reported that he had already received three hundred thousand francs in revenues and that Lowicz would surely bring in four hundred thousand francs a year.[52] This revenue came at a very advantageous time, as the Davouts were financially hard-pressed by the summer of 1807. The spring of the following year witnessed still another indication of imperial gratitude. On April 6, 1808, the Marshal received news that he was being raised to the dignity of Duke of the Empire.[53] His title, Duke of Auerstädt, gave full recognition to his greatest military achievement; and, at least in part, was Napoleon's way of restoring to the victor of Auerstädt the glory he had usurped in 1806 by considering that battle as merely the extended right flank of Jena.

The Duke of Auerstädt was well on his way to becoming not only one of the wealthier men in the Empire, but also a member of the highest strata of French society. Davout received more than nine hundred thousand francs in gifts from Napoleon—excluding the Polish lands and their income.[54] This figure is exceeded only by the amount received by Marshal Berthier. The relationship which had developed between the Marshal and the Emperor was by no means a one-sided affair. Davout's social and economic gains were more than balanced by his loyal service. An Empire based upon its military might was in constant need of skilled field commanders and military administrators, and Davout probably filled both positions better than any man in France. Yet despite this mutual need there was not always complete agreement between the two men.

The question of Polish independence was one point which tended to separate the Emperor and his newly created Duke. Davout had always been sympathetic toward the cause of Polish independence. "An ally is worth much more than a slave" he had frequently advised the Emperor.[55] Furthermore, he tended to take Napoleon at his word, as indeed did many Poles, when the Emperor spoke of reestablishing the Polish kingdom. This genuine sympathy gradually became suspect during 1809–10 as personal ambitions became involved. Was Davout's interest in Poland motivated by his desire to ascend the Polish throne, or was it simply on behalf of the Polish people? If it had started as the latter, there were few in Europe by 1812 who did not believe that Davout was actively seeking a crown. After all could he not reason that lesser men than himself had become kings merely because of their relationship to the Emperor. Joseph Bonaparte had become King of Spain, Louis, King of Holland, Jérôme, King of Westphalia, and even Murat, who was only the Emperor's brother-in-law, had been made King of Naples. Then too, there was Jean Baptiste Bernadotte, a man of *petit bourgeois* origins, of questionable military talent, and an opportunist of the first magnitude, who had become the crown prince of Sweden. Surely Davout must have reasoned that if these men could sit upon a throne, why not himself!

It is impossible to ascertain precisely when Davout first began to think seriously of kingship. In fact there is no statement in his correspondence, either official or personal, which indicated that he actually sought the Polish crown. Furthermore, the following conversation between Napoleon and the Marshal is recorded by his daughter, the Countess de Blocqueville, in an unconvincing attempt to prove that her father had not sought the throne. "'*Eh bien!* Davout, gossip has it that you have become obsessed with ambition and that you are working to become king of that country [Poland].'

The *duc d'Auerstaëdt,* shrugging his shoulders, responded casually: 'And have you forgotten sire! . . . Poniatowski is there . . . completely devoted to your service, it is he who should ascend the throne of Poland, as I have so frequently said to your Majesty!'—'Yet suppose I gave it to you?'—'Your Majesty has not the right to impose it upon me! You may send me to command a single regiment at the end of the world and I will obey, but, when one has had the honor to be born a Frenchman, one could never stop being French!' "[56] The Countess de Blocqueville is completely alone in her campaign to show that the Marshal had not sought the throne of Poland.

There is no doubt but that Napoleon believed Davout aspired to kingship. Indeed, as he believed every soldier carried in his knapsack a marshal's baton, so he saw in the baggage train of every marshal a crown. Napoleon once declared to M. de Narbonne that Davout spoke of Polish affairs from personal interest, and concluded that this type of political egotism was always unpleasant.[57] By 1811 it had become common knowledge that the Marshal had designs on Poland's throne. M. de Bourrienne recounts the following from a conversation he had with Davout in that year: "On this occasion I said to him [Davout] that if his hopes were realized, and my sad predictions respecting the war with Russia overthrown, I hoped to see the restoration of the Kingdom of Poland. Davout replied that that event was probable, since he had Napoleon's promise of the Viceroyalty of that Kingdom, and as several of his comrades had been promised *starostes*. Davout made no secret of this, and it was generally known throughout Hamburg and the North of Germany." [58] But Bourrienne concluded that despite what Davout said, he himself did not consider these promises to be any more than conditional.

Davout's candidacy had much to support it. He was not only a good general—a quality both rare and advantageous during the Napoleonic period—but also a good administrator. His popularity among the Poles further enhanced his position. He was known as an honest man who was concerned about the well-being of the people. As one Polish historian wrote, he was a friend of the Poles.[59] The Countess de Blocqueville states quite frankly that there was a party in Poland which actively supported the Marshal's candidacy.[60] Furthermore, the Marshal made a conscious effort to win the support and the affection of the Polish people. The latter was somewhat difficult for a man of Davout's temperament and personality. Respected for his military abilities as he was, no one ever accused the "Iron Marshal" of being well liked—much less loved—by his comrades-in-arms. Yet, while in Poland he gave frequent dinners, banquets, and balls to which he invited the local dignitaries, both civil and military, in an ever increasing number. At one of these banquets, honoring the installation of the new Polish government, Davout rose and toasted "the good health of the inhabitants of the Grand Duchy of Poland." [61]

There is also evidence to show Davout was popular in the Duchy. The Poles recognized that the combined victories of Jena and Auerstädt marked the origin of their newly founded state, and the fourteenth of October was celebrated throughout the Duchy each year. On the third anniversary of these battles General Louis Kamieniecki (acting in the absence of Poniatowski), presiding over the banquet given in Warsaw, gave the following toast: "To the health of his Majesty the Emperor, our great protector and restorer! . . . To the heros who contributed so much to the victory of the 14th, to the field of Auerstaedt! Long live the duc d'Auerstaedt!" [62] It is particularly interesting to note here that while the Emperor is credited with having reestablished the Polish state, it is Auerstädt which is mentioned, not Jena, and long live Davout—not Napoleon—the cry which went up from the celebrators.

His popularity in Poland may well have been a factor in his feeling that he was the most likely candidate for the throne in the event one would be created. However, he was only one in a field of perhaps five or six possible choices from among whom Napoleon might have made his selection. Frederick Augustus, King of Saxony, was considered to be the "legitimate" heir to the throne. The reformed Polish Constitution of May 3, 1791, declared his dynasty to be entitled by inheritance to the throne. But as Napoleon did not recognize legitimacy, and as Alexander I cared little for the French puppet, there seemed to be no possibility that he would have been chosen. If the Polish people had been allowed to vote on the matter themselves after 1809, Prince Poniatowski would surely have carried the day. He became the nation's hero during the Austrian war of that year when, as minister of war, he led the Polish army in the defense of the Duchy. However, it would have been the Emperor

Napoleon I, not the Polish people, who would have created the kingdom and he would have chosen its monarch. That fact of life placed the candidacy of his younger brother Jérôme among the top of those seeking the nonexisting throne. It is true that Jérôme was already King of Westphalia, but he viewed the throne of Poland as a promotion, such as Joseph's when he moved from the throne of Naples to that of Spain. Still another asset to Jérôme's candidacy was the support of Alexander I, who undoubtedly recognized his ineptness. By the summer of 1812 this ungrateful and incompetent parasite had come to consider himself the "imperial candidate." This factor throws vital light upon the conflict which arose between Jérôme and Davout during the opening weeks of the Russian campaign and led to the King's departure from the army.[63] Of the two remaining candidates, the Emperor's stepson Eugène de Beauharnais and his brother-in-law Murat, the former did not want the throne, though he was considered by some a likely nominee, and the latter lost interest in it after he became King of Naples because he hoped to become king of all Italy. The failure of the "Second Polish War of Liberation," as Napoleon called the Russian campaign of 1812, brought a sudden end to the aspirations of the would-be candidates; and as the Allied armies occupied the Duchy of Warsaw, Davout also lost his Polish estates.

The Marshal had become very much attached to these lands during his residency in Poland. He frequently retreated from Warsaw, a city which he never grew to like, to Skierniewice, where he established a country residence. Here it was that his wife joined him in April 1808. He had not seen Aimée since his hasty departure from Paris to rejoin the army at the beginning of the Prussian campaign in the fall of 1806. The Emperor had denied his request for a leave of absence late in 1807 deeming that his presence was essential to the continued effective functioning of the Duchy.

During this prolonged absence Madame Davout gave birth to another girl, Adèle Napoléonie (June 1807). The Marshal, who had hoped this child would have been a son, wrote from Tilsit: "I have only one regret, it is that I was not with you to receive this dear child, you would have been able to judge from my caresses that a son could not have been more welcomed."[64] The early death of their first two children and the poor health of their third caused the Davouts much anxiety over the new arrival. Nevertheless little

Adèle, whose own illnesses added further justification to his concern, was able to make the strenuous journey to Poland with her sister Josephine in the early spring of 1808. On April 22, Davout saw his new daughter for the first time.

The year 1807 had also been one of financial worry for the Davouts. The maintenance of Savigny posed a particularly heavy burden on their resources during the years since they had acquired the beautiful estate. Providing virtually no income of its own, Savigny had, in fact, become somewhat of a golden millstone about their necks. In May of 1807 the Marshal wrote to his wife, who dearly loved the stately manor and its not-so-well-kept grounds, that though they might regret having purchased it, the harm had already been done and only the good will of the Emperor could now repair the damage.[65] By August of the same year the cloud had grown even darker. "You will find enclosed a draft for 15,000 francs," he wrote his wife, "it is all that I was able to save . . . I hope that His Majesty, knowing your embarrassment, will remove this anguish."[66] Despite this financial embarrassment there is no indication, nor even any accusations, that the Marshal used his position or influence to alleviate it by dubious means. "I prefer poverty to a fortune which I would have acquired by means that would make me blush," he wrote during this troubled time. "Nothing will change me. My Aimée will never have to be embarrassed about her husband."[67] Napoleon, himself, bore witness to this flawless honesty when he confided to the Comte de Narbonne: "It is necessary that I give to him . . . for he does not take for himself."[68]

In August of 1807 Napoleon came to the rescue of his hard-pressed Marshal with the bequest of extensive land in Poland. In addition to the three to four hundred thousand francs which he realized annually from these estates, the Emperor continued to bestow upon him evidence of his gratitude. In the fall of the same year Napoleon made him a gift of fifty thousand francs for the purchase of a permanent residence in Paris. The Emperor was already in the process of creating a court to go with his Empire and wished his new nobility to establish itself in a manner befitting its new position. The Davouts thereupon acquired the hôtel Monaco from the Turkish ambassador early in 1808. This splendid mansion, the remodeling of which was closely supervised by Madame Davout, was never able to take the place of Savigny as her preferred residence. The Marshal was not himself to see the new Paris house until 1810 when he returned to the capital after a three-and-one-half year absence. Nevertheless, in the spring of 1808 he was reunited with his family.

The strenuous journey from Paris made in the early weeks of spring was particularly hard on Madame Davout, but her reception in Poland was warm. Her arrival was the signal for the commencement of a round of dinners, balls, and parties. She was entertained in the homes of Poland's most influential families, and a lasting friendship was established with the Poniatowskis. When she gave birth to her next son in 1809, the Countess Tyszkiewicz, sister of Prince Poniatowski, assisted her and was the first to write the joyous news to the Marshal.[69] Yet Aimée Davout was not socially inclined. She much preferred a quiet life with her husband, children, and a small group of intimate friends to the gaiety of Parisian, or any other, society. This was borne out time and again as she turned her back on the imperial court and took refuge behind the moat which encircled Savigny.

During the months she spent in Poland she made few friends; for while she performed her social duties as the wife of the military commander, she did not make her house a center of social activity.[70] The result of her antisocial inclinations was that she was not particularly popular in Poland. Nevertheless, her husband, himself possessing neither social grace nor charm, managed to maintain his popularity—a necessary asset for his royal candidacy. This is not to be interpreted to mean that the Duchess of Auerstädt was any less desirous of becoming a queen than her husband a king. Indeed, she was always more conscious of her social status than was the Marshal.

While the conduct of Madame Davout was very much in keeping with her character during her Polish visit, the Marshal is accused of conduct which, if true, was equally incompatible with his own. In her *Memoirs* the Countess Potocka wrote: "He [Davout], like all the Frenchmen, raved over the Polish women, and seemed ill convenienced by the presence of his wife, and he had, besides, a Frenchwoman who was supposed to be his wife's image, and who, thanks to these legitimate externals, had followed the army, to the Emperor's profound displeasure."[71] Only General Thiébault, who openly acknowledged his hatred of Davout, and who was in Spain at the time, echoes this accusation of infidelity on the part of the Marshal, and his account contains errors which make it unreliable.[72] Davout's abrupt and frequently rude manner, and the strict discipline which he imposed upon officers and men alike under his command, earned him few friends during his career, while he could count among his enemies kings and princes from Stockholm to Naples. Yet of all the criticisms and derogatory statements which his enemies leveled against the man, only these two are to be found accusing him of infidelity.

9

The Wagram Campaign

THE YEAR 1809 was one marked by intrigue in France and fighting in Germany, Italy, Austria, Portugal, and Spain. For Davout it brought laurels and a princely title. For Napoleon it brought troubles and a decline in his military prestige, although on the surface he appeared at least to be holdings his own. His armies were able to win battles and eventually the campaign on the Danube. Even in Spain, despite reversals the previous year, hopes ran high for a complete victory. Furthermore, English trade with the Continent reached a low point during this year before it began to recover from the initial effects of the Continental System.[1] But there were also indications that all was not going well. Fighting on two fronts proved to be an enormous strain upon the resources of the Empire and the abilities of the Emperor. He could not be all places at once; and when he spent the year involved in central Europe, his position in the Iberian Peninsula began again to deteriorate. Nor did his relations improve with the Tsar Alexander. Russia's lack of support during the Austrian war would clearly indicate that Tilsit and Erfurt had been hollow triumphs.

The year began with Napoleon's return to Paris amid the not-so-hollow rumors of the treasonous plot of Talleyrand, Fouché, and followers, and increased sword-rattling on the part of the growing Austrian war party. He had gone to Spain in November of 1808 at the head of an army of seasoned veterans to put an end to the national uprising which had driven his brother Joseph from the

Spanish throne upon which he had just placed him. But before the task could be completed, it became apparent that his presence in Paris was more vital to the security of the Empire. Domestic affairs were quickly put in order with the dismissal of Talleyrand and the temporary subjugation of Fouché. Austria, on the other hand, was quite another matter; one which would have to be settled on the battlefield.

With two hundred thousand of his best troops, including the Young Guard, tied down in Spain, Napoleon did not want war in central Europe. Temporarily, at least, he wished to maintain the *status quo* in Germany, Italy, and Poland. It was for this express reason that he had traveled to Erfurt in October 1808 to meet with the Russian tsar. Here Alexander had promised to support France in the event Austria insisted upon war. Napoleon counted on this agreement not merely to assure the neutrality of Russia, but he expected it actually to deter the Austrians from pursuing their hostile diplomacy to its ultimate end. On the strength of this Erfurt agreement Napoleon persisted well into February 1809 in his belief that Austria would not be so foolish as to undertake war with France supported by Russia. What the French emperor did not know was that his "brother" Emperors—Alexander and Francis—had made a secret agreement, the substance of which was that Russia would not take an active part in the event of war. Alexander had come to realize that it would not be in the best interest of Russia to have Austria weakened and France's position in east-central Europe strengthened. Austria thus hastened her preparations for war with the assurance that Russia, whatever her verbal pronouncements, would remain neutral.

Austria had been more than defeated in 1805, she had been humiliated, but her leaders refused to accept the Treaty of Pressburg as anything more than a temporary setback. Everyone in Vienna agreed that the struggle with France would have to be renewed; the only point upon which they differed was when and how the next campaign would be conducted. The Ulm-Austerlitz campaign had pointed out clearly that the antiquated Austrian army would have to undergo major reorganization and training before it could again challenge the highly polished war machine which had been forged by the Revolution and Napoleon.

This task was begun early in 1806 under Austria's most able military leader, the Archduke Charles. He had been named Supreme Commander of the Austrian army as it was disintegrating during the terrible days following Austerlitz. Charles's determination to rebuild the military might of the once-respected imperial Austrian army was hampered by the decadent Aulic Council.[2] Nevertheless, he was able to introduce a number of changes which the French army had proven effective in its recent victorious campaigns. The infantry was reorganized into army corps, the artillery was greatly improved and the number of guns substantially increased, and the old drill book, based on the outdated principles of Frederick the Great, was updated to incorporate new French innovations such as skirmishing tactics. The one major drawback which Charles was unable to correct was the lack of able experienced senior commanders.

Austria had not been ready to renew the struggle with France in the fall of 1806, nor did the spring of 1807 seem appropriate to the temporarily cautious Viennese court. But by the fall of 1808, there had developed a strong war party which was encouraged as much by the events in Spain and the accomplishments of Charles's diligent labors, as by promises of English gold. The Archduke himself was not to be found in their ranks, nor were the majority of his generals. They were aware that there was still much to be done before the army could face the French on the upper Danube with a good chance of success. The Emperor was forced to listen to his military advisors in 1808; however by the early months of 1809 the council of the hawks prevailed and the generals, themselves encouraged by the French buildup in Spain, made last-minute preparations for the opening of hostilities.

The original Austrian plan, and the one favored by Charles, called for a bold onslaught into central Germany by a strong force based in Bohemia, with substantially weaker forces south of the Danube and in Italy. To this end some six army corps were concentrated in western Bohemia by February 1809, two more south of the Danube on the Inn, and an additional two south of the Alps. But the more conservative Aulic Council, fearing that the road was being left open to Vienna, prevailed upon the Emperor to modify the overall strategy so as to shift the main theater of war to the south bank of the Danube. Here Charles would lead six army corps into Bavaria while two other corps would debouch from Bohemia. These two armies would join forces between Ratisbon and Ingolstadt on the Danube and advance up the river toward the Rhine. This latter plan, which prevailed despite Charles's opposition, was much less daring and was unlikely to bring about an early decision in the campaign. Rather it was believed to be by far the safer course of action.

The new Austrian threat imposed an enormous burden on France, her allies, and her Emperor. With the heavy commitment in Spain, Napoleon was not really prepared to undertake major military operations in central Europe. Yet within a few months he was able to field a respectable army. Beginning with Davout's Army of the Rhine, of which the III Corps was the backbone, he added German units, the Old Guard (which was recalled from Spain), and newly created French divisions to form the Army of Germany. This new *Grande Armée* stood at approximately one hundred and seventy thousand men [3] when the campaign opened, but they were supported by fewer than three hundred and fifty guns.[4] The shortage of artillery was made even more critical by the general low quality of the troops. As Napoleon put it in a letter to his minister of war: "The worse the troops are, the more artillery they require." [5] Except for the tried and proven veterans of Davout's III Corps and the Guard, the army was made up of young and inexperienced French conscripts and reluctant German allies. In addition to this army, Napoleon could oppose Austria with some sixty-eight thousand men under arms in Italy, seventeen thousand Poles in the Duchy, and sixteen thousand Saxons in the vicinity of Dresden. While it is true that these troops would tie down more than an equal number of Austrians, they could not be counted upon to give direct support to the main theater of operations on the upper Danube.

Davout's command consisted of four infantry divisions (commanded by Morand, Friant, Gudin, and St. Hilaire), two divisions of heavy cavalry (St. Sulpice and Montbrun), and light cavalry (Jacquinot)—in all a formidable force of sixty-seven thousand well-equipped men.[6] This army corps was nearly twice the size of any the Marshal had commanded in the past, a fact resulting largely from the shortage of experienced corps commanders in central Europe. In mid-March the III Corps was in winter quarters in the general vicinity of Erfurt and Bamberg. The three infantry divisions of Morand, Friant, and Gudin were composed of the seasoned veterans of Austerlitz, Auerstädt, and Eylau. The cavalry was also made up of veterans of earlier campaigns, and it, too, was in superb combat readiness. On the other hand, the rapid expansion of the newly created Army of Germany had been made possible only by calling up the 1809 and 1810 classes of recruits. While the 1809 class had received some training during the winter months, it had yet to face an enemy on the field of battle. The younger men of the class of 1810 were merely clothed and armed before being sent to join combat units in preparation for the approaching clash. Even many of the junior officers were fresh from the military academies and completely lacking in experience and maturity. Davout absorbed some of this raw material into his seasoned III Corps as best he could in the limited time available.

Two new army corps were formed in February and March of 1809. The IV Corps was entrusted to the experienced and capable Marshal Masséna, while the II Corps went to the not quite so experienced but exceedingly brave General—soon to be Marshal—Oudinot. Both of these corps were made up of large numbers of recruits and noncombat veterans. The remaining units were composed of troops from various allied states—Württemberg, Westphalia, Bavaria, Saxony, and Poland. The quality of many of these somewhat reluctant troops left much to be desired. Speaking of the entire Saxon army in the late summer of 1808, Davout said that its officer corps was so aged that he doubted it could actually be used in combat.[7] Marshal Bernadotte was sent to care for these elderly gentlemen and their sixteen thousand men.

Davout had rejoined his command in central Germany by the middle of March following the birth of a son, Napoleon. He immediately set into motion the well-tried machinery which brought the III Corps to combat readiness. Establishing his headquarters at Bamberg, he began to move his divisions southward toward the Danube between Ratisbon and Ingolstadt. All leaves had been canceled, and on March 20, in a letter to his brother-in-law General Friant, he ordered that all women be sent back to France beginning with those of the generals and colonels.[8] War had not been declared, but the campaign had begun.

The Austrian attack did not come until April 10, and when it did it achieved at least minimal surprise. Although no one believed peace could be prolonged into May, Napoleon did not think Charles would be able to commence hostilities before April 15, and strongly hoped that it would not be before the last week of that month. Davout, on the other hand, was in a much better position to ascertain the intent of their hostile neighbor than his imperial master, who remained in Paris—in order to avoid any changes of aggressive action—until Austrian troops actually crossed the Bavarian frontier. Throughout the winter and early spring the Marshal had developed an excellent network of intelligence. Not only did he take full advantage of all travelers crossing the frontier from Austria to gain information of troop movements and concentrations, he also sent out spies to secure additional data and to check the validity of less reliable sources.[9] He actually formed what he himself called his "secret police" with the sole task of discovering and reporting Austrian military activities.[10]

So successful was his intelligence service that he was able to keep Napoleon accurately informed of the position of the Austrian army during March and early April.[11] As the impending attack approached, Davout relayed to Paris the movement of major Austrian forces from Bohemia southward to the Bavarian frontier, and predicted that the enemy's attack would be two-pronged—out of the Bohemian mountains into the upper Palatinate (that is to the north of the Danube) and across the Inn River into Bavaria south of the Danube.[12] This espionage was not restricted solely to the Austrian empire. His intelligence operations covered Prussia and Russia as well.

On March 26, the Marshal reported that the Prussian king had refused to cooperate with the Austrian ministers who were striving to bring him into the coalition against France. In the same correspondence he informed the Emperor that there was absolutely no activity of a military nature in western Russia. Neither troop movements nor a buildup of supplies could be detected by the spies he had sent into that country. Every indication was that the Tsar Alexander, despite his military alliance with France, had no intention of taking the field against Austria in the coming struggle.[13] The latter news was even more discomforting than the former was encouraging. Napoleon had counted upon the neutrality of Prussia. Any news to the contrary would have come as a surprise. However, he was also expecting the Russian tsar to honor the commitments he had made at Erfurt to support France in the event Austria should turn upon her. Davout's reports clearly indicated that Napoleon had been duped by

Alexander and that he would have to face the superior numbers of the Austrian army without the support he had counted upon the previous fall when he marched two hundred thousand men across the Pyrenees.

The exact timing of the Austrian attack was a closely guarded secret which Davout's intelligence service was unable to acquire. But he was able to report on March 27, that the Archduke Charles had left Vienna on the twenty-first to join the army,[14] and three days before the attack was launched (April 7) he wrote: "One is no longer able to gain Austrian intelligence. All communication has been interrupted. . . . The news that circulates here strongly supposes that hostilities are imminent."[15] Despite Napoleon's strong desire for more time to finish his preparations, Davout's steady flow of dispatches made him ever aware of the rapid approach of the commencement of hostilities.

Austria lost her golden opportunity to catch the French unprepared when she changed her strategy in March 1809. Had Charles been allowed to launch six army corps into central Germany from their bases in Bohemia, where they had been assembled during the winter months, he would have found only Davout's III Corps to oppose him. The weeks of delay, which resulted when the decision was made to direct the major attack from south of the Danube, gave Napoleon the time he so desperately needed to assemble his army and move it into position to receive the attack. Nevertheless, the French were still not completely ready when Charles crossed the Inn. Had he advanced rapidly on the Danube from the south at the same time as General Heinrich Bellegarde (commanding two corps) moved southwest from Bohemia, he might still have achieved an initial success. But, despite the reorganization and retraining of the Austrian army, it still marched at a snail's pace.

Numerically the Austrians had an advantage in the Danube theater of operations. The Archduke commanded two hundred thousand men, whereas Napoleon had been able to muster only one hundred and sixty-five thousand men by the time the campaign opened. However, Charles's force was divided into two parts. He had only one hundred and fifty-one thousand men south of the Danube under his direct command, while the remaining forty-nine thousand men commanded by Bellegarde were some fifty to seventy-five miles to the north. Only the closest coordination of these two armies could bring this superiority to bear at the critical point of impact.[16]

On April 9 the Archduke Charles delivered a brief note to the commander in chief of the French army in Bavaria declaring simply: "In conformity with a declaration made by His Majesty the Emperor of Austria to the Emperor Napoleon, I hereby apprise the general-in-chief of the French army that I have orders to advance with my troops and to treat as enemies all who oppose me." [17] No formal declaration of war was made, and the following morning the Austrian army began operations by crossing the Bavarian frontier at Braunau. Marshal Berthier, nominally in command of the Army of Germany, received this news at Strasbourg on the eleventh, and transmitted it on to Paris where it reached the Emperor at seven o'clock on the morning of the thirteenth. In accordance with his orders Berthier moved his headquarters forward to Donauwörth and began issuing orders to the scattered French corps commanders, most of whom were already aware of the Austrian attack.

The first week of the campaign (April 10–17) was marked by the failure on the part of the Austrians to capitalize on the advantage gained by their having seized the initiative, and by misunderstanding and confusion in the French camp which would have led to sure catastrophe in the face of a more aggressive opponent. The confusion in the French ranks stemmed from the absence of the commander in chief. The transmittal of orders from the capital to Berthier to the field commanders did not operate efficiently. As information of the movement of Austrian troops from Bohemia southward had been relayed back to Napoleon during March and early April, he began to issue the necessary orders to counter the apparent change in enemy strategy. The result was a flood of orders and counterorders from Berthier's headquarters which bewildered the corps commander.

Napoleon's overall plan for the campaign called for checking the initial Austrian attack and then seizing the initiative to advance down the Danube while Eugène held off the Archduke John in Italy and Poniatowski defended Poland. More specifically his strategy for the Danube theater called for a concentration of the army in the Nuremberg-Ratisbon-Augsburg triangle, where it would be able to face either Bohemia or Bavaria as necessity would dictate. As the

French army took shape in the last days of March, the Emperor sent two specific sets of instructions for the eventuality of an Austrian attack before or after April 15. If the attack came before the fifteenth, the army would concentrate behind the river Lech with its headquarters at Donauwörth. However, Napoleon did not believe that the Austrians would move so rapidly, and so called for a concentration on Ratisbon in the event the attack developed after the fifteenth. With the later timetable in mind the various corps were moving toward Ingolstadt and Ratisbon when the Austrian attack was launched.

Davout pushed his army corps southeast from the Bamberg district through Nuremberg and Amberg in a fanlike formation toward the Danube. On April 6 the Marshal reached Nuremberg and reported that St. Hilaire's division would occupy Ratisbon on the ninth, while the other divisions were converging on the city.[18] By the tenth the III Corps occupied the following positions: Friant was at Amberg, Gudin at Neumarkt, Morand at Hemau, St. Hilaire at Nansouty, and Montbrun at Ratisbon.[19] Marshal Lefebvre's VII Corps, primarily Bavarians, was extended from the Danube to the Alps through eastern Bavaria with its center at Landshut. It was originally designed to hold up a secondary Austrian army which might push across the Inn. Oudinot's II Corps was between Augsburg and Pfaffenhofen, with Masséna's IV Corps coming up from Ulm. Other divisions, such as Vandamme's and Demont's, were east and north of Donauwörth.

The opening of hostilities threw the French army into confusion. Napoleon had received news from Davout[20] and other sources on the seventh—that the major attack was expected any day from Austria rather than Bohemia. On the tenth, unaware that the Austrian army had attacked, he sent the following message to Berthier by semaphore telegraph: "I think that the Emperor of Austria will soon attack . . . and if the enemy attacks before the 15th, concentrate the army on Augsburg and Donauwörth, and have everything ready to march."[21] In good weather this message could have been transmitted from Paris to Strasbourg in six minutes, but due to rain and fog it took three days, and did not reach Berthier, who had moved his headquarters forward to join the army, until the sixteenth.[22] This semaphore message was followed within hours by a more lengthy horse-carried dispatch. In the first paragraph of this poorly worded order Napoleon wrote: "In order for you to forestall that which everyone thinks the Austrians are going to attack, and that if they attack before the 15th, all should fall back on the Lech." Then in the second paragraph he went on to write: "If the enemy makes no move . . . the duc d'Auerstaëdt will have his headquarters at Ratisbon; his army will huddle within one day's march on this city, *and this in every event.*"[23] This dispatch reached Berthier on April 13—three days before the telegraph message! Had he received the straightforward telegram first there could have been no question of the Emperor's intentions. But the Major General interpreted the more lengthy dispatch to mean that Davout's III Corps should be concentrated at Ratisbon regardless of when hostilities commenced, whereas the Emperor meant for this to take place only if the campaign opened after the fifteenth.

Davout realized immediately the dangerous position of his corps at Ratisbon. Bellegarde's two corps were advancing on his left flank while the main Austrian army threatened his right. If he remained at Ratisbon he would surely be caught between these two forces. Therefore, on April 12 he informed the Major General that he was falling back upon Ingolstadt.[24] The following day three of his divisions (Morand, Gudin and Demont, the latter temporarily under his command) reached Ingolstadt as did the Marshal himself. But then, much to his horror, he received orders from Berthier to march back to Ratisbon! The astonished Davout began to retrace his steps back down the Danube despite his awareness of the increasing danger which was approaching from both sides, but not without expressing his belief that the maneuver was an error. "I will depart tonight for Ratisbon," he wrote Berthier at 7:00 P.M. April 14 from Ingolstadt, adding that he would do what he could to reunite his army corps the following day. But, he went on to say, "It seems to me that the best maneuver would be to concentrate on Ingolstadt." The Marshal then asked the Major General to reaffirm his instruction, assuring him at the same time that "if Your Highness persists in the execution of his orders, I will execute them and not fear the results."[25] The morning of the fifteenth witnessed the divisions of the III Corps once again converging on Ratisbon. The Marshal spent that night at Hemau and arrived at his destination the morning of the sixteenth. By evening he had assembled in the Ratisbon vicinity three divisions of infantry (Gudin, Morand, and St. Hilaire) and two of cavalry

(Montbrun and St. Sulpice), with Friant's division protecting his left rear at Nemau.

On the morning of April 17 the situation of the French army was critical. The Archduke Charles had secured several bridgeheads across the Isar between Munich and the Danube, while Bellegarde's two corps were advancing unopposed upon Neumarkt (thirty-five miles northwest of Ratisbon). The French army had not been concentrated behind the Lech as Napoleon had intended, but rather was scattered from Augsburg to Ratisbon—a distance of more than eighty miles. Davout was already outflanked south of the Danube, and greatly concerned for the safety of Ingolstadt and his lines of communication to the rear.[26] Furthermore, Kollowrat's II Austrian Corps (part of Bellegarde's command) had engaged his outpost to the north and serious fighting was developing. "I am anxiously awaiting your orders," he wrote Berthier nervously on the seventeenth, "for if I use my ammunition against General Bellegarde, I will find myself in an embarrassing position for whatever movements you may direct." [27]

Fortunately for Davout, and the entire French army, the Emperor arrived at Berthier's headquarters (Donauwörth) early on the morning of the seventeenth. Having left Paris well before dawn on the morning of the thirteenth, and stopping only for fresh horses, Napoleon reached the army in time to avoid the impending disaster only because of the slowness of the Austrian advance. By the seventeenth Charles should have been at Ingolstadt and Davout's position at Ratisbon hopeless. Berthier was overjoyed at the Emperor's arrival. As always, the faithful clerk had tried to carry out to the best of his abilities his chief's orders. Napoleon did not always confide his overall plan to the Major General, so that the latter feared to take upon himself the responsibility of acting in an independent manner—even when he somewhat belatedly came to the realization of the dangerous disposition of the various army corps.

Berthier had gone south on the Augsburg road on the sixteenth in hope of meeting the Emperor, whom he knew to be near. Thus when Napoleon arrived via another route at his headquarters he could find no one who was able to brief him on the position of the various corps. "I am absolutely ignorant of the whereabouts of the Duke of Auerstädt," he wrote Berthier shortly after his arrival, "and no one here knows precisely where he is. General Vandamme assures me that the enemy is at Ratisbon." [28] Then the picture gradually became clearer as he read Berthier's correspondence. With this clarification came the awareness of the danger confronting the army, and, in particular, the III Corps. "I have just learned that you occupy Ratisbon," he wrote Davout at 10:00 A.M. "My intention had always been to concentrate my troops behind the Lech. You will withdraw with all of your troops towards Ingolstadt." [29] Davout did not receive these instructions until 8:00 P.M. He immediately assembled his corps south of the river—in accordance with his orders—and began the withdrawal. Then on the nineteenth he was attacked by two Austrian corps (Hohenzollern and Rosenberg), supported by a third (Lichtenstein), as he moved westward along the right bank of the Danube.

Napoleon had not been well informed of the movements of Charles's corps since they had crossed the Bavarian frontier. Thus to order Davout to march across the enemy's front was to expose him to grave danger. It would have been much less dangerous for the III Corps to have fallen back along the north bank of the Danube while keeping Bellegarde at bay. The Archduke Charles, seeing Davout's vulnerable position, now became determined to pin him against the river and destroy him. Indeed he surely would have done so had his army hastened forward from Landshut. But whereas the French were on the move by five o'clock the morning of the nineteenth and pressed on by forced marches, the Austrians were late getting under way and advanced at their customary leisurely pace. Davout's baggage train and the artillery were assigned to the only good road running from Ratisbon to Ingolstadt. The infantry and cavalry had to use secondary ones which wound through the hilly woodlands and villages between the river and the plains of Eckmühl.[30] Davout's main concern was to pass through the Saal defile (just east of that village) and make contact with Lefebvre's left. The latter's VII Corps had fallen back before the enemy advance into the vicinity of Abensberg with instructions to aid Davout. By evening the divisions of Wrede, Demont, and Nansouty had moved up to support the operation.

It was not until almost noon of the nineteenth that the corps of Hohenzollern and Rosenberg were in position to interfere with Davout's march. But the Austrian commanders did not throw their full weight against the exposed flank of the III Corps. Furthermore,

Morand and Gudin had been rushed forward to secure the vulnerable defile at the first sound of gunfire, and did not take part in the fighting until evening. As it developed, St. Hilaire and units of Friant (perhaps thirteen thousand men) held off Hohenzollern's III Corps (eighteen thousand), while Montbrun's cavalry kept Rosenberg's IV Corps (twenty-five thousand) at bay throughout the afternoon. Despite the thunder of guns on the plains north of Eckmühl, Lichtenstein calmly marched his reserve corps of some twenty-six thousand men behind Rosenberg and up the Eckmühl-Ratisbon road taking no part in the battle. At dusk Davout attacked Hohenzollern on both flanks simultaneously, and drove him beyond Hausen in confusion. As darkness closed in on the battlefield heavy rains put an end to the fighting. Before midnight the III Corps was linked solidly with Lefebvre and was temporarily out of danger. This successful withdrawal from Ratisbon was due primarily to the ineffectiveness of the Austrian command. Davout handled his corps with skill and efficiency, taking full advantage of his adversary's mistakes, but Charles should have reached the Saal defile before the French and driven the III Corps into the Danube.

On April 20 Napoleon reorganized the army. A new provisional corps was created of the divisions of Morand, Gudin, Nansouty, and St. Sulpice, and the cavalry brigade of Jocquinot. Commanded by Marshal Lannes, who had just arrived from Spain; it held the section of the line between Davout's reduced III Corps—only consisting of the infantry divisions of Friant and St. Hilaire, the cavalry divisions of Montbrun, and a brigade of St. Sulpice's cavalry—and Lefebvre's VII Corps. With their backs to the Danube these three corps extended from Abbach on their left (held by Montbrun) through Abenberg to Siegenburg. Opposing them were the Austrian corps of Rosenberg, before Friant; Hohenzollern, before St. Hilaire and Lannes's left; and the Archduke Louis (V Corps), facing Lannes's right and Lefebvre. Behind Louis was Kienmaier's II Reserve Corps and behind him was Hiller's VI Corps. The latter two corps formed the Austrian left. Their fronts faced west toward the advancing corps of Oudinot and Masséna. The city of Ratisbon was still held by a regiment of the III Corps under Colonel Coutard. But he was hopelessly caught between Kollowrat's II Corps on the north and Lichtenstein's I Corps on the south.

Napoleon now executed one of his favorite tactical maneuvers.

He ordered Lannes to break through the enemy's center, while Masséna struck his left flank-rear. Davout was to fix Rosenberg and as much of Hohenzollern as he could, and Lefebvre would tie down Louis and support Lannes. The plan was executed with skill. The outnumbered Austrian center gave way and fell into disorder. Lefebvre then overran Archduke Louis's V Corps and threw it back upon Kienmaier. With the approach of Oudinot from the west Hiller decided that rather than move eastward to Eckmühl and join the main Austrian army, he would retire on Landshut in order to cover the road to Vienna. The French now pivoted upon Davout and pushed the Austrians back on to a line running south from Ratisbon through Eckmühl.

At this point Napoleon misinterpreted his success. "Yesterday and today have been another Jena," he wrote Davout. "The Duke of Rivoli reached Landshut yesterday at 3 P.M. You have nothing before you but a curtain of three infantry regiments." [31] He believed the battle had been won and was preparing the pursuit. Nor was the Emperor's enthusiasm lessened by Davout's more pessimistic reports which reached imperial headquarters during the morning of the twenty-first. The enemy remained before him in force on the plains of Eckmühl, the Marshal reported, and added that there were no signs whatsoever of his retreat.[32] As a result Davout, who still commanded only Friant, St. Hilaire and Montbrun, and Lefebvre, now reduced to two divisions, faced the greater part of the Austrian army while the rest of the French forces at Landshut prepared to pursue what Napoleon believed to be a fleeing foe. Therefore, he ordered Davout to attack the enemy "screen" before him with the support of Lefebvre—if help was needed! Skeptically but vigorously, Davout sent Friant and St. Hilaire clashing headlong into Rosenberg's entire corps, while on his left Montbrun kept the relatively inactive Lichtenstein at bay. But within an hour the Marshal sent an urgent note to the Emperor: "Sire, the entire Austrian army is before me, the battle is extremely heavy." [33] Still Napoleon persisted in his belief that Davout faced only a rearguard action and that the Austrian army was merely covering its retreat.

Davout stood his ground throughout the twenty-first though the fighting grew heavier as the day wore on. Lefebvre came into the line on his right to prevent his flank from being turned, but the Emperor sent no supporting units. By nightfall his troops were exhausted, yet he was able to inform imperial headquarters that "we have held our position," adding that "everything confirms the fact that the Archduke Charles is here with practically his entire army." [34] Munitions were running low, he informed Napoleon after the battle, and the enemy still showed no signs whatever of withdrawing.[35] By 2:30 A.M. of the twenty-second, Napoleon, who had been receiving confirming reports of the position of the Austrian army, decided to march on Eckmühl. "I have sent General Oudinot with the divisions of Tharreau and Boudet," he wrote Davout; and authorized him to retire toward Rohr-Rottenburg if he deemed his position untenable.[36] He had also received the unpleasant news—from Davout [37]—that Coutard, after expending all of his ammunition, had been forced to surrender Ratisbon, with its bridge intact, on the twenty-first. Thus the Austrian army had two possible lines of retreat across the Danube: one over the Straubing bridge, which it had always held, and now one over the Ratisbon bridge. Furthermore, the fall of Ratisbon enabled Kollowrat's II Corps to cross the river and join the main army, increasing its numbers by some twenty thousand men.

The fighting on the twenty-first convinced Charles that he had only two reduced French corps before him at Eckmühl, and he became determined that on the twenty-second he would attack and destroy them. The Austrian commander would be able to mount four corps against the French. Kollowrat and Lichtenstein were to turn Davout's left flank while Hohenzollern and Rosenberg fixed the French front and right. Fortunately for the two French marshals help was on its way. "I will be at Eckmühl at noon," the Emperor wrote early on the twenty-second, "and in position to attack the enemy vigorously by 3 P.M." [38] He then set up a signal with Davout in order to coordinate their efforts to destroy the Austrian army during the late afternoon. "I will be at Ergoldsbach in person at noon. If I hear a cannonnade, it will tell me to attack at once. If I do not hear one and you are in position to attack, fire a volley of ten guns at noon, another at 1 P.M. and a third at 2 P.M." [39] An attack would then follow in which Davout and Lefebvre would fix the Austrian center and Napoleon would turn their left.

The Austrians again had the advantage of time and again threw it to the winds. Kollowrat did not bring his corps into action against

Montbrun's left until mid-morning—at least three hours late. Lichtenstein, who was in position early, decided to wait for Kollowrat before advancing. Even Rosenberg, who had remained opposite Davout through the night, did not engage the III Corps until he heard the guns on his right. Thus it was nearly 10:00 A.M. before the battle was well underway. During these critical morning hours Napoleon was marching north from Landshut with forty thousand men. Davout's outnumbered and hard-pressed divisions were able to hold their ground during the first hours of the fighting, but by 1:30 P.M. Montbrun was falling back fighting, and Friant, his left being threatened, also started to give ground.

Optimism was running high in the Austrian camp as Charles appeared to be in complete command of the battlefield. Then just when victory seemed to be in his grasp, it was snatched from him by the guns of Marshal Lannes, which had been placed in position on the heights south of Eckmühl. With the divisions of Gudin and Morand leading the attack, Lannes began turning the Austrian flank. Rosenberg's IV Corps bore the brunt of the French onslaught as Lefebvre and Davout also began to move forward. Shortly after 5:00 P.M. the Austrian left broke. Overwhelmed by numbers, Rosenberg's troops, who had fought well throughout the day, now fled northward toward Ratisbon. Kollowrat and Lichtenstein had been ordered to halt their turning action as Lannes's attack grew serious. To stop the French advance, on his left, Charles threw all available cavalry between his fleeing IV Corps and the French. As darkness consumed the battle area, Napoleon halted his weary infantry and ordered the cavalry to take up the pursuit. The French horsemen clashed with the Austrians in the darkness, and in the fierce fighting which followed the French gradually gained the upper hand and pushed the enemy back to within eight miles of Ratisbon.

The victory had been complete, but the French army was totally exhausted. There were no fresh troops available for a pursuit such as followed Jena-Auerstädt. Davout's weary men dropped on the battlefield and slept where they lay. They had borne the heaviest burden of the four days fighting and had accounted well of themselves. Yet the victory did not end the campaign. The Austrian army was still intact; defeated, shaken, demoralized, and in retreat—but still an army. After two days of hard fighting before Ratisbon, during which time Charles crossed to the north bank of the Danube, the town was taken by storm. The III Corps, which had been given a well-deserved rest during the attack, was now assigned the task of pursuing the enemy in order to harass his withdrawal into the Bohemian mountains and delay as long as possible his reorganization. The rest of the army turned eastward and marched down the right bank of the Danube toward Vienna.

The Archduke Charles had two days march on Davout, and there was little chance of the Marshal overtaking him. Actually, the III Corps had been directed to "escort" the badly maimed Austrian army out of Germany, and had no intentions of giving battle to more than the rear guard. Led by Montbrun's cavalry, Davout followed Charles, with the divisions of Friant, Gudin, and Morand, as far north as Nittenau. On April 26 Montbrun came upon the enemy in a strong defensive position at Bruck. This proved to be Bellegarde's I Corps, still some twenty-eight thousand men, marching to join Charles in Bohemia. Bellegarde had remained on the north bank of the Danube during the previous week's fighting and had posed somewhat of a threat to Ingolstadt from the north and the French lines of communications to the rear. Davout did not attack the Austrian position and Bellegarde, who was simply covering the Archduke's withdrawal, evacuated Bruck during the night of April 26–27 and moved off into Bohemia.[40] When it became evident that the entire Austrian army had crossed into Bohemia, Davout retraced his steps to Ratisbon and followed the other French corps along the south bank of the Danube toward Vienna.

The Austrian capital opened its gates to Marshal Lannes on May 13 under the threat of an artillery bombardment. The city itself had little military significance as the Austrians occupied the north bank of the Danube and all bridges had been destroyed. The French position was somewhat delicate despite the victory at Eckmühl and the triumphant march to Vienna. Contrary to Napoleon's customary strategy, he had not pursued the enemy's army, but had marched to his political capital. Furthermore, and equally contrary to his own rules of war, he had seriously overextended and scattered his army. The Emperor himself was at Vienna with two

THE LION OF ECKMÜHL. This monument commemorates the Battle of Eckmühl, April 21–22, 1809. Marshal Davout was rewarded with the title Prince of Eckmühl for his distinguished service here.—*Courtesy of Donald D. Horward*

army corps (Lannes and Masséna) and the Guard. The remaining units of the Army of Germany were scattered between the Austrian capital and Augsburg. Davout was at St. Poelten with the III Corps, Vandamme at Linz, Bernadotte—who had joined the army from Dresden with the IX Corps (Saxons)—at Passau, and Lefebvre was in southern Bavaria. On the other hand, the Archduke Charles, who had virtually his entire army reassembled, was on the left bank of the Danube in the vicinity of Vienna.

The French emperor was aware of this Austrian concentration, and, despite warnings that the river was subject to rapid rising and even flooding during the late spring, he decided to cross the Danube and attack the enemy. Between May 18 and 20 the river was bridged just south of Vienna at Kaiser-Ebersdorf, and the army began its passage. The operation was hampered by repeated breaks in the pontoon bridge caused by the combination of rising waters, strong currents, and flooding between Aspern and Essling.

Davout was informed on the eighteenth that bridging operations were under way and he was ordered to prepare the divisions of Friant and Gudin to move to Vienna.[41] The following day the Emperor wrote: "Be ready with the divisions of Friant, Morand, and Gudin, to depart at 2 A.M. for whatever destination will be necessary."[42] The Marshal was then ordered to march from St. Poelten to Vienna, which city he reached at noon on the twentieth. At the same time his engineers and sappers were sent to Nussdorf (just north of Vienna) where they began to construct a bridge over the Danube.[43] This latter move was designed as a diversion to cover the crossing downstream. Then at 9:00 A.M. on the twenty-first Berthier sent an urgent dispatch: "The bridge has broken, much time has been lost. The enemy has attacked with all of his force, and we are only 20,000 men.[44] The fighting has been fierce, but the battlefield has remained in our hands. It is necessary that you send all of your artillery and as much of your munitions as possible. Send also as many troops as you are able."[45] Although the bridge was repaired on the twenty-first it was again broken between 10:00 A.M. and 11:00 A.M. the following morning, and could not be used throughout the day of the most critical fighting. Davout arrived at Ebersdorf on the morning of the twenty-second in ample time to take part in the battle of Aspern-Essling, but owing to the destruction of the bridge his badly needed divisions sat idly on the right bank while across the Danube their comrades fought for their lives. The Marshal crossed the river in a small boat and offered his services to the Emperor, but without his troops or artillery the only contribution he could make was of an advisory nature, and what Napoleon needed was not advice—he needed the III Corps.[46] When the sun set on the bloody battlefield the French still held their position, but, without hope of reinforcements, the Emperor withdrew his outnumbered army to the island of Lobau and, when the bridge was repaired, to the right bank of the Danube.

Napoleon blamed the loss of success on the Danube in his "Twenty-first Bulletin,"[47] and in at least one sense he was correct. Had the bridge held through the twenty-second and Davout's III Corps arrived on the battlefield during the morning—which it would have done—when Lannes had penetrated the Austrian center,[48] the battle might well have been won. But as a commander reaps the glory of victory regardless of how it was won, so he must bear the burden of defeat—regardless of how it was lost. Napoleon had acted in too great a haste, without sufficient intelligence of the enemy's strength or exact position, and without uniting his own army. It is for these reasons that he was forced to withdraw under cover of night to the island of Lobau and eventually (May 27) to recross the main arm of the river to the south bank. The French army performed an extraordinary feat. It had faced superior numbers of men and guns and held its ground. This, however, is simply to say that the Battle of Aspern-Essling was not a disaster—merely a costly failure. Certainly one of the most costly aspects of the battle was the loss of Marshal Lannes, who died several days after the battle of wounds he received on the twenty-second.

The battle had little effect on the military situation as a whole. The Archduke Charles continued to hold the north bank of the Danube, as he had before May 20, and Napoleon still controlled the south bank. But from the point of view of European politics and Austrian morale, it was a major setback for the French. Napoleon was fully aware that he must now recross the Danube and destroy the Austrian army in order to reestablish his military supremacy in Europe, for only in this manner could he hope to continue to dominate the Continent. He therefore set about making his preparations. The entire army was united in the vicinity of Vienna, and the island of Lobau was turned into a fortress and arsenal. A permanent bridge was constructed from the south bank of the river to Lobau with a line of piles upstream to protect it from fire boats and other floating objects. All available artillery was assembled, for the Emperor was determined that his troops would not be forced to face a superior number of Austrian guns as they had on May 21–22.

During this period of preparation—the entire month of June—the III Corps was in the vicinity of Pressburg. Following the re-establishment of the bridge linking Lobau and the south bank, Davout moved down the river to protect the army's right flank. By June 3 Jean Dominique Compans's division, now attached to the III Corps, had reached a point opposite Pressburg and the Marshal had set up his headquarters at Wolfstadt.[49] The Austrians not only occupied Pressburg, which is on the north side of the river, and fortified the heights which dominated the city, but they had fortified several islands in the immediate vicinity and held a strong position on the right bank at Engerau.[50] After an unsuccessful assault on Engerau, Davout was forced to lay siege to the town. On June 21 he occupied the island opposite Teber which the Austrians had held.[51] But the enemy's strong position in the vicinity of Pressburg ruled out any easy victory. Furthermore, the Archduke John, with his Army of Italy, was falling back to the Danube at Raab and forced Davout to divide his attention.

John had been pursued vigorously by the French Army of Italy under the able command of Eugène. During the second week of June the Emperor's stepson closed in on John, who decided to make a stand at Raab where he expected to be reinforced by Hungarian troops. However the Hungarians welcomed the embarrassment of the Vienna government and its armies, and raised the standard of rebellion. The battle took place on June 14—the anniversary of Marengo and Friedland. Eugène was victorious and the Austrian army retreated eastward to Konorn where it crossed to the north bank of the Danube. Davout had sent the divisions of Lasalle and Jacob François Marulaz to support Eugène, and actually started Gudin, at the head of six thousand men and fourteen guns, toward Raab on the fifteenth.[52] News of the enemy's defeat brought Gudin back to Pressburg, and a brief siege of the ancient fortified city of Raab eliminated that Austrian foothold south of the Danube.

On the morning of June 24 Davout received orders from Napoleon to bombard the city of Pressburg.[53] The Archduke John, who had arrived at Pressburg shortly after his defeat at Raab, was strengthening the fortifications of the city and the heights which dominated it, and gathering boats and material for bridges. Davout had reported these activities, but he did not believe that the Austrians would attempt a crossing in the face of the fifteen thousand men he had to oppose them. He thought it more likely that they would wait until the French had crossed to the north bank in force, leaving only a screen opposite Pressburg, and then cross the river and threaten their rear.[54] Napoleon ordered the bombardment to delay such an offensive, and at the same time create a diversion from his preparations to recross the Danube from Lobau. He gave the Marshal very precise instructions. Davout was to send an officer to John demanding that he stop at once all work on the fortifications and that he withdraw all troops from the Danube islands in the vicinity of Pressburg. If he did not agree to this ultimatum, the bombardment was to commence. After firing some one thousand rounds (later changed to two thousand) a halt would be called and another officer sent to Pressburg with the same demands. If again rejected, the guns would resume their deadly work. Periodically the bombardment was to be stopped and the demands renewed, until such time as the Archduke accepted the terms or the city was destroyed.[55] These instructions were repeated, with slight modification, on the twenty-fourth and twenty-sixth.[56]

Napoleon had hoped that this operation would get under way by the twenty-fourth or the twenty-fifth at the latest. But delay in the arrival of siege guns and munitions made it impossible to fire the first round before the night of June 26.[57] Davout carried out the Emperor's instructions to the letter, though he did not believe John would accept such terms. "General Desailly will present a new demand which will be phrased as your Majesty desires," he wrote on the twenty-seventh, but "I doubt that it will produce any results." [58] Nevertheless, the obedient Marshal continued to alternate between bombardments and demands until he began to run dangerously short of munitions on the twenty-ninth.[59] Despite the severe damage to the city, the Austrian commander refused to accept the French demands. His only answer was to direct heavy artillery fire against the French positions.

By June 30 Napoleon was ready to begin operations against the

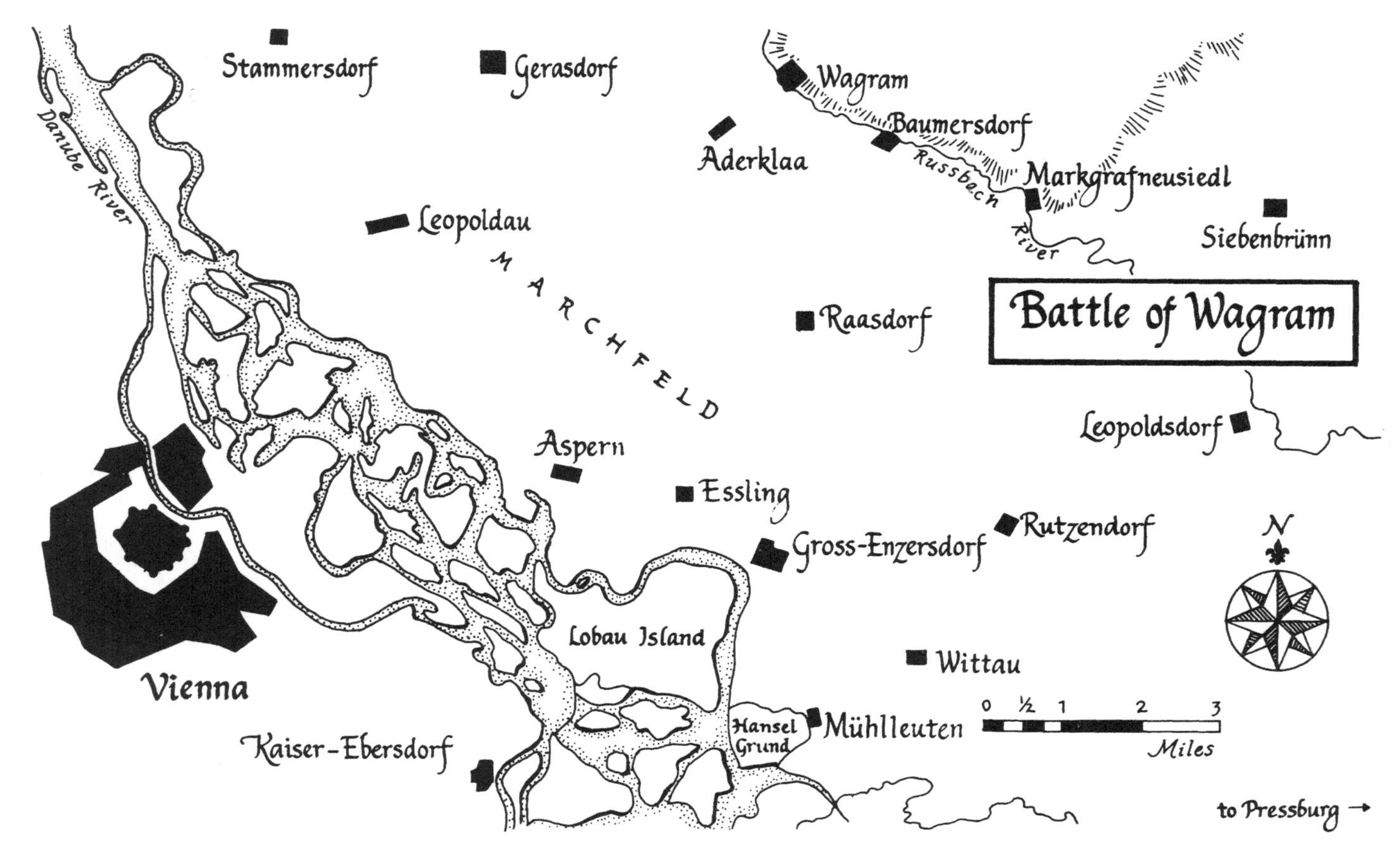

Battle of Wagram
Stammersdorf
Gerasdorf
Wagram
Baumersdorf
Aderklaa
Russbach River
Markgrafneusiedl
Siebenbrünn
Leopoldau
MARCHFELD
Raasdorf
Leopoldsdorf
Aspern
Essling
Gross-Enzersdorf
Rutzendorf
N
Danube River
Lobau Island
Wittau
Vienna
Hansel Grund
Mühlleuten
Kaiser-Ebersdorf
0 ½ 1 2 3
Miles
to Pressburg →

main enemy army in the vicinity of Vienna. On that date he sent Davout the following instruction: "You will be relieved of your post by a division of the Viceroy's [Eugène], on July 1 or 2 and you will march to Ebersdorf, at which place you will arrive on the 3rd. On the 4th the corps of the Viceroy will arrive. On the 5th I will attack the enemy."[60] After successfully attacking one of the islands held by the Austrians and taking two hundred prisoners on June 29–30,[61] Davout prepared to join the reassembling army south of Vienna in preparations for the Battle of Wagram.

The III Corps, part of which had been at Vienna during the month of June, arrived at Ebersdorf during the night of July 3–4. The various divisions were in excellent combat readiness.[62] The army had already begun to move onto the island of Lobau under cover of darkness. Oudinot's (formerly Lannes's) II Corps, Masséna's IV Corps and Davout's III Corps were designated to make the initial crossings during the night of July 4–5. Since the Austrians had fortified the Aspern-Essling-Gross-Enzersdorf area to prevent a crossing from Lobau northward, Napoleon directed his efforts to the east toward Mühlleuten and Wittau from the southeast corner of the island.

The Archduke Charles had done little in the way of utilizing the weeks following his victory at Aspern-Essling. Nor did he have any real indication of what his enemy might be about until July 1.[63] Even then there was much debate and uncertainty in high Austrian circles. Davout's increased activities before Pressburg had led the high command to believe that the French would attack at that point so as to avoid crossing the river in the presence of their entire army. When it became increasingly clear that the French buildup was once again on Lobau during the first days of July, and that the attack would undoubtedly come from the island as it had in May, Charles drew his army corps up in a line from the Danube through Stammersdorf, and Gerasdorf, to Wagram, and then along the heights on the north bank of the Russbach to Markgrafneusiedl. This position was taken up because it was believed that the French superiority in artillery made it unadvisable to oppose them at the river or on the open Marchfeld behind Aspern and Essling.

Napoleon had expected to outflank the Austrians, whom he was sure would take up approximately the same positions they had in May, that is in the vicinity of Aspern and Essling. He would land below Essling and attack the village on the flank and rear. Oudinot led the shore-to-shore operation and gained a foothold in the Mühlleuten vicinity (actually the island of Hansel-Grund) during the predawn hours of July 5. Once his operation was well under way Masséna bridged the hundred-and-seventy-five-foot arm of the Danube some three-quarters of a mile upstream, and reaching the north bank swung to his left and advanced on Gross-Enzersdorf. Then, as the sun began to rise in the east, Davout constructed his bridge below Masséna's and moved toward Wittau. By midmorning Napoleon had three army corps on the north bank and began to push them out into the open plain between Gross-Enzersdorf and Wittau. The operations of the fifth had gone smoothly and according to the Emperor's timetable. Oudinot had to cross the line of march of Davout's Corps in order for the latter to assume his position as the army's right flank and the former to occupy the center, but as the enemy made no serious attempt to interfere with this maneuver, it was carried out with a minimum of delay.

The remaining units of the French army continued to move across the dozen or more bridges which spanned the narrow arm of the Danube throughout the day. Davout advanced toward Markrafneusiedl, Oudinot toward Wagram, and Masséna cleared the enemy from Essling and Aspern, while Eugène's Army of Italy and Bernadotte's IX Corps moved into line between Oudinot and Masséna. By evening the Guard, Marmont's XI Corps and various other units had joined the main force.[64] But even before the last divisions had left the island Napoleon ordered an attack on the Russbach heights. Surveying the Austrian position late in the afternoon, he noticed that it had been taken up hurriedly and with little advance preparation. Hoping to catch the enemy before he had time to prepare defensive earthworks, he ordered four corps to attack. The premature assault was not well coordinated, nor was it supported by artillery—which had not had time to move forward. Only Oudinot's II Corps, the first to engage the enemy, made any headway against the stubborn resistance of the Austrian infantry. Eugène's Army of Italy also attacked with vigor, but with less success. Bernadotte's belated attack on Wagram gained initial success before he withdrew to his original position. On the extreme right Davout had not received his orders until the sun had already set. Yet this mixup did not prevent the III Corps from moving forward in the fading light.

Here again, as all along the front, the victors of Aspern-Essling held their ground. As darkness moved over the battlefield, the French broke off the engagement and bivouacked for the night. The untimely attack had not only been unsuccessful, but when General Etienne-Jacques Macdonald's men fired upon one another in the confusion, and the Archduke Charles personally led a counterattack with fresh troops, the French had broken and fled to the rear. The gap was quickly filled, and the enemy was unable to exploit the incident. Nevertheless, it gives much insight into the unreliability of some of the troops comprising the army. There is no question but that this "Grand Army" was not the *Grande Armée* of Austerlitz and Jena-Auerstädt.

The Austrian left flank had held its ground so well against the French attack on the evening of July 5 that the Archduke Charles decided to seize the initiative early on the sixth. Klenau's VI Corps (the extreme right) was ordered to push south along the Danube and to clear the French out of Aspern and Essling. He would then destroy the enemy's bridges and cut off Napoleon's line of communications and retreat. With Klenau well under way Kollowrat's III Corps (on his left) and Lichtenstein's reserve Corps would pivot on Bellegarde, who held Wagram, and roll back the French left. As the offensive began to gain ground Bellegarde would attack southward from Wagram supported by Hohenzollern's II Corps (the left-center of the line) who would debouch from Baumersdorf. Rosenberg's IV Corps on the extreme left would fix whatever French troops were in front of it by a diversionary attack. Thus by midmorning the entire Austrian army—136,200 men and 446 guns [65]—would be advancing. One last aspect of Charles's tactics was to summon his brother John from Pressburg to fall upon the enemy's rear with his 12,500-man Army of Italy. If the French were routed on the plains before Wagram and cut off from the Danube bridges, they could be completely destroyed between the two Austrian armies. Tactically the plan was daring but sound. Against a less formidable foe it would likely have succeeded.

The French emperor also spent the night of July 5–6 planning for the resumption of the battle. Perhaps the greatest single difference was that Napoleon had been planning for this occasion since his defeat at Aspern-Essling, whereas Charles had wasted most of the interval. The result was that the Emperor already outmanned (188,900 to 136,200) and outgunned (488 to 446)[66] his opponent, and now would outmaneuver him as well. With this superior strength he intended to exploit the weakness of the Austrian center in the Wagram vicinity. During the early part of the night he pulled Masséna's divisions to the right, closing them up on Bernadotte's IX Corps at Aderklaa. Eugène and Oudinot faced the Russbach between Wagram and Markgrafneusiedl and Davout moved somewhat to his right so as to face the village Markgrafneusiedl and extended his right flank to the east of the Russbach toward Siebenbrunn. The reserve cavalry under Bessières and the Guard were at Raasdorf where they could easily be deployed to any sector. Only one division, commanded by General Boudet (IV Corps), remained before Aspern and another under General Reynier on the island of Lobau to hold the Danube bridgehead.

Napoleon had not planned to begin the battle before six o'clock on the morning of July 6, but at 4:00 A.M. Davout's slumbering men were rudely awakened by Rosenberg's artillery. Charles's orders to Klenau and Kollowrat were apparently delayed so that they had not yet broken camp when Rosenberg began his diversionary action. Napoleon at once thought of the Archduke John. Had he arrived on the battlefield and immediately attacked his exposed flank? The Emperor set out at once in person for Davout's headquarters followed by two divisions of cavalry (commanded by Generals Nansouty and Arrighi) and the Guard. Rosenberg had the element of surprise with him, and his men, encouraged by their own steadfastness the evening before and remembering their feats of arms before Essling, fell on Davout's Corps with determination. The French were driven out of their forward positions, but quickly regained their composure and rose to the occasion like the veterans of Austerlitz and Auerstaedt which they were. The Austrian attack collapsed on the bayonets of "Caesar's X Legion." Before Rosenberg could regroup his men to defend the ground he had won, Davout ordered his men forward. By 6:00 A.M. they had not only regained their original position, but had reached the foot of the Russbach heights which ran northeast from Markgrafneusiedl perpendicular to the stream. At this point the fighting died down while both corps commanders undertook the reorganization of their divisions necessitated by the three-hour struggle. Napoleon, quite satisfied that Davout had the situation well in hand, returned to his headquarters at Raasdorf with Nansouty and the Guard, neither of which had been engaged. Arrighi's cavalry remained behind the III Corps to keep a watchful eye for the Archduke John, who might still appear at any time and disrupt the French right-rear. Before leaving Davout the Emperor ordered the Marshal to prepare an attack on the Austrian left as quickly as possible, but the earliest his lieutenant could promise was two hours hence (about 9:00 A.M.).

Meanwhile, the Austrian right was on the march. Klenau had belatedly, and almost leisurely, moved on Aspern with practically no opposition. Boudet made no attempt to defend the village, but rather fell back into a prepared position in a bend in the river. Kollowrat also moved south through Breitenlee and then swung to the east toward Raasdorf. He also was unopposed. In the center a vacuum had been created in the French line by Bernadotte's evacuation of Aderklaa, presumedly to shorten the line between Eugène and Masséna which had formed an arch. Bellegarde quickly pulled his right around and occupied the strategically located village as Lichtenstein unhurriedly moved forward on his right. Furious at Bernadotte's unauthorized action, Napoleon ordered him to retake Aderklaa with the assistance of Masséna. The village changed hands twice in the hard fighting that followed. Then for the second time in as many days Napoleon's allied troops broke and fled to the rear. Apparently while attempting to rally his fleeing Saxons the unfortunate Bernadotte met the Emperor while riding hard with his back to the enemy. Angrily, Napoleon relieved him of his command and ordered him off the field of battle.[67] The future King of Sweden thus concluded [68] a military career in the service of France which he had begun as a private in the army of Louis XVI. Within four years he was back on the battlefield—this time at the head of a Swedish army fighting to destroy the military power of his native France, which had been the instrument of his elevation to royalty.

The gap created by this unfortunate affair was filled by Masséna who, after hard fighting, regained and held Aderklaa. This crisis had hardly been met when the Emperor received startling news from his exposed left flank. Klenau and Kollowrat were advancing steadily, if slowly, and the situation was reaching the critical point. Napoleon now displayed those qualities which distinguished him from his contemporaries. Calmly he ordered Masséna to disengage his infantry from the Aderklaa sector and to march south—across the front of the advancing enemy—toward Essling to form a new left flank from the Danube north. This movement was covered by extending Eugène to his left, massing 112 guns against Lichtenstein, and throwing his cavalry reserve (Bessières and the Guard) against Kollowrat. In this manner Masséna was able to take up a position running north and south through Essling and to check Klenau's advance. The Austrian VI Corps had already come under the deadly fire of Reynier's massed artillery on the northern side of Lobau as it approached Aspern. Klenau retired to Aspern and this sector of the line was stabilized temporarily as Masséna prepared to attack.

While Masséna was marching across the enemy's front, Davout, at the opposite end of the inverted "S" line, was developing a full-scale assault on Rosenberg's position. Pressed hard by Napoleon, he launched his III Corps against Markgrafneusiedl, the key to the Austrian left flank, at about 9:30 A.M. The Austrian infantry gave a good account of itself, and Davout's men paid dearly for every foot of ground they gained throughout the morning. The Marshal himself had his horse shot out from under him, while General Gudin, who was at his side, was seriously wounded.[69] Still the French line continued to move forward with Gudin's determined men meeting their stiffest resistance west of Markgrafneusiedl and Friant scaling the heights to the east of the town. On the extreme right Morand's division, which had seen action during the early morning attack and counterattack, threatened to turn Rosenberg's flank. The Austrian commander countered with an energetic attack —during which Morand was wounded—but was unable to halt the forward motion of the French infantry. General Jacques Pierre Marie Puthod's division, temporarily attached to the III Corps and positioned between Friant and Morand, supported the attacks on his left and right. At about 11:00 A.M. the Archduke Charles personally led his cavalry reserve against Gudin and Friant in a desperate attempt to turn back the French tide which was now becoming a serious threat. The Austrian horsemen broke through the center of the first line and would have routed the entire corps had not the second line of reserves stood their ground. The enemy attack was halted, and Davout quickly regrouped his men and reestablished his line. Before noon all four divisions, supported on their far right by the cavalry divisions of Montbrun, Grouchy, and Arrighi, were again advancing. This time Charles lacked the reserves to stop them.[70]

The final crisis had been met and overcome. Napoleon had averted disaster on his left flank, stabilized the front in the center, and now Davout was turning the enemy's left. As the III Corps moved north beyond Markgrafneusiedl Rosenberg's hard-pressed men began to give ground more readily. Charles realized by 1:00 P.M. that his situation was critical. His left flank was being rolled back and would soon be completely routed; his brother John had not appeared on the battlefield; and his right and center could make no headway. When Napoleon, who was also aware of the enemy's plight, threw his reserves against Charles's center for the *coup de grâce,* the latter ordered a general withdrawal. There was no panic in the Austrian ranks, nor was Macdonald able to break through their center. The battle was won on the French right, and what started as an orderly phased withdrawal only gradually became a full scale retreat.

Wagram was a complete French victory. The enemy had been driven from the field in full retreat, but he had not been completely destroyed. Napoleon had used his last reserves during the final phase of the struggle and had no fresh troops to exploit his victory in a headlong pursuit. His army was exhausted. Though they remained close on the enemy's heels through the better part of the afternoon, by nightfall they could follow no longer. Charles was thus allowed to disengage under cover of darkness and retreat unmolested to the north. The following morning the French pursuit was again underway and by the tenth had overtaken the bulk of Charles's disheartened army at Znäim. Rather than give battle, Charles, himself slightly wounded at Wagram, asked for an armistice. Thus the campaign actually came to an end on July 12 with the signing of a convention.

The Battle of Wagram served the two main purposes for which the French emperor had crossed the Danube. It reestablished his military domination in central Europe—though Aspern-Essling could not be completely eradicated from men's minds—and it brought the Austrian emperor to the peace table with hat in hand. However, the battle as well as the campaign had been hard fought, and casualties ran high. French losses were between thirty-two thousand five hundred and thirty-four thousand men killed or wounded [71] in a single day. Austrian losses were somewhat heavier than those of the French—forty to forty-three thousand men [72]—but even Napoleon had gained a new respect for this army which he had hitherto looked upon as degenerate. In a meeting of the Imperial Council called in 1810 to discuss his proposed marriage with an Austrian princess, Lacuee de Cessac opposed the union saying that "Austria is no longer a great power." Napoleon cut him down curtly with a single sentence: "It is easy to see that you were not at Wagram!" [73]

Napoleon had indeed salvaged the Campaign of 1809 which on two occasions had been on the verge of disaster. During the opening weeks the army had almost been lost, but he rose to the challenge and turned near defeat into victory. Again at Aspern-Essling he saved his army from what should have been annihilation. Even at Wagram he had narrowly escaped defeat before winning the day. These factors, and other errors made between April and July, have caused many military historians to conclude that the military genius of 1805–6 had begun his decline.[74] Nor was his army of the superior quality of that of the Austerlitz, Jena, or Friedland campaigns. The incorporation of an increased number of foreign troops and of young inexperienced French recruits was apparent when the pressures of combat were greatest. Davout's command suffered least from these weaknesses, and, as might therefore be expected, turned in an excellent account of itself. It was indeed the III Corps that played the decisive role during the Eckmühl phase of the campaign, and pressed home the decisive attack which destroyed the Austrian left flank at Wagram.

When darkness had brought an end to the fighting on July 6, and Napoleon realized that his army was in no condition to undertake a pursuit, Davout bivouacked at Deutsch-Wagram. As the French army moved north the following morning, the III Corps continued to make up its extreme right flank. When the main force overtook Charles at Znäim on the tenth, Davout was occupying Nikolsburg and forcing a passage of the Thaya. With Grouchy's cavalry leading the way, the III Corps was in hot pursuit of Rosenberg's badly mauled IX Corps which was fleeing toward Brünn. Not until July 13 did Davout receive news of the armistice and orders to occupy Brünn. General C. P. Pajol was already in possession of the city, which was to form the advance post of the French army until the Treaty of Schönbrunn was signed on October 14.

10

The Good Years

THE AUSTRIAN CAMPAIGN of 1809 actually came to a close with the signing of the armistice on July 12, even though the peace treaty was not concluded until October. During this three month interval the Austrian government struggled desperately to reorganize its shattered military forces in the unrealistic hope that they would be able to continue the war. But when it became unmistakably clear that no help could be expected from England or Prussia, and that the Austrian army could not survive another major engagement, the Treaty of Schönbrunn was concluded.

The III Corps passed these three months in the vicinity of Brünn, where Davout undertook the reorganization of his command. There was always the possibility of a renewal of hostilities—even though the dismissal of the Archduke Charles by his brother shortly after the armistice made such a move on the part of the Austrians quite unlikely from a leadership point of view. Nevertheless, Davout made all necessary preparations to continue the campaign. Replacements were trained, equipment replaced, and the citadel of Brünn strengthened and stocked with stores so as to serve as a base for future operations.[1] The Marshal's perpetual concern with the health of his men caused him to remove Morand's division from the immediate vicinity of the Thaya River, as he attributed the sharp increase of sickness to the location of its camp.[2] In mid-September the Emperor made a five-day tour of inspection of the army in Moravia, during which he visited Davout at Brünn and reviewed several divisions of the III

Corps.[3] Davout also razed the fortifications of Goeding in accordance with the Emperor's instructions. The destruction of these extensive works, which included sixteen to eighteen "redoubts," required the labor of two thousand peasants and three regiments of Morand's division. The Marshal himself went to Goeding to witness this undertaking during the second week of August.[4]

On the Emperor Napoleon's fortieth birthday (August 15) he displayed his gratitude to the men who had served him well over the years. Included in this number was Marshal Davout, who was given the title Prince of Eckmühl[5] in recognition of the major role he played in the victorious combat of April 19–22. Accompanying the title was the chateau of Brühl with its parks, lands, and domains.[6] This display of gratitude marks the high point in the relationship between Napoleon and his loyal Marshal. In the declining years of the Empire, Davout remained faithful to the Emperor, even during the darkest days of 1813 and 1814; but Napoleon began to find fault with him—as with virtually all of his marshals—and their relationship was strained during the disaster of 1812.

In mid-October the Treaty of Schönbrunn[7] brought peace once again to central Europe. Napoleon felt that the terms of the treaty were not unreasonable considering the fact that the Austrians had taken advantage of his commitments in Spain to wage a war which he had not wanted, but Austria viewed the loss of the Duchy of Salzburg and Engadine Valley to Bavaria, her Polish province of Galicia to the Duchy of Warsaw and Russia, and her Illyrian provinces to France as a humiliating catastrophe. The reduction of her standing army to 150,000 men was designed to prevent her from repeating the 1809 attack, while her recognition of Napoleonic changes in Italy, Spain, and Portugal served to deepen Austrian resentment. The ink on the document was hardly dry when Napoleon took his leave of the Austrian capital to return to Paris. Before his departure, he appointed Davout responsible for the orderly evacuation of Austrian territory in accordance with the treaty and named his III Corps as the rear guard.[8]

The French withdrawal took place in three stages according to imperial orders.[9] Those army corps which were closest to France began to pull back first. During the first phase of the withdrawal (October 15–November 15) all French troops were withdrawn west of St. Poelten. The Austrian capital was evacuated between November 15–19. In the second phase the III Corps fell back behind Linz, while the final phase (December 15–January 4, 1810) resulted in the complete evacuation of all Austrian territory. The operation was carried out in such a manner as to prevent any possible foul play on the part of the Austrians. Davout was ready at all times for a renewal of hostilities should Austria decide to take advantage of the withdrawal to launch a surprise attack. But the Austrian army followed the III Corps at a respectable twenty-four hours' march, and the only problem which beset the Marshal was that of supplying his hungry troops in a hostile country that had already been ravaged by eight months of war and occupation.[10]

With the successful completion of the evacuation,[11] Napoleon reorganized his forces in Germany and sent them into winter quarters.[12] As a prelude to this regrouping, Marshal Berthier was transferred to the Army of Spain (November 1809).[13] This left Davout in command of the Army of Germany. He established his headquarters at Ratisbon to facilitate the observation of the new Austrian frontier. As winter drew on into 1810, the problem of feeding the army grew more critical in some quarters.

The detached Austrian province of Salzburg had been exhausted during the campaign of 1809. By January it was incapable of sustaining the troops stationed there, and Davout had to ask for supplies.[14] Furthermore, he complained about the poor conditions of the Portuguese troops which had been attached to his command in mid-January. "They are in the worse state," he wrote to the minister of war, "without shoes or clothing." [15] At the same time the Marshal placed these troops under the command of General Friant with the hope that with good care and training their morale would be raised.

Early in 1810 Davout had his first official clashes with the Emperor's brother Jérôme, the recently appointed King of Westphalia. The troops under the Marshal's command which were stationed in the Kingdom of Westphalia were not being properly cared for by the local officials whose responsibility they were. "I entreat Your Excellency," he wrote to the minister of war on January 29, "to make it known to me if it is the intention of the Emperor that the troops which are stationed in Westphalia should be treated differently from those which occupy the other parts of Germany. I wish to point out to Your Excellency that in a foreign land, and in particular Magdebourg, if a soldier does not receive his war ration, he will be unable to maintain his health on his army pay which is consumed by his other needs. If this sort of treatment will provide some economic benefits for the government of Westphalia, it will, on the other hand, cause misery to the French soldiers." [16] This mistreatment of the troops under his command, coupled with a general dislike for the playboy king, whose only claim to the throne of Westphalia was his relationship to the Emperor, generated a dislike which reached its climax in the opening month of the Russian campaign (1812). Davout had absolutely no respect for King Jérôme, who, unfortunately, had little ability either as an administrator or as a general, although Napoleon vainly attempted to cast him in both roles.

With central Europe restored to Napoleonic submission, the Army of Germany was placed on a "half peace footing" (January 30, 1810).[17] Davout settled his affair, placed General Compans, his chief of staff, in command of his headquarters, and departed for Paris. The year 1810 was to be one of peace for the Marshal, and for the first time in seven years he was able to spend nearly ten months in the vicinity of the capital, much of it with his wife and children. His official position as Colonel General of the Guard required that he spend weeks at a time with the Emperor at Fontainebleau, Paris, or St. Cloud. Occasionally his wife accompanied him but more frequently she remained at Savigny. When his official duties did not claim his time, the Marshal would join his family on their spacious estate south of Paris.

The first and, without a doubt, the principal event of the year 1810 was the marriage of the Emperor and the Austrian Princess Marie Louise. It was not that Napoleon no longer cared for Josephine but there was no romance left in their marriage, and the necessity of a Bonaparte heir to the throne of France was of the utmost importance. Josephine had had two children by her first marriage to the late General de Beauharnais. When no child was born of her second marriage with Napoleon, it was assumed by all—including the unhappy husband—that it was the Emperor who was sterile. However, the birth of an illegitimate son in December of 1807, who came to be known as the Comte de Léon, changed all of this. The event proved beyond any doubt that it was Josephine, now forty-six years of age, who could not bear children. This fact was again confirmed in the winter of 1809–10 when it became known that the Emperor's Polish mistress, Madame Walewska, would give birth to a child in the spring (May 4). Napoleon, therefore, decided to divorce his wife, for "reasons of State," and to take a younger woman who could provide France with an heir to the imperial throne.

The Emperor's first choice had been Ann, sister of the Emperor Alexander I of Russia. But neither she nor her mother, nor, it appears, her brother favored the union.[18] Therefore, Napoleon turned quickly to Austria and received, without hesitation, the hand of the eldest daughter of the Emperor Francis I. The divorce had taken place quietly and with a minimum of publicity. The marriage took place amid great celebration and joy. Napoleon did not travel to Vienna, where the ceremony took place by proxy on March 11, 1810. However, when Marie Louise arrived in France a civil marriage was performed (April 1), followed by a religious ceremony.

The Prince of Eckmühl, Colonel General of the Imperial Guard, played an active role in the reception of the new Empress and in the round of festivities which followed. Despite the affection which both he and his wife had for Josephine, who had been instrumental in bringing the Davouts together in 1801, the divorce and remarriage was beyond any but the most private criticism, and it was absolutely essential that this *fait accompli* be completely accepted by all who hoped to continue in the service of the Emperor. Thus when the Princess of Eckmühl was invited—or perhaps more correctly "ordered"—to court to present herself to the Empress upon her arrival, she complied.[19] Aimée Davout had never developed an attachment to Napoleon, and the replacement of Josephine by the young and flighty Austrian girl, grandniece of Marie Antoinette, did nothing to draw the quiet, refined Madame Davout out of her desired seclusion.

On the other hand, both of the Davouts were very well aware of their position. They had received virtually all of their worldly possessions directly from the Emperor. Titles, estates, annual income, and social position, all of this Napoleon had bestowed upon them. Not that Davout was any less deserving than others who had benefited from the Empire. Few had rendered greater services to France and the Emperor during the first decade of the nineteenth century. Nor had any been more loyal to Napoleon or expressed this loyalty in more willing service than Louis Davout. He had given himself almost entirely to the will of the Emperor, for he equated his will with that of the nation. Thus, despite their personal sympathy for the deposed Josephine, the Marshal and his wife completely accepted the young Austrian princess as the new Empress and accorded her all of the dignity, respect, and honor which her title demanded.

Marie Louise left Vienna on March 13 and after a two-week journey, which included elegant receptions at the courts of the southern German states, she arrived at Campiègne. Amid much pompous ceremony Madame Davout, with the wives of the generals of the guard, was presented on the twenty-ninth.[20] Davout was himself present when the new Empress arrived and played a major role in the pageantry which heralded her arrival. Though Marie Louise did not have the charm of a Josephine, she did please the Emperor; and the members of the court made every effort to gain her favor. The Davouts' relationship with the Empress was satisfactory. The Marshal's very nature virtually rendered impossible anything that might even border on a familiar relationship, and Aimée Davout, while ever mindful of social position, continued to shun the court. During 1811 her husband was once again suggesting that she spend more time in Paris and that she should attend court and social affairs.

The year 1810 was marked with tragedy and sorrow for the Davouts. In June their son, Napoleon, died shortly before his first birthday. Aimée Davout, overcome once again with grief, was virtually inconsolable. Her health, which was continuously a concern to her husband, worsened, and as the summer wore on she began to feel the effects of pregnancy. The death of this child, the third of five children, was particularly hard on the Marshal as it was their only son. Just as Napoleon desired a male heir to perpetuate the dynasty, so also Davout sought a son who would inherit his titles and estates. It was not surprising that he found it difficult to conceal his desire that the child his wife was carrying would be a boy.

The death of the Marshal's mother in the first week of August further grieved the Davouts. Louis reached her bedside at Ravières several days before she died; but Aimée, who was forced to travel more cautiously because of her pregnancy, arrived too late to see her mother-in-law alive.[21] The relationship between the two women had been an amiable one, and the Maréchale was grieved by the loss. Perhaps the premature death of the Marshal's father had caused him to turn more to his mother than he might otherwise have, for he was deeply attached to her and keenly felt her death. In a letter to his younger brother Alexandre, who was unable to reach Ravières in time, Davout displayed a tenderness of which few of his friends and certainly none of his enemies would have thought him capable.[22]

The sorrow which had accompanied the death of their second son was all but eradicated with the birth of another male child on January 6, 1811. Louis would be their only son to reach manhood. (He died in 1851.) The news of this joyous event reached Davout in Hamburg at two o'clock on the morning of the seventh. Unable to sleep the rest of the night, he poured out his joy in a letter to his equally pleased wife.[23] Then putting his affairs in order he returned to Paris as quickly as possible to spend four weeks with his family. While the new baby unquestionably brought much happiness into the lives of Aimée and Louis Davout, he did nothing to improve the health of his mother. "You cause me much unhappiness by neglecting your health," Davout later wrote from Hamburg.[24] And again: "You continue to be quite unreasonable, my Aimée, your health will never improve."[25] He further offered advice with respect to the health of the children. "Do you not think, my Aimée, that the unpleasant [bad] heating pipes contribute to the colds of our children? ... Perhaps they are also caused by too much heat in their room. Remember when we were children, we had no heat, and we got along very well."[26] Then with particular reference to their son the annoyed father added: "It is quite necessary to take care so as not to weaken our little Louis' stamina; he must have that of his father's. He must also form good habits so as to make him strong, and it will not be in heated rooms that he will acquire the necessary health to serve well the King of Rome."[27]

The Davouts had other problems which were by no means unique—money! Being a Prince did not solve the Marshal's financial difficulties which tended to keep pace with his increased income. Scrupulously honest, Davout did not profit from the influential positions he held during the Empire. Despite the false accusation of Désirée Clary Bernadotte,[28] the Davouts were not among the wealthiest families of French society. Quoting the Swedish princess, Davout's wife wrote him in mid-November 1811: "You have acquired a greater fortune than any other person composing the Imperial family."[29] The truth of the matter was that during 1810–12 Davout found it difficult to maintain the standard of living which Napoleon required of one in his position. The greater part of his wealth was in the form of land in Poland and the Germanies.

These rendered a generous annual income; but still the Marshal was unable to meet all of his obligations. The upkeep of Savigny and their townhouse in Paris, the partial support of members of his family, and the maintenance of his quarters with the army in time of peace more than equaled his income. In 1812 it was necessary for him to ask Napoleon for a year's postponement of "the 120,000 francs which I was to pay this year [1812] in taxes." [30] Neither the Marshal nor his wife could be called extravagant. Madame Davout had, to be sure, quickly acquired the habits and tastes of the French aristocracy, but her husband tended to cling to the simplicity of the Revolution. Neither cared much for grand parties or balls, but rather looked upon such affairs as a necessity which accompanied their social position. On the other hand, both were ambitious. He strove for military recognition; being a *Duke* or a *Prince* meant less to him than being the Duke of *Auerstädt* and the Prince of *Eckmühl*. She was extremely conscious of social position. Coming from good pre-Revolutionary bourgeois stock the Princess of Eckmühl was always a *Princess*. Thus with Davout living as a Marshal and dignitary of the Empire, and his wife living as a Princess, their financial problems more than kept pace with their increasing wealth.

This increase in wealth, military fame, and social standing did nothing to improve Marshal Davout's disposition or win for him friends. The fact is that he did not seek popularity—neither among the rank and file of the men under his command nor from the officer corps. That which did concern him was that he had the respect of officers and men, and even this could be secondary if it came in conflict with what he considered *Devoir*. His devotion to "duty" was almost fanatical. General de Laville is reported to have best captured Davout's worship of duty. "He is a good husband and father," Thiébault quotes de Laville as saying, "and in his own home hardly has any will of his own; yet he would without hesitation sacrifice his wife and children in the performance of what he thought his duty." [31] This devotion to duty, if overstated by de Laville, nevertheless deeply affected every decision Davout made and explains his passion for justice.

To say that Davout was a "just man" requires a qualifying explanation, for justice was always seen in the light of duty. In 1813, for example, he was displeased when a military court found Count Bentinck innocent of charges of treason. "You were to have made a much-needed example of Count Bentinck," he scolded General Thiébault, who had been a member of the court, "and you preferred to make the case into a triumph for the Emperor's enemies!" [32] Whether or not the Count was innocent seems to be overshadowed by the necessity of an example to bolster the sagging Empire. On the other hand, his sense of justice could take the form of public apology for a wrong committed against an individual.

The Marshal's paternal treatment of his men caused a mixed feeling among them with respect to their commander. In time of war their strict discipline and good training made them the pride of the army and brought down upon them the coveted praise of the Emperor. Furthermore, the excellent supply system and superb condition of their equipment, which they also owed to their commander, made them the envy of the rest of the army. But in time of peace, when other commanders relaxed restrictions and closed their eyes to infractions of regulations, the Iron Marshal continued to ride hard on his command. At all times he displayed a deep and genuine interest for the well-being of his men. Whether it was their health, food, clothing, equipment, or quarters, he made it his concern and demanded that it be the concern of every officer under him. The higher the rank of the officer the less tolerant he was of error or negligence. He demanded that the same driving sense of duty which motivated his own actions should be foremost in the minds of the officers under him. When his own cousin, Colonel Coutard, surrendered the city of Ratisbon (1809) at a time when the Marshal believed his duty called for him to hold on despite all hardships and odds, he immediately demanded his resignation. Then in October of 1811, by which time Davout was more fully apprised of the impossibility of continuing the resistance at Ratisbon, he invited Coutard and his wife (a d'Avout), with seven other prominent officers and their ladies, to a dinner in an effort to display his acceptance of the Colonel's actions in 1809, and to right the wrong he had committed. Later, in 1815, when Davout was minister of war, he offered the former Colonel a generalship and command. Wisely his cousin refused and was duly rewarded in 1816 with the title of Count and served in the army of Louis XVIII with the rank of General.[33]

Davout's relationship with the trilogy of division commanders who were the most direct instruments of his glory was somewhat mixed. Though Friant was married to his wife's sister, and Morand was the most capable commander, it was Gudin for whom the Marshal held the greatest affection. A series of events in August 1809 illustrated not only his deep attachment to Gudin, but also his ability to mistreat a high-ranking officer and to overcome his pride to right the injustice. General Gudin's wounds, received on the field of battle at Wagram, forced him temporarily to relinquish his command of the 3rd Division of the III Corps. Napoleon therefore sent General Puthod, an able commander, to take his place. The news of Gudin's replacement reached the Marshal at Brünn on Bastille Day while he was attending mass. As he left the church to return to his quarters he came upon Puthod, who had just arrived. The Marshal stamped up to the elegantly dressed General, who was wearing all of his decorations in honor of the day, and without so much as a cordial greeting began to insult him. "So you are the one, monsieur," he began, "who pretends to replace General Gudin and do you really think you are capable! Before I would remove this heroic general from command of the brave division which he has led at least twenty times to victory, I will break my marshal's baton." [34] During the course of the day Davout came to realize that Puthod had not merited the chastisement he had given him; that, in fact, the General had not even known at the time that he was to replace Gudin. Without hesitation the Marshal sent one of his aides-de-camp to Puthod to implore him to attend the reception which he was giving that night for the officers of his command. There, before the entire gathering, he took the unjustly offended General's hand and asked to be forgiven for an outburst stimulated by his affection for Gudin. Puthod was so impressed by this public act of repentance that he remained attached to Davout from that time forward.[35]

The death of Gudin during the Russian campaign of 1812 was a grievous loss to Davout, and one from which he did not so readily recover. While convalescing in Moscow from wounds he had himself received during the battle of Borodino (September 8), he wrote to his wife: "Assure her [Madame Gudin] that I will be true to the promises which I made to the General during his last moments, and that I will have the same interest for their children as for our own. Rarely in my life have I experienced such painful sentiments as these caused me by the death of Gudin . . . I will remain faithful to the friendship and esteem which I had for him." [36]

The relationship between brothers-in-law was also a most cordial one. Friant was an excellent and seasoned commander. He was already at the head of a division by the end of the Egyptian campaign, at a time when Davout was but a general of brigade. On occasion the Marshal vigorously defended him against the criticism of his sister-in-law, Madame Davout, and took every occasion to praise him and recommend him to the generosity of the Emperor.[37] The two men never seriously quarreled and remained on the best of terms until the Marshal's death.

Morand, unlike his two comrades, grew to dislike his commander. The early years of their relationship were amiable enough; however, following the Austrian campaign of 1809, friction began to develop. To be sure, the General was somewhat envious of the Marshal, as were many ambitious subordinates. But there was more to it than this. Davout was not an easy man to serve under and the years of inactivity in Germany between 1809 and 1812 brought to the foreground differences and led to quarrels which would have been overshadowed or overlooked in time of war. Indeed, the two men functioned in harmony during the rigorous Russian campaign; and the Marshal, in a letter to his wife from Doubrowna (August 11, 1812) wrote: "General Gudin has just rejoined me . . . Generals Friant and Morand are also returning. I feel as though my moral courage has been tripled." [38]

When Morand joined the III Corps in February 1806, Davout expressed a genuine sentiment when he wrote: "You cannot doubt, my dear General, the pleasure which I felt when I received the news that you would command one of the divisions of the III corps; the esteem and friendship which I have for you is your proof." [39] This same warm sentiment was again expressed in January 1808, when the General was married: "The sincere friendship which I hold for you is your guarantee that I will never be a stranger." [40] But by 1810 their relationship had worn so thin that Morand requested a transfer out from under the order of the Prince of Eckmühl.

The climax of the antagonism was triggered by a brutal chastisement of Morand by the Marshal. Davout had given strict orders that all correspondence from his command should be directed to Paris through him, and that no commander would write directly to the minister of war or the major general of the army. This he did primarily so that he would be fully informed of events during his prolonged absence in Paris during most of 1810. Thus when Morand, either intentionally or through neglect—it made little difference which to Davout—wrote directly to the minister of war, his commander reacted quickly and very sharply. On November 18, 1810, the outraged General sought the intercession of the minister of war (General Clarke, Duke of Feltre): "I had the honor of writing on the 16th to Your Excellency the Minister of War to request your protection and justice and to obtain for me from His Majesty the Emperor my retirement, my resignation, or to employ me elsewhere rather than under the command of the Prince of Eckmühl . . . I beseech Your Excellency to remove me from the painful situation in which I find myself. I swear to you that it is impossible for me to serve in the future under the orders of the Prince of Eckmühl . . . I must be separated from him; *I must obtain another command or retire and abandon my career* [italics mine]. . . . After the disgrace of the Emperor, the loss of my wife and children, the worse thing that could happen to me would be to die under the orders of the Prince of Eckmühl."[41]

But despite Morand's pleas for reassignment Napoleon refused to break up the combination which had so successfully served him on the battlefields of central Europe since the establishment of his Empire. Nor did Morand give up his military career. The two men were never again on good terms, but with the approach of the Russian conflict and the actual campaign itself, they were able to work together in harmony for the good of the army and the glory of the Empire.

Davout's relationship with his fellow marshals was also of a mixed nature. While it is true that none of them ever really forgave him for the tremendous prestige and glory he acquired as the result of the Battle of Auerstädt, he counted only Bernadotte (after 1806), Berthier (after 1809), and Murat (after 1812) as his enemies. Oudinot, Ney, and St.-Cyr were perhaps on best terms with him during and after the Empire, though even with these men there were periods of discord. In general, his peers considered him poor company for social affairs and too strict a disciplinarian but a capable field commander.

By 1813 General Vandamme had become the most undisciplined divisional commander in the entire French army. An extremely capable officer, he had become frustrated and embittered because the

Emperor had not seen fit to grant him a marshal's baton. He had been the despair of every commander under whom he served. Nevertheless, Napoleon was in need of every good officer available. After the disastrous campaign of 1812 he sent Vandamme to join Davout's command at Hamburg. Under the mailed fist of the Iron Marshal the maverick General was harnessed and his talents put to good use.[42] Vandamme had no love for his harsh commander, but he did respect his military judgment, and though slow at times, he carried out his orders.

Another of Davout's divisional commanders in 1813, General Thiébault, was undoubtedly his most outspoken critic. The *Mémoires du général baron Thiébault* are frequently quoted in order to paint a dark picture of the Prince of Eckmühl. "Thus my request to leave the dullest and least estimable commanders in the Army of Spain," he wrote of his transfer to Davout's Corps, "resulted only in bringing me under the orders of the *most detestable commander in the Grand Army* [italics mine]."[43] And again he concluded that "in order to be worthy of serving under him [Davout], one ought to have killed one's father and mother."[44] Thiébault cannot be accused of hypocrisy. He never pretended to be a friend of Davout's, neither when under the Marshal's orders nor in his later writings. The General was, like Vandamme, disillusioned that he had not received a marshal's baton and considered himself more intelligent and more capable than Davout. He tended to believe, as did many other Napoleonic generals, that fate had simply not placed him at the head of an army facing the King of Prussia.

Davout's departure from France was delayed at the beginning of 1812 by the birth of his second son, Jules d'Auerstädt d'Eckmühl (died 1813) on January 11. When he reached his headquarters at Hamburg Davout began in earnest to forge the "Army of Observation of the Elbe" into the I Corps of the Grand Army of 1812. New recruits were trained and assimilated into existing units; new regiments were formed; and non-French troops, Spanish and German for the most part, were organized into battalions and regiments.[45] The continental blockade was enforced as usual and a sharp eye was kept on the activities of Prussia. Davout reported the importation of arms through Prussia's Baltic ports[46] and complained that this *ally* continually encouraged and aided desertion from his command.[47]

Prussia's generally unfriendly attitude, which stemmed from an increasingly obvious desire to throw off the heavy hand of Napoleonic domination and to regain control of her own destiny, led the French emperor to force that unhappy nation into a military alliance requiring her to provide troops for the projected invasion of Russia. If Frederick William refused cooperation Napoleon was bent on the complete occupation of his state. To this end he wrote to Davout on November 14, 1811, ordering him to make the necessary preparations for marching on Berlin and for occupying Prussia's major seaports and cities.[48] The presence of well over one hundred thousand men, and the Prussian king's presumption that Napoleon would use them if he should attempt to follow an independent course, resulted in an alliance between the two powers and improved relations, at least on the surface, for the next thirteen months. At the same time that Prussia was displaying moderate anti-French feelings resistance in other parts of Germany were taking place.

During the early years of the French Revolution there had been widespread sympathy in the German states for the ideals of the Revolution and the aspirations of the French bourgeoisie and the peasant class. But as the struggle for political and social rights gave way to the imperial ambitions of the Emperor Napoleon, the German people came to look upon the French as their oppressive and hated masters. The arrival of Marshal Davout at Hamburg had the immediate effect of overcoming most obstacles to French rule. His reputation had preceded him and, according to General Bourrienne, his very name spread terror throughout northern Germany.[49] As military commander he became increasingly aware of this anti-French feeling. Desertion from the German regiments under his command had increased almost geometrically through 1810–11. In March 1811 he found it necessary to encircle one German regiment at night with French patrols to prevent desertion,[50] and in November of the same year an entire German regiment, the 129th Line, raised the standard of rebellion. The unsympathetic Marshal took immediate steps to restore discipline, but not before the mutiny had spread to the 127th and 128th Lines.[51] Another indication of anti-French feelings may be seen in an incident which occurred at a Westphalian border post in February 1811. A French convoy en route to Cologne was stopped and the Westphalian officer refused to allow it to pass until customs were paid. In the scuffle that followed one French trooper and a number of horses were wounded. Again Davout acted swiftly. He dispatched General Bruyère to Minden, where the episode had taken place, with orders to take whatever steps were necessary to place the officer responsible under arrest and to prevent the reoccurrence of such a "revolt." [52]

Franco-Swedish relations had also deteriorated throughout 1810–12. It was hoped by many, Napoleon included, that the election of a French marshal, Jean Baptiste Bernadotte, in 1810 as the Prince Royal and heir to the Swedish throne would improve relations between the two nations. Sweden had recently been victimized by Russia in a war in which she lost Finland, and there was no tradition of friendship with England. But Bernadotte, to whom the aging and ailing Charles XIII gave control of the government in 1811, followed a hard and hostile line in his dealings with the French government. In November 1811 he publicly insulted the French ambassador, Alquier, and violently attacked France and the Emperor.[53] Under the pretext, which was well founded, that Swedish Pomerania was not adhering to the continental blockade and that it was serving as a port of entry for British goods into northern Europe, Napoleon ordered Davout to occupy the Swedish territory.[54] On January 26, 1812, General Friant's 2nd Division entered Sweden's last outpost on the south shore of the Baltic Sea with orders to put down any resistance.[55] All communications were severed with Stockholm, all British goods were confiscated, and the twelve hundred Swedish troops in the territory were disarmed.[56] This action was undoubtedly a mistake in foreign policy from a French point of view. On the brink of a major war with Russia, Napoleon needed every ally he could attract. And while it may be argued that by January 1812 there was no possibility of Swedish support in the forthcoming campaign, there still remained the hope of her complete neutrality. Besides, if Russia could be brought into line with French foreign policy, Sweden would have no choice but to follow her example. As it was, the Swedes did not take part in the war, but neither did they remain strictly neutral. The ex-French sergeant *Belle-Jambe* gave comfort and advice to Sweden's traditional enemy and, in 1813, openly declared war on France.

11

The March to Moscow

THE WAR with England was entering its nineteenth year in 1812, with but a brief truce following the Treaty of Amiens, and there seemed little possibility of a settlement in the near future. All serious thoughts of a direct attack upon the island kingdom had vanished beneath the waves off Cape Trafalgar. Still, Napoleon continued to consider England his principal enemy, and the Continental System his principal weapon. The blockade of the Continent had been in effect more than five years, at least on paper, yet it had no apparent effect on the "nation of shopkeepers." Goods continued to flow into the Continent. Despite the annexation of Holland and the mouth of the Elbe, despite the captivity of Pope Pius VII for his refusal to cooperate, despite the agreements made at Tilsit (1807) and Erfurt (1808), British exports remained at a consistently high level. The tightening of the blockade in 1811 had resulted in a decline in British exports to European nations, but this loss was almost compensated for by increased trade with North and South America. Furthermore, what angered the French emperor most of all was that imports of British goods continued at a high level in those continental countries where his influence was weakest—notably Portugal and Russia.[1]

The Tsar Alexander had agreed to the blockade at Tilsit and had reaffirmed this agreement at Erfurt. However it was clearly not in the best interest of Russia to cut economic ties with England. By 1812 British imports were approaching their pre-Tilsit level and the Tsar showed no indications of enforcing the unpopular and unprofitable ordinances. Notwithstanding the apparent failure of the Berlin and Milan Decrees, Napoleon continued to hold to the theory that England could be forced to come to terms if he could destroy her trade. Thus he reasoned aloud that it was only necessary to subdue and control Spain and Portugal and force Alexander to live up to his agreement in order to defeat England. But the clash between France and Russia is not quite so easily explained. War clouds had begun to gather over eastern Europe as early as 1810. Among the causes of discord may be cited the refusal of the hand of the Tsar's sister Ann in marriage to Napoleon, the annexation to France of the Grand Duchy of Oldenburg over the protests of Alexander on behalf of his brother-in-law, and of primary importance the conflict of interest over Poland.

As both nations prepared for war Napoleon launched a diplomatic campaign aimed at isolating Russia and dragging all of Europe into a coalition against the Tsar. Reluctantly, first Austria and then Prussia signed offensive-defensive alliances with their former enemy against their former ally. Frederick William III would have resisted except for the presence of one hundred thousand men in central Germany under the command of Davout. The lesser states of Europe joined the great "crusade" against Russia without a murmur as French satellites. Of all the nations which took part in the campaign of 1812, only the Poles were enthusiastic. Napoleon called it the "Second War of Polish Liberation," and the inhabitants of the Duchy of Warsaw looked not only to the long-awaited establishment of an independent Polish state at the victorious conclusion of the war, but also the extension of their eastern border to include the Polish population of western Russia.

Napoleon's overall strategy for the Russian campaign called for the use of Turkey and Sweden to form his extreme flanks. However he was unable to exercise the control or influence necessary at such distances from Paris. Sweden, protected from the French army by English domination of the Baltic Sea, and led by her former French marshal, Bernadotte, threw in her lot with her former enemy Russia in the expectation of acquiring Norway from pro-French Denmark. On the Bosporus there was little trust or confidence in the French ruler. Turkey was still at war with Russia in the spring of 1812, and she would have seemed at first glance to have been a natural French ally. But the war had not been going well for the Turks, and the nation was exhausted. Though French armies were moving east, Napoleon was still talking peace. As late as May 1812 he sent Narbonne to Vilna to talk peace with Alexander. Narbonne's real mission was to prevent the Russians from launching an offensive before the French army was in position on the Niemen; however, the Russian negotiators used his mission to convince the Turks that Napoleon did not intend war and that they would have to continue the struggle alone. The Treaty of Bucharest, which ended the Russo-Turkish war, removed the danger on Russia's extreme left flank.

The French army was scattered from Cadiz to Danzig. More than two hundred thousand of France's best troops, the veterans of Austerlitz and Jena, were being wasted in a futile attempt to subdue the Iberian Peninsula. The greater part of the remaining French troops were spread out through Germany. Davout commanded the major portion of these troops which were designated the Army of Observation of the Elbe. With his headquarters at Hamburg he became the chief architect of the new *Grande Armée* which was beginning to take shape by the fall of 1811. It was hoped that the extensive preparations would intimidate the Russian tsar and convince him of the futility of waging war with France. If, on the other hand, Alexander was bent on resistance, the necessary military force would be ready to settle their "misunderstandings" on the battlefield.

In his position as commander of the Army of Observation of the Elbe, Davout once again put to use those organizational and administrative talents which he had displayed at Bruges (1803–5) and in Poland (1807–9). With more than one hundred thousand men directly under his command and central Europe as his main source of supplies, he set about this new task with typical energy. A field commander at heart, he never liked the "detestable desk work" which occupied him into the long hours of those winter nights.[2] The buying of horses for the cavalry and supply train,[3] the recruiting of men in Poland,[4] and the buildup of great quantities of food and equipment in centers in eastern Europe,[5] together required so much of his time that he wrote his wife on February 12 that he could not even ask the Emperor's permission to take leave so that he might attend the ball she was giving in Paris.[6]

The first major steps toward the reorganization of the French army were taken in January 1812. In this month Marshal Berthier

The Russian Campaign
N
Baltic Sea
Riga
Dwina River
Dünaburg
Drissa
Vitebsk
Kovno
Prenn
Vilna
Smorgonie
Ochmiana
Grodno
Niemen River
Mir
Zembik
Studenka
Borisov
Minsk
Svisloch
Slutsk
Bobruisk
Berezina River
PRIPET MARSHES
Orsha
Krasny
Mogilev
Fatowa
Novo Bykhow
Dnieper River
Smolensk
Dorogobuzh
Elnya
Dnieper River
Viazma
Gshatsk
Dubrovno
Borodino
Moskva River
Moscow
Mozhaisk
Louges e
Borowsk
Maloyaroslavets
Medyn
Kaluga
Oka River
0 25 50 100
Miles

was informed that he would take up his customary post as *Major général de la Grande Armée* to become effective February 1.[7] The army was regrouped into four corps with Davout in command of the I Corps. Consisting of five infantry divisions and one cavalry brigade, it was more than twice the size of the other three. The II Corps was commanded by Marshal Oudinot; Ney was given the III Corps; and part of the former Army of Italy became the IV Corps with the Viceroy, Prince Eugène, at its head.[8] With the first signs of spring these corps were marching eastward—Ney from northern France and the Low Countries, Eugène from Italy, Oudinot and Davout from Germany. All were converging on the Vistula where the Grand Army was to assemble.

On March 8 Davout arrived at Stettin where he received orders to be on the Vistula with his entire army corps by April 1.[9] Once established in northern Poland, with his headquarters at Thorn, his corps became the bulwark against a possible Russian offensive. Yet as Napoleon did not want this war to begin until he himself was ready, he wrote to Berthier on March 25: "The language of the Prince d'Eckmühl must be very *pacifique;* he must avoid all reconnaissance or military movement beyond the Vistula; none of his patrols may go as far as the Osterode." [10] Then in May the I Corps was ordered into East Prussia between Elbing and Königsberg. Davout established his headquarters at Elbing while the final organization of the army progressed, more or less, on schedule. The artillery and portable pontoon bridges began to catch up with the rest of the army early in June, and final preparations were made for the advance on the Niemen.

Meanwhile, Napoleon had remained in Paris until the last possible moment so as to continue the illusion that he still hoped for peace. Then on May 9 he set out for Dresden under the pretext "of going to inspect the Grand Army reunited on the Vistula." [11] On the same day the *Moniteur* published the first article in a study entitled *Recherches sur les lieux où périt Varus avec ses légions*.[12] The contemporary Varus was ready to lead his legions against the "barbarians." The eleven days he passed at Dresden were designed to impress the Russians with the solidarity of his coalition. But while the Austrian emperor was paying his respects to his son-in-law, Prince Metternich was sending friendly agents to Russia and England. Leaving Dresden, Napoleon continued his premature victory march to Thorn where he began inspecting the army. On June 7 the Emperor arrived at Marienburg where he met Davout.

This meeting proved somewhat of a landmark in the relationship between the Emperor and his loyal lieutenant, for it provided the occasion for the renewal and embitterment of the hostility between Davout and Berthier. Ill feeling had prevailed between these two Marshals since the opening of the Austrian campaign in 1809 when Davout's tactical brilliance on the field had saved the army from Berthier's strategic blunder.[13] During the years that followed, the alienation diminished as the two antagonists were not obliged to work together. At Hamburg, Davout reported directly to the Emperor or the minister of war; while Berthier spent the majority of the time in Paris as Major General of the Army of Spain. By the end of 1811 the marshals had been separated for more than two years and both men were making somewhat of an effort to maintain a cordial relationship. When, in February 1812, Madame Davout was obliged to give a ball, and her husband was unable to be present, he wrote her the following concerning Berthier: "I am sensitive about all matters which involve the Prince of Neuchâtel; ask him on my part to help you with your ball. . . . I am counting on his friendship to render you this service." [14] However the Russian campaign once again brought the two marshals into close contact. As Major General of the Grand Army, Berthier became the intermediate between Davout and the Emperor. He was still an excellent chief of staff, despite the fact that he had lost his enthusiasm for war and would have much preferred to remain at home rather than undergo the rigor of a campaign in Russia. The renewed strain on this relationship can be seen in Davout's letter of April 19 to his wife: "Since our separation, the Major General's correspondence has become very bitter." [15]

Davout now received virtually all of his instructions directly from the Major General. He came to feel more and more that these orders were in bad taste, and that Berthier was endangering the opening operations of the campaign as he had in 1809. Davout had in fact lost all confidence in the man whom Napoleon had chosen as his second-in-command. At Marienburg, "Davout expressed himself harshly, and even went so far as to accuse Berthier of incapacity or treachery." [16] The Emperor, in whose presence this quarrel took place, and who was well aware of Berthier's lack of enthusiasm, tended to side with Davout whose ardent support of the campaign was well known to all. But Davout's triumph over his old enemy was short-lived. Napoleon went on to Danzig the following morning where he was joined by his Major General. Here Davout's enemies were able to gain the Emperor's ear without the Marshal present to defend himself. They twisted his diligent preparations, his endless labor, and his enthusiasm, and used them against him. " 'The marshal,' said they, 'wishes to have it thought that he has foreseen, arranged, and executed everything. Is the emperor, then, to be no more than a spectator of this expedition? Must the glory of it devolve on Davoust [*sic*]?' " To which Napoleon exclaimed: " 'One would think it was he who commanded the army.' " [17] Nor did his enemies stop short at this point. Once they realized they had the Emperor's attention they launched a full scale attack on the absent Marshal. " 'Was it not Davoust [sic] who, after the victory of Jena, drew the emperor into Poland? Is it not he who is now anxious for this new Polish war?—He who already possesses such large property in that country, whose accurate and severe probity has won over the Poles, and who is suspected of aspiring to their throne?' " [18]

Thus it was that doubt was sown in the Emperor's mind; doubt which was to deprive him of the advice and counsel of one of his best tactical commanders. One cannot be sure that it was pride and selfishness, as is implied by Davout's apologists,[19] which drove the wedge between the Marshal and his Emperor. But there is no question of Napoleon's jealousy of his military glory. His reluctance to share with Davout their conquest of the Prussian army in the autumn of 1806, his refusal to grant Marshal Soult the title Duke of Austerlitz, gives evidence of Napoleon's covetousness of these great victories. The conquest of Russia was to be his greatest military triumph. Davout was but one corps commander, one of his best to be sure—but nevertheless, merely one of many cogs in *his* war machine. Napoleon himself was quick to admit that his domination of Europe, and France itself, was based on his military achievements and reputation. He was in need of good generals, but he could not tolerate a rival within his own camp.

In the days that followed his meeting with the Emperor at Marienbourg Davout occupied himself with last-minute preparations. His army corps was in excellent condition and well supplied. General Caulaincourt, who passed Davout's men on their way to the

Niemen, wrote of them: "The men of the First Corps [Davout's] were noticeable for their fine bearing and general smartness. Coming from excellent quarters, fresh from the hands of a commander who had drilled them long and well, they could rival the Guard. All this mass of youth was full of ardour and good health. In their knapsacks the men of this corps carried rations for a fortnight." [20]

The entire army was now poised along the Russian frontier from the Baltic Sea to the Austrian province of Galicia. It was not a *French* army in the same sense as were the armies General Bonaparte commanded in Italy and Egypt, or which Napoleon I led at Austerlitz and Jena. These armies had been either exclusively French or merely supported by foreign auxiliary troops. This army of 1812 on the other hand, was hardly more than half French. More than fifty percent of the infantry and one-third of the cavalry were Austrian, Prussian, German (non-Prussian), Spanish, Italian, Portuguese, Dutch, Polish, and Croatian.[21] Some of these allies were reluctant to take an energetic part in the campaign—notably the Austrian and Prussian corps. Others, such as the Dutch, Spanish and Portuguese, were at best indifferent. They fought with bravery on the advance to Moscow, but were among the first to throw away their arms and break ranks when the retreat began. The Italians, Bavarians, Saxons, and Poles were the most loyal of the foreign troops, and served with distinction. But as the campaign degenerated into a rout, they also broke ranks. Davout's I Corps consisted primarily of French troops, but he also had five and one-half regiments of foreigners—three and a half regiments of Germans, one of Spaniards, and one of Poles.[22]

The left flank of this European army was made up primarily of Prussians, Poles, and Germans. It was designated the X Corps, and commanded by Marshal Macdonald. Its left rested on the Baltic Sea, and its point of crossing on the Niemen was Tilsit. On the other extreme was the Austrian corps commanded by Prince Schwarzenberg. The main part of the army was directly under the control of the Emperor, and comprised the first three corps—Davout, Oudinot, and Ney—and Murat's cavalry. This center was closely supported by the Viceroy (Eugène) who had under him the corps of St.-Cyr (VI corps), Grouchy (a cavalry corps), as well as his own IV Corps. Napoleon would cross at Kovno while Eugène would pass the river near Prenn. The King of Westphalia (Jérôme Bonaparte) commanded the left flank of the actual striking force. It is true that

Prince Karl von Schwarzenberg was to his right, but the Austrians were assigned the mission of protecting Poland from an invasion by the southern Russian army of Tormassov which was forming below the Pripet Marshes. Jérôme had under him Poniatowski's V Corps (Polish), the VIII Corps (Westphalians) commanded by General Vandamme, and General Reynier's VII Corps (Saxons). This army was destined to enter Russia by way of Grodno. In all, the Grand Army stood at about four hundred and thirty thousand men.[23] It was the largest force yet assembled in modern history.

To oppose this formidable host Alexander was able to field only approximately two hundred and eighteen thousand troops.[24] This army was divided into three commands. The First Army of the West, which was the main Russian force, numbered some one hundred and twenty-seven thousand men and was commanded by General Prince Michael Barclay de Tolly. It covered an extended front from Tilsit south to Grodno. General Ludwig Wittgenstein formed its right while Platov's Cossacks made up its left. The Second Army of the West was considerably smaller. Commanded by General Prince Peter Bagration, it numbered no more than forty-eight thousand men. The left flank of this army rested on the Pripet Marshes, while its right met Platov on the upper Niemen. The third Russian army was being assembled south of the Pripet Marshes. This force numbering some forty-three thousand men was commanded by Tormassov. Together they comprised the actual fighting force of the Russian army. There were perhaps an additional thirty-five thousand men in garrison towns between Riga and Kiev, but these would only join the main armies as they fell back across the Dwina-Dnieper line.

Napoleon hoped—and even seemed to have expected—that the Russian army would give battle shortly after he had passed their frontier. In fact he was counting on a decisive engagement—another Austerlitz or Jena-Auerstädt—which would bring Alexander to the peace table without the necessity of a prolonged campaign. Interestingly enough the Tsar also planned to fight, not immediately, but on the Dwina at Drissa. Napoleonic strategy called for a rapid advance from Kavno to Vilna. If the Russians refused battle he would divide their forces by advancing on Minsk and Drissa. His right wing (Jérôme) would delay its crossing at Grodno so as to lull Bagration into a false sense of security. Then with Jérôme pressing hard from the west and the right of Napoleon's central army advancing south on the Russian's rear, Bagration would be pinned against the Pripet Marshes and destroyed. At the same time the Emperor himself would continue to seek a decisive battle with Barclay. Macdonald was assigned the task of pinning down Barclay's right by an advance on Riga which would also threaten St. Petersburg.

The Russians had little in the way of a strategic plan. Alexander had no intention of taking the offensive and crossing the Niemen himself. If attacked, the Russian army was to fall back. But from this point on there was no agreement between the Tsar and his generals. Alexander had come under the influence of a former Prussian staff officer, General E. von Phull. Phull convinced the Tsar of the merits of a fortified camp at Drissa which would protect both the road to Moscow and the road to St. Petersburg. Almost two years of labor had gone into the preparation of this camp, and Alexander intended Barclay to fall back under the safety of its guns.[25] But Barclay, supported by all of his lieutenants, saw in Drissa a trap which would result in the encirclement and eventual capitulation of the army.[26] The General himself did not seem to have any plan of operation other than to avoid the destruction of his army. He wished to fall back behind the Dwina and have Bagration join him. Then with the two Russian armies united, and Napoleon's forces scattered and his lines of communications extended, he would choose a suitable site and give battle.

Preparations thus proceeded on both sides of the Niemen through the month of June. Then on the night of June 23–24 the ill-fated invasion was launched. Davout's I Corps led the way across three hastily constructed bridges at Kovno. With Morand's division at its head, and supported by Murat's cavalry, the French advanced into Polish Lithuania. Only roaming Cossack patrols were sighted and these had no intentions of obstructing the enemy's advance. The march on Vilna was uninterrupted. The Russian army evacuated the Lithuanian capital well in advance of the French columns. On the night of June 24 Davout's lead division had entered Rumschiski. By evening of the twenty-eighth it was at the gates of Vilna. The following day the Marshal wrote to his wife: "We have taken Vilna without a fight, and have obliged the Russians to evacuate all of Poland; this beginning of the campaign has been a great victory." [27] On the twenty-ninth the Emperor arrived and at once dispatched the I Corps to the southeast toward Minsk.

This maneuver was designed to cut off Bagration, since it was believed he would try to retreat northeastwardly onto Barclay who was preparing to take up an unwanted position at Drissa. Napoleon had apparently underestimated Bagration's strength for he detached three of Davout's divisions (Morand, Friant, and Gudin) and sent them with Murat's cavalry in pursuit of Barclay.[28] As a result of this reorganization of the I Corps there remained under Davout's direct command only Compans's infantry division (Dessaix having also been detached) of the five he had led across the frontier. To make this force respectable the Emperor attached to Davout the cuirassier division of General Valence and the light cavalry brigade of General Pajol. Furthermore, General Grouchy's cavalry corps and the cavalry of General Nansouty were to support him—one on each of his flanks.[29] On paper this gave Davout a substantial force with which to maneuver against Bagration's right flank and rear; but in practice it did not work so. Murat, believing that he had made contact with Barclay's main army, pulled Nansouty off to the north leaving Davout's left vulnerable, and reducing his numbers. Then Grouchy engaged a portion of the Russian IV Corps (under Shuvalov) which he mistook for Bagration, and lost contact with Davout. Thus the I Corps advanced on Minsk reduced in strength and with both of its flanks exposed. At Ochmiana it captured a large quantity of medical supplies which the Russians, in their hasty retreat, had not destroyed.[30]

Bagration had no news of the French advance on Vilna until after they had occupied the city. And as Jérôme remained inactive before him, he was furiously indignant when Barclay, who was also minister of war and therefore his superior, ordered him to retire on Drissa. The General hurled unjustifiable accusations against the Minister, and complained loudly to anyone who would listen.[31] Yet, in obedience, he set out for the fortified camp along the shortest route, which led midway between Vilna and Minsk. But Davout had already crossed his projected line of march, and a brief skirmish with patrols of the I Corps caused the Russian commander to veer to his right in an attempt to gain Minsk ahead of the French. This time Davout outmarched his opponent. Entering the city on July 8, he prepared to defend it despite the fact that he had only a portion of his army corps and was inferior in numbers to the enemy.

Davout had executed the first part of the plan with clocklike precision. He had placed himself in a position between the two Russian armies and was ready for battle. But for the plan to succeed it was now necessary that the King of Westphalia execute his role in an energetic manner. The three army corps under Jérôme were to attack Bagration so as to harass his withdrawal and drive him into the waiting arms of Davout before Minsk. It was not a complicated maneuver requiring extraordinary tactical or strategical skills, nevertheless it did call for an energetic general with experience as an independent commander—the more so as communication between the armies was via the Emperor's general headquarters. Jérôme not only lacked the necessary experience, he was also devoid of basic military knowledge. In justice it must be admitted that the King wanted to do what was necessary to win the campaign, the problem was that he had been miscast by his all-powerful brother. As King of Westphalia he could get into little trouble out of which Napoleon could not bail him. On the battlefield it was quite another story. Against a clever, experienced, and active commander such as Bagration, Napoleon should have sent a tried and proven professional military man. In the first place the troops under Jérôme were poorly organized, drilled, and equipped. The King was also completely lacking in all talents of this nature, and the efforts of his staff proved inadequate. In the second place his army was inadequately supplied, and even before it reached the Niemen was in bad shape. Plundering its way across Poland, discipline had broken down and food became scarce. Arriving late at its crossing point—Grodno—the army halted to rest and regroup. In this manner Jérôme fell five days behind schedule.

During the first week of July, while Davout was marching on Minsk and Bagration was organizing his retreat, Napoleon repeatedly urged his brother to attack the enemy before him with vigor. "My cousin," he instructed Berthier on July 5, "write to the King of Westphalia . . . that it is impossible to maneuver worse than he has done. Tell him [also] that the fate of my maneuvers and the best occasion of the war have escaped by this single omission of the elementary principles of war." [32] When Jérôme attempted to justify his delays on grounds that the roads were bad, his troops exhausted, and the weather miserable, the Emperor retorted "if your soldiers are unable to march, what about those of Bagration and

Davout."[33] And the following day he ordered Berthier to write: "The two or three days which the troops of Your Majesty [Jérôme] have lost have perhaps saved Bagration."[34]

Disappointed in his younger brother's handling of the army under his command, and fully aware of the unquestionable superiority of the talents of Davout, Napoleon issued the following order on July 6: "His Majesty orders that, in case of a reunion of the V, VII, and VIII army corps and the IV reserve cavalry corps with the corps commanded by the Prince of Eckmühl, command should be taken over by the Prince of Eckmühl as the senior general. The Emperor orders His Majesty the King of Westphalia to recognize the Prince of Eckmühl as supreme commander so long as the army corps remain united."[35] These orders were dispatched to Marshal Davout at once, but were not sent to the King of Westphalia. Davout was not to make them known until such time as the two armies were joined, and unity of command was necessary. Thus Jérôme continued to exercise supreme command over his three army corps after July 6.

Jérôme's advance guard had not left Grodno until July 5, and only the following day was the entire right wing of the army at last on the march. On July 10 his most advanced units engaged the enemy's rear guard, but because of their weakness they caused Bagration little damage or concern. Napoleon again criticized his brother severely for his lack of initiative and told him that he should have been with his advance columns and fallen on the enemy in force.[36] The King finally arrived at Mir on July 12. But it was too late to force a decision before Minsk. While Davout was waiting in vain for Jérôme to force the enemy upon him, Bagration filed off to the south unmolested.

All was not yet lost. The Marshal still stood between the two Russian armies. For Bagration to join Barclay—which was still his prime objective—he must either outmarch or outfight Davout. On his part Davout found himself too weak to attack the Russians alone. Therefore, when Jérôme established direct communications with him on July 12 from Mir, Davout assumed supreme command of the entire right flank. On the fourteenth he sent a copy of the July sixth order to Jérôme accompanied by Berthier's letters.[37] If he could bring the entire right to bear on Bagration, Davout believed he could still crush him. To this end he ordered Jérôme's corps to redouble their pursuit of the enemy, who was now marching on Bobruisk with the intention of crossing the Berezina.

Jérôme's reaction startled the entire army. He flatly refused to serve under the orders of the victor of Auerstädt and Eckmühl. At first he made feeble excuses to the Emperor: Davout was only a prince whereas he was a king and could take orders only from the Emperor. But to Berthier he was more to the point: "I can not see in this disposition anything but a total lack of confidence on the part of the Emperor, a firm desire on the part of His Majesty to humiliate me, especially after what has passed between myself and the Prince of Eckmühl."[38] The reference to the Prince of Eckmühl was in fact what lay at the bottom of Jérôme's refusal.

During the winter of 1811–12 the Kingdom of Westphalia had been the organizational ground for the Grand Army. Davout, as the main architect in the field exercised his authority in an arbitrary, aggressive, and often tyrannical manner. The mere prince, who had won his title on the battlefields of Europe and North Africa, had little respect for the puppet King, who owed his title to his relationship to the Emperor. When trouble broke out in Magdeburg and Brunswick in February 1812, the Emperor ordered Davout to restore tranquility. The abrupt Marshal took highhanded measures to crush all opposition, leaving scars which could only further separate the German population from their uninvited French king.[39] In addition there was what had become almost a perennial source of ill will between the Prince and the King—the crown of Poland. To be sure, it was more subtle, but nonetheless real. With Jérôme assuming the role of imperial candidate and hoping to win the fame and glory in this "Second Polish War" necessary to justify the crown of "liberated" Poland, Davout could hardly avoid seeing his dream vanish before his eyes while that of his rival was enhanced.

Insulted by his brother's continual criticism and humiliated by being placed under the orders of Davout, Jérôme requested permission to leave the army and began to make preparation for his departure. He had halted his army corps on the fourteenth upon receiving Davout's dispatch, and turned over his command to his chief of staff, General Jean Gabriel Marchand. The immediate result was that Poniatowski's V Corps and Marie Victor Nicolas Latour-Maubourg's cavalry corps lost a full day before Marchand could order them to renew the pursuit of the enemy. When Davout realized (after receiving a dispatch from Jérôme on July fifteenth) that the King was personally offended and intent on leaving the army, he wrote a conciliatory letter trying to persuade him to stay.[40] But Jérôme had already left his headquarters, and had no intention of returning. Thus a second letter from the Marshal, dated the sixteenth, had no effect upon the wounded pride of the King.

To ascertain the effects of Jérôme's refusal to serve under Davout is not an easy task. There was no longer any question of forcing Bagration to fight a battle on two fronts at once. Nor was it likely that his army could be destroyed. It is also highly questionable that the end result (Bagration's linking up with Barclay at Smolensk) would have been any different had Jérôme remained with his army and cooperated with Davout. Bagration had already escaped. Only the most vigorous pursuit of the enemy would have enabled Poniatowski and Latour-Maubourg to support Davout at the Battle of Solta-Nawka (July 22).

Napoleon blamed his brother for the escape of Bagration's army, and allowed him to retire, with his guard, to Westphalia. Nevertheless, he was not above accusing Davout at a later date "of suffering the escape of the left wing of the Russians by remaining four days in Minsk." [41] The initial error was undoubtedly on the part of the supreme commander himself. The appointment of an incapable relative, one who had already demonstrated his military inabilities during the campaign of 1809, best explains the failure of the operations against Bagration.[42]

There is, on the other hand, more justification in the charge which the Emperor brought against his Marshal for prematurely assuming command of Jérôme's army. "My cousin," he wrote to Berthier on July 20, "write to the Prince of Eckmühl that I am not satisfied with his conduct towards the King of Westphalia; that I had not given him command except in case the reunion would have taken place and the two armies being on the field of battle, one commander had been necessary; . . . that after having done so, and after having learned that the King of Westphalia had retired, he should keep the command and send orders to Prince Poniatowski; that today I no longer know how conditions are on my right; . . . that since he has taken command, he should keep it, but that he would have done better not to have taken it, because he had not united with the King."[43] Yet even here Davout's defense is solid. Joint action and unity of command were necessary if the full weight of the French force was to be brought against the enemy. With Jérôme at Mir, and in direct communication, Davout assumed their forces to be "united." The orders of July 6 were not so explicit as the criticism of July 20.

Though Bagration could no longer be driven into the Pripet Marshes or forced to fight at a disadvantage, he still did not have a clear road to Vitebsk where he now hoped to join Barclay. The latter had abandoned the fortified camp at Drissa and was falling back on Vitebsk with Napoleon in pursuit. Bagration had crossed the Berezina at Bobruisk and turned again northward. He intended to march by way of Mogilev and Orsha to Vitebsk, thus avoiding the necessity of crossing and recrossing the Dnieper. Davout had moved south from Minsk on July 14, and reached Svisloch on the Berezina as the Russians were crossing the river further to the south. He realized what his adversary planned to do and in a series of forced marches arrived at Mogilev on the twentieth determined to block the road to Orsha.

Davout had directed Poniatowski's Polish corps to move north and east from Slutsk to join his I Corps, while Latour-Maubourg was to continue to follow Bagration. But neither of these corps could arrive in time to support him before Mogilev. Thus he would have to face Bagration's entire army with but a portion of his own command. On July 21, he pushed General Bouistry's regiment south on a reconnaissance mission to locate the main enemy force. The General ran headlong into a strong Russian advance guard under General Raeffskoi, and was roughly handled.[44] Suffering heavy losses he fell back onto the outer defenses of Mogilev where, reinforced, he stopped the enemy. Davout now attacked Raeffskoi in force and drove him south. Realizing that he would have to give battle to Bagration's superior force the next morning, the Marshal sought a strong defensive position.

Drawing up behind a ravine which was both deep and wide, the French had the Dnieper on their left and the hamlet of Fatowa on their right. Here Davout awaited the onslaught of the Russian army with his twelve thousand men.[45] Though Bagration's force numbered at least thirty-five thousand—other estimates place the figure as high as forty-five thousand with the reserve units and garrison troops he had picked up during his retreat—he attacked the French position with only twenty thousand men.[46] So confident was he of victory, for he knew that Davout had only a portion of his army corps before him, that he sent his aide-de-camp to the Marshal to suggest that he give way and avoid a useless battle for "he intended to sleep the following night in Mogilev." [47] Davout's only reply was to strengthen his position.

On the morning of the twenty-third Bagration launched his infantry against the French lines; but the combination of a staunch defense and the ravine were more than the Russians could overcome. Counterattack followed attack, and throughout the long hot day the battle raged. Neither army could successfully cross the natural barrier in the face of his enemy's determined resistance. Davout could afford a stalemate—and even consider it a victory. But Bagration had either to break through the French position or retreat. Davout would be reinforced by the following morning and the Russian's situation substantially worsened. To renew the battle on the twenty-fourth was therefore out of the question for Bagration. When he saw that he could not pass Davout, he broke off the action in the late afternoon, and retracing his steps to Novo Bykhow, he crossed the Dnieper on the twenty-sixth and set a course for Smolensk. Davout remained in position of the field of battle, but his weakened army was in no condition to pursue an enemy which was superior in numbers and had not been defeated. He had suffered relatively heavy losses in the fierce fighting; and though they were fewer than his opponent's, so also was his army.[48]

Davout remained in Mogilev for four days while he regrouped his forces. Poniatowski and Latour-Maubourg both directed their corps so as to join him there. Davout did not cross the Dnieper and march on eastward—thus remaining between Bagration and Barclay—because he was not in sufficient strength. Caught by Bagration's full force on the left bank of the Dnieper, without the possibility of immediate support, he would have placed the entire right wing of the army in jeopardy. Furthermore, as the main Russian army was still at Vitebsk, he believed that Bagration would have to recross the Dnieper to join him.[49] However, unknown to Davout, Barclay retired along the main Smolensk road and the long-delayed junction was at last effected.

It had now been more than five weeks since the French army had crossed the Niemen. The heat, dust, bad roads, and shortage of supplies of every kind had taken their toll. The artillery and supply trains were unable to keep pace with the infantry, so that even those supplies which were moving with the army frequently were not up with the troops when they were needed. This resulted in additional hardships for the men. It became almost impossible to prevent marauding and pillaging, which always lead directly to a weakening of discipline.[50] The Emperor was no longer sure exactly what his effective striking force was at any given time. Stragglers and deserters roamed the countryside. The sick and wounded further depleted the ranks.

Davout's I Corps—and to some extent, Eugène's IV Corps—were exceptions to the general rule. "As we marched from Orsha to Liady," wrote Ségur, "the first corps, that of Davoust [*sic*], was distinguished by the order and harmony which prevailed in its divisions. The fine appearance of the troops, the care with which they were supplied, and the attention that was paid to make them careful of their provisions, which the improvident soldier is apt to waste; lastly, the strength of these divisions, the happy result of this severe discipline, all caused them to be acknowledged as the model of the whole army."[51] The Baron de Marbot also gives testimony to the fine condition of the I Corps. "Davout's corps was, however, for a long time a fortunate exception to this rule," Marbot wrote concerning the poor condition of the army as a whole, "since that marshal, who was no less great as an administrator than as a leader, had organized before the passage of the Niemen huge trains of small carts to follow the army. These carts, filled with biscuits, salted meat, and vegatables, were drawn by oxen, a certain number of which were slaughtered every evening. This while assuring a supply of provisions, had a great effect in keeping the soldiers in their ranks."[52]

Ségur also wrote a lengthy commentary on the organization and supply system of the I Corps:

> It was remarked now [at Vitebsk] as well as before we reached Smolensk, that the divisions of the first corps continued to be the most numerous; their detachments were better disciplined, brought back more, and did less injury to the inhabitants. Those who remained with their

colours lived on the contents of their knapsacks, the regular appearance of which relieved the eye, fatigued with a disorder that was nearly universal.

Each of these knapsacks, reduced to what was strictly necessary in point of apparel, contained two shirts, two pair of shoes with nails, and a pair of extra soles, a pair of pantaloons and half-gaiters of cloth; a few articles requisite to personal cleanliness, a bandage, and a quantity of lint, and sixty cartridges.

In the two sides were placed four biscuits of sixteen ounces each; under these, and at the bottom was a long, narrow linen bag, filled with ten pounds of flour. The whole knapsack and its contents, together with the straps and the hood, rolled up and fastened at top, weighed thirty-three pounds twelve ounces.

Each soldier carried also a linen bag, slung in the form of a shoulder-belt, containing two loaves of three pounds each. Thus with his sabre, his loaded knapsack, three flints, his turn-screw, his belt and musket, he had to carry fifty-eight pounds weight, and was provided with bread for four days, biscuit for four, flour for seven, and sixty rounds of ammunition.

Behind were carriages laden with provisions for six more days; but it was impossible to reckon with confidence on these vehicles, picked up on the spot, which would have been so convenient in any other country with a smaller army, and in a more regular war.

They were colonies uniting the character of civilized and nomadic. The Emperor had first conceived the idea, which the genius of the Prince of Eckmühl made his own; he had everything he wanted, time, place, and men to carry it into execution; but these three elements of success were less at the disposal of the other chiefs. Besides, their characters, being more impetuous and less methodical, would scarcely have derived the same advantages from it; with a less organizing genius, they would therefore have had more obstacles to surmount; the Emperor had not paid sufficient attention to these differences, which were productive of baneful effects.[53]

At Vitebsk Napoleon halted the army and gave it several days of much-needed rest. Davout had departed from Mogilev on July 29, the same day Poniatowski arrived, and marched north along the Dnieper to Orsha. When the Emperor was satisfied that Barclay, even though Bagration had joined him, would not take the offensive, he ordered a general advance on Smolensk via the right bank of the Dnieper. By August 16, Ney and Murat had reached the outer works of the city; and the former, to test the strength of its defenses, had launched an attack—unsuccessfully—against the citadel.

On the seventeenth Smolensk was invested by the French on three sides. Ney's III Corps faced the citadel on the west with its left resting on the Dnieper. Davout faced the city on the south with Poniatowski's Poles on his right. Murat held the ground to the east of the city along the river. The north (right) bank was occupied by the Russians. Both Bagration and Barclay, who had been maneuvering north of the city, hurried back in a series of forced marches. Arriving north of the city on the seventeenth, they reinforced the garrison; but Barclay had no real intention of defending the holy city in a major battle. Smolensk had lost its military significance except as a crossing point for the French army. Nevertheless, Napoleon ordered a general assault (noon of the seventeenth). It may have been that he wished to test Russian determination to defend the city, however militarily the attack was unnecessary. A flanking movement on either side would have forced the enemy to evacuate.

The main attack was led by Davout's three divisions—Friant, Morand, and Gudin—which had rejoined the I Corps several days earlier during the advance on Smolensk. The vigorous and determined attack was met by an equally stubborn defense. The Russian artillery, which was on the north bank of the Dnieper, was unable to bring Davout's divisions under fire; and the French, taking full advantage of this, pressed their attack. The suburbs on the south were occupied and artillery was brought up to breach the walls of the old city. When these twelve-pounders—the largest available—proved incapable of the task, Napoleon called a halt to the attack. The battle had raged four hours, and losses had been heavy on both sides. Still the Emperor had not given up the hope of taking the city by storm. Davout regrouped his forces and prepared to launch an all-out assault on the walls before dawn the next morning. Poniatowski and Ney had also been heavily engaged during the battle but with even less success than Davout. By midnight, having gained the time needed to get his artillery and baggage on the high road to Moscow, Barclay ordered the evacuation of the disputed city. At dawn Smolensk was occupied without firing a shot; and the Russians continued their evasive retreat.[54]

The French began crossing to the north bank of the Dnieper on the nineteenth. Ney's III Corps led the way, followed by Murat's cavalry and Davout. Because the low road—the main road—to Moscow ran along the right bank of the river, and was covered by French artillery in place on the other side, it had been necessary for Barclay to send his baggage and artillery on the high road, which was longer and slower. To give his cumbersome baggage train time to regain the main Moscow road, he reinforced his rear guard and ordered it to hold along the Dolodnia, a small stream running from north to south into the Dnieper. Here Ney engaged the enemy in a pitched battle on the afternoon of the nineteenth. Napoleon ordered Gudin's division to support Ney in this action. Arriving shortly before nightfall, Gudin immediately led his men against the enemy in an all-out attack. The Russians stubbornly held their ground until dark, and then began to fall back under the mounting pressure. They had gained what they needed most—time—despite extremely heavy losses (between seven and nine thousand men). French losses were less in number, but the death of General Gudin, one of the truly fine divisional commanders of the army, marked the Battle of Kolodnia as a tragedy.[55]

The death of Gudin was more than the loss of an excellent divisional commander to Davout—it was the loss of a friend and companion of more than ten years. Only eight days before his tragic death, the Marshal had written to his wife: "My dear Aimée, General Gudin has just rejoined me; this reunion gives me the greatest pleasure." [56] On August 20, after the battle but before the General died, he wrote his wife the following melancholy letter:

> I have to give you, my dear Aimée, an unpleasant task, that of preparing Madame the Comtesse Gudin to receive bad news which will soon arrive concerning her husband in a combat in which his division covered itself with glory. He has had one leg amputated and the muscle of the other leg shattered by a canon ball which exploded near him. There is little chance that he will survive. He took the amputation with rare courage: I saw him shortly after his misfortune, and it was he who tried to console me. . . . I cried like a child. Gudin said that I need

> not cry; he spoke to me of his wife and children, saying that he died peacefully on their part, because he knew the benevolence of the Emperor towards his servants, and that he took with him the certainty that I would do that which was necessary for his family. You may assure Madame Gudin, that if she has the misfortune to lose her husband, that I will justify on every occasion the sentiment and confidence of her husband.[57]

Gudin's division was taken over by General Gérard, the future Marshal of France,[58] and the advance continued. The Russian army was retreating along the main Smolensk-Moscow road. Barclay intended to give battle now that Bagration had joined him, and he was seeking favorable ground. Napoleon pushed Murat's cavalry forward to maintain contact with the enemy. As Ney's corps had sustained relatively heavy losses on the nineteenth, Davout was ordered to support Murat. By the twenty-third the entire army was again on the march. It now moved in three columns. The principal army marched along the main road, led by Murat and Davout and followed closely by Ney and the Guard. Grouchy's cavalry and Eugène's IV Corps marched parallel to the Moscow road to the north, while Junot, Poniatowski, and Latour-Maubourg paralleled it to the south. These three columns were to march in such a manner as to be able to concentrate their force within twenty-four hours at whatever point the enemy might present itself in strength.[59]

Murat harassed the Russian rear guard with reckless enthusiasm. Much to the displeasure of Davout, who supported him, he attacked every temporary position he came upon. It was not surprising that within a few days these two contrasting soldiers found themselves in complete disagreement as to how the pursuit should be conducted. The Emperor had not placed the Prince under the orders of the King, but Davout was to give Murat's cavalry infantry support when it was required. The difficulties which arose generally centered around the question of who—in the absence of a supreme commander—was to decide when support was needed and in what form.

In a letter to Davout dated August 22, Napoleon had written: "I recommended to the King of Naples not to overtire the troops in this extreme heat, to engage only the [enemy's] rear guard, and to take up a position in the event the enemy should take a stand to give battle."[60] And again on the twenty-sixth the Marshal received instructions: "It is necessary to make short marches and in good order. . . . The marches should be such as not to overtire the infantry. It must finish [the day's march] at an early hour. In all probability the enemy will await us at Viazma [Vyazma]; it is necessary to arrive there in order." [61] In following these instructions, and his own good judgment, Davout tried as best he could to keep his men in good condition so that they would be ready for that decisive battle which now seemed closer at hand than at any other time since the crossing of the Niemen. Yet while Davout was husbanding his troops, Murat was destroying his cavalry and attempting to do the same to the I Corps.

The conflict erupted on August 28. The preceding day Murat had attacked the Russian rear guard in a strong position which they would presumably abandon at nightfall, as was their custom. At the height of this futile engagement one of Davout's batteries refused to take orders from the King of Naples. The commanding officer declared that he had the strictest orders from the Marshal not to engage in offensive action without his permission. This permission was immediately given, but Murat declared that it arrived too late to be effective. The next day there occurred a violent quarrel between Murat and Davout at Slawkowo in the presence of the Emperor. Murat reproached the Marshal for his lack of cooperation and declared that "if there was any quarrel between them they ought to settle it by themselves, but that the army ought not to be made the sufferers for it." [62] Irritated by these remarks, Davout declared that Murat's thoughtless ardor was incessantly compromising his troops, and wasting to no purpose their lives, strength, and stores. He then proceeded to describe the manner in which he attacked a position which he could not possibly take, and which the enemy had no intention of holding except for a few hours so as to slow down the French advance. Murat, Davout went on, was wearing down the advance guard by keeping it under arms "all day without eating or drinking, amidst a cloud of dust, under a burning sky." [63]

After this lengthy oration on the manner in which the King was conducting the advance guard, Davout concluded by saying "that 'in this manner the whole of the cavalry would perish; Murat, however, might dispose of that as he pleased, but as for the infantry of the first corps, so long as he had the command of it, he would not suffer it to be thrown away in that manner.' " [64] The Emperor listened without interruption while his two lieutenants vented their anger on one another. Despite the fact that reason rested with the methodical prudence of Marshal Davout, the Emperor was inclined toward the impetuous King who suited his anxieties much better. When the audience had ended, and Murat was no longer present, Napoleon tried to soothe Davout by telling him that no one person could possess all aspects of merit; that while he certainly could conduct a battle better than Murat, the King of Naples knew how to push a rear guard. He then added that if it had been Murat, rather than Jérôme, who had been pursuing Bagration in Lithuania, the Russian army would probably not have escaped. "It is even asserted," wrote Ségur, "that he reproached the Marshal with his restless disposition, which made him desirous of appropriating to himself the entire command; less, indeed, from ambition than zeal, and that all might go on better; but yet this zeal had its inconveniences." [65]

Napoleon ordered the two commanders to return to their respective corps and to cooperate with one another in the future. But the fact remained that cooperation between them was impossible. One of them should have been given supreme command of the advance guard. However, as neither would have submitted to the authority of the other—and the Emperor knew this well—one of them should have been replaced.

The very next day trouble again arose on the battlefield. In a premature attempt to force the Viazma, Murat had completely engaged his cavalry, and seeing that it was in need of infantry support, he placed himself at the head of Compans's division and prepared to lead it into action. At that moment Davout rode up and countermanded the King's orders. Declaring that the enemy was in too strong a position to be dislodged, and that the cavalry attack had been a mistake, he refused to allow his men to be sacrificed in such a useless and futile undertaking. Despite the King's appeal to his superior military rank and the urgency of the situation, the Marshal would not give his consent. Murat therefore sent General Belliard, his chief of staff, to the Emperor to tell his brother-in-law that he must choose between himself and Davout. Napoleon was enraged! Davout had lost all mindfulness of subordination, he declared, and ordered Berthier to draw up at once orders detaching General Compans's division from the I Corps and placing it directly under the orders of the King of Naples.

This action tended to settle the military problem which had resulted from this clash, but it had little effect on the wounded pride of the two men. While Davout did not try to justify the manner of his conduct, he did vindicate his motives. On the other hand, Murat's anger was almost uncontrollable. Davout had publicly insulted him and he was determined to have satisfaction. Only the utmost energy on the part of Belliard, who pointed out the bad example it would set before the whole army at such a critical time, as well as the delight it would give to his enemies and the sorrow to his friends, prevented a duel between these two great soldiers.[66]

The pitfalls of a divided command in the presence of the enemy are most obvious in this affair. Had Napoleon himself been on the field of battle and ordered one of Davout's divisions to attack, the Marshal would have placed himself at its head and led them into the most forbidding inferno—as in fact he would do at Borodino. However the King of Naples was quite another matter. Davout did not recognize him as his superior in rank or in judgment. This was not the last public outburst between these two enemies. In October they would disagree on the route to be taken during the retreat from Moscow,[67] and again in December, after Napoleon left the army under Murat's command, they clashed.[68]

The lack of cooperation in the French advance guard had no real effect on the course of the enemy's retreat. The Russians had no definite plans for giving battle before Gshatsk, and even a closely coordinated pursuit would only have resulted in heavier casualties on both sides without altering the course of events. The Russians thus continued to fall back toward Moscow and the French to advance into the man-made wasteland of eastern Europe. From Dorogobuzh to Vyazma to Gshatsk to the headwaters of the Moskva, the unending march progressed. Finally the Russian army turned about, dug in above the village of Borodino, and prepared to meet the terrible onslaught of the invincible Napoleon.

Barclay had intended to fight a major battle in a good defensive position east of Smolensk on the Moscow road.[69] Then on the very day he had at last chosen a site, he was replaced by Mikhail Illarionovich Golenischev-Kutusov. Kutusov was the nation's choice, not the Tsar's. Alexander's dislike for him dated from the disaster of Austerlitz which Kutusov had done all within his power to forestall. Barclay had lost the support of the army, and, particularly after the

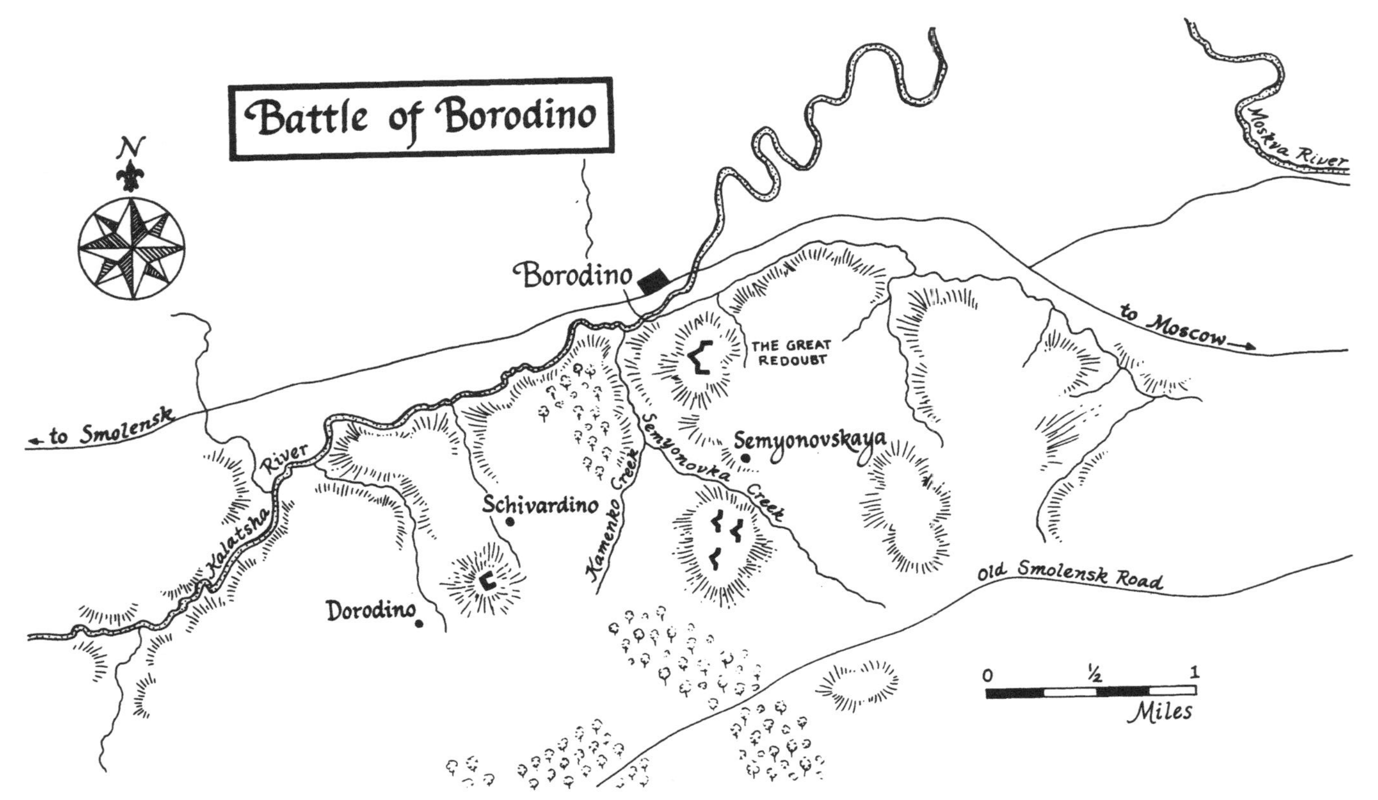

Battle of Borodino
N
Borodino
Moskva River
to Moscow
to Smolensk
THE GREAT REDOUBT
Semyonovskaya
Semyonovka Creek
Kamenko Creek
Schivardino
Dorodino
Kalatsha River
Old Smolensk Road
0
½
1
Miles

evacuation of Smolensk without a major battle, it had been necessary to find a new commander. Kutusov knew as well as Barclay that there must be a battle before Moscow; that ancient capital of Russia could not be abandoned as Smolensk had been. Furthermore, the two armies were approaching equality in numbers. Whereas the French had been able to face Smolensk with some one hundred and eighty thousand men, they arrived before Borodino with only one hundred and thirty thousand.[70] On the other hand, the Russian army, which had counted some one hundred and thirty thousand at Smolensk, was still able to put in the field one hundred and twenty thousand. This is not to say that the French had lost fifty thousand men and the Russians only ten thousand. The losses in the combined battles of Smolensk and Valutino were about equal—thirty thousand men on either side. But the French found it necessary to leave some six thousand men at Smolensk and to send ten thousand under General Dominique Pino to Vitebsk. At the same time the Russian army had been reinforced by twenty thousand as it drew near Moscow.[71] For the first time since the opening of the campaign the Russian army, in a good defensive position, stood a reasonable chance of stopping the enemy advance. Kutusov himself may have had little confidence in victory, but even a stalemate at this point could be considered a triumph from the Russians' point of view. The new commander had no intention of "fighting to the last man." If the French proved too strong he fully intended to retire, saving as much of his army as possible, and allowing Napoleon to enter Moscow.

The French took Gshatsk on September 1, and Napoleon gave his weary army a much-needed two-day rest. The central column in particular had suffered from lack of food and water. The weather had been extremely dry so that wells and streams had dried up causing an acute water shortage. The soldiers of the retreating Russian army, themselves suffering from a shortage of supplies,[72] devoured nearly everything that was to be found in the towns and villages along the main road; and what they were not able to use or take with them they destroyed. The flanking columns fared much better. The roads they had to use were not as good, but the villages through which they passed had not been emptied or burned by the enemy, and they ate relatively well. Thus it was necessary for the main army to remain inactive on September 2 and 3 while stragglers and supply wagons caught up.

On September 4 the army resumed its advance. Napoleon was confident that the enemy must fight before Moscow, and he intended to be prepared. Shortly after noon of the following day, Murat's advance guard came upon the Russian position to the south and west of the village of Borodino. The Russians had hastily constructed a redoubt on high ground near the hamlet of Schivardino and supported it with cavalry. Murat ordered an attack without waiting for support. He drove off the Russian horse and sent Compans's infantry, which was still under his orders, against the redoubt. Despite stubborn resistance, the enemy was forced to withdraw as Poniatowski moved forward to support the attack.

September 6 was used by both sides to prepare for battle. Napoleon was overjoyed with the thought that at last he would have the decisive engagement which had been eluding him. Kutusov's army was drawn up on high ground south of a small river (Kalatsha). His center, opposite the village of Borodino, was strengthened by a strong redoubt (referred to as the "Great Redoubt") at the highest point. His right lay along high ground on the south bank of the Kalatsha with the Moskva to its right and rear. Both the center and the right were commanded by Barclay. The Russian left, commanded by Bagration, extended to the south from the Great Redoubt across the old Smolensk-Moscow road. This flank was also strengthened by three smaller redoubts. Kutusov planned a strictly defensive battle with his one hundred and twenty thousand men.

Napoleon brought in his flanking columns so that Poniatowski formed his right and Eugène his left. His center was composed of the corps of Ney, Junot, and Davout, and was supported by Murat's cavalry. Grouchy's cavalry corps was attached to Eugène. The French left did not extend past Borodino except for a cavalry screen. Napoleon completely ignored the Russian right and concentrated against their center and left. Though his plans for the battle are somewhat uncertain, he apparently intended to break through the enemy's left and drive their center and right into the wedge formed by the junction of the Kalatsha and the Moskva.

During the late afternoon of the day before the battle, Davout joined the Emperor at the captured Schivardino redoubt, where he was making one last survey of the enemy's positions. Davout had himself just finished looking over the Russian defenses and made the following proposal to Napoleon: that he should be given command of the five divisions of his I Corps (he had only three—Friant, Compans, and Dessaix—at the time, Morand and Gerard having been attached to Eugène on the left); that to these thirty-five thousand should be added Poniatowski's Polish corps of the extreme right; and that together, well over forty thousand strong, they should march around the enemy's left flank during the night and fall on his rear at dawn as the main French army launched a frontal attack.

The plan was daring and tactically sound. With such an experienced and energetic commander as Davout it would undoubtedly have succeeded.[73] But after some deliberation, the master tactician rejected the proposal declaring that it would take him too far from his objective and cause him to lose too much time. Davout was not satisfied with this reply and continued to argue in favor of his plan. Finally, annoyed by being contradicted, the Emperor put an end to the discussion by exclaiming, "Ah! you are always for turning the enemy; it is too dangerous a maneuver!"[74] Still convinced of the soundness of his plan, but realizing that the Emperor would not accept it, Davout returned to his post perplexed at the unexpected prudence of the once daring commander.

Over one hundred French guns announced the opening of the battle at six o'clock on the morning of September 7. At seven Davout led two divisions in the initial assault against the southernmost of the three small redoubts. Dessaix approached it on the right while Compans moved on its side. The enemy fire was murderous. Compans was wounded before his battalions even reached the enemy position, and Davout himself took the General's place. He rallied the faltering troops and led them into the redoubt. But Napoleon had miscalculated the strength of the Russian left. Friant's division had been left behind in reserve, and the two divisions which were able to capture the enemy position were unable to hold it when Bagration counterattacked. Furthermore, Poniatowski's supporting attack on the extreme right had been delayed until 8:00 A.M., too late to aid Davout's attack.[75]

Ney's assault on the northernmost of the small redoubts met with the same success as did Davout's at the outset. As Bagration was now compelled to divert a portion of his reserves to meet Ney, the divisions of the I Corps were able to regroup. Despite a cavalry attack by the enemy which had followed their expulsion from the southern redoubt, Davout, still at the head of Compans's division, and Dessaix again moved forward. The Marshal's horse was killed under him and he was thrown to the ground with such force that he was temporarily knocked unconscious. As badly shaken up as he was, he refused to give up his command and leave the field of battle.[76] His troops swarmed back into the redoubt with renewed determination. During this second assault General Dessaix was seriously wounded and forced to leave the field. As General Rapp replaced him at the redoubt the Russians again counterattacked—this time unsuccessfully.

Both of the redoubts now occupied by the French were opened in the rear and afforded no protection from the heavy artillery fire now being directed against them from the third redoubt which lay behind the other two. Therefore Ney, with support from Davout's already weakened divisions, immediately overran this last stronghold on the Russian left. But Bagration now brought the entire force of his Second Army to bear on the French and drove them back. Napoleon sent Murat at the head of his cavalry (Latour-Maubourg and Nansouty) to support his right. The heights on which the three redoubts had been constructed became the focal point of the fiercest fighting. Friant's division was sent into the line in support of Ney, which enabled that Marshal to regain control of the disputed positions by one o'clock in the afternoon.

While this action, the main French effort, was taking place, Eugène had sent Alexis Joseph Delzons forward to capture the town of Borodino, which he did and held it against an enemy counterattack. The divisions of Droussier, Morand, and Gérard (formerly Gudin) were then sent against the Great Redoubt in the center of the Russian line. The position was staunchly defended by the enemy, and although counterattacks drove the French out twice, by early afternoon it was in the undisputed hands of Eugène's men. A flanking maneuver by the Russian cavalry (Platov and Uvarov) caused Eugène some concern and delayed his attack, but it had no effect on the course of the battle.

Kutusov had shifted his right flank from its original position along the Kalatsha southward to strengthen his hard-pressed left and center. During the early afternoon these troops arrived under murderous fire from the French artillery which then dominated the battlefield. Attacking in strength the Russians temporarily regained the heights about the three redoubts. But the combined forces of Ney (reinforced by Friant), Davout, and Murat eventually drove back this last supreme effort of the Russians. At the same time Junot, now in the line at Davot's right, and Poniatowski drove back the enemy's extreme left. The Russian left and left center were badly shattered and in some confusion. Bagration had been mortally wounded and was replaced by Docturov. Kutusov had committed all of his reserves to the battle. However, the French troops in the line were also in bad shape. Unable to deliver the *coup de grâce,* the marshals implored Napoleon to send forward the Guard and destroy the Russian army.

Thirty thousand men had taken little or no part in the fighting. The Old Guard had not yet fired a shot.[77] There are few dissenters from the theory that Borodino would have been, if not another Austerlitz, a complete Napoleonic victory had he thrown these fresh troops against the faltering Russian left. Yet despite the pleas of his marshals, the Guard was not committed to the battle. There are as many explanations of why Napoleon held back his reserves as there are accounts of the battle. They range from the Emperor's poor health—he was running a fever from the cold he had and was also suffering from another attack of uroedemo—to his belief that the Russians would stand their ground and he would have to fight again the following day. General Louis François Lejeune, aide-de-camp to Berthier at the time, gives what is perhaps the best explanation: "The Emperor, satisfied with all that had already been accomplished by General Friant and the other divisions under Davout, now thought the right moment had come to send his whole Guard to complete the victory, as yet only begun, when a timid counsellor remarked to him, 'Allow me to point out that your Majesty is at the present moment 700 leagues from Paris, and at the gates of Moscow.' "[78] Whatever the reason, the Russian army was saved! By four in the afternoon the only activity on the French right was an artillery duel which lasted several hours and died out as night came on.

Under cover of darkness Kutusov led the remnants of his army off to Moscow. His casualties had been staggering—more than forty-five thousand killed or wounded. And because he had left the battlefield in the hands of the French, virtually all of his wounded were taken prisoner. On the French side casualties were also heavy. Between twenty-eight and thirty-one thousand troops were put out of action. A portion of these would rejoin the army in Moscow, but the majority had either been killed or died later of their wounds.

One can only imagine the French emperor's disappointment on the morning of September 8, when he rose to find the Russians had once more slipped away during the night without having been completely destroyed. He might console himself with verbal declarations that the gates of Moscow had been opened, and that once in the capital of the old Muscovite state Alexander would sue for peace; but Borodino had been neither an Austerlitz, nor a Jena, nor a Friedland—it had in fact been an Eylau, and had settled nothing.

The divisions of the I Corps had taken a leading part in the fighting at Borodino, a fact reflected in their casualties. Even amongst the general officers the toll was high. Wounded were Compans, his replacement Rapp, Morand, Friant, Dessaix, and Davout himself. The Marshal's chief of staff, General Romeuf, was killed in the action. When the name of General Gudin, killed only a few days earlier at Valoutine, is added to this list, the corps was left without a single one of its original divisional commanders; and only General Gérard, of the five who took the field that bloody morning, survived the battle unharmed.

In addition to having his horse shot out from under him, the Marshal was wounded twice during the battle. Early in the morning he was struck in the abdomen by a cannon ball, which severely bruised him and rendered it painful for him to stay in the saddle the remaining long hours of the day. Later in the morning a bullet pierced his right thigh and he was unable even to put his horse to a trot by noon.[79] Yet, though he was in great pain throughout the greater part of the day, he did not leave the battle; nor even after the battle had ended did he give up his command. He remained with his corps, though unable to mount a horse, in order to give his men a good example and to encourage them. Not until his divisions were properly quartered at Moscow—that is, not until after the great fire—did the Marshal take to his bed for a long-overdue convalescence. "I had suffered a great deal until we entered Moscow," he wrote his wife on September 20, "but there, having been able to bathe and to rest, I began to get better. The inflammation disappeared at the end of forty-eight hours. The scabs have fallen off, the suppuration is well established, and now the two wounds are healing."[80]

The Russian army had been incapable of continuing the battle at Borodino on September 8. This is not to say Kutusov's army had been destroyed. On the contrary, he had executed a well-organized withdrawal under the cover of night and a strong rear guard. But he had been driven out of his prepared positions and lost the effectiveness of one third of his force. To have stood his ground, as some of his generals counseled, would undoubtedly have resulted in the complete destruction of his army. Thus he had fallen back giving lip service to another stand before the walls of Moscow, when in reality he knew that the ancient capital of the Tsars was already lost. His perception was broad enough to see clearly that the fall of Moscow did not put an end to the Empire. "The enemy's entry into Moscow," he wrote Alexander on September 16, "does not mean his conquest of Russia." [81]

On September 14 the dejected Russian army filed through the turbulent streets of Moscow, while the weary, but rejoicing, French troops prepared to enter the city. To the French, Moscow had become the symbol of the end of the campaign—peace, rest, and an abundance of all that had been lacking during the months of forced marches. Davout led his tired, hungry, battle-scarred corps through the Dorogomilov Gate into Moscow on September 15; but within less than twenty-four hours he was forced to evacuate the city as the fires, which had started as early as the night of the fourteenth, had turned it into a blazing inferno.

There is universal agreement as to the culprit responsible for the burning of Moscow. Count Fedor Vassilievitch Rostopchin, the governor-general of the capital, had given the orders to set the city afire before his departure.[82] The burning of the magnificent city was truly a tragic error. It unquestionably discomforted the French, who had expected to find all the necessities—and indeed pleasures—of Paris. Yet the real tragedy lies in the fact that it had no effect whatsoever on the outcome of the campaign. Napoleon's strategic position at Moscow was untenable whether the city was intact or in ashes. The great contemporary military historian Karl von Clausewitz summarized it in the following manner: "An army of 90,000 men, with exhausted troops and ruined horses, the end of a wedge driven 120 miles into Russia, an army of 110,000 men on their right, an armed people around them, compelled to show a front to all points of the compass, without magazine, with insufficient ammunition, with but one, entirely devastated, line of communication with its base—this is not a situation to pass a winter in." [83]

Nevertheless, three-quarters of the city was destroyed by the conflagration which raged from September 15 to 18. On the nineteenth the French reentered the smoldering city, and Davout's I Corps settled as best it could in the Kalouga and Toula quarters which had not been completely destroyed. Davout and his men were at last able to rest. Substantial stores of all kinds were found in Moscow despite the fire,[84] and though looters got more than their share, the army as a whole once again ate and drank well. During the five weeks spent in the Russian capital Davout was able to reorganize and, to some extent at least, reequip his men. By the middle of October the Corps was once again in better condition than any other unit, save the Guard, which had not taken part in the Battle of Borodino. Much was still lacking in the way of equipment—even essentials—but given the time and resources available, Davout had worked wonders.

During this interlude at Moscow, Napoleon saw fit to reward his deserving army. Numerous promotions were made in the general reorganization of the various army corps. In the I Corps, Gratien, Fredericks, and Gérard were promoted to the rank of general of division; Colonels Delort, Lejeune,[85] Dargens, and Buguet were named generals of brigade, and so on down through the ranks.[86] Davout, who received 300,000 francs from the Emperor, wrote his wife on September 27: "I have just received new proof of the generosity of his Majesty." [87]

12

The Retreat from Moscow

UPON HIS ARRIVAL in Moscow, Napoleon, and indeed the entire army, believed the campaign had come to a glorious conclusion. The Emperor had convinced himself that peace would be found in the ancient capital of the Tsars; and it was only the prolonged silence from St. Petersburg that brought him to the realization that he had misjudged Alexander. Though he made several attempts to open negotiations with the Tsar, the Russian monarch, much to his credit, stood by his pledge not to make peace so long as a single French soldier remained east of the Niemen. Without peace the French army could not winter in Moscow. Its lines of communication extended over six hundred miles through hostile country. There was only one good road, and it would soon be buried beneath a blanket of snow and harassed by raiding Cossacks and unfriendly peasants, who already were disrupting communications. But more important than these considerations was the Russian army. Kutusov had successfully saved the army from annihilation at Borodino. Evacuating Moscow he had led his mangled force south, first on the Ryazan road, and then on the Kaluga road. By the end of September he had taken up a position fifty to sixty miles south, and slightly west, of Moscow and had begun the difficult task of reorganization. In this excellent location, where he was able to be reinforced and supplied from the south, he posed a real threat to Napoleon's line of communication to Smolensk. Here Kutusov waited with his numbers increasing almost daily and winter coming on. Time was working in his favor.

Forced to reconsider his overall strategy, Napoleon decided to withdraw to the Smolensk-Minsk area where the Grand Army would go into winter quarters. Vast quantities of supplies had been stockpiled as far east as the Berezina and Dnieper, and the lines of communication into friendly territory (Lithuania and Poland) could be properly protected. The only question was the line of march the army should follow. The main road between Smolensk and Moscow had been devastated by the retreating Russians and the advancing French. Thus it was the least desirable route for the proposed withdrawal. Napoleon, therefore, decided upon a line of march which would take him southwest to Kaluga, and then west through Elnay to Smolensk. This would give him the double advantage of a route which had not been depleted of food and forage, and of not immediately allowing Kutusov to know his plan. It would appear as though he was marching against the enemy in order to renew the campaign, rather than retiring to the west.[1] Once Kutusov had been pushed south of Kaluga the French could move off to their right on the Smolensk road.

On paper the maneuver looked good. But before it could be put into action Kutusov took the offensive. He sent Bennigsen to attack Murat's force south of Moscow on October 18, and it was thrown back with substantial losses.[2] Murat was taken completely by surprise, in part because of a local cease-fire which the enemy had agreed upon and then violated without warning, and in part due to ineffective precautions. When Napoleon received news of this defeat he ordered the army to march at daybreak. Davout's I Corps left Moscow on October 19, and marched along the old Kaluga road followed by Ney's III Corps and the Guard. Davout's divisions were in better condition than any others in the army, with the exception of the Guard.[3] Each man carried bread and biscuits for seven days and flour for another week. Vehicles were provided for all who were unable to march; and they were sent back to Smolensk on the main road.[4] With the exception of the horses,[5] which were universally in poor condition throughout the French army, Davout's corps was ready to undertake the limited campaign which was planned.

Marching south from Moscow as if he intended to reinforce Murat, Napoleon suddenly veered to his right in order to gain the new Kaluga road and pushed on toward Maloyaroslavets. Despite his great superiority of cavalry, Kutusov lost contact with the French army on October 18 after the engagement with Murat and knew nothing of the whereabouts of his enemy. Not until the twenty-second did he again make contact, and then the French advance corps, Eugène's IV Corps, was mistaken for a foraging party in strength. But when General Doctorov was sent with his corps to drive the French back to Moscow, he discovered the error which had been made. Realizing Napoleon was heading for Maloyaroslavets, which was on Kutusov's left flank, he set out on a forced march to reach the town before him.

Eugène was first to arrive in the town, which is situated on the south bank of the river Louges (Luzha or Lutza). However, as it was late, he did not move his entire corps across the river; only two battalions were put in the town. Then Doctorov arrived in the hours just before dawn and took up a position astride the main roads south in an attempt to contain the enemy until reinforcements could arrive. At dawn when Eugène's advance guard moved forward it was met by heavy fire from Doctorov's Corps. Gradually the engagement developed into a battle as both sides committed themselves completely. During the afternoon units of Ney's III Corps and Davout's I Corps moved up to support Eugène. Ney's troops actually played a minor role in the fighting, but only Davout's artillery was engaged.[6] South of the burning town Doctorov was being supported by the arrival of Russian divisions as Kutusov slowly moved into position to block the French line of march. Maloyaroslavets changed hands eleven times in the course of the day. Eugène was unable to break out of the perimeter Doctorov had created, and the Russians were unable to throw the staunch Italian troops of the IV Corps back across the Louges. As the sun set on this decisive[7] battlefield Eugène still occupied the ruins of Maloyaroslavets and Kutusov the plains to the south.

That night in a shabby little farmhouse near the village of Ghorodnia the Emperor Napoleon held a council of war. It had not been customary in the past for him to hold such councils, but he was discouraged and depressed. The Russian army had defended Maloyaroslavets with a determination he had not expected. Even the rawest recruits, armed only with pikes, stood firm against the deadly fire of Eugène's battle-hardened veterans.[8] Should he commit his entire army to battle on the twenty-fifth in a major effort to throw the Russian army back on Kaluga as he had done at Borodino? Perhaps even more important: *could* he break out to the south and continue along the Kaluga road?

Present at this council were Murat, Eugène, Berthier, Davout, and Bessières. After a prolonged silence, Murat began the discussion by declaring himself in favor of attacking the enemy at sunrise and continuing the campaign. To this his brother-in-law replied that the only consideration at this point must be how to save the rest of the army. Bessières next pointed out how well the Russian soldiers had fought throughout the day; and that the morale of the French army, including the Guard which he commanded, was not up to the supreme effort which would be required to continue the offensive. He therefore concluded by voting in favor of retreating northward to the main Smolensk-Moscow road. The Emperor gave his approval to this view.

Davout then entered the discussion by observing that

> "as a retreat was decided upon, he proposed that it should be by Medyn and Smolensk." But Murat interrupted Davoust [*sic*], and whether from enmity, or from that discouragement which usually succeeds the rejection of a rash measure, he declared his astonishment, "that anyone should dare to propose so imprudent a step to the Emperor. Had Davoust sworn the destruction of the army? Would he have so long and so heavy a column trail along, without guides and in uncertainty, on an unknown track, within reach of Kutusoi [*sic*], presenting its flank to all the attacks of the enemy? Would he, Davoust, defend it? Why—when in our rear, Borowsk and Vererïa would lead us without danger to Mojaisk—why reject that safe route? There, provisions must have been collected, there everything was known to us, and we could not be misled by a traitor."
>
> At these words, Davoust, burning with a rage which he had great difficulty to repress, replied, that "he proposed a retreat through a fertile country, by an untouched, plentiful, and well-supplied route, villages still standing, and by the shortest road, that the enemy might not avail himself of it, to cut us off from the route from Majaisk to Smolensk, recommended by Murat. And what a route! a desert of sand and ashes, where convoys of wounded would increase our embarrassment, where we would meet with nothing but ruins, traces of blood, skeletons and famine!

"Moreover, though he deemed it his duty to give his opinion when it was asked, he was ready to obey orders contrary to it with the same zeal as if they were consonant with his suggestions; but that the Emperor alone had a right to impose silence on him and not Murat, who was not his sovereign, and never should be!"[9]

The old rivalry between Davout and Murat was again reaching a danger point when Bessières and Berthier intervened to prevent a serious clash at so critical a moment. Throughout these heated exchanges Napoleon had sat in silence, almost unaware of what was going on in the room about him. Finally he brought the council to an end by declaring that he would make the decision. The following day, after nearly being captured by Cossacks, he decided to retreat by way of Mozhaisk, not Medyn. A similar decision was made south of Maloyaroslavets. In the early hours before dawn Kutusov, who had moved his army in position for a general battle, suddenly lost his nerve and ordered a general withdrawal.[10] Thus it was that following what was in fact an inconclusive battle both armies retreated.

Davout's proposal to retire on Smolensk by way of Medyn had been sound and might well have resulted in the army's arrival at its destination several days earlier and in much better condition to continue the retreat. The route was shorter by nearly three days' march. It would also, as the Marshal had pointed out, have prevented the Russian army from using it, and would have forced them to march further to the south or behind the French.[11] As it was, Kutusov used the Medyn road himself, and the result was that he was able to cut off the French rear guard (Davout's I Corps) at Vyazma. With respect to the question raised by both Davout and Murat regarding provisions, each was half right. Sufficient provisions had not been stored along the Mozhaisk-Gshatsk-Vyazma route, so that the army arrived in Smolensk hungry. But Davout's suggestion that the army could live off the land as it passed through the untouched and plentiful regions along the Medyn road was also misleading. Clausewitz, in discussing Napoleon's plan to retire on Smolensk by way of Kaluga-Elnya, clearly saw the difficulties confronting an army retreating in a hostile country in the face of an enemy with superior cavalry. "What could an 'unexhausted country' do for an army which had no time to lose, and was forced to bivouac in great masses; what commissary could precede it to collect supplies; and what Russian authority would have obeyed his orders? The army would have been starved in a week." [12] He then went on to observe: "A man who retires from an enemy's country requires, by all rules, a prepared route; one who retires under very difficult circumstances has double need of it; one who has to retire 120 miles in Russia requires it threefold. By a prepared route, we mean one occupied by detachments, and in which magazines have been formed." [13] Unfortunately Napoleon had not sufficiently prepared a route for the retreat! But the inadequate stores along the chosen line were no substitute for the untouched towns and villages on the Medyn road. Further, as Davout pointed out, the sick and wounded, as well as various baggage trains, already cluttered the Mozhaisk road.

The remaining point to be considered is that which Murat brought up concerning the exposed flank of the army should it use the Medyn road. This was, of course, a factor which could not be lightly overlooked. Although Kutusov had fallen back on the twenty-fifth from Maloyaroslavets leaving the road to Medyn open, the French would have had to exercise great care. But having cleared the immediate vicinity of the town their situation would have been better than it was to be after Mozhaisk and Gshatsk. There would have been little possibility of the enemy's main army interfering with their advance on Smolensk, and they would have found supplies at Elnya. By the French taking the Mozhaisk route Kutusov was free to use the Medyn-Elnya road and pose a constant threat to the French army's left flank. It should further be noted that the failure of the Russian army to reach Smolensk ahead of Napoleon, although it had a shorter distance to cover, was due more to the fact that Kutusov did not wish to do so, rather than that he could not have done so.

Davout had not taken part in the fighting at Maloyaroslavets, but he came close to death the following day. General Lejeune, who had become the Marshal's chief of staff after the Battle of Borodino gives this account:

> On the morning of the 25th, Marshal Davout, Colonel Kobilinski, and I went the round of our outposts and saw with regret that the Russian army was drawn up in good order not far off, completely blocking

> the road to Kalouga, which we hoped to take. We made our dispositions for forcing a passage, and as we stood in a close group, bending over our maps, we offered an excellent mark for a Russian artilleryman. A ball from a twelve-pounder passed between the Marshal and me, and carried away one of Colonel Kobilinski's legs. The unfortunate officer fell against me, and we thought he was killed, but he recovered miraculously.[14]

On October 25 the French army began its retreat. Until this point Napoleon had always faced the enemy. Now he turned his back on the withdrawing Russian forces. Davout's I Corps was assigned the last place in the marching line. He pushed the enemy rear guard several miles south of Maloyaroslavets on the twenty-fifth, and the following morning began slowly moving to the north. All went well during the first days of the retreat. The enemy found it difficult to believe that after successfully maintaining his advantageous position at Maloyaroslavets Napoleon would not continue his advance on Kaluga. At the end of the third day Davout wrote the Major General from Vereya that he had crossed the Protwa without difficulty as only Cossacks were following him.[15]

Kutusov did not fully realize what had happened until the twenty-eighth. He then authorized Miloradovich and Platov to pursue the enemy while he himself led the main army through Medyn toward Dubrovno and Vyazma. Platov's cavalry, supported by Cossacks, caught up with Davout on the last day of October; but, as they lacked infantry, they were unable to cause serious damage. Miloradovich, on the other hand, reached the Moscow-Smolensk road twenty thousand strong, at a point four miles east of Vyazma as Eugène and Davout were approaching that city. On the morning of November 3 he attempted to cut off Davout and destroy the I Corps.

For four days Platov had been following on Davout's heels. The Marshal had retired unhurriedly and in good order. Eugène's IV Corps marched before him, preceded by Ney and Poniatowski. Napoleon led the march with the Guard and Junot's VIII Corps. The Emperor complained of Davout's slow withdrawal: "The Prince of Eckmühl," he wrote on November 3, "holds up the Viceroy [Eugène] and Prince Poniatowski for every Cossack charge that catches his eye."[16] He felt that the rear guard should have marched only three days behind the advance guard, rather than the five days distance which Davout had allowed to develop.[17] "The whole army," declares Ségur, "and the corps of Prince Eugène in particular, repeated these complaints."[18] Davout was criticized in general for having allowed the enemy to overtake the army because of his spirit of order and obstinacy.

The Marshal readily admitted his natural horror of every kind of disorder had at first slowed his march; but he believed it necessary to impose respect upon Platov so as to conceal from him the true condition of the French army, which, had he known, would only have served to encourage him and make him all the more aggressive.[19] Furthermore, his task was infinitely complicated by the scorched earth policy being carried out not by his rear guard but by the army before him which destroyed even the bridges he depended upon. Stragglers from every corps in the army, on foot, on horseback, and in vehicles, also compromised his work. "Every day he had to march between these wretches and the Cossacks, driving forward the one, and pressed by the other."[20] But Napoleon was not as interested in explanations as he was in results. By November 3 he had decided to replace Davout with Ney as commander of the rear guard.[21]

Before these corps could exchange marching positions, which was to have taken place at Vyazma, Miloradovich attacked in force. On the night of November 2, he moved into the gap between I and IV Corps. The action was lively from the beginning. Davout was threatened in front and on his flank by Miloradovich, and in the rear by Platov. He might well have recalled the words he wrote to his wife from Moscow less than a month ago: "Only peace can now save them [the Russian army] from total ruin; their army is no longer able to give battle; it is very tired, diminished and disorganized by the loss of generals and officers."[22] A complete about-face was now in the making. He it was who must fight to survive, and the worst was yet to come. Without the support of Eugène, his army corps, between fifteen and twenty thousand men, would have suffered enormous losses cutting its way through to Vyazma. But the Viceroy halted his Corps as soon as he heard gunfire behind him, and ascertaining that Davout was in difficulty, he sent a division back to attack the Russian units blocking the road from behind. The Marshal was able to ward off the attacks on his rear by

Platov with little effort; and the enemy blocking his advance astride the Smolensk road, caught in a cross fire, was forced to evacuate its position. Thus Davout was able to pass behind Eugène, who had taken up a defensive position, and move in on the Viceroy's right so that together they formed a front facing Miloradovich. This maneuver was not accomplished without units of the I Corps falling into momentary disorder. The Emperor's Master of the Horses and former ambassador to Russia, General Caulaincourt, wrote the following of this affair: "They [the Russians] inflicted severe damage on the I Corps, in which some disorder was shown when it passed ahead of the Viceroy's army. This disorder was still greater at the crossing of the bridge [over the Wiasma]. Until then—as long, that is, as it had to withstand alone the attack of the enemy—the I Corps had maintained its honor and reputation, although it was fiercely attacked and its formation broken by artillery. This momentary disorder was conspicuous because it was the first time that these gallant infantry broke their ranks and compelled their dogged commander to give ground. . . . The I Corps, which on taking the field was the largest and finest, a rival to the Guard, was thenceforward the hardest hit; and the evil spread." [23] In writing to Berthier the following day (November 4) Davout also mentioned the stragglers: "On this day order has been restored on the march; but there are four thousand men, belonging to every regiment of the army, who will not move with regularity; on the slightest attack on the part of the enemy they fly, and endanger the steadiness of my columns." [24]

The incident of the disorder is particularly important as the I Corps, along with the Guard, had formed the backbone of the Grand Army. It marked the beginning of disorganization and dissolution of the army.[25] This is not to imply cause but rather to single out the earliest indication of the pending disaster. The army was retreating. This was the first time that a substantial force was threatened with complete destruction. However, disaster was avoided at this point and the I Corps completely regained its order and poise while still under enemy fire. Then together with the IV Corps it withdrew to Vyazma in good order.

Passing through the already burning city, Davout took his new place in the marching line between Eugène and Ney. Ney, "the bravest of the brave," as Napoleon was to dub him, was better suited for the task of commanding a rear guard than the methodical Prince of Eckmühl. The army now passed through Dorogobuzh and moved on toward Smolensk. The weather turned colder and snow fell during the first week of November, but it was by no means severe. Food also became scarce, but, again, it was not acute before arriving at Smolensk. The army had departed from Moscow with fifteen day's rations and had found some supplies along the way. Yet the fact remains that it reached Smolensk in bad condition.

It was, nevertheless, still an army that reached Smolensk though an army on the point of despair and disintegration. Already the weak, sick, and seriously wounded were falling behind the retreating column and being killed by the Cossacks and peasants or dying of hunger and exposure. The leading corps found the warehouses well-stocked and eating their fill were able to rest "comfortably" for a few days. But as discipline broke down, and disorder and confusion took its place, plundering quickly depleted every kind of necessity. As the trailing corps entered the unhappy city it became increasingly difficult to find food. The army had been looking to Smolensk as the end of the "withdrawal." Here there was to be plenty!—food, rest, and shelter from the increasing cold. Here they would go into winter quarters and forget about war until the spring. But such was not to be their happy lot. Smolensk had become strategically untenable. Kutusov's now-aggressive army, superior in numbers and morale, was moving on the city from the south and east. Wittgenstein's Army of the North and Tshitshagov's Army of the South were attempting to force a junction at Minsk and completely sever all communications with Poland. Napoleon was therefore obliged to turn his eyes further west—to Vilna, or even the Niemen!

The French army numbered no more than fifty thousand effectives at Smolensk, including those troops which had been in the immediate vicinity.[26] In addition there were thousands of stragglers from every division in the army, who, without arms, seriously hampered the orderly movement of the various corps. Napoleon had sent Junot and Poniatowski ahead on November 12–13, and followed himself with the Guard on the fourteenth. Eugène marched out of the disorderly city on the fifteenth; while Davout and Ney were to depart on the Sixteenth. Ney would continue to form the rear guard. That marshal was instructed to blow up the city's defenses and everything of value to the enemy before leaving. If he deemed it necessary, he might delay his departure until the seventeenth.[27]

Davout had entered Smolensk on November 11. Most of his baggage train had been captured or destroyed in the combat before Vyazma. Arriving late at Smolensk, and realizing that the retreat was to continue, his troops supplied themselves as best they could. There were still provisions to be distributed, but they did not receive the six days' rations which those corps preceding them had received. (It might be noted that the Guard had received fifteen days' rations at Smolensk.) When Ney's hard-pressed III Corps arrived in the turbulent city on the fifteenth, they found even less than had the I Corps. Thousands of looters roamed the streets. The commissary staff had departed with the Emperor, and even a large portion of the flour which had been set aside for the rear guard had been pillaged. Ney immediately accused Davout of allowing his men free rein to loot the city and thus deprive his hungry and exhausted troops of the stores needed to enable them to continue the retreat. Davout denied the charges, declaring that not the men of the I Corps, who had been issued only a portion of the stores set aside for them, but the stragglers and civilians who roamed the streets, were the culprits. This reply did not satisfy the angry Ney, and a heated quarrel followed.[28]

On the sixteenth of November Davout marched his I Corps out of Smolensk along the Orsha road. Ney remained behind as was his option in accord with the orders he received from the Emperor.[29] The situation now became critical. The Russian army had overtaken the advanced French units at Krasny (Krasnoe). A determined and energetic commander could undoubtedly have brought the campaign to an end at this point. However, Kutusov declined, as he had at Maloyaroslavets, to engage in an all-out battle with the "invincible" Emperor. Whether because he believed that the winter would soon destroy the French army, or because he feared he would only compromise his reputation and that of the army by another defeat, is still a matter of conjecture. But the Russians allowed Napoleon and his Guard to pass almost unharmed.

Closing the road behind the Emperor, with a relatively weak force, Miloradovich, who commanded in the field, forced Eugène to fight his way through. Napoleon supported the IV Corps by sending back a battalion of the Guard which took the enemy in the rear.

With Eugène safely at Krasny, and the road once again closed by the enemy, the Emperor became concerned for the safety of Davout and Ney. The former realized by early afternoon on the sixteenth that trouble lay ahead. As the picture became clearer to Davout, he dispatched couriers to Ney at Smolensk informing him that the enemy was attempting to cut off their retreat—and that for him to delay any longer would seriously compromise his entire corps. He therefore strongly urged that marshal to march at once.[30] On the fifteenth and sixteenth Napoleon had repeatedly ordered both Davout and Ney to "quicken their pace" [31] as the danger was growing more acute. Despite Davout's warning, Ney remained in Smolensk until the morning of the seventeenth, declaring "that all the Cossacks in the universe should not prevent him from executing his instructions." [32] Ségur suggests that it was "an angry feeling against Davout" that caused Ney to reply in such a manner.[33] Yet he could hardly have departed before dark, which in November came in the late afternoon. Thus the most practical time for him to march was the morning of the seventeenth.

On the seventeenth Davout ran head-on into Miloradovich astride the high road. When Eugène heard the battle raging behind him, he countermarched one of his divisions and helped the trapped corps to cut its way through. Davout was outnumbered nearly three to one, "and it was only by the bravery and skill of the Prince of Eckmühl," wrote Labaume, "that the troops under his command were saved from absolute destruction." [34] The I Corps was also aided by Kutuzov's decision to concentrate on cutting off the rear guard. Had the Russian marshal committed his entire force to this action, Davout could not have broken through as he did—even if Eugène had countermarched with his entire command. The I Corps had again survived, but not without heavy losses. Davout had, in fact, waited too long for Ney to join him; and when at last Davout broke through to Krasny his own rear guard was cut off and forced back toward Smolensk. It joined Ney the following day and shared the fate of his unfortunate corps.[35]

When Ney reached Miloradovich's position on the eighteenth he found virtually the entire Russian army blocking his path. Believing at first that it was only a portion of Kutusov's force, he attacked it straight on. Thrown back with staggering losses, he took up a defensive position. When called upon to surrender, he refused. As dusk came on he withdrew several miles toward Smolensk and ordered his troops to build their fires for the night. After the men had eaten and rested a few hours, he left his fires burning and marched off to the north. Crossing the thin ice of the Dnieper he gained its right bank; but he had had to leave all baggage and artillery behind, as the ice would barely support the weight of a man. Though he avoided the main Russian army by this skillful maneuver, he was harassed all the way to Orsha by Platov's cavalry and Cossacks. On the afternoon of November 21, a Polish officer reached Orsha and informed Eugène that Ney was approaching the city on the right bank of the river under attack and in need of support. The Viceroy immediately marched out with the remnants of his corps and meeting Ney after dark brought him to Orsha. Ney had returned; but his corps had been reduced from six thousand to nine hundred effective troops.

Ney at once blamed Davout for having deserted him at Krasny. When the latter attempted to justify his action to the still-angry Marshal, he was cut short with: "Monsieur le maréchal, I have no reproaches to make to you; God is our witness and your judge!"[36] But judgment was not left to God; the entire army judged the unfortunate Davout, and his enemies at once found him guilty. He had never been popular with the army and had, in fact, made numerous enemies in high places, while on the other hand, Ney had become the hero of the campaign. He was loved by his men and admired by his officers. When he was believed lost Napoleon expressed profound sorrow.

It was then easy for the army in its grief over the assumed loss of Ney to vent its rage against Davout. Napoleon and Berthier had more personal reasons to saddle Davout with full responsibility for Ney's misfortune, for in doing so they might relieve themselves of the burden of guilt. So Davout became the scapegoat—the whipping boy for the entire army. With the Emperor setting the tone, wrote Caulaincourt, "It is impossible to describe the unbridled rage and fury that everyone showed towards Marshal Eckmühl, and scarcely any [restraint] even when he came into the presence of the Emperor, or when anyone met him face to face."[37] Nothing could have pleased Berthier and Murat more than this opportunity to take vengeance against their old enemy. Berthier in particular, wishing to vindicate himself and turn all against Davout, showed everyone who would look the orders he had sent to that Marshal to support Ney. Both he and Napoleon said Davout had direct orders to support the rear guard;[38] that as the rear guard set the pace of the retreat, depending on the obstacles with which the enemy confronted it, Davout should have modified his pace accordingly.[39]

All things being equal, Davout should indeed have modified his pace. Why he did not is explained, not justified, by the presence of the enemy astride the main road west. Davout had warned Ney of the danger and believed that he was unnecessarily jeapardizing the safety of his entire army corps. For Davout to wait for Ney would thus place the I Corps in the greatest of danger as the result of his colleague's poor judgment. Furthermore, Davout had no knowledge of the enemy's plans for destroying the rear guard, and could reasonably have expected Ney to fight his way through the enemy position if the I Corps could do so. However, the situation changed rapidly once Davout had passed the Russian position. He was driven on west by the enemy making it impossible for him to turn back and give Ney the kind of support which Eugène had given to him.

The news of Ney's safety served to lessen the attacks on Davout. Nevertheless, he had clearly fallen out of favor with the Emperor, a fact which enabled his enemies to drive him into the background. He had continually quarreled with kings, princes, and marshals. So long as the campaign had been successful—at least on the surface—the Emperor had been willing to overlook these petty jealousies and rivalries. Now however, disaster had overtaken the army. Since Napoleon could never bring himself to accept the responsibility for failure, Davout came under heavy attack. Despite the whole unpleasant affair, the retreat had to continue. And because Ney's corps had lost its effectiveness, Davout was again entrusted with the rear guard.[40]

The I Corps was now in wretched condition—as was the entire French army. Davout himself was hardly any better off than his troops. He had lost all of his personal belongings when the Russians captured the corps's baggage train at Krasny. His arrival at Orsha is described by Ségur in graphic terms: "This marshal had lost everything, was actually without linen, and emaciated with hunger. He seized upon a loaf which was offered him by one of his comrades, and voraciously devoured it. A handkerchief was given him to wipe his face, which was covered with grime."[41] There was some slight improvement at Orsha, for there the army found provisions of all kinds which were so desperately needed. The arsenal even contained thirty-six pieces of artillery which were distributed, complete with fresh horses, between Davout, Eugène, and Latour-Maubourg.

The army had suffered heavy losses in the march from Smolensk to Orsha. Its effective strength had been cut in half.[42] The I Corps could barely muster four thousand men for roll call. The distribution of food at Orsha and the opportunity to rest out of the range of Russian guns brought many stragglers back to their regiments—but this proved only to be temporary. As the doomed army approached the Berezina the number of stragglers again increased. The once proud army corps which had numbered between thirty and seventy thousand men was now reckoned in the hundreds.

Kutusov had fallen behind the fleeing French as a result of his attempt to cut off Ney at Krasny. Only light cavalry and Cossacks harassed Davout as he withdrew along the high road toward Borisov. Napoleon had planned to retreat behind the Berezina. Then with Minsk as a supply base, and reinforced by Victor's IX Corps, Oudinot's II Corps, which had joined him, and Schwarzenberg's Austrian Corps, he would hold the line along that river. Together with Wrede's VI Corps, which was in the vcinity of the headwaters of the Berezina, and the stragglers he hoped to rally about Minsk, the Emperor believed he could once again command an army of one hundred and twenty thousand men.[43] Nor did he abruptly alter this plan when he received news on November 18 that Minsk had been captured by Tshitshagov.

All hope of wintering in Russia was by now unrealistic. The northern Russian army under Wittgenstein, thirty thousand strong, and the southern army under Tshitshagov, thirty-four thousand strong, were converging on Borisov; while Kutusov, though he had fallen nearly two days behind the French and was making little effort to overtake them, still commanded some sixty-five thousand men. Napoleon was in the center of this triangle, and unless he could cross the Berezina all would be lost. Then on November 22 he received news from Oudinot that Tshitshagov had reached the Berezina and had crossed it to occupy Borisov. Though Oudinot was able to recapture the town, the Russians succeeded in burning the only bridge that offered the army a sure means of escape. To add to the rapidly deteriorating situation, a warming trend was breaking up the ice on the river. Oudinot was at once ordered to find suitable fording points. He found one north of Borisov at Studenka, and another south of the town at Bolshoi-Stakhov. Feinting south to draw Tshitshagov's attention, Napoleon threw two bridges across the Berezina at Studenka during the night of November 25–26. By one o'clock the following afternoon the infantry-cavalry bridge was completed, and Oudinot's corps began to file across. Taking up a position on the west bank of the river he defended the bridgehead, together with Ney (whose command had been substantially strengthened by units from the V Corps) while the rest of the army crossed on the twenty-seventh and twenty-eighth.

Davout had continued to bring up the rear along the Orsha-Borisov road. He was not pressed by the enemy, only harassed by their light troops. At night the Cossacks would shell his camp, and though this caused little damage, it did unnerve his men. The real problem which faced the Marshal was the enormous number of stragglers whom he was ordered to herd along before him. They stayed close to his troops for protection, but the least alarm caused them to panic and spread confusion in Davout's ranks.[44] Reaching Studenka on the night of the twenty-seventh, Davout crossed the Berezina the following day ahead of Victor, who had taken up a strong position to defend the eastern approaches to the bridgehead. The last corps (Victor's) crossed before dark. The bridges, which had several times broken and been repaired during the three days in use, were at last burned on the morning of the twenty-ninth as the Russian army approached. Although thousands of unarmed men, women, and even some children had been allowed to pass over the bridges between the various corps, perhaps some ten thousand were abandoned on the snow-covered east bank of the Berezina, as it was necessary to destroy the bridges before they fell into the hands of the enemy.

Napoleon now altered his plan of marching on Minsk, where he had hoped to gain support from Schwarzenberg in opening the way to the west. Instead, he set his course directly for Vilna, by way of Zembik. With Ney again replacing Davout as the rear guard, the bedraggled army passed over the marshes which covered the right bank of the Berezina. By burning the wooden bridges over the marshes the French succeeded in breaking contact with the main Russian armies. Only light cavalry and Cossacks now harassed them.

Where the enemy guns left off the Russian winter now picked up. The extreme cold which plagued the last weeks of the retreat has become legendary. Though it is difficult to exaggerate its ultimate effect on the French army, there are several aspects which are often misunderstood. One misconception is that winter came early in 1812 and was a major hardship throughout the retreat. "General Kreitz, who took part in the whole campaign, wrote: 'French writers unjustly declare that the cold was the cause of the destruction of Napoleon's army. From Maloyaroslavets to Vyazma, the weather was quite warm. Between Vyazma and Smolensk we had light frosts, and near Elna [November four] the first snow fell, but it was light. The Dnieper, however, was covered with a thin crust of ice, which no one ventured to walk on before Ney arrived there [November 15]. Between Smolensk and Borisov [November 26], the cold was more intense but still bearable; we camped at night without shelter.' General Kreitz spent his first night under a roof at Borisov. 'Between Borisov and Vilna the frost was extremely severe, and most of the French died on that stretch.' "[45] The Grand Army had begun to disintegrate shortly after Maloyaroslavets and was in an advanced state of decay *before* the weather became a major factor. To be sure it was the subzero temperatures, reaching 35–40 degrees below zero (Fahrenheit), which finished the army; but the weather may simply have done the Russians' work for them.

Most historians have stressed the effects of the cold on the French army, ignoring the fact that it was just as cold for the Russians. Kutusov's army had not been issued winter clothing and it suffered almost as severely from the freezing winds as the pursued. "After the crossing of the Berezina," wrote Baron Löwenstern who was with Kutusov, "terrible frosts set in. I was unable to remain on my horse for more than ten minutes, and as the snow made it very difficult to walk, I alternately mounted and dismounted, and allowed my Hussars to do the same. To keep my feet from freezing, I stuck them in the fur caps of the French grenadiers, which littered the road. My Hussars suffered severely. . . . The Sumsky regiment had no more than 70 horses capable of charging when we arrived at Vilna. . . . Our infantry was visibly disorganized. . . .

When our soldiers managed to get under a roof somewhere, it was absolutely impossible to get them out. They preferred to die." And again he wrote: "Only vodka sustained our strength. We suffered no less than the enemy." [46]

The Russian army was rapidly losing strength. Before Maloyaroslavets it had numbered some 97,000 men and 622 guns. When it reached Vilna in the second week of December only 27,464 men answered roll, and they had fewer than 200 guns.[47] But if the Russian army's sufferings were great, those of the French were truly unbearable. After the Berezina little thought was given to the enemy. Survival depended upon one's ability to defend himself from the cold, not the Russians. The most lively fighting between the rear guard and their pursuers was for the possession of a town or village in which both desired to spend the night, since it had become impossible to live through the long hours of darkness without shelter. The French soldiers who reached Vilna on December 8–10 no longer constituted an army. Even the Guard, which had "passed through our Cossacks like a hundred-gun warship through fishing boats," [48] had all but ceased to exist.

On December 5 Napoleon announced that he was leaving the army. There was nothing more he could do for the unhappy survivors by remaining with them. Whereas in Paris he could organize an army of one hundred thousand men for the spring campaign which would determine the fate of central Europe. Furthermore, the Malet Plot [49] indicated that his presence was needed in the capital to stabilize the government once the full details of the Russian disaster became known. The announcement was first made to the corps commanders at a dinner the Emperor gave for them at Smorgonie. He wished to win over all of his marshals to his plan, and to leave behind him as loyal and homogeneous a group as possible. Ségur describes his reception of Davout as follows: "Thus it was, that on perceiving Davout, he ran forward to meet him, and asked him why it was that he never saw him, and if he had entirely deserted him? And upon Davout's reply that he fancied he had incurred his displeasure, the Emperor explained himself mildly, receiving his answers favorably, confided to him the road he meant to travel, and took his advice, respecting its details." [50] He was kind and flattering to all present, and did what he could to create an amiable atmosphere on his last night with the army. After dinner he announced that he was leaving Murat in command of the army, and that Berthier would stay on as Major General. He asked them all to render to the King of Naples the same obedience that they had to him and to cooperate in every way possible for the good of the army. The following morning he departed for Paris. It was more than two years (June 20, 1815) before Davout would again see the Emperor.

The remnants of the army dragged on to Vilna, but it was in too degenerate a state to defend the city. The soldiers were able to eat and rest well for several nights. But with the Russian approach in force, Murat ordered the retreat to continue toward the Niemen on December 10 in the desperate hope that the enemy would end the pursuit at their frontier. Five miles west of Vilna an icy hill proved the final obstacle to all wheeled vehicles, including the artillery. The French horses had not been rough-shod, as was the custom in Russia, and the exhausted animals were unable to keep their footing. Nevertheless the loss of these vehicles did serve the purpose of detaining the pursuing Cossacks, who stopped to pillage the wagons. On December 13 Murat reached the Niemen at Kovno. Here he found the river frozen solid, and of no value whatsoever defensively. The condition of the army had worsened—if that were possible. There was nothing for him to do but to order the retreat to continue. However, the main Russian army did not cross the Prussian frontier in strength. Kutuzov went into winter quarters at Vilna, and Tshitshagov on the east bank of the Niemen. Only Platov was authorized to follow the enemy as far as possible. Wittgenstein was sent north to intercept Macdonald, who was retiring from Riga. In fact, however, there was no French army after Vilna, only fleeing soldiers.

When Murat reached Gumbinnen he found himself only lightly pursued. Therefore, he gave the men several days needed rest and held a council of war on December 17, which was attended by the marshals and corps commanders. The King of Naples had reached the point of despair. This brave warrior, who had daily faced death as readily as the least soldier of his vanguard, was at the breaking point. To lead a cavalry charge against overwhelming odds was one thing; to command a ruined and fleeing army was quite another. Denouncing his brother-in-law as a madman, he declared that there was no longer any safety in supporting his cause, and that no monarch in Europe could rely on his word.[51] Repenting that he had not made his peace with England as Bernadotte had done, he reflected on the manner in which Napoleon had removed his younger brother Louis from the throne of Holland. "Seeing that the Prince of Neufchatel [Berthier] remained silent," wrote Davout shortly after the incident, "I pointed out to the King, without forgetting for one instant the respect which I owed to a sovereign, and in particular to a King-brother-in-law *dumien,* that duty required that I remind him that he was only King by the grace of the Emperor and the blood of Frenchmen, that he was also a French prince and that his duty prescribed that he not make peace with the enemies of the Emperor without his consent." [52]

Murat persisted in his opinion and added "that he was King of Naples just as the Austrian Emperor was Emperor of Austria, and he could do as he pleased." [53] This was the last encounter between these two antagonists. After Davout's departure for Thorn, Murat quit the army, turning over his command to the Viceroy. These two great soldiers were never again to see one another before the King was executed by a Neapolitan firing squad on October 13, 1815.

13

The Siege of Hamburg

NAPOLEON'S DEPARTURE from the doomed army on December 6, 1812, was truly its death blow. Since the crossing of the Berezina, the presence of the Emperor had been the sole force around which the weary troops had rallied. The news of his departure, coupled with an extreme cold wave, led to the complete disintegration of the Grand Army. The flight into Poland was headlong and without any consideration of establishing a line of defense. Napoleon had first hoped to hold the Niemen. When this proved unrealistic, he ordered the "army" to defend the Vistula. Time was what he needed most now for back in Paris he was busily stamping out of the ground an army for the forthcoming spring campaign.

As the debris of the once-mighty army trudged westward from Vilna, rallying points were established along the Vistula in the hope that the soldiers would rejoin their corps. The I Corps was assigned Thorn, and Davout, with a handful of officers, reached that city on December twenty-fourth. As the last week of 1812 wore on, the wretched remains of the corps staggered into the Polish city. Of the nearly seventy thousand men who had crossed the Niemen under his command only eight hundred officers and fifteen hundred men could now be counted, and many of these were sick or wounded.[1] Even those soldiers who were capable of bearing arms were lacking the most basic equipment, having discarded everything but food and clothing in the last phase of the retreat. The plain truth was, as Napoleon soon learned, that all corps were in as bad—or worse—

condition as the I Corps; and even with the reserve units, such as General Wrede's corps,[2] the Vistula could not be held.

Davout remained four weeks in Thorn during which time he strengthened and reorganized the city's defenses, and fought minor engagements with advanced Russian patrols and bands of Cossacks. But when the enemy advanced in force, the French abandoned the Vistula and withdrew, this time in good order, to the west. The Marshal, having left a garrison of eighteen hundred men to hold Thorn, marched on Jaunary 21 toward Posen. Here, on January 31, he received orders from Eugène, who had succeeded Murat as commander of the army, to fall back on Magdeburg.[3] Retiring through Küstrin and Stettin he reached his destination on February 14. The retreat, which had begun from Moscow, had at last come to an end; and the French army, reinforced, reorganized, and reequipped, now took up a defensive position along the Elbe which it could reasonably hope to hold.

In the first phase of the campaign of 1813 Davout played a secondary role. Confusion, which resulted primarily from Napoleon's absence from army headquarters and the necessity for Eugène to make decisions on the scene—decisions which did not always fit into his stepfather's plans—caused Davout to travel to Leipzig and Dresden. Then in mid-April he was given command of the 32nd Military Division,[4] which included the whole of the lower Elbe from Magdeburg to Hamburg. This move was prompted by unfavorable reports from the north. General Carre St.-Cyr, who commanded the garrison in Hamburg, had evacuated that strategically important city on March 12. Faced with a popular revolt,[5] he had received false rumors which led him to believe that large enemy forces were approaching. The fact was that Wittgenstein had dispatched several small "free corps" into Mecklenburg to harass and confuse the French. One of these, led by Tettenborn, occupied Hamburg on March 18 as Carre St.-Cyr fell back on Bremen.

Napoleon was extremely displeased by the news of the loss of Hamburg, and reprimanded Carre St.-Cyr for having surrendered the key to the north without having fired a shot.[6] Davout would thus have to fight his way into his new command. This task the Marshal gave to General Vandamme, who had recently been placed under his orders. Vandamme, a general of division of long standing, was an outspoken maverick who had proven himself uncontrollable by marshals and kings under whom he had served in past years. Yet he was an excellent field commander, whose services Napoleon needed in these difficult days. The Emperor thus placed him under the orders of the one marshal who, by virtue of his own military and disciplinary reputation, Vandamme would obey. There was no love between these two soldiers, but there was an accord. Davout dealt with the General in a respectful manner, but as a subordinate; and Vandamme obeyed without his customary sarcasm and insubordination.

Advancing on Hamburg from the southwest Vandamme attacked and captured Harburg (April 29), and then turned his attention to the islands below Hamburg which were formed by the arms of the Elbe. These were taken during the second week of May. On the eighteenth the Danish garrison at Altona (on the north bank of the Elbe) received orders to support the French in accordance with a reassurance treaty signed between their two governments. The citizens of Hamburg and their Russian allies quickly requested Swedish help. The Swedish general Dobeln answered by sending two battalions to the hard-pressed city, but when Bernadotte, who now commanded an Allied Army of the North, heard of this he deemed it too risky and ordered their withdrawal (May 26). Increased French pressure supported by a Danish division and coupled with the news of French victories between the upper Elbe and Oder, caused Tettenborn to evacuate Hamburg on May 30 without signing a capitulation. That same day the citizens opened the city's gates to the Danes. After two and a half months Hamburg was once again in French hands.

The unfortunate inhabitants of Hamburg, who had enjoyed the advantages—as well as the disadvantages—of having been annexed to France, and who were therefore French citizens, were now treated as rebellious stepchildren. Davout, who had been holding the lower Elbe between Hamburg and Magdeburg, entered the newly won city on May 31. In his knapsack he brought the vengeance of the Emperor in the form of a decree suspending constitutional rule, and a letter of instructions from Berthier. Napoleon was fearful that the various German states, which had lost their independence during the course of France's rise to dominance in the past twenty years, would follow the example of Hamburg and proclaim their sovereignty once again and support his enemies. He therefore was determined to make an example of the city, which had set up a senatorial government and invited the Russians to aid them in their defiance of French rule. The letter of instructions to Berthier—assuming the Emperor put his wishes in writing—has not been preserved; but that of the Prince de Neufchatel to Davout spelled out in unmistakable terms the vengeance of the Emperor. When General Vandamme would capture Hamburg, wrote Berthier in code on May 7, 1813:

> This is what you will do:
>
> You will arrest immediately those subjects of Hamburg who have taken service under the title of Senators. You will hand them over to a military commission, and you will shoot the five most guilty. You will send the others under heavy escort to France to be retained in a state prison. You will sequester their belongings, and declare them confiscated. The state will take possession of their houses, land, etc.
>
> You will disarm the city, have all officers of the "Anseatique Legion" shot, and you will send all enlisted men to France to be put in the galleys.
>
> You will make a list of 1500 of the wealthiest rebels in the 34th [*sic*] Division; have them arrested, sequester their belongings and then confiscate them. This measure will also be necessary in the city of Oldenburg.
>
> You will impose a contribution of 50 million on the cities of Hamburg and Lubeck. You will take measures to have this sum apportioned, and to assure its prompt payment.
>
> You will disarm the countryside and arrest all who are traitors. Their property will be confiscated. . . .
>
> All of these actions are rigorous; the Emperor does not leave you free to modify them in any way.[7]

In order to be sure that these instructions reached Davout, Berthier wrote a second letter on the same day (May 7), shorter than the first but containing essentially the same message, and sent it by a separate courier.[8]

Davout was shocked by the severity of these measures, and recognizing in them Napoleon's impulsive reactions at a time when all was not going well politically or militarily, he played for time so as to soften the punishment of the unfortunate German population under his authority.[9]

By his actions, rather than by words, Davout circumvented the harshest provisions of the Emperor's revenge; but Napoleon was not quick to allow his lieutenant to exercise moderation. On June 7, 1813, he wrote to Davout: "I am in agreement with the coded letter of the Major General of May 7."[10] This was followed on June 17, by: "Carry out the military trials, and, to make an example, have the first person who will be convicted of having concealed his gun shot."[11] But the Marshal was determined not to execute civilians, and to do the least amount of harm possible.[12]

Davout, the soldier and administrator, cared little for the command with which he was now burdened. He would have preferred to have been with the Emperor in the main theater of fighting, rather than punishing German civilians for not being good Frenchmen. Napoleon sent him to Hamburg because he needed an administrator who knew the district and the people,[13] and a soldier who could—and would—carry out orders effectively in his absences. Indeed, the Marshal did act in the best interest of the Emperor—if not in exact accordance with his instructions.

First of all, none of the Senators who had formed the "rebel" government in Hamburg fell into Davout's hands.[14] This eliminated the possibility of their executions. Secondly, though he did make arrests upon his arrival, there were no deportations. Virtually all of the officers of the Hanseatic Legion fled the city with the Senators before effective French controls could be imposed.

Immediately following his arrival in the city, Davout began his own campaign to secure an amnesty for all civilians in Hamburg as well as those who would return from their self-imposed exile. These efforts culminated in his letter of June 20: "Sire, I have the honor of sending to Your Majesty a copy of the order which I issued on the first day of the occupation of Hamburg. During the necessary intervals which elapsed before the lists were drawn up, and before I had named the secret commission to designate the five most guilty persons to be judged by a military commission was announced, I had received a letter from the Major General relative to the return of those who had fled the city under pain of having their belongings confiscated. . . . I am convinced that the order for these people to return should imply the promise that there will be no punitive action taken against them if they obey the injunction. . . . I regard it as my duty to inform Your Majesty that I believe that it would be in your best interest to punish these people by fines only. . . . I assure you Sire that if I were authorized to issue a clemency that it would produce the best effect on the collection of the contribution, while at the same time improving the morale of the inhabitants." [15]

Napoleon, who was in greater need of money than he was of vengeance, saw the wisdom of the Marshal's words. "My cousin," he wrote Davout on July 1, "I leave you master of the situation, if you judge it to be in my best interest to publish an amnesty for those who will return within forty-five days, it will meet with my approval. The best way to punish merchants is, in fact, to make them pay." [16] But making the "sugar merchants of Hamburg" [17] pay forty-eighty million francs, which Napoleon levied upon the district, proved a somewhat difficult task. When Davout sent a report indicating that the city could not raise such a large sum before 1815,[18] the needy Emperor countered with a formula. It called for ten million to be paid at once in hard cash—Davout already had six million of this—then the Bank of Hamburg would put up twenty million to be paid at the rate of two million a month beginning October 1, 1813. An additional fifteen million was to be paid in kind: cloth, linen, wine, brandy, spices, etc. The three million francs balance would be paid in the form of wages for the troops of the 32nd Military Division.[19]

This solution to the "War Contribution" demanded by the Emperor represented a concession on his part, but not the one which the leading citizens of Hamburg were seeking. They had hoped to have the amount reduced, and indicated a lack of willingness to cooperate. They sent a deputation to Dresden to plead their case before the Emperor. Napoleon became angry when he learned of their reaction to his "generous" offer. He refused to see the deputation and ordered them to leave Dresden within twenty-four hours. He then wrote Davout: "The crime of rebellion and treachery which they [the people of Hamburg] have committed has stripped them of all their properties and civil rights, the war contribution is their redemption." [20] He also demanded that the full contribution—48 million francs—be collected without delay. To expedite payment he ordered Davout to confiscate all shops, stores, warehouses, and so forth, in Hamburg, and if necessary to ship their goods to France or other parts of Germany to be sold in order to raise the money. Only after full payment had been made would he "give them back their civil rights, and their property." [21]

The Emperor was forcing the hand of his hesitating Marshal. The result was that the severe military government became even more burdensome despite Davout's efforts toward moderation. While it is true that only ten million francs of the contribution was paid before the city was encircled in November,[22] the Marshal did collect additional monies to support his army during the siege of 1813–14. Furthermore, Napoleon, whose anger was tempered to some extent during the summer of 1813, allowed Davout a rather free hand in issuing an amnesty. Promulgated on July 24, the document stated: "An amnesty is accorded for all acts of insurrection, rebellion and desertion committed up to this date in the thirty-second Military Division." [23] Article 2 then listed the twenty-eight men who were exceptions to the amnesty,[24] all of whom had gone into exile when the French reoccupied Hamburg and Lübeck. In this manner Davout was able to satisfy the Emperor's earlier instructions without actually making political arrests. However, the property and belongings of the twenty-eight persons were confiscated. Contrary to the Marshal's expectations the amnesty did not serve the purpose of enticing those who had fled from the reoccupied cities to return. Very few reentered Hamburg before the siege. Almost without exception those in exile waited to see the outcome of the fall campaign, and, after the French defeat at Leipzig, decided to await Davout's expulsion. It would be a full year before the Hamburg exiles would be able to reenter their native city, but Davout's absence from Savigny would be more than three years.

At the conclusion of the Russian campaign, when many of the marshals and generals had returned to France to spend time with their families, Davout had remained with the army. As anxious as anyone, and with far better reason than most, he desired to be with his wife who, in January, was about to give birth to their seventh child. She wrote to him in mid-February that "everyone is arriving: soon you will be the only marshal with the army." [25] He repeatedly requested leave,[26] but the Emperor did not grant his wish. The remnants of the shattered army pouring westward from Russia required regrouping and reorganizing. After pulling together the stragglers of his I Corps, and expanding its ranks with replacements, the Marshal was ordered back to the Elbe to continue the formation of the new army. When in midsummer the I Corps was again one of the finest in the army, Napoleon called it to Dresden. But he placed General Vandamme in command of the Corps; and creating a new corps, the XIII, he assigned the task of its formation, organization, and supplying to Davout.[27] It becomes quite clear at this point that the Emperor felt in greater need of the proven administrative service of the Marshal than of his equally proven military services.

Both the Davouts were disappointed when the Marshal was informed that he would be given leave as soon as the situation made possible his absence. However, both submitted their wills to the Emperor and began to think in terms of Madame Davout's going to Germany rather than his returning to France. On June 4 an armistice was signed by the belligerents which proved to be the timely catalyst that made the long overdue reunion possible. After much correspondence[28] and delays caused by the illnesses of Jules and Madame Leclerc, the reunion was realized. Leaving the baby at home, but bringing the other small children, Aimée arrived in Hamburg on July 21. The length of her visit was determined by the negotiations at Prague. When on August 11 the Marshal received word from the Emperor that the armistice would most likely be denounced by the enemy on the tenth and fighting would resume by the sixteenth or seventeenth, Aimée, whose bags had been packed for several days, made her final preparation to leave the war zone. The Marshal crossed the Elbe with his family on the twelfth and bade them farewell at the outskirts of Harburg. This reunion had been a happy one, filled with hope for the future.

The Marshal's faith in Napoleon's ability to solve his—and France's—problems on the battlefield had not been shaken by the events of the preceding year.[29] He continued to place full blame for Europe's troubles squarely on the shoulders of England. "I believe that France and Europe desire peace;" he had written just before the armistice, "but with the petty passions of our enemies [England], the Emperor is not able to conclude it as quickly as he wishes."[30] After the resumption of hostilities he declared: "The Emperor is unable to make peace; England dominates the coalition."[31]

By 1813 Marshal Davout had developed a hatred for both England and Russia, and in a letter to his wife he gives full vent to the new brand of nationalism which was inspired by the French Revolution and Empire. "I am perfectly satisfied with the educational methods used for our daughters," he wrote Aimée on April 7, 1813. "I would recommend to you that you inspire in our two sons a strong hatred for the English and the Russians. Louis should direct all of his hate against the Russians, and Jules against the English: I wish to inspire in him [Jules] a desire for service in the navy. I know that these sentiments of which I speak are not to be found in the heart of a woman, but *they must enter into the heart of a Frenchman* [italics author's]." [32] But if the French disliked the Russians and cared less for the English, it was war that they had truly come to hate. The renewal of hostilities in mid-August was received throughout France with great disappointment.

Davout had been kept informed of the peace negotiations and the likelihood of their failure. But the most disheartening news was not that the fight was resuming—this he had come to expect—rather it was the entry of Austria into the war on the side of the Allies. This increased the enemy's strength by some two hundred and forty thousand men on the Emperor's exposed right flank. In a letter to the Marshal dated August 5, at Dresden, Napoleon spelled out his strategy for the opening of the new campaign. Marshal Oudinot, with an army of sixty thousand men, would march north from the Lübben-Luckau vicinity to Berlin. At the same time Davout would advance his XIII Corps (thirty thousand men) eastward through Mecklenburg toward Stettin. It was hoped that this combined move of ninety thousand men would push the Allies' Army of the North, commanded by the Swedish crown prince (Bernadotte), back across the Oder and relieve the encircled garrison at Stettin.[33]

The XIII Corps was composed of three divisions: the 3rd Division commanded by General Henri-Louis Loison, the 40th Division commanded by General Thiébault, and the 50th with General Vechery in command. In addition to these troops the Marshal had the Danish division of Prince Frederick of Hesse under his orders.[34] Davout's total strength was approximately forty-three thousand men when the campaign was renewed.[35] However, with eight thousand men in the Hamburg and Harburg garrisons, three thousand more spread out in the towns and cities of the 32nd Military Division, and five thousand in the hospital, the Marshal's actual field command stood at only twenty-seven thousand men.[36]

Davout began operations on August 17. Fighting was light as

the Swedish corps before him under General Wegesack fell back in good order. By the twenty-third the French had reached Schwerin and occupied most of western Mecklenburg. Davout now halted his small army and sent out only reconnaissance patrols. He had very little information of the enemy's strength or position. Nor had he received any word from Oudinot, who should have been in Berlin on August 20 or 21. Oudinot had advanced on the Prussian capital, but when one of his unsupported corps (Reynier's) was stopped at Grossbeeren (within twenty miles of Berlin) and pushed back, he quickly retired on Wittenberg. This premature retreat, for Oudinot had not been defeated, left Napoleon's left flank dangerously exposed, and Davout's right flank seriously exposed.[37]

News of Oudinot's failure and of Bernadotte's advance toward the Elbe filtered north to Davout's headquarters by the end of August. Cooperation with Oudinot was now out of the question as far as offensive operations were concerned, and the position of the XIII Corps at Schwerin was a weak one from a defensive point of view. Therefore, Davout, who was now left completely without new orders, reverted to his secondary mission—that of the defense of Hamburg and Holstein. On September 2, his army began to fall back to a defensible line.[38] This new position rested on the Elbe above Hamburg, and ran north along the old Stecknitz Canal through Ratzeburg to the Baltic. Here Davout awaited new orders and the news of new French victories from the upper Elbe-Oder theater of operations. The Marshal still had complete confidence that the Emperor would attain a military solution to his problem. However, if he was surprised by the "solution" which was rendered by the Battle of Leipzig (October 16–18), he was not caught unprepared.

Since his entry into Hamburg at the end of May 1813, Davout had been preparing the defenses of the city. It had become his principal base of supplies and the focal point of his command. During the summer months he viewed Hamburg as a base of operations for a drive on Berlin and the lower Oder. But early in September, with no news from the Emperor on the conduct of the war in the Dresden-Leipzig theater and with the failure of Oudinot's advance on the Prussian capital, he began to think more seriously about the defensive aspects of Hamburg. On September 8, he wrote to the Count de Chaban, quartermaster general of finances at Hamburg:

"It is important to take immediate measures to have . . . provisions for 30,000 men for 7 to 8 months, and forage for 5,000 horses for the same length of time."[39] Then on October 16, as Napoleon was fighting for Germany at Leipzig and ten days before the news of the battle reached his headquarters, Davout issued orders for the civilian population of Hamburg to stock enough supplies to enable them to sustain a prolonged siege which could last until July 1814.[40] Unfortunately, the inhabitants did not take this warning seriously, and the Marshal did not have the means to force them to act. By the end of the first week of November his position at the mouth of the Elbe looked dark indeed. On the ninth of that month he re-instructed the civilian authorities in Hamburg that the city's population must either make provisions for an eight-month siege or leave the city.

Davout's line of retreat was cut by the advancing Allied armies early in November. The XIII Corps was isolated from France and the orders of the Emperor. The last set of instructions from Napoleon came in the form of a letter from General Carre St.-Cyr, the former commander of Hamburg. Dated November 5, but not arriving at Davout's headquarters until the eleventh, it read: "Monsieur Marshal, it is the intention of the Emperor, by his orders from Mayence, dated November 1st that you leave a strong garrison at Hamburg, and fall back into Holland, or, if there was not time to make this movement, to maneuver on Hamburg."[41] In the justification of his actions during 1813–14, which Davout addressed to Louis XVIII in the summer of 1814, he declared that it was no longer possible for him to retire on Holland as the enemy occupied the left bank of the Elbe in force. Furthermore, to have left a strong garrison in Hamburg would have been to sacrifice them for they could not have held out long against the vast numerical supperiority of the enemy.[42] He therefore concluded that the only course of action open to him was to fall back upon the prepared defenses of Hamburg and to hold that strategic city until the Emperor could reorganize his military strength in the spring of 1814, drive the Allied armies back across the Elbe, and raise the siege.

Though he realized early in November that he would have to retreat to within the fortified circumference of greater Hamburg, the Marshal ordered the Stecknitz line to be held until the river and canal would freeze solid and no longer serve as a defensive barrier.

This gave the defenders an additional three weeks to gather supplies for the coming siege and to work on the defenses. When the temperature dropped sharply on December 2 all was ready, and the XIII Corps retired in an orderly fashion into Hamburg.

The position which Davout had prepared at the mouth of the Elbe was by no means limited to the city of Hamburg. It also included the suburbs adjacent to the city and even some of the small villages on the right bank of the river. Several hamlets on the left bank of the Elbe were also an intricate part of this fortified system, as well as some strategic islands in the river which were deemed necessary for the protection of Hamburg and the lines of communication with Harburg. The total strength of the besieged garrison was forty-two thousand men, but eight thousand of this number were already in hospitals. Only a small percentage of these men had been wounded in combat, as there had been only minor engagements with the enemy during the months of October and November. Dysentery was the army's principal disabler, and a large majority of the men eventually were returned to active duty. The defenders were supported by adequate artillery. The three hundred and fifty heavy-caliber guns which ringed the impregnable position were supported by an additional seventy-six six- and twelve-pound fieldpieces which could be concentrated at any point of attack. The number of horses—seventy-five hundred—was more than adequate for defensive purposes, and, in fact, supplemented the meat ration for the army during the winter months. The thirty-eight hundred cavalry mounts had been carefully selected from the ten thousand horses purchased in Denmark during the summer. They were well cared for throughout the siege and made up the bulk of the four thousand animals which returned to France with the Corps in 1814.[43]

The name of Marshal Davout became synonymous with all of the misfortunes and sufferings of the civilian population of Hamburg during the siege. Not since the wars of religion of the seventeenth century had a German city come to hate one man as Hamburg came to hate Davout. The ordinary miseries of a prolonged siege through winter months would have been sufficient by themselves to render his name odious, but there were some particular aspects of this siege which compounded the resentment. The principal problem was that the German population did not consider this struggle to be theirs, or to be in their best interest. It was an unwelcome French army in their city being attacked by what they considered to be a friendly Russian army. They wished to see the siege ended by the defeat of the defending forces. Thus they were unwilling to make any sacrifice in order to prolong the siege, and the discomforts forced upon them were deeply resented. This basic attitude was also an underlying factor in their strong resentment of the destruction of parts of the city's suburbs by order of the commanding officer, his acquisition of funds from the Bank of Hamburg, and his expulsion of twenty-five thousand inhabitants during the course of the siege.[44]

The defenses of the city of Hamburg had been allowed to fall into decay by its commercially minded leaders. What defenses did exist in 1813 were antiquated and totally inadequate. Davout was therefore forced to start almost from scratch in June when the Emperor ordered him to prepare the city as a defensive strongpoint in the north. Major earthworks were constructed and the old ramparts strengthened or replaced. Some buildings had to be leveled, but not many in number. Then in the beginning of November, when it became certain that there would be a winter siege and that the enemy forces would outnumber the defenders by at least two to one, Davout further undertook to strengthen his position. More houses were torn down in order to clear fields of fire for the artillery.[45] By the end of December it became clear to the Marshal that the enemy had found the weak link in his chain of defense. This was the section of the front facing Altona. It thus became "necessary" from a military point of view—the only point of view ever held by Marshal Davout—to destroy the suburbs of Hamburgerberg and St. Pauli[46] in the first week of 1814.[47] The suffering of the unfortunate civilians was made particularly grievous because of the short notice they were given to gather their valuables and evacuate their homes in the dead of winter. The most regrettable aspect of this operation was the destruction of a hospital. The sick were evacuated to Eppendorf, but as a result of the move several of them died.[48] Davout justified these actions, which he had hoped would not have been necessary and had therefore postponed them until the last possible moment, on the grounds that the city of Hamburg could not sustain a major attack at this point unless they were carried out. The authority for such an undertaking was based upon Article 95 of the imperial decree dated December 24, 1811: "The Governor or Commander of a fortress is armed with sufficient power to destroy everything in the interior of the place which would hinder the movement of troops or artillery, as well as all of that outside of the place, which would serve to facilitate the enemy's approach." [49]

The dismantling of the suburbs before and during the siege affected primarily the working-class population. The criticism which was directed against Davout by the vocal middle and upper classes following the French evacuation was of a moral and philosophical nature. But it is not surprising that the act for which the Marshal was most bitterly and passionately attacked is that of having laid hands on the funds of the Bank of Hamburg. By his own accounting Davout took 12,542,664.80 francs from the bank during 1813–14.[50] Napoleon, whose shortage of money had become critical by the summer of 1813, had agreed on June 16 to accept in lieu of the full forty-eight million franc war contribution levied on Hamburg ten million francs in cash at that time and the balance in merchandise and time payments. These time payments were to be two million francs a month beginning October 1, 1813, and continuing until August 10, 1814. The Bank of Hamburg was designated as the responsible agency for these payments.[51] Napoleon believed that Davout's financial needs would thus be taken care of as the Marshal collected the contribution. But even before Hamburg was cut off from France in November, it had become perfectly clear that no more could be collected from the local population without inflicting disastrous economic harm. Therefore, Davout decided to use the funds in the Bank of Hamburg to meet the obligations of the army and French government in the besieged city. The money was used to continue the work of preparing the city's fortifications, to support the military hospitals, to pay the army, and to run the government.[52]

The moneyed class of Hamburg immediately raised the cry of theft, despite the careful and thoroughly legal method in which all transactions were carried out with the bank. Attempts were made after the siege to have the government of Louis XVIII repay the twelve million francs, and some irresponsible individuals went so far as to accuse Davout of having personally profited from the transaction—a statement for which there is absolutely no evidence. Yet the name of Davout continued to be associated with this affair throughout the nineteenth century. On May 14, 1890, Field Marshal

Count von Moltke—the famed chief of the German General Staff—declared before the German Reichstag: "Did we not see in 1813, when he was already in full retreat, a Marshal of France put his hands on the funds of the Bank of Hamburg, during that vile French period." [53] But when Davout's daughter, the Marquise of Blocqueville, called upon the aging Field Marshal to clarify his statement, he was quick to write to her: "In my discourse before the Reichstag I mentioned the seizure of the Bank of Hamburg which is a historical fact. It is evident that the French General in this case acted only on the orders of his government, which he was obliged to obey. If, however, the expression which I used was able to be interpreted to imply that Marshal Davout had been guided by personal interest, I regret to have badly chosen my words." [54]

The citizens of Hamburg who had not—or who were unable to—provide sufficient food for themselves were ordered out of the city on December 19, 1813. "All of those who are unable to provide for themselves six months of food," the order read, "must leave the city 48 hours after the publication of this order." [55] In addition to those persons the Marshal also ordered that "all persons who were born outside of the walls of Hamburg must leave the city within 24 hours, that is to say between noon and 2 P.M. of the 20th." [56] The abruptness with which this expulsion was carried out added to the misery of those involved and can hardly be justified. Davout undoubtedly knew in advance that this action would have to be taken, and even if he arrived at the decision on December 19, he could have reduced the suffering of the twenty-five thousand civilians involved by allowing them more time to prepare for their departure.

Davout justified the expulsion on the grounds of military expediency. "In all places in a state of siege," reads Article 95 of the imperial decree of December 24, 1811, "when the enemy is within three days march of the place, the governor or commander is authorized without waiting to declare a state of siege, the expulsion of useless mouths, foreigners and individuals singled out by the civil and military police." [57] To have allowed twenty-five thousand men, women and children to remain in the besieged city, Davout pointed out in his *Mémoire au Roi* (1814), would have resulted in one of two eventualities: either he would have had to feed them from the army's rations, or they would have died of starvation. If he had followed the first solution, it would have shortened the length of time which he could possibly hold the city from seven to four months. Thus he would have had to surrender Hamburg to the enemy by the end of March. Since he could not expect the Emperor to rally his forces and launch an offensive before May, there would have been little to gain from holding the city through the winter. This solution was, therefore, not deemed acceptable. On the other hand, should he have allowed this mass of *bouches inutiles* to remain in the city without feeding them, the degree of suffering would have been infinitely greater than that endured as the result of their expulsion.[58]

Davout carried out what he believed to be his duty. "I would have liked to have abandoned Hamburg," he declared later, but "to follow my instruction, [I] had to make Hamburg a respectable fortress."[59] Thus he followed that course of action which would allow the longest possible siege and least amount of suffering. That this least amount of suffering was nevertheless enormous for the civilian population he did not deny, but rather declared that it could not be avoided. He had his orders, and as a soldier they had to be carried out. Civilian discomforts were of secondary importance. During the Nuremburg trials of the post–World War II years, German officers were sentenced to life imprisonment when they based their defense on following the orders of their superiors. Indeed had Davout been tried by a war crimes court in Germany in 1814, he would surely have been found guilty of crimes against the people of Hamburg. But to have followed orders was still sufficient at that time to vindicate the commander of an army, and, as a matter of fact, Napoleon himself was not even imprisoned after his first abdication in 1814. "I was severe, it is true," Davout admitted publicly in his *Mémoire,*[60] however, he believed that the situation in which he found himself demanded the actions he took.

The principal concern of Marshal Davout, and the one which overshadowed all others was that of rendering "the French name respectable to the enemy."[61] While he did not look upon the German population of Hamburg as his ally, none the less he did not consider them to be his enemy as he did the Allied armies besieging him. Bennigsen, and in particular ex-Marshal Bernadotte, would know that they had indeed engaged a French army whatever might be the outcome. With communications severed between France and Hamburg, and with no possibility of fighting his way back across the Rhine, Davout was determined that he and the XIII Corps would write a chapter of military history which could stand with honor along side those of Austerlitz, Auerstädt, Eckmühl, and Wagram.

The defensive military operations of Hamburg were carried out with such skill and success as to make them the classic example to be studied throughout the next half century. The besieged garrison not only tied down three times its own number throughout the last five months of the war, it also beat back determined efforts to break the city. Davout was untiring in his efforts to strengthen his position, and work was still going on in April 1814 when the fighting came to an end. His troops were well cared for in virtually every respect. They had good housing, were well clothed and shod, and never missed a meal. The quality of the wine may have declined as the siege was prolonged into the spring, and the amount of horse meat may have increased, but hunger—the bitterest enemy of a besieged garrison—was unknown. In the hospitals conditions were good. The best food and wine was served to the men there.[62] As the number of wounded increased sharply with the heavy fighting in February, Davout pressed the unwilling doctors of the city into service. "The doctors, surgeons and pharmacists of Hamburg who will not fulfill their duty," Davout ordered on February 27, 1814, "will be arrested and confined in a house which will be prepared for this occasion and from which they will be conducted daily to the hospitals to make their visits; they will then be returned to this house."[63]

As was customary in Davout's command, and even more necessary under the extreme conditions of siege, discipline was "severe"—even by the Marshal's own admission.[64] This severity not only kept the garrison in trim fighting condition, but it also worked to the benefit of the civilian population. There was virtually no pillaging, stealing, or burning on the part of the French soldiers, and the women of the city were perfectly safe on the streets even during the long winter nights.[65]

There was little actual fighting during the month of December 1813. The Allied army, which was principally composed of Russian troops supported by German units, followed the French as they retired from the Stecknitz line early in the month. It was not until January that Bennigsen was ready to begin operations against the Hamburg defenses. At that time Bernadotte arrived before the city with his combined Swedish-German army. This raised the strength of the besieging army to better than one hundred and twenty thousand men,[66] and had they been wisely employed against the thirty thousand men Davout could have put into the lines, the city might well have been taken by storm. But the recently elected Crown Prince of Sweden knew only too well the Duke of Auerstädt–Prince of Eckmühl, and realized that the price of victory, if indeed victory could be gained over the stubborn Davout, would be the destruction of his own army. Therefore, after encouraging the German population of the city to rise up against their French oppressors, he marched his Swedes off to the Rhine in search of glory on a less costly field. Bennigsen was left with only his own army—still twice that of the French defenders—to carry on the siege. In January he undertook limited objectives. The French were forced to abandon all of their outposts and even some villages which they had held in strength. The garrison was also generally harassed, with the intention of wearing down its resistance. Then in February the major attacks took place.

The first general assault came on the ninth of the month. The fighting was heavy on all sides, but the principal effort was made against Harburg on the left bank of the Elbe. The enemy's attempt to gain an advantage by surprise was foiled by Davout's effective warning system. He had stationed two officers at all times in the highest church tower in the city, and because of the relatively flat terrain they were able to keep a watchful eye on all enemy troop movements. Being forewarned, the Marshal was able to strengthen his defenses about Harburg even before the battle had begun.[67] In organizing his command Davout had established a highly mobile reserve unit of picked men. These "flying companies," which were supported by horse-drawn artillery, proved to be most effective throughout the siege. On this particular day most of them were deployed on the left bank. The defenders were driven out of their forward positions before Harburg and extremely heavy pressure was put on the main system of defenses. However the crisis passed when the enemy, having suffered heavy losses, paused to regroup, and Davout, who had taken personal command of that section of the line, brought up reinforcements and bolstered the morale of his weary and outnumbered men. He had gone personally into the front lines and exposed himself to enemy fire while regrouping and encouraging his troops. But when his chief of staff, General Cesar de Laville, was wounded he retired in order to prevent any further loss among his staff officers, who refused to leave his side.[68] Then, in the late afternoon, a French counterattack before Harburg won back several strategic positions.

Bennigsen had had enough, and he did not continue the battle the next day. Not until February 17 did the Russian general again order a full-scale attack. But this new assault was no more successful than the one eight days earlier. Then, after a minor engagement on the twenty-fourth, Bennigsen attempted a night attack on February 27. Again Davout was ready. Flammable material was fired into the night sky, and the battlefield was sufficiently lighted for the French gunners to inflict heavy losses on the enemy. This was the last serious attempt made to penetrate the French lines. Bennigsen was now resigned to a sit-and-wait policy. Unable to reduce Hamburg by force of arms, he would allow hunger and disease to open the city's gates.[69] They might require a longer period of time, but they were surer and less costly in terms of casualties. Furthermore, even if Davout could hold out until midsummer it was becoming less likely that Napoleon could. Thus if the campaign of France was won on the Seine and peace forced upon the Emperor, there would be no need for further bloodshed on the Elbe.

French combat losses at Hamburg had not been heavy during the winter months despite the increased pace of the fighting in February. The bitter fighting on the ninth of that month had left twelve hundred killed and wounded,[70] but no other engagement even came near that figure. As Bennigsen rightly calculated it was the ordinary illnesses that attacked all besieged armies in the eighteenth century which cut down Davout's effective strength. February and March were the two worst months [71] with eighteen hundred and fifty deaths in less than sixty days.[72] In April this picture began to brighten. The men got more rest as the result of the comparative lull in the fighting, and the weather began to improve. The bitter cold which had characterized December through March gave way to more moderate temperatures and fairer skies. The total numbers in the hospitals declined sharply, while only three hundred and fifty deaths were recorded in March.[73]

The first two weeks of April passed much as those of March. The French regained some of the outposts which they had surrendered during the winter months. Davout even ordered one major operation against the enemy which enabled the besieged to gather forage for the horses.[74] Then on April 15 Lieutenant Colonel Aubert, of the Danish army, presented himself before a French outpost with a letter for Marshal Davout from General Bennigsen. "I believe it necessary, and also my duty," wrote the Russian General, "to communicate to your Excellence the official news which I have just received from Paris, so as not to be responsible for blood which would be shed uselessly by two nations which . . . no longer regard themselves as enemies. In accordance with the declaration of the French senate, you will see, sir, that Louis XVIII has been recognized as sovereign of France. Would you inform me of your disposition." [75] This was Davout's first indication that all was not going well in France. The last news he had received from Paris through the enemy blockade—on March 20—had announced that the enemy was being pushed back. This led the defenders of Hamburg to believe that they would soon be relieved.[76] Davout was, therefore, both cautious and suspicious. This might be no more than a trick on the part of Bennigsen designed to gain entrance to a city which he could not take by force of arms. On the very same day on which he received Bennigsen's letter, he wrote the following reply: "I am unable to respond to this letter other than a simple statement of reception; a man of honor does not regard himself released of his oaths of fidelity, because his sovereign may have suffered reverses." [77]

Davout had had no official instructions from France since the beginning of the siegee. Even if all had not gone well for Napoleon, and in fact he had abdicated (April 6, 1814), it was very questionable as to what action he should take. Whatever the events in Paris, the commander in chief of Hamburg felt honor bound to abide by the 1811 decree governing a besieged place of war. "Every governor or commander to whom we have confided a place of war," reads Article 110 of this decree, "must bear in mind that he holds in his hands one of the boulevards of the Empire or one of the points of support of the army, that his early surrender by just one day could have the greatest consequence for the defense of the State and well-being of the army. Therefore, he will be deaf to all rumors spread by the enemy of direct or indirect news which will reach him by way of the enemy. Thus should the enemy attempt to persuade him that the army has been beaten, or that Francc is conquered, he will resist these insinuations as an attack, he will not allow his courage or that of the garrison to be shaken." [78] The Marshal could readily bring to mind numerous examples of commanders who had negotiated with the enemy at a critical time and affected adversely either a campaign or a treaty. Kléber had so infuriated the First Consul by treating with the Turks and English in Egypt that Napoleon would not even allow his remains to be buried in France. Masséna's surrender of Genoa (1800) on the eve of the Battle of Marengo almost upset Bonaparte's well-laid plans in Italy. Coutard's surrender of Ratisbon (April 1809) allowed the Austrians to retreat safely into Bohemia after the defeat at Eckmühl. Davout, who had been highly critical of Kléber and Coutard, was determined that he would not himself be criticized for such actions at Hamburg. He would hold that place until he received orders from France to the contrary, or until hunger forced him to give it up.

On April 20 the enemy again made contact with the besieged garrison.[79] This time Davout was informed by the officer in command of the advanced posts before Altona that two Russian officers had presented themselves with dispatches from the French government. Remarking that it was unusual practice in time of war for a government to send its orders by way of the enemy, Davout sent word to the Russians that "the Emperor, of whose downfall I am unaware, was not in the habit of communicating with his general by way of the enemy."[80] This episode was followed by a meeting between the Marshal and Colonel Aubert at which the Danish officer gave Davout a letter addressed to Comte Bennigsen by the Emperor Alexander's chief of staff. This letter, dated Paris, April 1/13, 1814, announced the abdication of Napoleon, the establishment of a provisional government, and the presence of the Comte d'Artois, brother of Louis XVIII, in Paris.

This additional evidence, supported verbally by Colonel Aubert, whom Davout knew to be an honorable man, caused the Marshal to accept the letter from the French government, even though it had come by the way of the enemy. Dated in Paris on April 5 and addressed to *"Monsieur le Maréchal"* the letter announced the formation of the Provisional Government and asked for his support as a loyal and patriotic Frenchman.[81] It was signed by the five members of the new provisional government and the Secretary General.[82] However, since the letter had been written the day before Napoleon's abdication at Fontainbleau, there was no mention of the Emperor. Furthermore, there was no mention of Louis XVIII, as he had not yet been recognized by the Provisional Government as King of France. Thus the letter, even if Davout accepted it its face value, did not solve any of his problems, but rather complicated the picture since it presented him with a *coup d'état* against the imperial regime.

In order to determine what action he should take Davout was willing to agree to an armistice and requested permission from Bennigsen to send an officer to Paris to obtain orders from the "legitimate" government of France. But the negotiations, which continued through April 27, failed to produce any kind of agreement. The fighting did not stop, and though the Russian commander agreed in principle that General Victoire Joseph Delcambre be allowed to go to Paris, the conditions which he tied to this agreement (Russian occupation of key French positions) were not acceptable to Davout.[83] Then, just as it appeared that the negotiations had reached a stalemate, the Marshal was informed by the Russians that his cousin, François d'Avout,[84] had arrived in Altona with letters from his wife and the latest newspapers from Paris.

On April 28 Davout received his cousin with unquestionable information of the events which had occurred in France. There was no longer any doubt surrounding the abdication of Napoleon and the restoration of the House of Bourbon. On the twenty-ninth Davout informed the garrison of the change of government; and his entire command, including himself, swore fidelity and obedience to the new dynasty.[85] But François d'Avout had been sent to Hamburg by the Marshal's wife, not the new government. Thus he had no instructions from the new minister of war, and the position of the Hamburg garrison was still far from simple. Davout now requested and secured papers for General Delcambre to go to Paris, and an armistice was arranged. Delcambre departed on the thirtieth with an address to the King declaring the adherence of the XIII Corps to the military and civil administration of the new government,[86] and a letter from the Marshal to the Comte d'Artois, Lieutenant General of the Kingdom,[87] reaffirming the loyalty expressed in the address to the King.

The same day on which the garrison was informed of the restoration of Louis XVIII to the throne of France (April 29), the white flag of the House of Bourbon was flown from the highest towers of Hamburg in place of the Revolutionary tricolor. Upon his return to France, Davout would be charged by his enemies with having fired upon the white flag during the last days of the siege.[88] The fact was that he had. But the circumstances which surrounded the event put it in quite a different light from the treasonous act described to the King. Throughout the siege the enemy strove to sow seeds of discontent among the civilian population and the non-French troops of the Hamburg-Harburg position.[89] Then in the late months of the siege they tried to lower the morale of the French soldiers by informing them of Napoleonic defeats and the end of the war. In general these efforts were unsuccessful, but they did result in the defection of nine Dutch officers early in April.[90] In an effort to seal off Hamburg more perfectly from enemy propaganda Davout ordered his troops to fire on anyone who approached the advance posts, regardless of their pretext, unless they received orders to the contrary.[91]

Thus when Russian troops began an attack on the French outpost (April 20) waving white flags, the defenders, with the full knowledge of the commander, opened fire. Davout, in his explanation of this action to Louis XVIII (*Mémoire au Roi,* 1814) declared that he had no official knowledge of the restoration of the Bourbon dynasty at that time, and believed it to be a trick on the part of the enemy to confuse his troops and thereby gain a military victory. "We repulsed force with force," he wrote, and added, "I dare to say, Sire, that every man of heart and intelligence, would have acted in the same manner as I did in similar circumstances. . . . If there still remains any doubts in this regard in the heart of your Majesty, it would be easy for me to destroy them by recalling this undeniable fact, that by my own conviction, without having received orders from my government, and without having been forced by the enemy, I had that same white flag raised on the towers of Hamburg seven days before the arrival of your Majesty's commissioner." [92]

Not until May 5 did General Joseph Fouché arrive from Paris. As Royal Commissioner of the King he was authorized by the Comte d'Artois to undertake the transfer of Hamburg and Harburg to the Allies following the evacuation by the XIII Corps. This was the first official communication made by the new government—four weeks after the abdication of Napoleon. Then, on the eleventh of May, General Count Gérard arrived with orders from the minister of war to assume immediate command of the army. This action on the part of the Comte d'Artois, who was given a free hand in military affairs when his brother became King, was unquestionably meant to be an insult. The successful defense of Hamburg, in accordance with his orders, should have merited for Davout the honor of keeping his command until his return to France. General Gérard, who had served under the Marshal and respected him as a soldier, was extremely tactful in his unpleasant mission.[93] However, preparations were undertaken for the evacuation of the city.

The last weeks of May were used in preparation for the return to France. Negotiations were undertaken with the Russian commander; and Gérard, following the same hard line as Davout, secured honorable terms for the evacuation. The entire army and French administration were allowed to return to France. They took with them their arms, baggage, and artillery. Only the very sick, those who could not make the journey, remained behind, and they under a French officer, with the right to return home as soon as their health would permit.

On May 27 the first of three columns marched out of Harburg with its flags flying and its troops in high spirits. The two remaining columns marched behind at two-day intervals. The operations had been the last triumph of Napoleonic military glory. Hamburg had been the last city in Europe to lower the Revolutionary tricolor, and the enemy occupied it only after the garrison had been voluntarily withdrawn by the new French government. Davout had upheld his honor and that of the French army. He had, as he himself declared, "rendered the name of France respectable to the enemy."[94] Had Napoleon been successful in restoring his control over Europe, Davout's reward might have been great, but Louis XVIII saw no glory in the resistance of the Hamburg garrison. At best it postponed his return to France, and at worst proved that the Marshal was a loyal servant of the Corsican usurper and therefore suspect.

Davout, who marched with one of the columns of the Corps he had recently commanded, was fully aware that neither he nor his army would be received by the new government with open arms, much less as the heroes they felt themselves to be. Yet they approached France joyfully in the knowledge that the war had ended and they would soon be once again with their loved ones. The XIII Corps was still thirty-one thousand men strong. The three columns consisted of twenty-six thousand men, while some five thousand remained behind in hospitals. This represented a loss of eleven thousand men during the siege, most of whom died of disease. Though the heavy artillery was left behind in their positions about Hamburg, the French took with them one hundred pieces of field artillery (six- and twelve-pounders). Four thousand horses had also survived the siege. They provided teams for the artillery and wagons as well as a modest cavalry.[95]

The veterans of Hamburg were still at a considerable distance from Paris when a dispatcher arrived with orders for Marshal Davout. He was not to enter Paris, but rather to proceed directly to his estate at Savigny-sur-Orge and to remain there until he would receive further orders from the minister of war. This clear indication of disfavor was received with mixed emotions. The Marshal was overjoyed at the prospect of joining his family without delay, but not with the official attitude of the royal government. He was being treated as an enemy of the state rather than as a commander who had rallied his army to the King's side.

He had not long to wait before he was confronted with the charges against him. In a letter from Dupont-de-Nemours, minister of war, dated Paris, June 17, 1814, Davout was informed that the King had received complaints with respect to his command while at Hamburg. "The principal ones," Dupont declared, "are to have fired on the white flag after having had knowledge of the dethronement of Napoleon, and the re-establishment of the Bourbons to the throne; of having taken funds from the Bank of Hamburg; and of having committed arbitrary acts which tended to render the French name odious."[96] He concluded by inviting the accused to write a report of his actions during his command at Hamburg in order to clear himself of these specific charges. Davout undertook at once the task of clearing his name. In his report to the King, which he also had published under the title of *Mémoire de m. le maréchal Davout, prince d'Eckmühl, au roi,* he justified his actions on all three counts. Louis XVIII accepted Davout's explanations and no formal charges were brought against the Marshal.

14

The Minister of War

DAVOUT REMAINED out of favor throughout the First Restoration. His *Mémoire au Roi* was accepted by Louis XVIII as a satisfactory explanation of his actions while in command at Hamburg. Nevertheless it was well known in all quarters that the Marshal had been one of Napoleon's staunchest supporters, and that while he had accepted the white flag of the Bourbons, it had not been until he had received unquestionable proof that the Emperor had been removed from the scene. Furthermore, unlike the other marshals, he did not seek employment with the new government. Shunning Paris, he was quite content with putting his own affairs in order and seeing to the management of his estate at Savigny while at the same time enjoying the reunion with his family. His career as a soldier would have ended at this point had Napoleon not reappeared in France in March 1815.

Following the Emperor's abdication in April 1814, he had been exiled to the island of Elba, over which he ruled, but with the express understanding that he could not return to France. Yet in less than a year conditions had changed not only in France but in Europe. The French people had accepted the Bourbon Restoration not because they had any love of the old monarchy, but because the Empire had been destroyed and they desired peace. Once peace had been restored they began to view the monarchy as a threat to the gains which had been made as the result of the Revolution. The army was the least content element of society. It had remained loyal to the Emperor to the very end. Louis XVIII knew full well that it was the military might of the Allied armies which had placed him upon his throne over the opposition of the French army. Treated with suspicion, if not hostility, the army smarted under the unsympathetic Bourbon regime.

News from Vienna, where the victorious powers were leisurely and gaily reshaping the map of Europe, also seemed to favor a return to France by the exiled Emperor. A major split had occurred between Russia and Prussia on the one hand and Austria and England on the other. Their principal point of disagreement was over the fate of Poland and Saxony, which were coveted by the Emperor Alexander and the Prussian king respectively. So skillfully was Prince Talleyrand taking advantage of this split that France was becoming the balance of power. Believing that the major powers would be unable, or unwilling, to cooperate as they had in 1813 and 1814, and that France would welcome him back with open arms, Napoleon sailed from Elba with four hundred troops and landed on March 1, 1815, at Fréjus.

The Emperor was less than fully accurate in his estimation of the situation. The European powers at once put aside their quarrels and made common cause against him, while France accepted him with little fanfare and even open resistance in some provinces. The sentiment of the army is perhaps best seen in the fact that not one shot was fired at Napoleon or the troops he led. His march to Paris was hailed at every step by the rank and file and the majority of the officer corps. It is true that there were those among the upper ranks who for one reason or another refused to rally to the Emperor,[1] but they did not take up arms against him. Thus Napoleon arrived at the Tuileries on March 20 amidst the acclamation of his supporters.

Marshal Davout had not taken service under the Bourbon regime. His acceptance of Louis XVIII was the acceptance of the *de facto* government of France. Now that the King had fled the capital, Davout considered his government no longer to be that of France, and he had no reservations about offering his services to the Emperor. When the Marshal entered the courtyard of the Carrousel, the crowd that had gathered announced his arrival with an acclamation which was only surpassed by that rendered the Emperor himself. Though he was personally unpopular in many high military circles, he represented the finest qualities of honor, discipline, and glory to the masses of soldiers and civilians. When he came into the presence of Napoleon, whom he had not seen since December 1812, the Emperor greeted him warmly.[2]

Davout came to the Tuileries to seek a high command in the army, but Napoleon had already decided that he could best use the Marshal's talents, loyalty, and reputation as minister of war. When the other visitors had departed, he took Davout aside and explained to him that he needed him at the head of the war ministry. The Marshal immediately tried to refuse the position declaring that he could best serve the Emperor and France on the battlefield. He pointed out that he had many enemies in the army, that dealing with people was not one of his strong points, and that he tended to be severe. Napoleon discounted his arguments and then added: " 'Eh bien! I will speak to you with an open heart and tell you all. I have let it be known and must continue to let it be known that I act in harmony with my brother-in-law, the Emperor of Austria. It has been widely announced that the Empress is on her way bringing with her the King of Rome, that they will arrive any day now. The truth is that this is false, that I am alone, alone before Europe. This is my situation! Will you also abandon me?' To this the Marshal immediately replied without hesitation: 'Sire, there is only one answer I can make, I accept the ministry!' "[3] Reluctantly, Napoleon's most capable field commander became an administrator.[4]

The loss of Davout to the Army of the North was not noticeable until the army took the field in June, but his administrative efficiency and capability were at once taxed to the utmost. Napoleon declared his peaceful intentions upon his return. Yet, from the beginning, it was extremely doubtful that the European powers would allow him to regain his throne without a battle. As the weeks passed it became clear that war was unavoidable. In March the assembled powers in Vienna declared him an outlaw and formed the Seventh Coalition against him. It was, therefore, imperative that the army be put on a war footing in the shortest possible period of time. But even more pressing than this was the necessity of extending and consolidating imperial control throughout France.

In general the northern and eastern regions of the nation rallied to the new government, while the southern and western sections showed pro-Bourbon sympathies. On the morning following his appointment as minister of war, Davout sent a deluge of couriers with dispatches announcing the reestablishment of the Empire and calling for acknowledgment of the new government.[5] He was most concerned with the fortified towns along the frontier. There was fear that if their garrisons remained loyal to the King they would open their gates to the enemy, and in this manner deprive the imperial army of strategic defensive positions in case of attack, or of staging areas if the Emperor decided that the best defense was an offense.[6]

The efforts to win over the frontier cities were crowned with immediate success, but those directed toward the control of the south and the west were quite another matter. In the south the Duke of Angoulême led the resistance. Gathering a small army of regular troops in the Marseilles district, he undertook a "campaign" up the Rhône. This threat was met with imperial troops commanded by General Grouchy—soon to be Marshal for his services. The Duke was forced to flee the country when the soldiers he led showed little willingness to fight for the Bourbon cause, but the cities of Marseilles and Toulon displayed more genuine royalist sympathies. Not until substantial military pressure was brought to bear in the form of an actual siege did Marshal Masséna, who had tried to remain neutral in a most difficult situation, hoist the tricolor and deliver Marseilles to the Emperor.[7]

At Bordeaux, royalist resistance centered about the Duchess of Angoulême. It was not as militant as that led by her husband, yet it required the presence of imperial troops before the city submitted to the Paris government. Toulouse was a third center of resistance in the south, but here again the opposition collapsed before a show of force.

In the west the Vendée posed still another problem. During the Revolution it had been the stronghold of monarchism, and, until the advent of Napoleon, had successfully withstood attempts by the central government to bring it under control. In mid-March the Duke of Bourbon was sent to the Loire to organize and lead the supporters of the monarchy. But he proved to have been a poor choice. Moreover, both the monarchists and Bonapartists misjudged the temperament of the Vendée. The larger towns and cities came out openly in support of the Emperor. The Duke of Bourbon was advised to leave Angers because of the pro-imperial enthusiasm displayed by the inhabitants, and shortly after his arrival in Rennes a bust of Napoleon was paraded through the streets.[8] Even among the peasants, where the strongest support for the King was to be found, the younger men who had served in the imperial army did not aspire to fight against their former comrades-in-arms for Louis XVIII. This is not to say that there was not substantial support for the monarchy, but the Vendée was not of one mind on the subject and time was needed to stimulate and organize the Bourbon cause. The Duke of Bourbon was not slow in grasping the situation, and on March 27, just one week after Napoleon's arrival in Paris, he sailed for Spain leaving word that when the insurrection was ready he would return to place himself at its head.

The departure of the Duke by no means meant the end of resistance in the Vendée, but it did mean that for the most part resistance went underground. The royalists set to work organizing resistance and collecting arms and munitions. The government's strategy, as put into operation by the new minister of war, was to concentrate its strength in the cities where its greatest support was to be found, and from these to attempt to control the countryside. Davout dispatched loyal generals to take command of the regular army units, but there were insufficient troops in these questionable departments of the west to bring them under complete control. Nor was the Emperor inclined to send enough reinforcements to assure domination of the Vendée. Quite correctly he ascertained that the real threat to the Empire would come from the north, not the west. Wellington was at the head of an army in Belgium and Blücher's Prussian army was moving into position in the German districts west of the Rhine. Together they would outnumber him in the coming campaign. Any troops sent to the west could only lessen his odds in the north. If he could gain a crushing decision over these forces before the Austrians and Russians made their presence felt, he would then be able to deal with the hard-core royalist faction in the west which would not accept the reestablished Empire. On the other hand, if he were to be defeated by the Allies, it would make little difference whether the Vendée had been subjugated or not—all would be lost. Thus Davout was left with insufficient troops, so that he could do little more than maintain the *status quo* while awaiting the decision of arms in the north. With every effort being made to extend and consolidate imperial control throughout the nation, the enormous task of rebuilding the army was also undertaken.

Louis XVIII had had no intention of becoming involved in war. Indeed, he owed his throne to his brother monarchs, and asked of them and the French people no more than to live out the remaining years of his life as King. Quite understandably he had cut back the army to two hundred and twenty-four thousand men, and in an effort to economize had allowed even this number to sink well below the level of combat readiness. No more than one-fifth of the army was ready for field service by March, 1815.

The tasks of doubling the size of the army, equipping, training, and reorganizing it fell heavily on the shoulders of the minister of war. There was a shortage of everything—arms, clothing, shoes, and in particular horses. The latter posed a major problem, one which had weakened the army during the 1813 and 1814 campaigns. Every effort was made to acquire all available animals, but still the army entered upon the Waterloo campaign with a pronounced shortage of cavalry. Furthermore, while a recruit could be trained for the infantry in a relatively short period of time, cavalrymen required a considerably longer period. Inexperienced soldiers in any branch of the service weaken the combat effectiveness of that service, but this is particularly true as the necessary skills increase in difficulty. Despite every effort, the cavalry was to go into combat lacking in numbers and experience.

Supplying the necessary materials of war was a difficult, but not insurmountable, task. Old arms factories were reopened, and orders went out for uniforms, shoes, and all types of military necessities. These efforts were hampered somewhat by the reluctance of the bourgeoisie to extend credit to a goverment which would have to consolidate its position on the battlefield, especially in the light of the disastrous campaigns of 1812–14. Nevertheless, the army was reasonably equipped and supplied when it went into battle in mid-June.[9]

The reorganization of the army was made more complicated by a number of factors. During the Restoration when the army was drastically reduced in size, it had been necessary to eliminate some units while combining others. Davout now had to sort out the regiments, create new divisions, and form them into corps. Recruiting men to fill the ranks of the expanding army proved to be more of a job than might have been imagined. Theoretically, there was an ample supply of veterans, both officers and men, who had been discharged in the spring of 1814. But while the officers were willing enough to return to their regiments, the enlisted men were hesitant. The last three campaigns had been marked with failure and defeat, and many an old soldier, enjoying for the first time the pleasures and comforts of civilian life, had no desire to take up arms again. Nor was it easy to raise raw recruits. In the south and the west it often proved impossible. Young men were hidden by their families or took refuge in the forests. Despite these drawbacks Davout was able to produce two hundred and eighty thousand men, veterans and new recruits, within eight weeks.[10]

The training of these new men was in the hands of competent commanders. The officer corps, with the exception of its highest ranking members—the marshals—rallied in large numbers to the Emperor. Of the few marshals (Davout, Ney, Brune, Suchet) who were employed, none was given field command when the Army of the North was formed; and only Ney led troops in battle during the brief campaign. (Grouchy, who received his marshal's baton in April 1815, after rallying to the imperial cause, was given command of the right wing of the army.) Command of the five corps which formed the bulk of the new army was given to capable and experienced division commanders. The I Corps was given to Jean Baptiste Drouet, Comte d'Erlon; the II went to Honoré Charles Reille; the III to Vandamme; the IV to Gérard; and the VI to Lobau.[11] Command of the cavalry corps was given to Generals Claude-Pierre Pajol, Rémi-Joseph Exelmans, François-Etienne Kellermann, and Edouard Jean Baptiste Milhaud. The ability of these officers equaled and in some instances surpassed, that of the older marshals. The new corps commanders also had the additional incentive of a marshal's baton. Indeed, the promotion in April of General Grouchy to the rank of marshal for his services along the Rhône clearly indicated that upon the conclusion of a victorious campaign there would be promotions, titles, and wealth for those who had taken part. Thus what may have been lacking in experience in commanding large numbers of troops was more than made up for in enthusiasm. With few exceptions Napoleon suffered no loss as a result of the absence of his marshals. The most noticeable loss, even more so than that of Davout as a field commander, was Marshal Berthier. The former chief of staff did not offer his services to his old master after the king had fled, and on June 1, he died under mysterious circumstances.[12] His place as major general of the army was taken by Marshal Soult, but he had neither the ability nor the experience of his predecessor.

The military picture was not the only one which had changed during the First Restoration. Politically Louis XVIII had granted to the French people a Charter which set up a form of constitutional monarchy. Upon his return, Napoleon had the "Appendix to the Constitutions of the Empire" tacked on to the old Constitution. The "Additional Act" as the Appendix was called, was no more than the reaffirmation of the King's Charter, that is, it established a constitutional Empire with an elected assembly. The opening of the Parliament on June 7 was one of his last official acts before he joined the army. These gestures were calculated to win the support of the liberals and moderates. However, few were taken in, and all realized that the fate of the restored empire would be decided on the battlefield, not on the floor of an elected assembly. Still the Emperor needed all the support at home he could muster.

As April gave way to May and the opening of the inevitable campaign approached, tensions built up in Paris. Davout, who would have much preferred to be with the army rather than organizing it, began to clash with field commanders, the major general of the army, and the Emperor himself. His conflict with General Rapp occurred during early May. Rapp, whose original dislike for the minister of war dated back to 1811, when he commanded at Danzig under the latter's authority, not only questioned the appointment of an officer to his command, but did so in insulting terms. The infuriated—and frustrated—Davout penned a sharp reply to the General: "My dear Rapp, I am limiting myself to returning to you the commission of the officer in question, but I declare to you in friendship, that if I receive from you a second letter in this style, I will cease to be Minister of War, or you will cease to command an army corps. . . . I did not know this officer from Adam or Eve, I signed his commission like so many others, on confidence. If he is unworthy of wearing our uniform, send me the complaints and justice will be rendered . . . but not in this style, nor in this manner of action. I tell you once again that I will not endure it." [13] This reprimand proved sufficient to bring the general back into line, and there was no further difficulty between the two men.

The problem which rose between Davout and Soult was less dramatic but of a much more serious nature. Fundamentally it was caused by both men issuing orders to the Army of the North and to other units without any form of coordination. Marshal Soult, as major general of the army, assumed that he was in command in a direct line from the Emperor. The minister of war based his authority on the fact that he was responsible to the Emperor for preparing the army to take the field. Since the Army of the North had not embarked upon a campaign, was not even assembled during the month of May, and was still on French soil, Davout assumed that it was his responsibility along with other units—under the direct orders of the Emperor. The matter was clarified on May 16 on which date Napoleon decreed: "The Major General will give orders only to the Army of the North, except when transmitting a special order while the Emperor is present with the army." [14] This division af authority left Soult in direct command of the Army of the North and Davout in charge of all other units. But four days later Soult was still dispatching orders to commanders not directly under him.

The confusion resulting from the conflicting orders caused Davout to threaten again to resign his ministerial post. On May 22 he wrote to Soult: "Marshal, I have just received your four letters of May 20th, in which you give orders to the generals of the Army of the North and all other commanding officers. I wish to point out to you that, despite your wishes, this manner of action will cause the greatest confusion. I bring to your attention the Emperor's order of May 16, which determines your powers and which was sent to you. . . . I ask you, sir, to abide by the decision of the Emperor. In general, if you give orders on your part and I on mine, the results can only lead to the greatest confusion, and I will resign my position as Minister of War. I accepted the ministry reluctantly, and it would give me the greatest pleasure to remove from myself this burden." [15] The air was somewhat cleared after this, but it was not until the Emperor joined the army in the second week of June that the matter was completely settled.

Davout's conflict with Rapp and Soult and in particular his

threat to resign as minister of war reflect the strained relationship between himself and Napoleon. The Emperor had need of the Marshal, for of all who rallied to him in 1815, Davout commanded the greatest respect from the army. But since the Russian campaign, the Prince of Eckmühl had not been in the Emperor's favor. As the imperial government established its authority throughout the nation and the army took shape in preparation for the coming campaign, the personal relationship between Davout and Napoleon became less amiable. This is not to say that the Emperor came to regret the Marshal's appointment as minister of war. Quite the contrary, he continued to depend heavily upon Davout. Yet, at the same time, the Emperor criticized him, quarreled with him, and even spied upon him.

The Emperor wrote to Davout on May 2: "My cousin, you have in your department men of inferior quality. It is my intention that tomorrow, Wednesday, you will bring to me a list of individuals to be dismissed." [16] This letter is viewed as a rebuke to Davout and a tribute to the effectiveness of the Count of Flahaut, a *général de boudoir* whom Napoleon imposed on Davout.[17] The appointment of officers provided other occasions for friction between the Emperor and his minister. The most unpleasant of these was with respect to General Louis A. V. Bourmont. Napoleon suggested to Davout that the Count of Bourmont, who was known to be a royalist sympathizer, be given employment with the Army of the North. As this did not constitute a direct order, the Marshal, who was vehemently opposed to the appointment, took no action. When the Emperor demanded an explanation for the delay, Davout declared that while he readily acknowledged the General's abilities as an officer, he had no confidence in the man's loyalty to the Emperor. Nevertheless Napoleon insisted upon his appointment. Whereupon Davout replied: "Sire, if these were ordinary times, your Majesty would not force the hand of his Minister of War, who would respectfully offer his resignation rather than subscribe to that which he believes would compromise the best interests of the Emperor and his nation. I will obey, regretfully and I wish, though with little hope, that your Majesty will not have to repent for it." [18] Few weeks were to pass before Napoleon did in fact regret his decision. On June 15, just three days before the Battle of Waterloo, General Bourmont defected to the enemy.

Davout's repeated threats of resignation were expressions of frustration with his job and with the Emperor himself. He stayed because Napoleon wanted him to stay, and because he still equated the man with the nation. To Davout Napoleon was France. He represented the consolidation of the Revolution, the glory of the Empire at its height, and the instrument of his own position and wealth. Despite the setbacks of 1812–14 Davout still believed in the "destiny" of the Emperor. He had not been with Napoleon at Leipzig, nor had he felt the defeat of the other marshals during the campaign of 1814. His own experience had been quite different. Rather than witnessing the defeats which had led to the Emperor's first abdication, he had successfully withstood the enemy's siege of Hamburg. Thus in 1815 he was one of the few who strongly believed in the possibility of reestablishing the Empire on the battlefields. He did not comprehend the vast changes which had come over Europe since 1812, nor did he understand the magnitude of the forces which were drawn up against France in the summer of 1815.

The Emperor spoke of peace during the first weeks of his return because it was politically advantageous, not because he sincerely believed there would not be war. He had hoped that peace might prevail long enough for him to consolidate his position at home and prepare the army for war. But by mid-April this possibility, which had never been very plausible, had completely faded. There would be war. The questions to be answered were when and where? To wait for the enemy to attack would have given Napoleon more time to strengthen the French army, particularly to increase its numbers. It would also have given the Allies time to bring to bear the full weight of their numbers. Because of the enormous potential of the strength of the combined armies of England, Prussia, Austria, and Russia, who would have been able to field more than one million men, Napoleon wisely decided to attack at the earliest possible moment. By taking the field before the Austrian and Russian armies could arrive on the Rhine, he would only have to face the Anglo-Dutch and Prussian armies, neither of which represented the full commitment of their respective nations.

General mobilization was ordered on April 8, and before the month had ended the hated conscription was once again introduced. Neither of these measures were received warmly by the French nation. Conscription was not only unwelcome, it was resisted both passively and actively. Nevertheless, two hundred and eighty thousand men were raised. The regular army was to be supported by the National Guard and the creation of *Fédérés*.[19] The organization of these auxiliary troops became the task of the minister of war. Military supplies and equipment had first to be sent to the regular army. What was left went to the National Guard and the *Fédérés*. Their principal function was to protect the homeland while the army carried the war to the enemy on his own ground. In order to make available a maximum number of regular troops for the Army of the North and the other armies and corps of observation (along the Rhine, the Alps, and the Pyrenees), Napoleon ordered the garrisons of the fortified cities and towns to be incorporated in line units and their places taken by the National Guard, supported by the *Fédérés*.[20] Davout's preoccupation with this reorganization throughout the months of May and June is exemplified by the flood of orders which poured forth from the Ministry of War.[21] By a decree dated May 15 Paris alone was to raise twenty-four battalions of *Fédérés*[22] to defend the city should the Allies attack it as they had in 1814.

The *Fédérés* in the western departments had no sooner come into existence than they were put to the test. On May 15 the signal was given in the Vendée for open insurrection. The royalist forces had had time to organize and supply themselves. To meet this new threat Davout secured the Emperor's reluctant permission to dispatch additional troops to the southwest.[23] By the beginning of June there was an army of twenty-five thousand men supported by artillery on the Loire.[24] The actual fighting was on a relatively small scale. On May 17 an insurgent force was routed near the village of Echaubroignes, and two days later General Travot surprised a sizable royalist force at Aizenay and put it to flight.[25] But the campaign did not go as well as Davout believed it should have. On June 1 he criticized General Lamarque, who commanded the major portion of the troops on the Loire, for his "defensive attitude" in conducting the war.[26] With the additional troops that had been sent to him the minister of war urged him to be active and to carry the fighting to the enemy rather than sitting in the safety of his defensive position at Angers. Nevertheless, there were no pitched battles in the Vendée during June as neither side felt strong enough to attack the other, and efforts for peace talks were undertaken by the second week of the month.[27]

The Vendée was not the only section of France which was growing restless as war approached. "All of Marshal Brune's reports announce that the government's authority is ignored at Marseilles," Davout wrote to Marshal Suchet, the Duke of Albufera, "orders are torn-up, the military is insulted and the city is in a state of constant disorder which borders on revolt." [28] To cope with these conditions the minister of war ordered Brune to place the city under a state of siege and to arrest fifty to sixty of the leading trouble-makers, disarm the National Guard, and restore law and order.[29] These measures, backed up by Suchet's army corps, proved sufficient to control Marseilles until the news of Waterloo and the Emperor's second abdication unleashed a "White Terror" which was to cost Marshal Brune his life.

By the second week of June all preparations had been made for the Army of the North to take the field. Davout wrote to all corps commanders on the sixth that "hostilities were imminent"; [30] and six days later, on June 12, Napoleon left Paris to join the army. Well before his departure the Emperor had made clear the position of the minister of war during his absence. On April 30 he had written to Davout: "My Cousin, if we have war and I am obliged to depart, it is my intention to leave you in Paris as Minister of War, governor of Paris and commander in chief of the National Guard, the *levées en masse* [*Fédérés*] and the troops of the line which will be in the city." [31] The uncertainty of the political situation in France required Napoleon to leave behind him a soldier whom he could trust. Paris had been turned over to the Allies in 1814, not because the defending garrison had been overwhelmed by military might, but because Marshal Marmont saw no point in resistance. Davout's able defense of Hamburg and loyalty to the Emperor made him the most logical choice—had he not been needed on the battlefield.

Napoleon had withheld troops from the Vendée on the sound judgment that the decisive action upon which the Empire would stand or fall would be with the Army of the North on the plains of Belgium, not on the Loire. This same sound judgment should have caused him to give Davout a command in the army where he would have been able to have direct influence on the course of events in the principal theater of operations. Napoleon should have realized that he would have need once again of the services of the man who had held the Austrians at bay of Eckmühl, destroyed a Prussian army twice the size of his own at Auerstädt, and withstood the crushing assault of the Russians at Austerlitz.

The events of the third week of June 1815, are familiar to every student of European history. The French army crossed the frontier into Dutch-controlled Belgium on the fifteenth and gained an immediate victory over the Prussians at Ligny on the sixteenth. Two days later Napoleon attacked the Anglo-Dutch army under the command of the Duke of Wellington just south of Brussels. The outcome of the battle was still undecided when Blücher arrived on the scene with his Prussian corps in the late afternoon. Outnumbered and outflanked, the French army was driven from the field and scattered over the countryside. It was the Prussians' answer to Jena and, indeed, it had the same devastating effect. Napoleon fled to Paris in the hope of rallying the nation around him in a last desperate attempt to save the Empire.

The capital had been quiet since the Emperor's departure, with everyone eagerly awaiting news from the front which would set them at ease. On the eighteenth news of the victory of Ligny reached Paris and was received joyously. Then there were two days without news. During June 20 the rumors of the defeat of the army at Waterloo began to filter into the capital. Fouché was perhaps the first to know.[32] The Council of Ministers was informed by Prince Joseph who read to it a letter sent by the Emperor from Philippeville. Three of the ministers (Decrès, Caulaincourt, and Combacérès) were appalled and dejected; Carnot, the "Organizer of Victory" of 1792–93, and Davout stood ready to continue the struggle; Fouché concealed his thoughts and emotions.[33]

The night of June 20–21 was one of confusion, plotting, and despair. No one knew the extent of the disaster, only that the army had suffered a defeat. Napoleon arrived at the Elysée about eight o'clock on the morning of the twenty-first. He was exhausted both physically and mentally. Still dressed in his dirty uniform from the battlefield, he greeted those present and went directly to the suite of rooms he had been occupying since mid-May. While soaking in a hot bath he summoned the minister of war. When the Marshal presented himself the Emperor, raising his arm and letting it drop uncontrolled back into the water in such a manner as to splash his visitor, exclaimed repeatedly: "Well? Davout, Well?" Davout replied: "Well, Sire, I presume that your Majesty has sent for me to make known the whereabouts of the debris of the army and the orders which are to be given in these circumstances." But Napoleon merely asked, "what are they saying in Paris?" to which the Marshal replied, "they have not yet had time to know of the events." [34]

The Marshal then informed the Emperor that the ministers were all gathered in the next room. He pointed out that there was not a moment to lose and urged Napoleon to take the steps necessary in order to dominate the situation. The most important measure in the opinion of the minister of war was to prorogue the two Chambers in order to concentrate the government in the hands of the Emperor in this time of crisis. Napoleon replied that he would dress at once and meet with his Council. Davout rejoined the other ministers and informed them of the Emperor's intention. When, however, a considerable time elapsed and he did not arrive, Davout returned to Napoleon's private quarters to implore him to join the Council as time was of an essence. Napoleon replied that since his brother Joseph was present the deliberation should begin without him and he would come in time. But the Marshal was persistent. The gravity of the situation was such that the Emperor's presence was imperative and that the authority of his brother was completely inadequate for the decisions which would have to be made if the nation was to be saved.[35]

The Emperor at last joined the Council, which was opened by the reading of the last bulletin of the *Grande Armée*. Then Napoleon declared that the situation was grave. In order to save France he would have to be given great powers. He could take them, but he preferred that they be given to him by the Chambers. Discussion followed with the ministers expressing various views. Davout again expressed the opinion that there should be a single head of the government; and that, therefore, the Emperor should prorogue the Chambers. But the deliberations were inconclusive. Napoleon refused to go himself to the Chamber of Representatives, and in his place sent one of his ministers to request that the Chamber vote him dictatorial powers.

The Chamber of Representatives met shortly after noon on the twenty-first. Fouché, fearing that Napoleon might rise to the occasion and, with the support of the nation, continue the struggle, had warned his friends in the Chamber "that the Emperor supported by Carnot, Davout and Lucien Bonaparte, was preparing for a dictatorship, that danger threatened the representatives."[36] The first to address the session was Lafayette, that spirit of 1789 who for three generations played significant roles in French revolutions. He proposed that the Chamber adopt the following measures as a preliminary step in meeting the crisis at hand:

> ARTICLE 1. The Chamber of Representatives declares the independence of the country is threatened.
>
> ARTICLE 2. The Chamber declares itself in permanent session. Any attempt to dissolve it is high treason; whoever may be guilty of such an attempt is a traitor to the country and may summarily be judged as such.
>
> . . . .
>
> ARTICLE 5. The Ministers of War, of External Affairs, of the Police and of the Interior are requested to present themselves to the Assembly immediately.[37]

The articles were accepted without opposition from the Bonapartist members of the Chamber.

Napoleon had waited too long to act. The Chamber had assumed supreme power. It was, in fact, a *coup d'état* against the Emperor and the Constitution. Napoleon could only regain control of the government by the use of force. If he decided to follow that course of action, the full support of the minister of war, who was also in command of all troops in and about Paris, was essential. During a late afternoon meeting of the ministers the Emperor was informed of the action taken by the Chamber of Representatives. He was outraged and stormed against the representatives. But the mood of his ministers was polarizing in opposition to force. Davout, who in the morning had counseled the Emperor to seize power, now declared "that the time to act had passed. The resolution of the representatives," he declared, "was illegal and unconstitutional; but it was a completed act against which there now remained only the use of brutal force."[38]

When the emotion and the confusion which marked those June

days had evaporated and the Bourbon dynasty was once again restored, the exiled Davout explained his unwillingness to support the use of force against the representatives of the people. His motives were not generated by respect for the Chamber of Deputies—indeed he had little faith in representative government—rather they were based on a sound evaluation of the situation. Conditions were not the same as they had been on the eighteenth of Brumaire. At that time the Assembly had been prudently moved from Paris to Saint-Cloud, whereas in 1815, action would have to be taken in the capital. Even more important, the risk of civil war was much greater than it had been fifteen years earlier. Even if the imperial government were victorious, the victory would be both incomplete and illusory in the face of the Allied armies which were advancing on the city and the royalists who accompanied them.[39]

On the evening of the twenty-first still another meeting took place at the Elysée. The Emperor's brother Joseph presided at this session which included some thirty persons: Lucien Bonaparte; six ministers with portfolio; four ministers of state; nine representatives from the Chamber of Peers; and nine from the Chamber of Representatives. They discussed at length the pressing governmental, military, and financial problems. Then the question of a second abdication on the part of the Emperor was inevitably raised. Davout voted with the narrow majority (seventeen to thirteen) against abdication.[40] However, no one could fail to notice that thirteen of the eighteen representatives from the two Chambers openly advocated that the Emperor step down.

That same evening, the twenty-first, Napoleon made one last attempt to gain control of the government through parliamentary methods. He sent his brother Lucien, who had been the presiding officer in the Assembly of Five Hundred on the eighteenth of Brumaire (1799), to the Chamber of Representatives to request that they vote him extraordinary powers, so that he might save the nation in its great hour of need. Lucien's mission was doomed to failure before he had left the Elysée. The coalition of constitutionalists, moderates, republicans, and opportunists was already in control. They told Lucien to go back to his brother and ask him to abdicate if he truly wished to save France; adding that if he refused to do so he would be deposed at dawn of the following day.

Napoleon was again outraged and poured out his contempt for

the representatives of the people. He also denounced the ingratitude of the Peers, whom he had appointed and who had accepted Lafayette's five articles which subjugated the executive to the legislative. Yet he realized that only at the head of an army and at the cost of civil war could he now do what Davout had counseled that morning. His self-confidence shattered by three disastrous military campaigns and the events of his first abdication, Napoleon resigned himself to the inevitable. At noon, June 22, he abdicated in favor of his son Napoleon II.

Davout stood by in silence as he watched the Emperor sign his name to the document which ended his career. The Marshal supported this course of action as being in the best interest of the nation. Had Napoleon moved at once on the morning of the twenty-first to prorogue the Chambers and seize dictatorial powers, Davout would have supported him and worked for a military victory. However, the minister of war believed that the Emperor made his first and greatest error when he returned to Paris after the defeat at Waterloo. He should have retired to Laon and there regrouped and reorganized the army. At the head of such a force—sixty thousand men including Grouchy's undefeated corps—he could have dealt with the political crisis in Paris from a position of strength.[41] When Napoleon realized that he could not gain this support he withdrew, hesitantly, from the political scene. Davout considered that Napoleon's abdication absolved him from all official allegiance to the man whom he had faithfully served for fifteen years.

Davout's personal relationship with Napoleon, as indicated earlier, had been strained well before the defeat at Waterloo and the second abdication. He had reluctantly accepted the portfolio of the Minister of War and had clashed with the Emperor during the Hundred Days. Napoleon had insisted that he accept the position not out of any affection for the Prince of Eckmühl, but because he needed his reputation to help reestablish the Empire. In March 1815, Davout still equated Napoleon with France. By serving the Emperor he believed he was serving the best interests of the nation. Yet there was little affection for the returning exile on the part of the Marshal. Memories of past glory could still be brought to mind, but they were dulled by Napoleon's unjust treatment during the retreat from Moscow, the futility of the defense of Hamburg, and the disasters of Leipzig and Waterloo. Bonapartist sympathizers,[42] pointing to the events of the second abdication and the days immediately following, accused Davout of ingratitude. But Davout's relationship with the Emperor during the Hundred Days had been strictly of an official nature—not of a personal one. By the evening of June 21, Davout no longer associated the destiny of France with that of the Emperor. With the army in shambles and the enemy marching on Paris it was in the best interest of the nation to make peace with the enemies of Napoleon and obtain the best possible terms for France. If this could be accomplished by removing the Emperor from the scene, then Davout was willing to work for this end, even if it meant cooperating with Fouché, whom he detested.

The Duke of Otrante (Fouché) was the principal figure in the intrigue to restore Louis XVIII to the throne of France. It was not that the former regicide was a Bourbonist—he was a "Fouchéist"—but rather that he wished to be the instrument by which the King was restored and thus receive from the grateful monarch the portfolio of the Minister of Police. He cared nothing for Napoleon, having plotted against him as early as 1809. The fate of the fallen Emperor concerned him only to the extent that it might further his own plans. So well did he engineer the course of events that he emerged president of the Commission of the Government which the Chamber of Representatives appointed after accepting the Emperor's abdication.

In the first actual meeting of the Commission of the Government (June 24) the five Commissioners (Fouché, Carnot, Ouinette, Caulaincourt, and General Grenier) entrusted Davout, still the minister of war, with the defense of the city of Paris.[43] The military situation was serious. Efforts to regroup the defeated army north of Paris had been carried out in a haphazard manner. Morale was low among officers and men alike, and the absence of the Emperor had only added to the confusion. The one bright spot in the picture was the army's right wing under the command of Marshal Grouchy. These troops had not been at Waterloo—a fact which caused Napoleon to blame his defeat on the unfortunate Grouchy—nor had they come in contact with the fleeing remnants of the main army. Retiring from Belgium in good order with twenty-five thousand men, Grouchy had become the principal commander in the field.

Napoleon had left Marshal Soult in command of the Army of the North when he returned to Paris. Designating Laon as the rallying point he had been able to collect approximately thirty thousand men by June 23.[44] On that day Davout wrote to Grouchy to inform him that the new government was appointing him commander of the Army of the North.[45] This dispatch fell first into the hands of Soult, who opened it, read it, and sent it on to Grouchy with a disgruntled note saying that he would remain at army headquarters only until the new commander would make contact with the troops under him.

Following their victory on the battlefield Blücher and Wellington pursued the shattered French army toward Paris. The Prussians, who had taken a lesser part in the fighting at Waterloo, were the more aggressive, while Wellington, who had borne the brunt of that immortal day's fighting, advanced with more respect. Along the Rhine and the Alps there was still little activity as the Austrians had launched only a minor offensive.

In Paris the situation remained uncertain. The accession of Napoleon II was not taken seriously by anyone other than those who wished to be deceived. There was almost continuous agitation about the Elysée and even some talk of the ex-Emperor putting himself at the head of the army in order to "save the nation." By June 23 the Chambers, urged on by Fouché, decided that it was necessary to remove Napoleon from the capital. The former Minister of Police convinced Davout that this move was necessary for the safety of Napoleon as well as the good of France. Reluctantly, the minister of war, under orders from the Commission of the Government and supported by the Chamber of Representatives, went to the Elysée on the twenty-fourth to carry out his unpleasant task.

When he arrived in the courtyard of the Elysée, he found it filled with "officers on half pay, deserters from the army, and those people whom one encounters in such circumstances," agitating and milling about. Addressing himself to the officers, the Marshal reprimanded them for their conduct. He told them that "they were bringing disgrace upon their uniform by their idleness far from danger when the nation's danger called every man to his post, when their duty was to give an example of courage, of firmness and military virtue which alone could save France."[46] Having thus chastised his embarrassed listeners, he was presented to the former Emperor. He respectfully explained his mission, placing the emphasis on the good of the nation.

Napoleon expressed immediate anger. Referring to the shouts of "Long live the Emperor," which could be heard coming from the crowd beneath his windows, he angrily exclaimed: "If I had wished to put myself at the head of these good and brave people who have the greatest instinct for the nation's true needs, I would have put an end to those who had the courage to stand up against me only when they saw I was defenseless." [47] Then, after he had calmed down, Davout reminded him that the conditions which had led him to abdicate still existed and that the danger of civil war could only be averted by his withdrawal from the capital. If his departure from Paris had been only to relieve the personal anxieties of the representatives who, having forced his abdication, still feared him, he, Davout, would not have undertaken his present mission. However, the presence of the former Emperor in the capital raised grave doubts in the Allied camps as to the sincerity of his intentions. Since one of the strong bargaining points of the government in its attempts to make peace was the Emperor's abdication, it was absolutely necessary for the good of France that he retire to Malmaison at once.[48]

Napoleon knew full well that he was at the mercy of the government unless he was willing to plunge the already unhappy nation into civil war. He had rejected this course of action at a time when his chances of success were much greater, and though he would continue for the next week to talk of the possibility of placing himself at the head of the army to fight one last battle, he had already decided that he would only act with the approval of the Chambers. He, therefore, bowed to the will of the government and began to make preparations to depart from Paris, which he was never to see again. Davout took his leave without even so much as a handshake. In the words of the Marshal himself, "the interview had been cold." [49] The two men never saw one another after that day.

On June 25 Napoleon moved to Malmaison, where he remained until July 1 at which time he departed for Rochefort with the intention of embarking for America. The same evening that he arrived at the country home which he and Josephine had shared during the height of the Empire, General Becker appeared with a letter from the minister of war naming him commander of the Emperor's guard.[50] Becker had risen through the ranks to general of division by 1809 at which time his military career was impaired by the

Emperor. He had boldly criticized Napoleon's orders and was first put on half pay, and then in 1811, retired from the army. On June 20, 1815, by order of the Emperor, he had been recalled to service for the defense of Paris.[51]

Becker's selection was the work of Fouché, but Davout was the willing instrument. The President of the Commission of the Government wished to make a prisoner of the ex-Emperor and use him in the negotiations with the Allies. He picked Becker because he could be counted upon to carry out the orders of the government and would not be won over by the charm and personality of his "prisoner." Davout was more concerned with Napoleon's safety. He knew that the Allies would do all they could to take him captive. General Becker was a capable officer who would do all in his power to escort his ward to Rochefort and safety. Therefore, despite the General's objections to his mission, Davout, who had known him well during the Prussian and Polish campaigns of 1806–7, insisted that he accept.[52]

Napoleon's departure from the capital removed any serious threat that he might have posed to the government and strengthened its hand in negotiating with the Allies, who had declared that they were making war against the man not the nation. By June 25 Davout had come to the conclusion that it was useless to prolong the war. He was disgusted with the political intrigues about him, and, being uninterested in personal gain as a result of the national catastrophe, he directed all of his efforts to obtaining the best possible settlement. As minister of war—and a soldier—he was particularly concerned for the well-being of the army, which had not been treated well following the first abdication. As a realist he was seeking an honorable solution for France, one which would neither reflect unfavorably upon himself nor upon the army. Undoubtedly his long-time friend and comrade-in-arms, Marshal Oudinot, played an influential role in his decision to support the restoration of Louis XVIII.

Oudinot was denounced to Davout by the minister of police as being one of several known royalists who were meeting secretly at the house of Baron de Vitrolles. Vitrolles, an avowed Bourbonist, had been released from prison by Fouché in the hope that he might serve as an intermediary between the king and the former regicide. The minister of war sent at once for Marshal Oudinot to explain his actions, and was completely satisfied when the latter gave his word of honor that he would not lead a royalist *coup d'état.* This business settled, the two men discussed the innumerable problems facing the nation. Oudinot then told Davout that "he was authorized to tell him on the part of the king that he [Louis XVIII] regarded him as a man useful to France in the position in which the nation found itself." [53] The King was, therefore, asking the minister of war if he did not have a proposition to make to him. "The Prince of Eckmühl drafted at once, in the presence of the Marshal [Oudinot], a series of demands in thirteen articles, and gave his assurance that if these demands were accepted, he would present them to the Provisional Government and the Chambers, as the only means of saving France." [54]

No written record has survived of the conditions stipulated by Davout at this meeting, but in his memoires he states the principal ones as follows: "The king must enter Paris without the aid of foreign troops, which must not approach within thirty leagues of the capital; the two Chambers must be conserved and the army until peace is concluded; a total disregard of all votes, discussions and legislative acts of the last events which would be passed, and an assurance of the security of Napoleon and his family." [55] In these conditions Davout believed that the honor and dignity of all concerned would be upheld. His naïveté in believing that the King would accept such compromising terms, or that the Allies would allow him to do so, indicates his lack of experience in politics. The man who had been a lion on the field of battle was proving himself to be an amateur in the political arena.

Oudinot took Davout's proposition to Vitrolles and returned several hours later with rather vague and obscure assurances. The minister of war was told that Vitrolles had "full powers" to speak for the King, but that he was somewhat surprised at the Marshal's demands. After all, everyone was aware of the King's generosity upon his return in 1814. Such a proposition as that drawn up by Davout would be considered an outrage in the light of Louis's past benevolence. Both parties were in agreement that it was in the best interest of all that the King should be accepted by the government and reenter Paris without the aid of foreign troops. However, Vitrolles, who in fact could speak with no real authority, said that he could guarantee the proposition which Davout put forward.[56] Time was now all-important.

The Prussian army was advancing upon the capital from the north and Grouchy had not yet arrived in strength with his troops. On the morning of June 27 Davout attended a conference at the Tuileries which included the Commission of the Government, the Council of Ministers, and the leading representatives of the two Chambers. Fouché presided over the gathering and opened it with a brief, but discouraging, description of the existing state of affairs. He saw little hope of resistance and declared that the Commission of the Government desired the opinions of the ministers and members of the Chambers. "When all of these persons, of whom some had nothing to say and others dared not speak, had exchanged vague words, Davout demanded to be heard." [57] He declared that after having studied thoroughly the military situation from the points of view of numbers, material, and morale of the French army, and the rapid advance of the enemy, he was convinced that there was little point in resistance. "In order to evade the greatest catastrophe," he said outrightly, "it is necessary to rally to the king upon obtaining from him certain essential guarantees." [58] He then set forth, article by article, the guarantees which he believed necessary to accompany the Bourbon restoration. The majority of the assembly was in agreement with the minister of war. Only a few, notably Carnot and Thibaudeau, expressed opposition.[59]

Davout's bold, and to many surprising, position in favor of the return of Louis XVIII was not motivated by self-interest. His actions were stimulated by his deep concern for France—particularly in this case the city of Paris—and the army. He had come to the belief that the restoration of the Bourbon dynasty was in the best interests of the nation, and that it should, therefore, be brought about as painlessly as possible. The military situation, upon which he based his judgments, was in the long run hopeless. This is not to say that he could not have held Paris for several weeks—perhaps several months. But in the end France could not hope to win the war. Time was on the side of the Allies, and with each passing day their numbers would increase. The main French army, indeed the only formidable French army, had been defeated by the English and Prussian forces. When the Austrian and Russian armies would reach France in full force, sheer numerical superiority would win the day as it had in 1814. Furthermore, Davout knew that the French people were unwilling to repeat the sacrifices of 1792–94 which had turned back the invaders. Thus, if the king was to be restored, better by a French government than an enemy army, and better on conditions laid down by that government than by those that might emanate from London, Berlin, or Vienna.

The military situation continued to deteriorate as the government floundered. By June 28 the Prussian cavalry had reached the plains of Saint Denis and were pushing hard their advance on the capital. Wellington was moving at a more leisurely pace, but within a week he too would be at the gates of Paris. The remnants of the French army which had fought at Waterloo were arriving to bolster the defenses of the threatened city; however, their reorganization had been hasty and was incomplete, and their morale was low. The principal forces upon which the defense of the city depended were Grouchy's three corps (Vandamme, Gérard, and Exelmans) and they had not yet arrived. During the twenty-eighth Vandamme's III Corps marched south from Soissons toward Meaux, and that evening the General wrote that his men were exhausted from forced marches and rearguard actions. He reported that it would be forty-eight hours before they could take up positions about Paris and become an integral part of the city's defenses.[60] Paris had not been prepared for a major, prolonged siege. Its defenses on the right bank of the Seine were in good condition and adequately manned. If the Seine became the line of defense the city was not in serious danger. This presumed, however, an army operating both to the east and west of the capital, completely independent of the city's own garrison, and capable of preventing the enemy from crossing the river. But Paris had not been fortified on the left bank of the river prior to Waterloo. Some measures were taken during the last week of June; but, as Davout reported to the government, defenses on the left bank were virtually nonexistent.[61] Thoroughly convinced of the futility of continuing the struggle, Davout became one of the strongest advocates of an armistice which would halt the Allied advance on Paris.

To secure such an armistice he entered into negotiations with Vitrolles and Oudinot on the one hand and the government on the other. The difficulties proved to be insurmountable. The members of the Commission of the Government and the representatives in the Chambers did not want to be responsible for an armistice unless they could point to the military as being incapable of defending the capital. Davout knew that he could, in fact, defend the city but only temporarily. Furthermore, Fouché did not want to see a military solution until he had achieved his own personal political ends. The picture was further complicated, though it was not known in Paris, by Blücher's determination to enter the French capital at the head of his victorious army. He cared nothing for the political intrigues of his enemy, having in mind only the humiliation of 1806.

Davout was becoming increasingly disgusted with the intrigues of Fouché and his immediate circle, and the increasing number of peers and representatives, all of whom were more interested in their own personal welfare than in that of the nation as a whole. His own aims were straightforward—to save Paris, the nation, and the army from the catastrophe which was about to engulf them. To do this it was necessary to stop the fighting and bring back the King. Neither of these solutions came easily or willingly to a professional soldier and long-time Bonapartist. Yet, as he wrote to Fouché on June 28: "My motives are inspired by the future; I have conquered my prejudices and my convictions. The greatest necessity and inward conviction have led me to believe that there is no other way to save our nation." [62]

On the same day Fouché answered the minister of war by authorizing him to enter into negotiations with the enemy for a cessation of hostilities and to make "all sacrifices which are compatible with your duty and dignity." [63] The latter statement was designed to give the President of the Commission an escape in the event all did not go well. On June 30 Davout dispatched General Kellermann and the Major-General of the Paris National Guard, General Tourton, to Wellington and Blücher with a request for an armistice.[64] This desperate effort to stop the enemy's advance was coupled with continued efforts to reach a political solution of internal affairs through talks with Vitrolles.

Vitrolles was with Davout at his forward headquarters at Villette on the evening of the twenty-ninth when a delegation of representatives from the two Chambers [65] arrived with a patriotic address to the army.[66] The Marshal was in an upper room with Vitrolles when they arrived. If he had wished to do so, he could have easily concealed the identity of his unpopular visitor. But the straightforward Davout received the representatives in the same room with the royalist agent. The presence of Vitrolles at army headquarters caused much alarm among the newcomers. They spoke out with passion against Fouché, Vitrolles, and Davout himself. To calm them the Marshal declared that he would never act against the interest of the nation or the will of its representatives. Then in order to reassure the generals who accompanied the deputies he stated forcefully that he would always act in accord with his comrades-in-arms.[67]

The representatives departed after inspecting troops from the army corps which had taken part in the Battle of Waterloo. In their report to the Chamber of Representatives the next day they made no mention of Vitrolles's presence at Villette. However, a number of the generals were profoundly disturbed. In order to reassure themselves, the government, and the army as a whole, they drew up an address during the night of June 29–30 which, according to Davout,[68] asserted the patriotism of the army and its desire to be in accord with the nation's representatives to save France, but which was completely devoid of any political statement or inference. After the Marshal read and signed the address it was realized that there had been an omission and that several modifications were necessary. As it was necessary for him to inspect the city's defenses in anticipation of an enemy attack in the morning, Davout signed a blank piece of paper on which was to be written the modified address. In the final draft, written in above his signature, a statement was added declaring that the army would never accept the restoration of the Bourbons.[69] The address, with its rejection of the King, was read before the Chamber of Representatives on July 1.[70]

When Davout learned that the address, which bore his signature, had been altered so as to make it a major political statement rather than a patriotic reassurance, he immediately denounced it. In a lengthy letter addressed to the Chamber of Representatives he vainly explained that his signature on the document which had been read to them did not express his political sentiments. "It is for you, the guardians of this great nation's destiny, to choose a head of government who will restore happiness; it is for us, devoted warriors, that it is reserved to execute without question the resolutions which you dictate."[71]

Davout's repudiation of the controversial address, written on July 2, was not received by the Chamber of Representatives until after the capitulation of the city of Paris. It was interpreted by some, not all of whom could be classified as his "enemies," as merely a political expediency by one who had championed a losing cause, and now that he saw clearly that the King would be restored he hoped to save his career.[72] The Marshal had not been enthusiastic about the address from the first. He was prepared to accept the restoration of the Bourbons with certain assurances. He signed the address because, as he later said: "As we were on the eve of a battle, the Marshal [Davout] feared that a display of dissension, a disagreement among the chiefs, would only serve to weaken and demoralize the army." [73]

On June 30 Davout was informed that Blücher and Wellington had refused to enter into negotiations for an armistice. It was becoming apparent to the Marshal that whether he liked it or not, he would have to fight a major engagement.[74] In the early hours of dawn on June 30 the Prussians attacked the northern defenses of the city to estimate their strength and the determination of the French to defend their capital. Finding them formidable and stoutly defended, Blücher decided to march around Paris by way of St. Germain and Versailles to attack the city from the south where his informants indicated the defenses were extremely weak.

The leading Prussian division crossed to the left bank of the Seine at Pecq and occupied St. Germain. On the morning of July 1, a cavalry brigade commanded by Colonel Sohr moved south toward Versailles with orders to swing eastward and cut the main road between Paris and Orléans. Davout, who was kept informed of the enemy's movements by the inhabitants, realized at once that Blücher's army was in an extremely vulnerable position. Stretched out from Versailles, through St. Germain, to St. Denis it could be attacked and forced to fight at a numerical and tactical disadvantage. Wellington's army was approaching Paris from the northeast, but could not have taken part in a battle west of the city before the second. The army wanted to fight. If they could defeat the Prussians and throw them back upon the English, they would be revenging Waterloo and checking the advance on Paris all in one blow. But Davout decided not to undertake a major engagement.

The Marshal felt the same desire for battle as did the officers and men under him. He was confident of victory and aware that it would bring new glory to his already illustrious career. However, realism continued to govern his actions. He still believed, and quite correctly so, that while he might be able to win a battle the campaign would be lost. The inevitable arrival of the Austrian and Russian armies would be the decisive factor. There was only glory to be had in a battle at this time, and perhaps for the first time in his life Davout rejected glory in the interest of the nation. He would content himself and appease the army by a limited engagement.[75]

Early on July 1 Davout ordered General Exelmans to assemble all of the cavalry on the left bank of the Seine and with it to attack the Prussian force moving toward Versailles. Exelmans deployed his forces skillfully. With one division he surprised the enemy at Villacoublay and threw him back into Versailles. Having been roughly handled by Exelmans's highly motivated men, Sohr ordered his brigade back toward St. Germain. At Rocquencourt Exelmans's second division lay in wait. When the already disorganized Prussian cavalry approached, the French fell upon them. In the ensuing battle virtually the entire Prussian brigade was either killed, wounded, or captured.[76] In some quarters of the army it was believed that this action was a prelude to an all-out attack on the Prussian army; but Davout, who was waiting for an answer to a new request for an armistice, had no such intention.

During the same morning, while Exelmans was marching to Versailles, a meeting of the Commission of the Government and military representatives from the Chambers was taking place at the Tuileries. As President of the Commission, Fouché presided over the meeting. He had already decided that it was necessary for the army to evacuate Paris and retire beyond the Loire. In order to convince the Chambers of the hopelessness of the military situation and of the necessity of recognizing Louis XVIII, Fouché sent a letter to Davout in which he asked the following questions: "Are you able to defend all of the approaches of Paris, those on the left bank of the Seine as well as the right? Are you able to fight at all points at the same time without compromising the fate of a million persons? In a word, for how much longer can you answer for the fate of the capital?"[77] At the end of the letter he invited the Marshal to attend the meeting that morning at the Tuileries to give answers to these questions. Davout recognized the skillful political maneuver. Fouché intended to put the blame for the evacuation of Paris on the Marshal and the military. Therefore, he neither attended the meeting nor answered the letter. But the political heads of the government would not be put off. They ordered Davout to call a council of war which would be attended by all marshals who were in Paris at the time, corps commanders, and the general officers in command of the artillery and the engineers.

This council of war met at nine o'clock on the evening of July 1 to discuss the specific questions put to it by the Commission of Government:

> 1. What is the state of entrenchments and their equipment, on the right as well as the left bank of the river?
>
> 2. Is the army able to defend all of the approaches of Paris—particularly on the left bank of the Seine?
>
> 3. Would the army be capable of fighting at all points at the same time?
>
> 4. In the event of a set-back, would the General-in-Chief be able to prevent an entrance by force?
>
> 5. Does there exist enough munitions for numerous battles?
>
> 6. Finally, can you control the fate of the capital, and for what length of time? [78]

The council was held at Davout's forward headquarters at Villette. Present were Marshals Masséna, Soult, Moncey, Mortier, Kellermann, Lefebvre, Sérurier, Oudinot, Gouvion St.-Cyr, and Grouchy, and Generals Vandamme, d'Erlon, Reille, Drouot, Gazan, Valée and Duponthon.[79] As presiding officer, Davout opened the council by reviewing the questions they were to discuss. Then General Valée, commander of the artillery, reported on the city's fortifications. For the next six hours the marshals and generals discussed the military and political situation. In the early hours of July 2 Davout penned the following reply to the government:

> *In answer to the demands posed by the government, the Council of War offers the following answers:*
>
> *To the first:* What is the state of the entrenchments and equipment on the right bank of the Seine. Although incomplete, they are in general satisfactory; of those on the left bank, the entrenchments are considered as non-existing.
>
> *To the second:* That the army is able [to defend the city] but not indefinitely and that it will not be exposed to a lack of food or shelter.

To the third: That it is difficult for the army to be attacked at all points simultaneously; but if that should occur, there would be no possibility of resistance.

To the fourth: That no general is able to predict the outcome of a battle.

To the fifth: That there are sufficient munitions.

To the sixth: That there can be no guarantee in this regard.[80]

Davout knew very well that his response would give the government the opportunity to shift the responsibility for whatever action it now wished to take onto the army. "I had no doubts," he wrote later, "but that a battle could be won beneath the walls of Paris and console by a momentary success the sorrow of the nation. If I had listened only to the interest of my own military glory, I would not have hesitated to profit from the opportunity that was offered me. But it would only have served my interests. The political and military situation had not changed, for the enemy had enormous reinforcements which would soon join them and give them a numerical superiority. We would still have been forced to treat [for terms] after a useless shedding of blood." [81]

The useless shedding of blood which the Marshal had hoped to avoid and which had already begun on June 30 was intensified during the morning of July 2. Exelmans's elimination of the Prussian cavalry brigade on the first had made the enemy more cautious but had not stopped his advance. By noon of the second, Prussian infantry had reached the heights of Sevres and were attacking the French positions protecting the bridge on the left bank of the Seine. Further east Issy was also attacked, and after heavy fighting the French were driven out of their advance posts. During the day Davout moved the bulk of the army to the left bank of the river. He knew that Blücher was the more dangerous of his two adversaries and that the southern approaches to the capital were the weakest. Wellington, he quite correctly judged, would hesitate before attacking the strong defenses on the right bank of the Seine. The night of July 2–3 was spent in preparing for the major battle which everyone believed would take place in the morning, by which time virtually the entire Prussian army would be on the left bank of the river and ready for action. But the military activities of the night were more than matched by those of the politicians.

Led by Fouché, the Commission of the Government, with the approval of the Chambers, sent one last delegate to the Allies. The Baron Bignon, as Under-Secretary of State for Foreign Affairs, led the three-man delegation.[82] Early on the morning of July 3, they found Davout at Montrouge. The Marshal was already on horseback and giving orders for last-minute preparations for an attack on the Prussian position at Issy. Firing had begun and the French divisions were under arms and awaiting the signal to advance.

Bignon explained his mission to Davout. The Marshal replied that he was in an excellent position for a general attack against the Prussian flank, and that the attack would surely be successful in driving Blücher back across the Seine for he was in a very unfavorable position with no possibility of receiving support from Wellington. This, continued Davout, would put the French plenipotentiaries in a much stronger bargaining position. Bignon replied that the Marshal would have to decide what he thought best in this situation. On hearing this Davout mounted his horse and galloped off along the French lines toward Vaugirard. Returning one hour later he informed Bignon that he had sent an officer to Blücher requesting a safe-conduct for the plenipotentiaries to negotiate an armistice.[83] The overall picture had not changed. A victory over the Prussians would only postpone, not alter, the inevitable.

The decision was again a difficult one for a man who had always chosen battle and never tasted defeat. The army wished to fight, if only to redeem its honor. Davout knew full well that there would be those who would accuse him of having lost his nerve and of having surrendered Paris without a fight. He could have sacrificed the army and the city for honor and glory, and, indeed, if it had been some ten or fifteen years earlier he might have done so. But Davout had compiled an excellent military record and could now afford to consider the effects of battle in terms other than his own reputation. He did what soldiers are seldom willing to do—he sacrificed the honor of the army for the good of the nation.

Fighting died down along the line during the morning of July 3 as negotiations for an armistice got under way. By afternoon an agreement had been reached (and signed on the fourth) by which the French army would evacuate Paris and withdraw south of the Loire. The Allied armies would occupy the city, while respecting the rights of citizens and property. Blücher cared nothing for the political settlement which would result from the Allied victory. He was satisfied with the occupation of Paris. Wellington, on the other hand, was careful not to make any commitments which would hinder in any way the restoration of Louis XVIII to the throne.[84]

The army began its withdrawal to the Loire on July 4. Marching in two columns by way of Etampes, one to Orléans the other to Blois, the once proud fighting men of France presented a sorry spectacle. Although their material condition was good, their morale had collapsed. Driven from the field at Waterloo, they had regrouped and reorganized about Paris. They desperately needed, and desired, one last battle to reestablish the honor of the army. When this was denied them by the capitulation of Paris, morale sank to a new low. Thousands of men deserted during the hot dusty march south. "I have 81 deserters from the 33rd, and 87 from the 86th," wrote General Berthezene, "in my artillery the desertion is so high that there remain only six men for each train." [85]

In order that he might accompany the army Davout resigned his post as minister of war, and in accordance with his request was given command of the Army of the Loire.[86] Included in this new army was not only the main French force retreating from Paris, but also the troops under the command of General Lamarque along the lower Loire which had hitherto been referred to as the "Army of the Loire," [87] and the troops in the various garrisons of the principal towns and cities south of the river. The army numbered between seventy-five and one hundred thousand men as it took up its position behind the Loire on July 11.[88] No mention had been made in the Capitulation of Paris relative to the occupation of the right bank of the Loire by the Allied army. Nevertheless, Blücher ordered his troops to follow the retreating French and did in fact occupy the right bank.

Before leaving the Paris area Davout, who spent several days at Savigny with his family while directing the withdrawal, appointed on July 7 a commission of three to represent the army in the capital and negotiate its submission to the new head of state.[89] In order that this commission be representative of the army, rather than himself as commander of the army, he appointed General Gérard (infantry); General Kellermann, Count of Valmy (cavalry); and General Haxo (special services). Gérard and Haxo arrived immediately in the capital, but Kellermann, feeling it necessary to remain with his troops until they were settled behind the Loire, did not join them until the tenth. The two representatives went first to see Fouché who was of little help to them. After telling them that the army would have to renounce the tricolors, he suggested that they see the new minister of war, Marshal Gouvion St.-Cyr, as the Executive Committee had ceased to function after July 7.

The army now found itself in a strange and awkward position. "By its sentiment, by its tradition," wrote Davout, "it was a national army, and yet it did not know whom to obey, or with which cause to place its devotion and courage. . . . An army without a government is a sort of monster which does not understand itself; it would be a reproduction of those bands, those great companies, with which Duquesclin liberated France during the darkest days of our history." [90] Its Commissioners found no sympathy in Paris, neither from civilians nor, as they might have hoped, from the military. St.-Cyr, who was completely submissive to the will of the King, received them coolly.[91] The press, which had become royalist almost overnight, referred to the army as the "Brigands of the Loire." Still Davout hoped to prevent civil war and strengthen the bargaining power of the King by delivering the army intact into his hands. This meant saving what was left of the army and rallying to Louis XVIII. It also meant to Davout receiving some kind of assurance that the army would not be purged.

On July 10 Kellermann arrived in Paris with new instructions for the Commission. "The army is ready to swear fidelity to the king and to the laws which govern the nation," Davout wrote, with the approval of twenty-two generals and forty-four colonels and senior officers, "it demands that which honor ordains: that no Frenchman be proscribed—neither of his rank nor his civil or military position; and that the army be conserved in its existing state until the foreigners have left France." [92] No mention was made of preserving the national colors. Davout knew very well that the army would have to accept the white cockade of the House of Bourbon, an act which would not be easy for the vast majority of the men.

When Gérard, Kellermann, and Haxo presented the army's demands to the minister of war, St.-Cyr told them that it would not be dignified for the King to bargain with the army and that it should submit unconditionally to His Majesty. He then added: "I promise you that you will be content with the king and that he will probably grant more than you demand." [93] When the commissionaires informed the minister that their instructions required guarantees, St.-Cyr arranged for their demands to be put before Louis and his ministers. On July 11 they received a negative reply. The new government absolutely refused to enter into any form of discussion with the representatives of the army until after it had submitted to the authority of the King. Louis and his ministers followed this hostile course of action because they believed that the army was no longer of one mind.

On July 9, without consulting or informing his commander in chief, General Milhaud wrote to the minister of war offering his own unconditional submission and that of the officers and men under him.[94] This independent course of action, by which Milhaud hoped to save his own political position, weakened the position of the army to such an extent that upon hearing of it from the commissioners in Paris Davout immediately realized that there was no longer any possibility of obtaining concessions from the King. On July 13 the Marshal wrote to Gérard, Kellermann, and Haxo: "You have acquired by your conduct the esteem of the entire French army. . . . If you judge that a pure and simple submission would be useful to our unhappy nation, make it; but save the honor of the army, because without that it would no longer be of any use, it would break up entirely." [95]

There was yet another factor to be taken into consideration in offering the submission of the army at this time. Neither Austria nor Russia had taken part in the negotiations which had led to the armistice and capitulation of Paris on July 3. Thus their armies were still advancing from the east toward the Loire. It was at best questionable as to whether or not they would stop at the river or force a crossing and continue the war. If the army placed itself under the King, whose government would then encompass the entire French nation, it would be difficult for his allies to continue hostilities against his army.

The unconditional submission of the army was dated on July 14.[96] Copies were made of it and sent to all military units to obtain the maximum number of signatures. Virtually all high-ranking officers of the Army of the Loire affixed their signatures to the document.[97] One might well imagine that this last act would bring down the curtain on the finale of this tragedy; but such was not the case.

There was still the acceptance of the very unpopular white cockade and the purging of the army by the Ordinance of July 24. The former had a major demoralizing effect on the masses of the troops, the latter on the officer corps.

The tricolor had been the rallying symbol of the Revolution and the Empire. It was associated with the social and political gains brought about by the turbulent decade of the 1790s and consolidated during the Empire. In addition, it was associated with the most glorious era of French military history. Its repudiation seemed to imply a rejection—even a condemnation—of the past quarter of a century.[98] This humiliation was keenly felt by the soldiers of the Army of the Loire and resulted in a sharp increase in the numbers of desertions during the last two weeks of July.[99] Discipline also reached a new low after having been reestablished to a reasonable degree following the capitulation of Paris and the march to the Loire.[100] The continued advance of the Austrian army toward the Loire, and its passage of the river at Bourbon-Lancy,[101] required Davout to make continuous preparations to defend his position. This threat helped to restore order, but low morale and poor discipline continued to plague the army throughout the summer.

The Ordinance of July 24 was a direct contradiction of the Proclamation of Cambrai which the King had issued upon his return from exile in the last week of June. In this document Louis had declared that he would leave it to the legislature to decide who should be punished for their actions during the Hundred Days, and that no one who had remained loyal until March 23 would be included. However, pressure from the Allies, who took a much harder line in 1815 than they had in 1814, coupled with a desire to relieve tension which had been building up as the result of rumors of which, and how many, names would be on such a list persuaded the King to act. The new minister of police, Fouché, was given the task of drawing up the list of those to be proscribed, and Talleyrand's cutting remark best described it: "We must give the Duke of Otrante credit for one thing, he did not forget any of his friends in drawing up the list."[102] As it finally appeared, after some revision, the proscription list contained the names of nineteen officers accused of treason and ordered to be tried by military courts, and thirty-eight other persons to be placed under arrest until such time as their fate could be determined by the legislature.

This was precisely what Davout had tried to prevent by attaching guarantees to the submission of the army. Realizing that he had been tricked, and despite the fact that with Fouché's assistance, he had made it possible for all of the officers on the list to avoid apprehension,[103] the Marshal resigned his post as commander of the Army of the Loire.[104] In a lengthy letter to the minister of war, dated July 27, Davout poured out his bitter disappointment. After citing the numerous assurances that there would be no proscription, but that at worst "several persons would be temporarily deprived of the right to reside in Paris or to approach the king," he wrote: "I see in the first article the names of generals Gilly, Grouchy, Clausel and Laborde. If they have been placed there for their conduct at Pont-Saint-Esprit, Lyon, Bordeux and Toulouse, it is an error, because they were only obeying orders which I addressed to them in my capacity as minister of war. It is therefore necessary to substitute my name for theirs. The same observation applies to General Allix, if he was proscribed for his conduct at Lille; for Colonel Marbot, for that which he did at Valenciennes; for General Lamarque, who could have no more against him than the pacification of the Vendée."[105]

Disappointed, disillusioned and angry, no longer able to influence the course of events, and determined not to preside over the dismemberment of the army he had worked so hard to preserve, Davout demanded that his replacement be sent immediately and that he be allowed to retire to his estate.[106] On August 1 Marshal Macdonald, Duke of Tarente, arrived at Bourges and assumed command of the Army of the Loire. During his last days with the army Davout had done everything within his power to warn those officers who were in danger of being arrested, and to aid them to leave France. "The victims," he later wrote, "such as Colonel Labedoyere and Marshal Ney, had had the possibility and the means of avoiding their fate."[107]

15

The Declining Years

RETURNING TO SAVIGNY in the first week of August, Davout prepared to resume the quiet life he had been leading when Napoleon arrived from Elba. During the Allied occupation of Paris, his wife had given birth to a baby girl, Adélaïde-Louise on July 8, 1815. Both mother and new daughter, as well as the other three children, were on hand to greet him. However, the reception was somewhat marred by the presence of the Prussian army which occupied the estate. The Prussian officers treated the Duke of Auerstädt with respect, and on several occasions the Marshal invited them to dinner. Still the whole affair was quite displeasing to a man who had himself commanded occupation troops in Germany for so many years. During the remaining weeks of the summer and fall of 1815 Davout settled once again into the life of a gentleman farmer, devoting his time and energy to the education of his children, the management of his lands, and the care of the new gardens about the chateau. However, this tranquility was once again interrupted.

The trial of Marshal Ney for treason, which opened on December 4, brought Davout out of seclusion and back into the limelight. Ney had been arrested in accordance with the Ordinance of July 24 and brought before a military court. However, the Prince of the Moskawa, exercising his right as a peer of France, demanded to be tried in the Chamber of Peers. Davout strongly recommended to the prisoner, as did many of his friends, that he stand trial before his military "peers" rather than before the Chamber; for it was unlikely that any soldier would have condemned the Prince of the Moskawa. Ney refused what, in retrospect, was excellent advice. Although Davout had not been on good terms with him since the retreat from Moscow, there had been somewhat of a reconciliation in the weeks before Waterloo. Thus, when he was called upon by the defense to testify on behalf of the accused man, Davout accepted without consideration of the effect such testimony might have on his own position under the Bourbon restoration.

The restored government of Louis XVIII was in desperate need of an example which would show the Allies that they were taking action against the responsible parties for the Hundred Days. Davout himself might have been a fine sacrificial gift but for the fact that he had never taken service with the King during the first Restoration and was thus free to serve under Napoleon when he returned. But Ney had not only sworn allegiance, he had accepted command of royal troops and had vowed to capture Napoleon and bring him back to Paris a prisoner. He was from the royalist point of view an ideal example. Before the trial was half over, the outcome was no longer in doubt.

Davout was called to the stand on December 5.[1] The president of the Chamber of Peers opened the examination by asking the Marshal if he knew Ney before the events which had led to his trial. Before Davout could answer, counsel for the defense (M. Berryer) rose and objected, declaring that the purpose of the Marshal's presence was to give the court his recollections on the Convention of July 3, 1815. Thereupon Davout related how he had prepared for battle on the night of July 2, and how, as a result of this, he had concluded a convention with the enemy for the evacuation of Paris.[2] M. Berryer then asked the witness what he would have done if the enemy had refused to sign the convention, and what were the possibilities of the success of his course of action. "I would have given battle," answered the Prince of Eckmühl. "I had 60,000 infantry, 25,000 cavalry, 400 to 500 pieces of artillery and as much expectation of success which a general commanding French troops could have."[3] Berryer next asked the Marshal to tell the Chamber what was the meaning of article 12 of the Convention which both he and the provisional government had signed. (This was the article which guaranteed to the Bonapartists that there would be no proscription for words or deeds after March 20, 1815.) At this point the prosecutor, M. Bellart, rose and declared that the question was irrelevant. Article 12 was concerned with the capitulation of the city of Paris whereas Marshal Ney was accused on the basis of acts performed which in no way had to do with that capitulation. "The opinion of the prince [of Eckmühl] can change nothing," concluded Bellart. "An act can not be altered by a declaration." [4]

Davout's testimony before the Chamber of Peers had no effect upon the outcome of the trial, and the "bravest of the brave" was condemned to death on December 6 and shot by a firing squad two days later. The death of Ney, however, did not end the affair as far as Davout was concerned. His testimony at the trial served to remind the royalists of his unyielding support of the adventurous usurper during the Hundred Days. "If Article 12 had not been included," the Marshal is quoted as having said, "I would never have concluded the convention of Paris." [5] The court circle which had the ear of the King needed no urging to implore Louis XVIII to take some action against this proven Bonapartist. The result was that on December 27, 1815, just three weeks after Ney's trial, the Prince of Eckmühl was ordered into exile. He was directed to take up residence in the city of Louviers and was forbidden to leave without the permission of the government.[6] The Minister of Police had originally designated Moutiers as the place of exile, but upon Davout's request he was allowed to move into a house owned by a cousin of his wife's in Louviers on the rue Royal.

The proud Marshal accepted his exile as an act of fate, but with the understanding that it would be temporary. He believed it to be a gross injustice, and bitterly resented the implications which accompanied such a "disgrace." He felt that his actions following the abdication of Napoleon had been in the best interest of France and the army. While he did not expect gratitude from the restored monarch, neither did he expect to be punished. His correspondence from Louviers makes it very clear that he considered his exile cruel and unnecessary.[7]

Madame Davout accompanied her husband to Louviers on the last day of January 1816, but she was unable to remain with him for more than two weeks. Returning to Paris she was occupied through the remaining months of the winter and the spring with negotiations to rent their Paris house, intrigue to secure her husband's return to Savigny, the care and education of their four children, and the management of their estate. The separation was all the more painful for both of the Davouts in that, unlike the prolonged absence of the Marshal during the Napoleonic era, there was neither duty, nor honor, nor glory, nor wealth to justify their loneliness. On the ninth of March Aimée returned to Louviers to spend two and one-half weeks with her husband, and again in mid-April she spent two weeks with the lonely exile. But these brief visits were all too short and the Marshal grew increasingly impatient through the spring of 1816 for news that he could return to Savigny.

During the seemingly endless days at Louviers, Davout took long walks in the country, read extensively in ancient history (Babylonian, Assyrian, and Roman), and, after March 10, undertook the education of his son who stayed with him several months.[8] He also concerned himself with affairs at Savigny and Paris. At first he did not like the idea of renting their Paris house, but pressing financial needs led him to approve his wife's negotiations with an American who wished a three-year lease on the magnificent structure on the rue St. Dominique. However, the house was never rented and their financial problems multiplied rapidly.

Davout's principal source of income throughout the Empire had been lands outside of France which the Emperor had given to him. With the collapse of the Empire, he was deprived of this revenue. Furthermore, he had been deprived of his military pay on October 27, 1815.[9] The only income which remained to him was derived from his land in France, and this was quite insufficient to maintain even the reduced standard of living which the Davouts had adopted. The result was that he continued to go into debt throughout 1816. Davout himself lived on 3.50 francs a day in Louviers,[10] and was unable to pay the wages of his faithful manservant M. Mayer,[11] who had accompanied him into exile. On April 5 his wife wrote from Paris: "All of our creditors are demanding their money; it is painful for me to refuse them, especially knowing their needs."[12] In these difficult days the Parisian furniture maker M. Jacob, who had made the furniture for the Hôtel Eckmühl (as their Paris house was called), offered to lend the Davouts money.[13] Although their need was great his offer was graciously refused.

By the first of April Davout was becoming impatient with the royal government because there had been no indication of when he might be allowed to return to Savigny. "I have just received, my dear Aimée, your letter of March 31," he wrote. "It has disappointed me very much. I have been waiting for definite news concerning my return to Savigny." [14] Yet despite this impatience, his wife, who was keeping well informed of the attitudes of the court, was unable to be encouraging. On the third of the same month she wrote that his isolation was necessary; that the minister of police received regular reports from the mayor of Louviers concerning him and his activities and that it was necessary that he saw no one, especially those who were hostile to the government.[15] This drew an angry reply from the exile in which he declared that he had seen only two or three persons since he was at Louviers and that he knew nothing of their political views.[16]

Shortly after Madame Davout's return from her April visit with her husband, she was at last able to write encouragingly concerning his return. Through the mediation of Marshal Macdonald, Duke of Taranto, and the Duke of Doudeauville the King was considering the return of Davout to Savigny. However, more than a month was to elapse before the formal order was issued. The marriage of the Duke of Berry, who was second in line to the throne, proved to be the final factor in Davout's return from exile. As one aspect of the celebration, he received the order (June 21, 1816) which allowed him to rejoin his family. Leaving Louviers that same evening and traveling through the night he arrived home the following day. Although he was allowed to reside on his estate just south of Paris, he was still far from a reconciliation with the royal government. He was forbidden to enter the city of Paris without royal permission, and this permission was denied him throughout the remainder of the summer and the fall of 1816. Furthermore, he remained under surveillance by the local authorities.[17] Although the commander of the police of Seine-et-Oise considered Davout to be a threat to the government and suggested maximum surveillance, the Prefect ordered merely a "precautionary surveillance." [18]

Davout occupied himself through the summer and fall of 1816 with the affairs of Savigny and his other holdings. He personally supervised the cutting of wood in the forest and the cultivation of his fields. He took a particular interest in the grape arbor which he had planted with vines imported from his native Burgundy. The wine which he produced from these grapes was so inferior that the Marshal alone was able to appreciate its qualities.[19] Yet, despite the careful management of their lands, the Davouts were unable to meet their financial obligations. "They no longer have any servants," wrote his mother-in-law, Mme. Leclerc, to her son on May 3, 1816, "that is to say very few." [20] Relief came at last on August 27, 1817, when Louis XVIII restored to Davout his military salary and four days later named him Marshal of France.[21] In addition to receiving the marshal's baton *fleurdelisé,* the King, in his generosity—or perhaps to ease his conscience—paid Davout's salary retroactively to January 7, 1816.[22] Thus the Marshal received one and a half year's back pay. The combination of back pay and the renewal of his salary enabled him to pay his debts and to reestablish the family's finances.

On August 31, 1817, before receiving the marshal's baton from the hands of Louis XVIII, Davout swore allegiance to the King. This marked the beginning of his return to public life. On February 11, 1819, Louis named him a Knight in the *Ordre royal et militaire de Saint-Louis.* This was followed on March 5 of the same year by his being named a Peer of the realm. He took his seat in the Chamber along with Marshals Jourdon, Lefebvre, Moncey, and Suchet who were equally honored at this time. Davout was thus completely reinstated and officially accepted by the restored Bourbon government. He did not seek acceptance in court circles or the upper strata of aristocratic society. Even if he had aspired to such social heights—which he did not—he would not have been accepted. Although he had come from good noble stock and won his titles on the battlefield in the best tradition of French nobility, he would always remain "Bonaparte nobility." Furthermore, though his wife may have been officially the "Princess of Eckmühl," the nobility of the Restoration would never forgive her for her bourgeois origins. Thus with few exceptions and no regrets, the Davouts associated primarily with the Imperial nobility.

The education of the Davout children was of the utmost concern to the Marshal. The two older girls, Josephine and Adèle, attended school in Paris. But young Louis, whose education was considered most important remained at home under the direct care of his father. Davout continued to work with his son until 1817 at which time he employed the services of James Gordon. Gordon, a twenty-five-year-old scholar, quickly gained the complete confidence of the elder Davout. By day he tutored young Louis, and after supper assisted the Marshal in putting his papers in order in preparation for the writing of his memoirs. It is in Gordon's hand that the manuscript of Davout's account of his role during the Hundred Days appears. During the long winter nights of 1818–19, the Marshal dictated to Gordon his account of the Hundred Days.[23] Gordon also assisted Davout in the preparation of the still-unpublished chapters of "Mémoires du maréchal Davout": chapter II, "Notes et pièces justificatives sur la campagne d'Egypte," and chapter III, "Notes sur la campagne d'Autriche—1800."[24] Chapter III on the Austrian campaign is in fairly good order, but the chapter on Egypt is more in the form of lengthy notes of ten to fifteen pages rather than a finished manuscript. If Davout and Gordon wrote a "Chapter I" it has been lost or misplaced since it is not to be found in the Davout Papers (K^1 to K^{100}) which were deposited in the War Archives (château de Vincennes) following the death of Madame Davout.

Davout's reentry into public life was quiet and unpretentious. His daughter, the Marquise de Blocqueville, declared emphatically that her father swore allegiance to the King and took an active part in affairs of state in order to assure the future of his son Louis.[25] In doing so, however, he also derived immediate financial rewards which undoubtedly saved Savigny and his Paris home from sale.

On March 13, 1819, Davout took his place in the Chamber of Peers. His political views led him to a seat in the midst of the loyal opposition, but he was in general ineffective in politics. His maiden speech in the Chamber (May 11, 1819) was made in defense of the army. On December 28 of the same year he spoke on behalf of prison reform, and on March 24, 1820, he defended the liberties of the individual. His final address before the Chamber of Peers was made on February 28, 1822, at which time he came to the defense of the muzzled press. When the Marshal's health began to fail in 1821–22, his attendance became irregular. By 1823 he had virtually ceased to attend the Chamber's deliberations. Yet despite the fact that his health was already beginning to fail in 1822, Davout accepted the position of mayor of Savigny on March 13.

Perhaps Davout's greatest joy in his waning years was the marriage of his oldest daughter Josephine, who was not yet sixteen years of age, to Count Achille Pierre Félix Vigier.[26] The ceremony took place at Savigny on August 5, 1820. Achille Vigier, born on May 22, 1801, in Paris, was the son of Pierre Vigier *ancien procureur au Parlement*. The elder Vigier had purchased extensive lands in the vicinity of Savigny during the Revolution and had expanded his holdings until his death in 1817, at which time young Achille inherited three hundred *arpents*. The marriage was the occasion of the greatest celebration the Davouts had ever had at Savigny. It brought together so large a number of high-ranking officers from the late Napoleonic army that it caused rumors of conspiracy in Paris.[27]

The joy which this marriage brought to the Davouts proved to be all too brief. Within one year—almost to the day—Josephine gave birth to a son Joseph Louis Jules Achille (August 12, 1821) and then seven days later, on the nineteenth, died of complications resulting from childbirth. The profound sorrow which engulfed Savigny was reflected on this occasion by Davout himself. In the past he had been a pillar of strength when death had overtaken the family, and his wife had depended completely upon him. But on this occasion he was unable to control his grief, and it had a telling effect upon his health.

The strain of twenty-two years of warfare, which had led him from the burning deserts of upper Egypt to the sub-zero temperatures of Russia, was beginning to show its effect. As early as 1816 there were indications that Davout's general health was beginning to fail. Despite his, and the family's, preference for the life at Savigny they began to spend the winter months at the Hôtel Eckmühl in Paris. With each passing year they retreated to Paris earlier in the fall and returned later in the spring. The Marshal made periodic visits to Savigny during the winter in order to oversee the care and management of his lands and chateau, but the cold damp air—the chateau was surrounded by water with a lake along one side—and the inability to heat the late-Renaissance structure made Savigny a health hazard during the greater part of the year.

The death of Josephine in 1821 caused Davout's health to take a turn for the worse. Upon the advice of his doctor he went to Vichy, accompanied by his wife, where they both underwent treatments. Although they returned to Paris as the weather became inclement, the Marshal's health failed to show substantial improvement. During the winter of 1821–22 he played an increasingly smaller role in the Chamber of Peers and gradually withdrew from public life. Even his return to Savigny for the summer months, which in the past had resulted in noticeable improvement, did not have the desired results. The winter of 1822–23 found him all but confined to the Hôtel Eckmühl. By spring it was apparent that the man who had survived the wars of the Revolution and the Empire was about to lose the final battle for life.

On May 21, 1823, Davout dictated his last will and testament.[28] In a sound state of mind, and fully aware that death was about to be rewarded for its patience, he bequested Savigny and the Hôtel Eckmühl to his wife. To his son Louis he left his library, maps, manuscripts, correspondence, and papers. Louis also received his father's arms, uniforms, decorations, and marshal's baton. These were to remain in the custody of the boy's mother until such time as she judged suitable for him to gain possession of them. His worldly possessions thus disposed of, Louis N. Davout prepared to meet his creator. Having received the last rites of the Roman Catholic church, he died on June 1, 1823, at the age of fifty-three.

Despite his request for a simple family funeral, the affair was in keeping with the dignity of a Marshal of France and Peer of the realm. A solemn requiem mass was celebrated at eleven o'clock on the morning of June 4 at the church of Sainte-Valère on the left bank of the Seine. The funeral procession, which was led by his son, the new Prince of Eckmühl, and which consisted of fourteen carriages and a military escort of two thousand men, bore the remains of the illustrious soldier on a caisson drawn by six horses. The dignitaries included marshals and generals from the army as well as members of both the Chamber of Peers and the Chamber of Deputies. At Père-Lachaise, Marshal Jourdan, his old comrade-in-arms, read an eulogy[29] worthy of the man being placed to rest. Davout was buried in the family plot next to his daughter Josephine.

Notes

Bibliography

Index

NOTES

CHAPTER I

1] Departmental Archives, Côte-d'Or, B. 10.471; B. 10.488; B. 10.574; E. 1251; and B. 10.598 as cited in Vicomte d'Avout, *Les d'Avouts: étude généalogique d'une famille d'ancienne chevalerie du duché de Bourgogne* (n.p., 1952).

2] See d'Avout, *Les d'Avouts,* p. 20.

3] Ibid., p. 18. The Vicomte d'Avout ties his family to that of du Vault by the marriage of Marguerite Davout to Eudes du Vault (d. 1272) and then traces Eudes's genealogy to 1230 (ibid., p. 20).

4] Davout changed the spelling of his name from "d'Avout" to "Davout" during the early years of the Revolution in conformance with the abolishment of titles of nobility. He continued to use this "common" spelling of his name until he was given the title of Duke of Auerstädt in 1808. From that time until his death he always used his title, styling himself Prince of Eckmühl after 1810. Other members of his family (excluding his own descendants) used the "Davout" spelling during the Revolution and Empire but returned to the noble spelling of "d'Avout" with the restoration of 1814.

5] See d'Avout, *Les d'Avouts,* pp. 9, 42–44.

6] Ibid., p. 10.

7] Marie-Louise's brother Etienne Minard died in the service of the King on the island of Saint-Dominque in 1763 during the Seven Years' War. It is interesting to note that Davout's brother-in-law, General Victoire Emmanuel Leclerc, also died on Saint-Dominque while commanding the French expedition to the island in 1801–2. Marie-Louise also had a sister, Anne-Edmée, who married Bernard Dominique Courtal de Cissey, a captain in the regiment of the Queen's dragoons.

8] François Eudes de Mézeray, *Histoire de France,* 3 vols. (Paris: M. Guillemot, 1643–51), 2: 718–19, as cited in Adélaïde-Louise de Blocqueville, *Le Maréchal Davout prince d'Eckmühl: raconté par les siens et par lui-même,* 4 vols. (Paris: Didier, 1879–80), 1: 82–83.

9] Julie was educated at the fashionable school at Saint-Cyr, which had been established in the second half of the seventeenth century by

Mme. de Maintenon. She later married the Comte de Beaumont, a general in the Napoleonic army.

10] Alexandre rose to the rank of general under the Empire, during which period he served many years as aide-de-camp to his brother, the Marshal.

11] Charles served in the French army and retired a colonel at the end of the Napoleonic wars. His younger son, General Léopold d'Avout, was named "Grand chancelier de la Legion d'honneur" by Napoleon III during the Second Empire. The Emperor also authorized him to revive the title of Duke of Auerstädt by which he and his descendants are known.

12] In a letter to his wife dated July 9, 1815, Davout wrote: "You have asked me, my Aimée, what name should be given our daughter; I would like it to be one of the names of my maternal grandmother, to whose memory, as you know, I have a religious attachment." Blocqueville, 4: 257.

13] The other eleven schools established at this time were in the cities of Beaumont, Brienne, Effiat, Dôle, Pont-a-Mousson, Pont-le-Voy, Rebais, Sorreze, Touron, Tyron, and Verdone. Actually the schools at Auxerre and Dôle were established seven months after the other ten. The law creating the ten schools was dated March 28, 1776, while that which brought Auxerre and Dôle into existance is dated October 31 of the same year. See Charles Moiset, "Le Collège royal militaire d'Auxerre," *Bulletin de la société des sciences historique et naturelles de l'Yonne* 47 (1893): 5–22.

14] Ibid., p. 8.

15] The school had been caught in the middle of the struggle between the Jesuits and the Jansenists during the 1760s and 1770s. Its enrollment had dropped from two hundred students in 1765 to about thirty in 1776. (Ibid., p. 12.) Nor were its troubles over when it was revitalized by the state in 1776. It was closed in November of 1793 by the revolutionary government in its attempt to secularize education. Reopened during the Empire, it continued to operate during the nineteenth century.

16] The Duke of Narbonne-Pelet (1771–1815) served Napoleon during the Empire.

17] As quoted in Charles Joly, *Le Maréchal Davout: prince d'Eckmühl* (Auxerre: Gustave Perriquet, 1864), p. 5.

18] As quoted in Comte Joseph Vigier, *Davout: maréchal d'empire, duc d'Auerstaedt, prince d'Eckmühl,* 2 vols. (Paris: Paul Ollendorff, 1898), 1: 14.

19] Louis Turreau, born at Orbec in 1761, was the son of Louis Turreau de Linières, advisor to the King and "siège presidial d'Evreux en Normandie, Cry, Pacy, Nonancout et justices en dependantes." His mother, Dame Marie-Antoinette d'Affray, was of noble birth.

CHAPTER 2

1] "Procès-verbal des officers de la 8e Compagnie due 3e Bataillon des Volontaires du Département de l'Yonne," Sept. 23, 1791. Archives de la département de l'Yonne, L 454 (hereafter cited as Arch. Yonne).

2] "Procès-verbal de la nomination de l'état-major au 3e Bataillon des Volontaires du Département de l'Yonne," Sept. 26, 1791. Arch. Yonne, L 454.

3] Ibid.

4] Alexandre Davout had a very respectable military career in his own right. He took part in many of the principal campaigns of the Revolution and Empire and rose to the rank of general of brigade before being retired from the army in 1813 for poor health. See André Rossigneux, "Officiers de la Grande Armée origenaires du départment de l'Yonne," *Bulletin de la société des sciences historiques et naturelles de l'Yonne* 66 (1912): 61–73.

5] D'Avout, *Les d'Avouts,* p. 46.

6] Arch. Yonne, L 459.

7] A full account of this episode was sent to the magistrates of the department of Yonne, dated April 21, 1791. The letter is reproduced in volume 1, pp. 295–97, of the four volume work published by his daughter Adélaïde-Louise, the Marquise de Blocqueville.

8] Arch. Yonne, L 461.

9] Davout to Administrators of Yonne, June 2, 1792. Arch. Yonne, L 461. See also letters from General Lafayette and the Administrators of Yonne to Davout in Arch. Yonne, L 461.

10] Lafayette was immediately imprisoned, first in Prussia and later in Austria, as he was believed to be one of the leading revolutionaries. He was not released until General Bonaparte made peace (Campo Formio) with the Austrians in 1797.

11] Arch. Yonne, L 461.

12] Davout to Administrators of Yonne, Nov. 19, 1792, Arch. Yonne, L 461.

13] *Moniteur,* Feb. 26, 1793.

14] Ramsay Weston Phipps, *The Armies of the First French Republic and the Rise of the Marshals of Napoleon I,* 5 vols. (Oxford: At the Clarendon Press, 1935–39), 1: 152.

15] Beurnouville and the four commissioners were exchanged in 1795 for the daughter of Louis XVI (the Duchesse d'Angoulême).

16] There are numerous accounts of this episode. The most reliable are to be found in the letter from Davout to the "Citoyens administrateurs" of Yonne (Arch. Yonne, L 461); and Phipps, *Armies of the First*

French Republic, 1: 158–70. The most extensive, and more romanticized account of Davout's movements is found in L.-J. Gabriel de Chénier's *Histoire de la vie politique, militaire et administrative du maréchal Davout* (Paris: Cosse, 1866), pp. 42–51.

17] Arthur Chuquet, *Les Guerres de la révolution,* vol. 11, *Hondschoote,* 3ᵉ serie (Paris: Léon Chailley, 1896).

18] Phipps, *Armies of the First French Republic,* 3: 18.

19] General Louis Antoine Pille had commanded the 1st Battalion of Volunteers from Côte-d'Or in the Army of the North. He and Davout had become good friends during the months preceding Dumouriez's defection. In the last critical days before the commanding general went over to the enemy, Dumouriez had placed Pille under arrest because he had refused to cooperate in the proposed march on Paris. Davout offered to free the general, but Pille refused saying that he had done no wrong and if he escaped it would imply some form of guilt. After Dumouriez's departure Pille was released and resumed command of his battalion.

20] Blocqueville, 4: 312–13.

21] Ibid.

CHAPTER 3

1] This may be seen in the arrest of General Bonaparte who corresponded with Augustin Robespierre and was known, at least by name, to his all-powerful brother Maximilian; and in the liberation of Josephine de Beauharnais who had been imprisoned for trying to aid her first husband, Alexandre, who had been arrested and executed by the Jacobins.

2] Letter from Turreau to General Pille, 20 *vendemiaire, an III*—October 11, 1794—as quoted in Vigier, *Davout: maréchal d'empire,* 1: 46.

3] The entire letter is given in Vigier, *Davout: maréchal d'empire,* 1: 44–45.

4] The entire letter is given in Vigier, *Davout: maréchal d'empire,* 1: 47.

5] Phipps, *Armies of the First French Republic,* 2: 199.

6] Gouvion St.-Cyr, *Mémoires sur les campagnes des armées du Rhin et de Rhin-et-Moselle de 1792 jusqu'à la paix de Campo-Formio,* 4 vols. (Paris: Anselin, 1829), 2: 385–86.

7] Two divisions from the Army of the Sambre and Meuse under the command of General Hatry continued the siege.

8] As quoted in Vigier, *Davout: maréchal d'empire,* 1: 51–55.

9] Davout to Marceau, July 2, 1795, as quoted in Vigier, *Davout: maréchal d'empire,* 1: 56.

10] Julie-Catherine-Charlotte-Françoise d'Avout was married to Général Comte Bonnin de la Bonniniere de Beaumont (1763–1830) on July 12, 1801.

11] St.-Cyr, *Mémoires,* 2: 333–34; and Baron Antoine Henri de Jomini, *Histoire des guerres de la révolution,* 15 vols. (Paris: Anselin et Pochard, 1820–24), 7: 62.

12] St.-Cyr, *Mémoires,* 2: 551; Jomini, *Histoire des guerres,* 7: 61–63.

13] Phipps, *Armies of the First French Republic,* 2: 211.

14] For this action Pichegru is most severely criticized by Jomini. For a fuller account of this phase of the campaign, see Jomini, *Histoire des guerres,* 7: 190 et seq.

15] St.-Cyr, *Mémoires,* 2: 102.

16] General Oudinot had fallen under five saber cuts and a ball and was taken to Ulm to recover from his wounds. He remained in Austrian hands until January 7, 1796, at which time he was exchanged for the Austrian General Zainiau. By the middle of April he was back on the active list of the Army of the Rhine and Moselle. (Phipps, *Armies of the First French Republic,* 2: 240–44.)

17] When Desaix assessed the situation late in the battle, he decided that a withdrawal into Mannheim was the only wise course open to the 6th Division; and, he therefore did not commit his own infantry.

18] The five Directors were Barras, Reubell, La Revelliere, Le Tourneur, and Carnot. As head of the war office Lazare Carnot continued to direct military affairs but not with the freedom of action he had had as a member of the Committee of Public Safety.

19] Phipps, *Armies of the First French Republic,* 2: 382–83, suggests that Davout may have taken part in the last phase of the retreat but says that there is no good evidence to prove that he joined the army before it was back behind the Rhine.

20] Huningue was evacuated on February 5, 1797.

21] The column commanded by Davout was made up of four battalion of infantry: three from the 31st Line and one from the 16th. Adjutant Generals Demont and Jardy commanded the two parts into which this force was divided.

CHAPTER 4

1] On Louis Desaix de Veygoux see Félix Martha-Beker, comte de Mons, *Le Général Desaix: étude historique* (Paris: Didier, 1852); Edmond Bonnal, *Histoire de Desaix: armées du Rhin, expédition d'Orient, Marengo, d'après les Archives du Dépot de la Guerre* (Paris: Dentu, 1881); and Armand Sauzet, *Desaix: le "sultan juste"* (Paris: Hachette, 1954).

2] Sauzet, *Desaix: le "sulant juste,"* p. 132.

3] J. Christopher Herold in his recently published *Bonaparte in Egypt* (New York: Harper & Row, 1962) builds a convincing case against Talleyrand while admitting that "historians have quarrelled over the question which of the two, Talleyrand or Bonaparte, initiated the Egyptian venture. Since it turned out to be a disaster, Talleyrand in his later years gave full credit for it to Bonaparte. Actually, it was thanks to Talleyrand's efforts rather than Bonaparte's that the Directory endorsed the plan" (p. 17).

4] Napoleon remarked at St. Helena that "Desaix was wholly wrapped up in war and glory. He was . . . always badly dressed, sometimes even ragged, and despising comfort and convenience." Barry Edward O'Meara, *Napoleon in Exile, or a Voice from St. Helena. The Opinions and Reflections of Napoleon on the Most Important Events of His Life and Government, in His Own Words,* 2 vols. (New York: Worthington, 1890), 1: 153–54.

5] The order had originated in the Holy Land during the Crusades. When the last Christian strongholds on the eastern Mediterranean coast were recaptured by the Moslems at the end of the thirteenth century, the Knights established their headquarters on the Island of Rhodes. They were driven from Rhodes by the Turks in the early sixteenth century, at which time (1530) the Emperor Charles V gave them the Island of Malta that they might continue their perpetual war against Islam.

6] There are actually two islands in the group. Gozo, twenty-five square miles and the smaller of the two, was occupied by the French on June 10.

7] There were only 332 knights on Malta at the time, and at least 50 of these were too old or too ill to fight. The native garrison consisted of about 1500 men, but they had little inclination to resist the well-trained and fully equipped French troops.

8] Berthier to Desaix, July 9, 1798, Archives de la Guerre (Service historique de l'état-major de l'armée, château de Vincennes), hereafter referred to as Arch. Guerre, K^1 100; and Berthier to Dumas, July 9, 1798, Arch. Guerre, K^1 100.

9] General Desvernois, who was at the time a captain in Desaix's division, wrote in his *Mémoires* of Mireur's death: "They wanted it to be said that he had been killed by the Arabs: that is not true. With several companions, I went to search for him and found him stretched out on the ground holding in his hand the pistol with which he had committed suicide. . . . His horse returned to camp which was another proof" (p. 111).

10] These figures have been taken from V. J. Esposito and J. R. Elting, *A Military History and Atlas of the Napoleonic Wars* (New York: Praeger, 1964), Map 32.

11] Arch. Guerre, K[1] 100.

12] Napoleon I, *La Correspondance de Napoléon Ier*, 32 vols. (Paris: Imprimerie Impériale, 1858–70), No. 3452, Order, Oct. 10, 1798, vol. 5, pp. 66–67. Hereafter cited as *Corresp. Nap.*

13] *Corresp. Nap.*, No. 3662, to Berthier, Nov. 23, 1798, vol. 5, p. 202; and Berthier to Davout, Nov. 23, 1798, Arch. Guerre, K[1] 100.

14] *Corresp. Nap.*, No. 3690, to Berthier, Nov. 30, 1798, vol. 5, p. 222.

15] *Corresp. Nap.*, No. 3715, to Desaix, Dec. 5, 1798, vol. 5, p. 237. There is a discrepancy in Davout's papers on these figures. In his "Notes sur la campagne du général Desaix dans la Haute-Egypte, écrites et transmises par le général Davout au général en chef Buonaparte" Davout quotes himself as having written "General Desaix, having received the 1000 cavalry which the General in Chief had sent to aid the conquest of Upper Egypt." Then, under the heading of "Fait militaire depuis le départ du Kaire jusqu'à la bataille de Samahoud—ou Samanhut ou Samanjour—1 janvier 1799–22 janvier 1799," he wrote "Buonaparte . . . gave orders to General Davout, who was in Cairo at the time, to leave that city with 1,200 cavalry, 300 infantry, supplies for Desaix's division and six pieces of artillery" (see Arch. Guerre, K[1] 100).

16] Desaix to Bonaparte, Aug. 7, 1799, Arch. Guerre, K[1] 100.

17] Davout, "Notes," Arch. Guerre, K[1] 100; and Nicolas P. Desvernois, *Mémoires du général baron Desvernois* (Paris: Plon-Nourrit, 1896), pp. 159–63. Desvernois took part in the battle, and was seriously wounded during the heavy fighting.

18] Desaix to Bonaparte, Aug. 7, 1799, Arch. Guerre K[1] 100 ("Combat de Thèbes").

19] Arch. Guerre, K[1] 100 ("Combat à Byr al barr").

20] Davout, "Notes," Arch. Guerre, K[1] 100.

21] Ibid.

22] Desvernois, *Mémoires*, p. 186.

23] *Corresp. Nap.*, No. 4173, to Davout, June 14, 1799, vol. 5, p. 579.

24] *Corresp. Nap.*, No. 4222, to Davout, June 27, 1799, vol. 5, p. 619.

25] *Corresp. Nap.*, No. 4243, to Desaix, July 2, 1799, vol. 5, pp. 634–35.

26] *Corresp. Nap.*, No. 4313, to Davout, July 25, 1799, vol. 5, pp. 688–89.

27] On the Battle of Aboukir see: Berthier to Minister of War, July 29, 1799, Arch. Guerre, K[1] 100; *Corresp. Nap.*, No. 4334, to the *Directoire Exécutif*, Aug. 4, 1799, vol. 5, pp. 705–6; and Clément Etienne de la Jonquière, *L'Expédition d'Egypte, 1798–1801*, 5 vols. (Paris: Charles-Lavauzelle, 1899–1907), 5: 433–81.

28] John Barrow, *The Life and Correspondence of Admiral Sir William Sidney Smith*, 2 vols. (London: Richard Bentley, 1848), 1: 364.

29] Davout to his mother, Aug. 11, 1799, as quoted in Vigier, *Davout: maréchal d'empire,* 1: 78–80.

30] Kléber to the Directors, Oct. 8, 1799, as quoted in François Rousseau, *Kléber et Menou en Egypte, depuis le départ de Bonaparte, août 1799–septembre 1801* (Paris: A. Picard, 1900), pp. 76–84.

31] General Menou had gone so far as to marry an Egyptian girl and adopt the Moslem faith.

32] When the army returned from Egypt in October 1801, Bonaparte refused to allow Kléber's body to be brought on to French soil. It was placed in the prison on the island of If off the coast of Marseilles.

33] *Corresp. Nap.,* No. 4364, to the Grand Vizier, Aug. 17, 1799, vol. 5, pp. 723–26.

34] Rousseau, *Kléber et Menou,* p. 89.

35] Ibid., p. 179.

36] Ibid., p. 186.

37] On January 4, 1800, the day after Kléber received news of the capture of El Arish, he wrote General Reynier, who commanded a full division at Datia (about twenty miles west of El Arish), to engage any Turkish forces advancing into Egypt (ibid., pp. 177–78).

38] Ibid., pp. 199–200.

39] Ibid., pp. 232–33.

40] General Damas to Kléber, Feb. 12, 1800, Arch. Guerre, K[1] 100.

41] Desaix to Minister of War, May 5, 1800, Arch. Guerre, K[1] 100.

CHAPTER 5

1] The Russian tsar, Paul I, was disturbed by the French expedition to the East, and particularly by the occupation of Malta, of which he considered himself protector by virtue of his having been elected the Grand Master of the Order. Furthermore, he had come to believe that revolutionary France had as one of its ultimate goals the revival of the Polish state with a government at least pro-French—if not controlled from Paris.

2] General Guillaume Brune had driven the Anglo-Russian invasion force out of Holland, and General Masséna had won a major victory over a combined Austro-Russian army in Switzerland at Zurich.

3] As First Consul Bonaparte could not command an army. General Berthier was, therefore, the actual commander though, in fact, he acted as chief of staff.

4] Duchesse d'Abrantès (Madame Junot), *Memoirs of Napoleon: His Court and Family,* 2 vols. (London, 1836), 2: 38–39.

5] Ibid., p. 39.

6] Bourrienne's concluding note on this conversation is also interesting: "The First Consul, very indiscreet as you know, quickly reported to Davout my opinion of him; his [Davout's] hatred of me died only when he did" (Louis Antoine Fauvelet de Bourrienne, *Memoirs of Napoleon Bonaparte,* 4 vols. [New York: Thomas Y. Cromwell, 1885], 4: 292), as also quoted in Le Commandant Vachée, *Etude du caractère militaire du maréchal Davout* (Paris: Berger-Levrault, 1907), p. 11, n. 2. There was indeed no love lost between Davout and Bourrienne. On April 1, 1801, General Sebastiani wrote from Paris to Davout who was still in Italy: "I believe, my General, that it is necessary for you to ask for leave in order to return to Paris, and the sooner the better. The intrigues of B . . . are such that he has not yet been able to attain an alteration of the esteem and the attachment the First Consul has for you. . . . This man is treacherous! You have no idea of the harm that he has tried to do to me: I have not been to see him and I avow to do to him that which he has done to me. But I tell you truthfully that I have served the government, and he has betrayed it. There is no one, my General, who is more loyal and attached to you than myself" (Sebastiani to Davout, Apr. 1, 1801, Blocqueville, 2: 8–9).

7] *Corresp. Nap.,* No. 4786, May 14, 1800, vol. 6, pp. 344–45.

8] D'Abrantès, *Memoirs of Napoleon,* 2: 39.

9] *Corresp. Nap.,* No. 4789, vol. 6, p. 346. Also see the *Moniteur, 29 floréal, an VIII* (May 19, 1800).

10] *Corresp. Nap.,* No. 4787, vol. 6, p. 345. At the same time Bonaparte wrote to Sieyès and Roger-Ducos: "I have written to Generals Desaix and Davout, who are two excellent generals, to come, by the shortest route, to me, as soon as their quarantine is finished" (*Corresp. Nap.,* No. 4786, May 14, 1800, vol. 6, pp. 344–45).

11] *Corresp. Nap.,* No. 4953, June 27, 1800, vol. 6, p. 491. Napoleon paid his respect to Desaix in the following testimony: "To such virtue and heroism, I wish to pay such homage as no other man has ever received; the tomb of Desaix shall have the Alps for its pedestal and for guardians the monks of Saint Bernard" (as quoted in Sauzet, *Desaix: le "sultan juste,"* p. 308). But perhaps it was Marshal Berthier who best summed up Desaix when, at his formal burial on June 14, 1805, he said: "Here lies the man whom the Orient hailed as the Just, his country as the Brave, his century as the Wise, and whom Napoleon has honored with a monument" (as quoted in Sauzet, *Desaix: le "sultan juste,"* p. 309).

12] The promotion order was dated the previous day, July 3, 1800.

13] Russia had withdrawn from the Coalition after the Battle of Zürich because the tsar, Paul I, was disgusted with the selfish policies of his Austrian ally.

14] The murder of Paul I, who had become somewhat of an admirer of Bonaparte, and the ascent of Alexander I, who was pro-English, also played a role in the collapse of the League.

15] As quoted in Vigier, *Davout: maréchal d'empire,* 1: 101.

16] Toussaint L'Ouverture had made himself master of the French half of the island, and though he pledged allegiance to France he had no intentions of taking orders from Paris.

17] See Madame Jeanne Louise Henriette Campan, *Journal anecdotique de Mme. Campan ou souvenirs recueillis dans ses entretiens,* ed. M. Maigne (Paris: Baudoin, 1824). Also available in English translation under the title of *The Private Journal of Madame Campan* (Philadelphia, 1825).

18] As quoted in Vigier, *Davout: maréchal d'empire,* 1: 107.

19] Ibid., p. 109.

20] Louis Bonaparte was removed from the kingship of Holland because he did not carry out the Emperor's orders. His brother Jérôme was placed under the command of Davout during the Russian campaign because of military incompetence.

21] As quoted in Vigier, *Davout: maréchal d'empire,* 1: 112.

22] Madame Davout continued to live at Savigny until her death in 1868, at which time the estate passed to M. le comte Vigier. He sold it in 1872 to M. de Durlodot. By 1898 it had passed into the hands of M. Duparchy. Today the chateau and immediate grounds are a local high school. (See Vigier, *Davout: maréchal d'empire,* 1: 110.)

23] Davout left Paris with Bonaparte on June 25 but returned a few days before the First Consul to be with his wife and dying son.

24] Louis N. Davout, *Correspondance du maréchal Davout prince d'Eckmühl: ses commandements, son ministère, 1801–15,* ed. Charles de Mazade, 4 vols. (Paris: Plon, Nourrit, 1885), 1: 3–6. Hereafter cited as *Corresp. Davout.*

25] The full organization of the III Corps is found in Berthier's letter to Davout dated August 29, 1803, found in *Corresp. Davout,* 1: 3–6.

26] The best account of the work on the coastal parts is found in Edouard Desbrière, *Projets et tentatives de débarquement aux Iles Britanniques,* 5 vols. (Paris: R. Chapelot, 1900–1902), 3: 139–78. Working exclusively from primary sources in the numerous Parisian archives, he has compiled an excellent account of the work done at Boulogne, Etaples, Ambleteuse, Wimereux, Calais, and Ostend.

27] *Corresp. Davout,* No. 4, to First Consul, Sept. 15, 1803, vol. 1, pp. 9–11. The letter is dated *28 fructidor an XI* and then incorrectly translated into the Gregorian calendar as 10 septembre 1803. Mazade is completely reliable when giving Revolutionary dates, which actually appeared on the documents he reproduced; but the translation of dates is at times careless.

28] *Corresp. Nap.,* No. 7172, to Davout, Oct. 6, 1803, vol. 9, pp. 35–36.

29] *Corresp. Davout,* to First Consul, Oct. 10, 1803, vol. 1, pp. 19–20.

30] *Corresp. Davout,* No. 5, to First Consul, Sept. 24, 1803, vol. 1, pp. 12–16.

31] *Corresp. Davout,* No. 13, Oct. 29, 1803, pp. 24–26.

32] *Corresp. Davout,* No. 15, Nov. 19, 1803, pp. 28–30.

33] *Corresp. Nap.,* No. 7306, to Davout, No. 23, 1803, vol. 9, p. 131.

34] *Corresp. Davout,* No. 21, to First Consul, Dec. 6, 1803, vol. 1, pp. 36–37.

35] *Corresp. Nap.,* No. 7139, to Davout, Sept. 28, 1803, vol. 9, p. 9.

36] *Corresp. Davout,* No. 4, to First Consul, Sept. 12, 1803, vol. 1, p. 11. (Mistranslated by Mazade from *28 fructidor an XI* as 10 septembre 1803.)

37] *Corresp. Nap.,* No. 7139, to Davout, Sept. 28, 1803, vol. 9, p. 9.

38] *Corresp. Davout,* Nos. 8–16, Oct. 1, 1803–Nov. 21, 1803, vol. 1, pp. 18–34.

39] See Registers of Davout's Correspondence, Arch. Guerre, K[1] 64–66.

40] *Corresp. Davout,* No. 63, to Napoleon, vol. 1, p. 95. (Davout began to address his letters "to the Emperor" after the establishment of the Empire on May 18, 1804.)

41] *Corresp. Davout,* No. 59, to Napoleon, Sept. 5, 1804, vol. 1, pp. 90–91.

42] *Corresp. Davout,* to Napoleon, Sept. 5, 1804, vol. 1, p. 92.

43] *Corresp. Davout,* No. 62, to Napoleon, Sept. 5, 1804, vol. 1, p. 94. It was not infrequent that Davout felt it necessary to take measures he believed in the best interest of the troops under his command but for which his superiors did not appropriate funds. When he ordered the troops in low-lying damp areas to be issued wooden shoes—sabots—the expense was born by his well-to-do aide-de-camp Trobriand. In all, during this period Davout himself spent some thirty thousand francs from his own pay on measures for which the government did not provide money.

44] As quoted in Vigier, *Davout: maréchal d'empire,* 1: 140.

45] *Corresp. Davout,* No. 49, vol. 1, pp. 79–80.

46] All high-ranking officers did not share Davout's enthusiasm for an empire or for Napoleon himself.

47] The title "Marshal of the Empire" was simply the restoration of "Marshal of France," a Capetian title abolished by the Convention on Feb. 21, 1793.

48] There were to be sixteen "active" marshals in all, but only fourteen were named in the decree of May 19, 1804. The two remaining batons were held in reserve by the Emperor to be awarded in recognition of service and heroism in future wars. Sixteen names may have been drawn up and at the last moment two scratched. If this was the situation, as Louis Chardigny (*Les Maréchaux de Napoléon* [Paris: Flammarion, 1946]) believes it was, it is most likely that it was Macdonald and Gouvion St.-Cyr who were eliminated. Both eventually were named marshals. (See Chardigny, p. 9.)

49] This figure does not include the three killed in battle—Lannes (1809), Bessieres (1813), and Poniatowski (1813), (the latter actually drowned while attempting to escape after the Battle of Leipzig)—nor Grouchy, who was made a marshal during the Hundred Days.

50] In addition to the previously cited four volume work entitled *Le Maréchal Davout prince d'Eckmühl: raconté par les siens et par lui-même,* the Marquise de Blocqueville edited *Le Maréchal Davout prince d'Eckmühl: correspondance inédite 1790–1815: Pologne, Russie, Hambourg* (Paris: Perrin, 1887).

51] See Anna Potocka, *Memoires of the Countess Potocka,* trans. Lionel Strachey (New York: Doubleday & McClure, 1900), pp. 99–100.

52] While it is true that this union with Aimée Leclerc was Davout's second marriage, it is usually treated as his only marriage because of the brevity of the first one. His two earliest biographers, Joly and Chenier (with the latter's work more than five hundred pages) make no reference whatsoever to his first marriage.

53] Blocqueville, 2: 83.

54] Ibid., pp. 83–84.

55] Ibid., p. 85, letter dated *4 floréal, an XII* (March 25, 1804).

56] Ibid., p. 102.

57] Ibid.

58] *Corresp. Nap.,* No. 8301, to Berthier, Jan. 31, 1805, vol. 10, p. 166.

59] D'Abrantès, *Memoirs of Napoleon,* 2: 149.

60] Mar. 25, 1805, Blocqueville, 2: 114.

61] Mar. 29, 1805, Blocqueville, 2: 116.

62] Mar. 31, 1805, Blocqueville, 2: 117–18.

63] In a letter to his wife dated April 13, Davout gave his agenda for the trip. (Blocqueville, 2: 124–25.)

64] See Charles Moiset, "Le Collège royal militaire d'Auxerre," *Bulletin de la société des sciences historiques et naturelles de l'Yonne* 47 (1893): 5–13.

65] Ibid.

66] As quoted in Vigier, *Davout: maréchal d'empire,* 1: 155–56.

67] July 4 and 5, 1805, Blocqueville, 2: 139–40.

68] Aug. 4, 1805, Blocqueville, 2: 151.

69] The naming of their first two daughters Josephine has led us to some confusion. This second daughter lived to marry the count Achille Vigier in 1820, only to die the following year on August 19 in childbirth.

CHAPTER 6

1] Louis-Antoine-Henri de Bourbon, Duke of Enghien, was a cousin of the deceased Bourbon King, Louis XVI. He was kidnapped in Ettenheim, Baden, and brought to France where he was tried for conspiracy and executed on March 21, 1804. This action enraged the courts throughout Europe and served to increase their distrust of Napoleon. It was an act of assassination for which Napoleon was held directly responsible.

2] It provided for England to pay £1.25 million for every 100,000 troops put into the field by the Russians. When Austria joined the Coalition later in the same year, England extended the same financial offer.

3] The Allies did in fact plan such an offensive which was destined to take Masséna in the rear. Still another diversion was planned in the North. A combined Anglo-Russian-Swedish army (the latter having also joined the Coalition) was to land in Hanover and threaten the northern French flank and hopefully persuade Prussia to join the Coalition.

4] Blocqueville, 2: 141; *Corresp. Davout,* vol. 1, p. 118, n. 1.

5] The best biographies of Louis Friant and Charles Etienne Gudin are in Georges Rivollet's *Général de bataille Charles Antoine Louis Morand, généraux Friant et Gudin du 3ᵉ Corps de la Grande Armée* (Paris: J. Peyronnet, 1863).

6] Esposito and Elting, *Military History and Atlas,* Map 47. Theodore A. Dodge, in *Napoleon: A History of the Art of War from the Beginning of the French Revolution to the End of the Eighteenth Century. With a Detailed Account of the Wars of the French Revolution,* 4 vols. (London: Gay and Bird, 1904–7), 2: 151, gives the III Corps' strength at twenty-seven thousand; and Chandler, twenty-six thousand (David Chandler, *The Campaigns of Napoleon* [New York: Macmillan Co., 1966], p. 1103).

7] *Corresp. Nap.,* No. 9227, to Davout, Sept. 17, 1805, vol. 11, p. 256.

8] *Corresp. Davout,* No. 88, to Napoleon, Sept. 29, 1805, vol. 1, pp. 141–44.

9] Davout's own account of this action, dated Lilienfeld, November twelfth, is found in Blocqueville's *Maréchal Davout: correspondance inédite,* pp. 70–74. This is the only surviving letter of Davout's correspondence between October 20 and November 17—that is, the period of his march from Bavaria to Vienna. It might also be noted that very few of his personal letters to his wife for the year of 1805 have survived.

10] *Corresp. Nap.*, No. 9502, "Bulletin de la Grande Armée," Nov. 16, 1805, vol. 11, pp. 509–12; No. 9499, to Davout, Nov. 16, 1805, vol. 11, p. 506; and *Corresp. Davout,* No. 115, to Napolean, Nov. 17, 1805, vol. 1, pp. 183–84.

11] *Corresp. Nap.*, Nos. 9512, 9519, and 9521, vol. 11, pp. 521, 526, 527–28.

12] Esposito and Elting, *Military History and Atlas,* Map 54.

13] Ibid.

14] In a letter to General Caffarelli dated Brünn, November 28, Berthier ordered him to prepare his division for the "great battle" which was about to take place. (See *Corresp. Nap.*, No. 9530, vol. 11, p. 533.)

15] Louis N. Davout, *Opérations du 3e Corps, 1806–1807. Rapport du maréchal Davout, duc d'Auerstaedt,* ed. Gen. Léopold Davout (Paris: Calmann Levy, 1896), Berthier to Davout, Nov. 28, 1805, p. v.

16] Ibid., pp. v–vi.

17] Troop figures are taken from Esposito and Elting, *Military History and Atlas,* Maps 54, 55, 56.

18] *Corresp. Davout,* No. 127, to Napoleon, Dec. 26, 1805, vol. 1, pp. 202–4. Davout wrote a lengthy account of his actions and those of the troops under his command on December 2 in answer to a direct request of Napoleon (see *Corresp. Nap.*, No. 9569, to Davout, Dec. 13, 1805, vol. 11, pp. 578–79).

19] Ibid., pp. 204–6.

20] In Baron Paul Charles Thiébault's *Mémoires du général baron Thiébault,* 5 vols. (Paris: Plon-Nourrit, 1895–97), which must be read with caution, there is a lively description of the action on the heights of Pratzen by an eyewitness who was wounded in the fighting. See vol. 2, pp. 159–70.

21] Louis Madelin, *Histoire du consulat et de l'empire,* 16 vols. (Paris: Hachette, 1937–51), 5: 331.

22] *Corresp. Davout,* No. 123, to Berthier, Dec. 2, 1805, vol. 1, pp. 192–95; No. 126, to Berthier, Dec. 6, 1805, vol. 1, pp. 199–202; No. 128, to Berthier, Dec. 27, 1805, vol. 1, pp. 208–12; Blocqueville, 2: 192–93.

23] Davout, *Opérations du 3e Corps,* p. vi.

24] General Friant received the *Grand Aigle* of the Legion of Honor on Dec. 27, 1805, in recognition of his service at Austerlitz. A "pension" of 200,000 franc accompanied the honor. (Rivollet, *Morand, Friant et Gudin,* p. 246.)

25] *Corresp. Davout,* No. 124, to Minister of War, Dec. 4, 1805, vol. 1, pp. 195–96.

26] See chapter 5.

27] *Corresp. Davout,* No. 124, to Minister of War, Dec. 4, 1805, vol. 1, pp. 195–96.

28] *Corresp. Davout,* Kutusov to Davout, Dec. 4, 1805, vol. 1, pp. 197–98.

29] *Corresp. Davout,* Alexander I to Davout, vol. 1, p. 198. In a footnote on this same page Mazade says that the note with Alexander's signature was sent on to Napoleon and was placed in the *portfeuille* with other documents relating to the campaign. It was then burned after the campaign of 1812 in order to prevent it from falling into the hands of the Russians, when the Empire collapsed. (See Claude François, baron de Meneval, *Souvenirs historiques du baron de Meneval* [Paris: A. Delahays, 1851].)

30] *Corresp. Davout,* No. 124, to Napoleon, Dec. 4, 1805, vol. 1, pp. 195–96.

31] *Corresp. Davout,* vol. 1, pp. 192–94, n. 1.

32] *Corresp. Davout,* No. 132, to Minister of War, Dec. 6, 1805, vol. 1, pp. 224–25.

33] *Corresp. Nap.,* No. 9587, to Davout, Dec. 18, 1805, vol. 11, p. 593.

34] Austria agreed to give up Vorarlberg, Breisgau, Tyrol, Constance, and Ortenau in Germany, Venetia in Italy, and Istria and Dalmatia on the Adriatic. Her only compensation was the city of Salzburg.

35] *Corresp. Nap.,* No. 9627, to Berthier, Dec. 27, 1805, vol. 11, pp. 621–27.

36] *Corresp. Davout,* Nos. 148, 149, and 150, all to Berthier, Jan. 28, 1806, Feb. 8, 1806, and Feb. 28, 1806, vol. 1, pp. 240–41.

37] *Corresp. Nap.,* No. 9973, to Berthier, Mar. 14, 1806, vol. 12, p. 231.

CHAPTER 7

1] See chapter 6.

2] The Confederation of the Rhine was made up of the major southern and western German states. The principal members were Baden, Bavaria, Berg, Hesse-Darmstadt, and Württemberg. To these were added ten smaller principalities.

3] Francis II renounced his title of Holy Roman Emperor following the Austerlitz campaign and became Francis I, Emperor of Austria.

4] Jean Thiry, *Iéna* (Paris: Berger-Levrault, 1964), p. 137.

5] Jean Baptiste Antoine Marcelin, baron de Marbot, *Mémoires du général baron de Marbot,* 3 vols. (Paris: Plon, 1891), 1: 283.

6] *Corresp. Nap.,* No. 10736, to Berthier, Sept. 4, 1806, vol. 13, pp. 177–78.

7] She became the comtesse Vigier after her marriage, but died in childbirth in 1821. See chapter 15.

8] *Corresp. Davout,* No. 170, to Friant, Sept. 15, 1806, vol. 1, pp. 264–66.

9] Ibid.

10] *Corresp. Nap.,* No. 10823, to Dejean, Sept. 19, 1806, vol. 13, pp. 270–71.

11] See Rivollet, *Morand, Friant et Gudin,* for the best biographical account of General Morand.

12] Rivollet's *Morand, Friant et Gudin* is primarily a biography of General Morand, with 231 of its 292 pages devoted to him and the remaining 61 to Friant and Gudin.

13] Davout, *Opérations du 3e Corps,* pp. 8–11. In these pages Davout gives a breakdown of the Corps into regiments, complete with figures and names of commanding officers and staff.

14] *Corresp. Nap.,* Nos. 10816 and 10818, to Berthier, Sept. 19, 1806, vol. 13, pp. 261–62 and 265–67.

15] The exact movements of the III Corps are given in great detail by Davout in his *Opérations du 3e Corps* and are the chief source for the military operations of the Corps during this campaign. Also see *Corresp. Davout,* No. 172, to Berthier, Oct. 2, 1806, vol. 1, pp. 267–68.

16] *Corresp. Davout,* No. 174, to Berthier, Oct. 5, 1806, vol. 1, pp. 168–69.

17] Karl von Clausewitz, *Notes sur la Prusse dans sa grande catastrophe: 1806,* trans. A. Niessel (Paris: R. Chapelot, 1903), pp. 19–20. With respect to Russian armament, Clausewitz actually said at the time that "the armament was worse than any in Europe" (p. 19).

18] These figures are given by Esposito and Elting, *Military History and Atlas,* Map 58. Other figures are readily available but less reliable. French accounts tend to run high in order to make the victory a greater one, while Prussian figures tend to reduce the strength of the Prussian army, thus lessening the poor showing it made.

19] One of the best discussions of the Prussian army on the eve of the 1806 campaign is found in Clausewitz's *Notes sur la Prusse,* pp. 10–56.

20] Davout himself gives the exact location of each division's camp for each night in his *Opérations du 3e Corps,* pp. 11–17.

21] Clausewitz, *Notes sur la Prusse,* pp. 115–16.

22] Clausewitz considers this to have been one of the major errors of this phase of the campaign, though he did not believe Rüchel's army (thirteen thousand men), even if it had supported Hohenlohe at Jena, could have turned the tide of battle (*Notes sur la Prusse,* p. 131).

23] A copy of this dispatch apparently did not survive the campaign. It is not to be found in Napoleon's published correspondence nor in the Parisian archives. The source for the dispatch is Davout's *Opérations du 3ᵉ Corps;* but only the portion concerning Bernadotte is in quotes (see pp. 29–30). It is also found in the form of a dispatch—implying that it is a copy of the original, but without documentation—in General Service School, Geneva Staff School, *The Jena Campaign. Source Book* (Fort Leavenworth: General Service Schools Press, 1922), p. 337. This is based on Davout's account.

24] Davout, *Opérations du 3ᵉ Corps,* p. 30.

25] Ibid.

26] Contemporaries did not agree so readily upon the strength of Brunswick's army as they did upon the strength of Davout's. The French Marshal, in a lengthy footnote in his *Opérations du 3ᵉ Corps* (pp. 30–31), gives the Prussian strength at sixty-six thousand men. On the other hand, Clausewitz puts its strength at only forty-five thousand (*Notes sur la Prusse,* p. 148). Napoleon's figures given in his "Fifth Bulletin," dated the day after the battles, are unreliable. He apparently still believed that the main enemy army had been before him at Jena, giving its strength at eighty thousand—double what it actually was, and that Davout had fought a smaller force, which he figured to have been fifty thousand, at Auerstädt. The figure given in the text is based on the calculations of Esposito and Elting, *Military History and Atlas,* Map 64.

27] Bruno V. Treuenfeld, *Auerstädt und Jena* (Hannover: Helwing'fche, 1895), p. 348.

28] The account given here of the Battle of Auerstädt is based primarily on Davout's own account in his *Opérations du 3ᵉ Corps;* Clausewitz's *Notes sur la Prusse;* and the General Service School, General Staff School, *Jena Campaign.*

29] *Corresp. Davout,* No. 179, vol. 1, pp. 276–78.

30] Ségur incorrectly accredits Colonel Bourke with having carried this dispatch to the Emperor and the error has been accepted by many nineteenth- and twentieth-century historians—including Jean Thiry. (See Thiry's *Iéna,* p. 219.) "Colonel Bourke," wrote Davout in his *Opérations du 3ᵉ Corps,* "received a ball in the upper arm which disabled him" (p. 53).

31] Lt. Col. Eugene Titeux, "Le Maréchal Bernadotte et la manoeuvre d'Jena," *Revue Napoléonienne* 4 (Apr.–Sept. 1903): 111.

32] *Corresp. Nap.*, No. 11014, to Davout, Oct. 16, 1806, vol. 13, p. 443.

33] *Corresp. Nap.*, No. 11011, to Murat, Oct. 15, 1806, vol. 13, pp. 441–42.

34] *Corresp. Nap.*, No. 11017, to Talleyrand, Oct. 15, 1806, vol. 13, p. 432.

35] *Corresp. Nap.*, No. 11009, "Fifth Bulletin of the Grand Army," Oct. 15, 1806, vol. 13, pp. 434–40.

36] Jacques-André Janvier, *Le Maréchal Davout et sa famille à Savigny-sur-Orge* (Essonnes: Typolino, 1951), p. 63.

37] Davout, *Opérations du 3ᵉ Corps,* pp. 29–30.

38] *Corresp. Nap.*, No. 11041, to Bernadotte, Oct. 21, 1806, vol. 13, p. 466.

39] Titeux, "Le Maréchal Bernadotte," p. 69.

40] Titeux's lengthy (eighty-four page) article "Le Maréchal Bernadotte" overstates Bernadotte's innocence of all charges brought against him.

41] The letter is quoted in Blocqueville, 2: 222–23. Blocqueville states that it was given to her by General Trobriand in 1861. But the only copy of this letter did not appear until 1861 when the aging Trobriand (in his eighties) made it available to the Marquise de Blocqueville (Davout's daughter). Some doubt as to its authenticity has, with justice, been raised, as there is neither a copy of the letter to be found in Davout's paper deposited in the War Archives at Vincennes, nor any reference to it prior to Blocqueville's publication of it in 1879.

42] *Corresp. Davout,* No. 189, to Berthier, Oct. 20, 1806, vol. 1, pp. 291–92; and Davout, *Opérations du 3ᵉ Corps,* pp. 61–62.

43] *Corresp. Davout,* No. 191, to Berthier, Oct. 21, 1806, vol. 1, p. 293.

44] Davout, *Opérations du 3ᵉ Corps,* p. 68.

45] *Corresp. Nap.*, No. 11058, to Davout, Oct. 23, 1806, vol. 13, pp. 481–83.

46] Davout, *Opérations du 3ᵉ Corps,* p. 70.

47] Ibid.

48] The "Second Polish War of Liberation" was the official Napoleonic terminology for the campaign against Russia in 1812.

49] Davout, *Opérations du 3ᵉ Corps,* pp. 73–79.

50] *Corresp. Davout,* No. 216, to Napoleon, Nov. 9, 1806, vol. 1, p. 324, n. 1; and Davout, *Opérations du 3ᵉ Corps,* p. 87.

51] Davout mistakenly refers to the lower Narew as the Bug in his correspondence and in his *Opérations du 3ᵉ Corps.* The Narew and Bug are of about equal size when they join some twenty-five miles east of the Vistula.

52] *Corresp. Davout,* No. 243, to Murat, Dec. 11, 1806, vol. 1, pp.

365–66; for a detailed account of the crossing of the Narew see Davout, *Opérations du 3e Corps*, pp. 106–13.

53] Actually two bridges were required as there was an island at the point chosen for the crossing. Morand crossed to the island and held it while the bridges were constructed. See Davout, *Opérations du 3e Corps*, pp. 115–21, and detailed maps opposite p. 120.

54] Davout, *Opérations du 3e Corps*, pp. 131–41; Jean Thiry, *Eylau, Friedland, Tilsit* (Paris: Berger-Levrault, 1964), pp. 40–46; Jean Rapp, *Mémoires des contemporains, pour servir à l'histoire de France, et principalement à celle de la république et de l'empire* (Paris: Bossange, 1823), pp. 124–29.

55] Thiry, *Eylau, Friedland, Tilsit*, p. 40.

56] A full description of the cantonment by regiments is given in Davout, *Opérations du 3e Corps*, pp. 143–48.

57] Ibid., p. 157.

58] The figures used for the Battle of Eylau are taken from Esposito and Elting, *Military History and Atlas*, Map 73; and Chandler, *Campaigns of Napoleon*, p. 1119.

59] Ibid.

60] Ibid.

61] For some unexplained reason the order for Ney to march on Eylau was not dispatched until the battle had actually begun—that is after 8:00 A.M.

62] Marbot, *Mémoires*, 1: 337–38; and Davout, *Opérations du 3e Corps*, p. 160.

63] See Marbot, *Mémoires*, 1: 339–40.

64] Davout, *Opérations du 3e Corps*, p. 168.

65] The following casualty figures are given by Davout (*Opérations du 3e Corps*, p. 171): 1st Division—killed, 275; wounded, 2,651; taken prisoner, 245 (total, 3,171); 2d Division—killed, 225; wounded, 1,111; taken prisoner, 71 (total, 1,407); 3d Division—killed, 77; wounded, 262 (total, 339); Cavalry—killed, 7; wounded, 83 (total, 90). Subtotals: killed, 584; wounded, 4,107; taken prisoner, 316; for a grand total of 5,007. In the "Fifty-eighth Bulletin of the Grand Army," written the day after the battle, Napoleon wrote: "Our losses were exactly 1,900 killed and 5,700 wounded." (*Corresp. Nap.*, No. 11796, Feb. 9, 1807, vol. 14, pp. 366–69.) This deliberate falsification of his losses was aimed at minimizing the effect of the battle on the French army—especially as it had not been a triumphant victory such as had come to be expected of him. The more reliable figures of "between 20,000 and 25,000 men" given by Esposito and Elting, *Military History and Atlas*, Map 75, and Chandler, *Campaigns of Napoleon*, p. 1119, tell the true story of Eylau.

66] *Corresp. Nap.,* No. 11816, Feb. 16, 1807, vol. 14, pp. 381–82.

67] This figure is given by Davout (*Opérations du 3ᵉ Corps,* p. 194) along with the following footnote: "Those absent are not counted in this figure. The 1st Division alone still had, at this time, 5,858 sick and wounded in the hospital." Esposito and Elting, *Military History and Atlas,* give the strength of the III Corps at 24,600 men (Map 76).

68] Davout, *Opérations du 3ᵉ Corps,* p. 191.

69] Ibid., p. 201.

CHAPTER 8

1] Nicolas Charles Oudinot, duc de Reggio, *Memoirs of Marshal Oudinot Duc de Reggio. Compiled from the Hitherto Unpublished Souvenirs of the Duchesse de Reggio,* ed. Gaston Stiegler, trans. Alexander Teixeira de Mattos (London: H. Henry, 1896), p. 50.

2] *Corresp. Davout,* No. 371, to Berthier, Sept. 4, 1807, vol. 2, pp. 46–47.

3] See for example *Corresp. Davout,* vol. 2, Nos. 391, pp. 84–85; 420, pp. 123–24; 421, pp. 125–26; 450, pp. 170–72; 462, pp. 197–98; 468, pp. 214–15; 469, pp. 221–22; 471, p. 224; 478, pp. 239–41; 482, pp. 246–47.

4] Polish volunteers had already fought and died in Italy during the campaign of 1800 and in St. Domingue (1801), but always as part of the French army.

5] Albert Vandal, *Napoléon et Alexandre Iᵉʳ: l'alliance russe sous le premier empire,* 3 vols. (Paris: Plon-Nourrit, 1911), 1: 88–92. On the question of the establishment of an independent Polish state Vandal says that from what Napoleon had seen of Polish politics during the war (1806–7) "it did not inspire in him confidence in the political spirit of the people. . . . Before Alexander I he denied any idea of an actual restoration" (1: 89).

6] See W. F. Reddaway, J. H. Penson, and O. Halecki, eds., *The Cambridge History of Poland from Augustus II to Pilsudski,* 2 vols. (Cambridge: At the University Press, 1951), 2: 237–38.

7] See Davout's correspondence during November and December, 1806. (*Corresp. Davout,* Nos. 228–57, vol. 1, pp. 345–81).

8] Blocqueville, 2: 247.

9] *Corresp. Davout,* No. 390, Note transmitted by Marshal Davout, Oct. 9, 1807, vol. 2, pp. 78–80.

10] *Corresp. Davout,* vol. 2, pp. 80–81.

11] See *Corresp. Davout,* vol. 2, pp. 69–273.

12] The academic question of the apex of the first French empire is one upon which historians may well never agree. The attitudes of French historians on this subject are perhaps best summed up in Pieter Geyl's *Napoleon For and Against* (New Haven: Yale University Press, 1949).

13] *Corresp. Nap.*, No. 13285, to Davout, Oct. 22, 1807, vol. 16, pp. 130–31.

14] Blocqueville, 2: 260.

15] For a discussion of this Constitution see Reddaway, Penson, and Halecki, eds., *The Cambridge History of Poland,* 2: 236–39.

16] *Corresp. Davout,* No. 389, to Napoleon, Oct. 9, 1807, vol. 2, p. 74.

17] Prince Poniatowski, a member of one of Poland's most illustrious families and a nephew of the last king (Stanislaus II), was to serve under Napoleon during the Russian campaign and was named Marshal of the Empire in 1813. He was to lose his life attempting to swim the Elster river after the Battle of Leipzig, during which he had been wounded.

18] *Corresp. Davout,* No. 390, Note transmitted by Marshal Davout, Oct. 9, 1807, vol. 2, p. 81.

19] *Corresp. Davout,* vol. 2, p. 83.

20] *Corresp. Davout,* No. 406, to Napoleon, Nov. 14, 1807, vol. 2, pp. 109–10.

21] See, for example, Davout's letter to Napoleon dated March 31, 1808. (*Corresp. Davout,* No. 456, vol. 2, p. 184.)

22] *Corresp. Davout,* No. 469, to Napoleon, June 22, 1808, vol. 2, p. 223.

23] *Corresp. Davout,* No. 496, to Napoleon, Aug. 26, 1808, vol. 2, pp. 269–70.

24] *Corresp. Davout,* No. 498, to Napoleon, Sept. 5, 1808, vol. 2, p. 275.

25] Reddaway, Penson, and Halecki, eds., *The Cambridge History of Poland,* 2: 229.

26] *Corresp. Davout,* No. 481, to Napoleon, July 26, 1808, vol. 2, p. 245.

27] *Corresp. Davout,* No. 433, to Napoleon, Mar. 1, 1808, vol. 2, pp. 146–47.

28] *Corresp. Davout,* No. 475, to Napoleon, July 9, 1808, vol. 2, p. 229.

29] "If my troops continue to remain in the Duchy of Warsaw, I refuse to take those measures which would cost Poland. I will pay them and feed them from my own stores and my own treasury." (*Corresp. Nap.*, No. 13599, to M. de Champagny, Feb. 24, 1808, vol. 16, p. 439.)

30] The actual number of Poles under arms at this time was closer to fifty thousand. The other twenty thousand were serving in Polish units of the French army, and were treated the same as any other men in the Napoleonic armed forces. For a general discussion of Poland's military efforts during the Napoleonic period see Reddaway, Penson, and Halecki, eds., *The Cambridge History of Poland,* 2: 220–35.

31] *Corresp. Davout,* No. 452, to Napoleon, Mar. 30, 1808, vol. 2, p. 176.

32] *Corresp. Nap.,* No. 13655, to M. de Champagny, Mar. 16, 1808, vol. 16, pp. 494–95.

33] *Corresp. Davout,* No. 466, to Napoleon, May 6, 1808, vol. 2, p. 209.

34] *Corresp. Davout,* No. 468, to Nap., June 15, 1808, vol. 2, p. 215. Napoleon had written to Davout on May 25, 1808: "In the position which you find yourself, it is necessary for you more than anyone else to have patience and *du sang-froid*" (*Corresp. Nap.,* No. 13987, to Davout, vol. 17, p. 234).

35] *Corresp. Davout,* No. 468, to Napoleon, June 15, 1808, vol. 2, pp. 216–17.

36] *Corresp. Davout,* No. 468, to Napoleon, June 15, 1808, vol. 2, pp. 214–17.

37] *Corresp. Davout,* No. 468, to Napoleon, June 15, 1808, vol. 2, p. 216.

38] *Corresp. Davout,* No. 475, to Napoleon, July 9, 1808, vol. 2, pp. 229–30.

39] *Corresp. Davout,* No. 475, to Napoleon, July 9, 1808, vol. 2, pp. 229–30.

40] *Corresp. Davout,* No. 462, to Napoleon, Apr. 12, 1808, vol. 2, pp. 194–96.

41] *Corresp. Nap.,* No. 13987, to Davout, May 25, 1808, vol. 17, p. 234.

42] *Corresp. Davout,* No. 469, to Napoleon, June 22, 1808, vol. 2, pp. 219–21.

43] *Corresp. Davout,* No. 458, to Napoleon, Apr. 6, 1808, vol. 2, pp. 186–87; No. 482, to Napoleon, July 26, 1808, vol. 2, p. 248; No. 427, to Napoleon, Feb. 1, 1808, vol. 2, p. 138.

44] *Corresp. Davout,* No. 378, to Napoleon, Sept. 22, 1807, vol. 2, pp. 54–55.

45] *Corresp. Davout,* No. 396, to Napoleon, Oct. 21, 1807, vol. 2, p. 91; No. 420, to Napoleon, Dec. 4, 1807, vol. 2, p. 123; No. 450, to Napoleon, Mar. 28, 1808, vol. 2, pp. 170–71.

46] *Corresp. Davout,* No. 468, to Napoleon, June 15, 1808, vol. 2, p. 214.

47] *Corresp. Davout,* No. 469, to Napoleon, June 22, 1808, vol. 2, p. 221.

48] *Corresp. Davout,* No. 495, to Napoleon, Aug. 25, 1808, vol. 2, p. 264.

49] *Corresp. Nap.,* No. 14269, to Davout, Aug. 23, 1808, vol. 17, pp. 539–40.

50] Ibid.

51] *Corresp. Nap.*, No. 12984, to Davout, Aug. 4, 1807, vol. 15, p. 588.

52] Blocqueville, 2: 308.

53] The *Lettre Patente de Titre de Duc d'Auerstaedt*, dated July 2, 1808, is reprinted in the appendix of Vigier, *Davout: maréchal d'empire*, 1: 295–96.

54] Murat undoubtedly derived greater wealth from his lands as King of Naples, but was not given a greater amount directly from the imperial treasury.

55] Blocqueville, 2: 260.

56] Ibid., p. 261.

57] Ibid., p. 262.

58] Bourrienne, *Memoirs of Napoleon*, 3: 330.

59] See Blocqueville, 2: 263.

60] Ibid., pp. 274–75.

61] Józef Zaluski, *La Pologne et les polonais. Les erreurs et les injustices des écrivains français mm. Thiers, Ségur, Lamartine* (Paris: Dumineray, 1856), p. 134.

62] As quoted in Blocqueville, 2: 269.

63] See chapter 11.

64] Davout to wife, July 2, 1807, Blocqueville, 2: 297.

65] Davout to wife, May 30, 1807, Blocqueville, 2: 296.

66] Davout to wife, Aug. 1807, Blocqueville, 2: 302.

67] Davout to wife, n.d., Blocqueville, 2: 304.

68] As quoted in Vigier, *Davout: maréchal d'empire*, 1: 257.

69] Tyszkiewicz to Davout, Dec. 7, 1809, Blocqueville, 2: 317.

70] Potocka, *Memoirs of the Countess Potocka*, p. 100.

71] Ibid.

72] Thiébault, *Mémoires*, 5: 369.

CHAPTER 9

1] J. P. Thompson, *Napoleon Bonaparte* (New York: Oxford University Press, 1952), pp. 256–57.

2] The Aulic Council, a remnant of the Holy Roman Empire, had lost virtually all of its former power even before the empire was formally dissolved in 1806. Yet it continued to exist as an advisory Council to the Austrian emperor and exerted some influence over Francis I.

3] Francis Loraine Petre, *Napoleon and the Archduke Charles* (London and New York: J. Lane, 1909) gives the figure one hundred and seventy-four thousand (p. 20), and this is used by Chandler, *Campaigns of Napoleon*, p. 670. The figure used in the text is from Esposito and Elting, *Military History and Atlas*, Map 93. For a detailed account of the makeup of the French army on the eve of the campaign, see C. de Renémont, *Campagne de 1809* (Paris: Charles-Lavauzelle, 1903), pp. 23–29.

4] Chandler, *Campaigns of Napoleon,* p. 670, gives the number of guns as "merely 311," which figure he took from Petre, *Napoleon and the Archduke Charles,* p. 19. The figure, three hundred and fifty, is from Esposito and Elting, *Military History and Atlas.*

5] *Corresp. Nap.,* No. 15678, to General Clarke, Aug. 18, 1809, vol. 19, p. 423.

6] *Corresp. Davout,* No. 652, to Berthier, Apr. 13, 1809, vol. 2, pp. 462–63; Esposito and Elting, *Military History and Atlas,* Map 93; and Chandler, *Campaigns of Napoleon,* p. 671 (which last source gives the figure as sixty-five thousand).

7] *Corresp. Davout,* No. 496, to Napoleon, Aug. 22, 1808, vol. 2, p. 263.

8] *Corresp. Davout,* No. 603, to Friant, Mar. 20, 1809, vol. 2, p. 410.

9] *Corresp. Davout,* No. 695, to Napoleon, Mar. 26, 1809, vol. 2, pp. 440–41.

10] *Corresp. Davout,* No. 633, to Napoleon, Mar. 29, 1809, vol. 2, p. 447.

11] See *Corresp. Davout,* 2: 393–459.

12] *Corresp. Davout,* No. 612, to Napoleon, Mar. 22, 1809, vol. 2, p. 423; and No. 625, to Napoleon, Mar. 26, 1809, vol. 2, p. 440.

13] *Corresp. Davout,* No. 625, to Napoleon, Mar. 26, 1809, vol. 2, pp. 440–41.

14] *Corresp. Davout,* No. 628, to Napoleon, Mar. 27, 1809, vol. 2, p. 444.

15] *Corresp. Davout,* No. 649, to Napoleon, Apr. 7, 1809, vol. 2, p. 458.

16] On figures for the Austrian army see de Renémont, *Campagne de 1809,* p. 59; Petre, *Napoleon and the Archduke Charles,* pp. 31–32; and Esposito and Elting, *Military History and Atlas,* Map 93. All three are in general agreement.

17] Bourrienne, *Memoirs of Napoleon,* 3: 88.

18] *Corresp. Davout,* No. 650, to Napoleon, Apr. 7, 1809, vol. 2, pp. 459–60.

19] *Corresp. Davout,* No. 651, to Berthier, Apr. 12, 1809, vol. 2, pp. 460–61.

20] *Corresp. Davout,* No. 647, to Berthier, Apr. 3, 1809, vol. 2, pp. 456–57. This dispatch should have reached Paris by the fifth, but for some unknown reason the Emperor did not see it until the seventh—four days after it had been written.

21] *Corresp. Nap.,* No. 15047, to Berthier, Apr. 10, 1809, vol. 18, p. 537.

22] Berthier wrote on the bottom of this dispatch the following: "I have the honor of pointing out to Your Majesty that this dispatch *telegraphique* did not reach me until today at Augsburg, April 16, at 6 A.M. [signed] Alexandre" (*Corresp. Nap.,* No. 15047, vol. 18, , p. 537*n*).

23] *Corresp. Nap.*, No. 15048, to Berthier, Apr. 10, 1809, vol. 18, pp. 537–38.

24] *Corresp. Davout,* No. 651, to Berthier, Apr. 12, 1809, vol. 2, pp. 460–62.

25] *Corresp. Davout,* No. 654, to Berthier, Apr. 14, 1809, vol. 2, pp. 465–66.

26] *Corresp. Davout,* No. 662, to Berthier, Apr. 17, 1809, vol. 2, p. 474.

27] *Corresp. Davout,* No. 662, to Berthier, Apr. 17, 1809, vol. 2, p. 475.

28] *Corresp. Nap.*, No. 15073, to Berthier, Apr. 17, 1809, vol. 18, p. 555.

29] *Corresp. Nap.*, No. 15075, to Davout, Apr. 17, 1809, vol. 18, p. 556.

30] The spelling *Eckmühl* will be used throughout, rather than Eggmühl, in order to conform with the title by which Davout is known—Prince of Eckmühl.

31] *Corresp. Nap.*, No. 15100, to Davout, 5:00 A.M., Apr. 21, 1809, vol. 18, p. 575.

32] *Corresp. Davout,* No. 671, to Napoleon, Apr. 20, 1809, vol. 2, p. 483; and No. 674, to Napoleon, 6:00 A.M., Apr. 21, 1809, vol. 2, p. 484.

33] *Corresp. Davout,* No. 675, to Napoleon, Apr. 21, 1809, vol. 2, p. 485.

34] *Corresp. Davout,* No. 677, to Napoleon, Apr. 21, 1809, vol. 2, pp. 486–87.

35] *Corresp. Davout,* No. 678, to Napoleon, Apr. 21, 1809, vol. 2, pp. 487–88.

36] *Corresp. Nap.*, No. 15104, to Davout, Apr. 22, 1809, vol. 18, pp. 577–78.

37] *Corresp. Davout,* No. 674, to Napoleon, Apr. 21, 1809, vol. 2, p. 484.

38] *Corresp. Nap.*, No. 15104, to Davout, Apr. 22, 1809, vol. 18, pp. 577–78.

39] Ibid.

40] See *Corresp. Davout,* Nos. 679–90, Apr. 23–29, vol. 2, pp. 488–98.

41] *Corresp. Nap.*, No. 15226, to Davout, May 18, 1809, vol. 19, pp. 23–24.

42] *Corresp. Nap.*, No. 15232, to Davout, May 19, 1809, vol. 19, pp. 28–29.

43] *Corresp. Nap.*, No. 15238, to Davout, May 19, 1809, vol. 19, p. 32.

44] Napoleon started the battle of Aspern-Essling with 17,830 men. By the evening of the twenty-first, this number had risen to 31,400 men. The Archduke Charles commanded 100,000 men, according to Petre, *Napoleon and the Archduke Charles,* p. 286.

45] *Corresp. Nap.*, No. 15242, to Davout, May 21, 1809, vol. 19, p. 37.

46] Unfortunately, it is impossible to trace Davout's exact movements after 2 A.M., on May twentieth as there is a gap in his correspondence from then until June 2.

47] "At Essling, 90,000 men had battled and contained 30,000 Frenchmen who would have completely routed and destroyed them, had the affairs of the bridge not produced a shortage of munitions" (*Corresp. Nap.*, No. 15409, "Twenty-first Bulletin of the Army of Germany," June 22, 1809, vol. 19, pp. 180–82).

48] See Petre, *Napoleon and the Archduke Charles,* pp. 288, 291, 312; and de Renémont, *Campagne de 1809,* pp. 245–49.

49] *Corresp. Davout,* No. 750, to Napoleon, June 2, 1809, and No. 751, to Napoleon, June 3, 1809, vol. 3, pp. 4–7.

50] Ibid.

51] *Corresp. Davout,* No. 791, to Napoleon, June 21, 1809, vol. 3, pp. 50–51.

52] *Corresp. Davout,* No. 779, to Napoleon, June 15, 1809, vol. 3, p. 37.

53] *Corresp. Nap.*, No. 15420, to Davout, June 23, 1809, vol. 19, pp. 190–91.

54] *Corresp. Davout,* No. 799, to Napoleon, June 24, 1809, vol. 3, pp. 59–60.

55] *Corresp. Nap.*, No. 15420, to Davout, June 22, 1809, vol. 19, pp. 190–91.

56] *Corresp. Nap.*, No. 15427, to Davout, June 24, 1809, vol. 19, pp. 195–96; and No. 15440, to Davout, June 26, 1809, vol. 19, p. 206.

57] *Corresp. Davout,* No. 805, to Napoleon, June 25, 1809, vol. 3, pp. 67–68; and No. 806, to Napoleon, June 26, 1809, vol. 3, p. 69.

58] *Corresp. Davout,* No. 807, to Napoleon, June 27, 1809, vol. 3, p. 71.

59] "There are only 200 shells remaining and these will be fired tonight and tomorrow, if the enemy does not evacuate the islands, after the new summons which I am sending" (*Corresp. Davout,* No. 809, to Napoleon, June 29, 1809, vol. 3, pp. 72–73).

60] *Corresp. Nap.*, No. 15465, to Davout, June 29, 1809, vol. 19, pp. 226–27.

61] *Corresp. Davout,* No. 812, to Napoleon, June 30, 1809, vol. 3, pp. 75–76.

62] "My cousin," wrote Napoleon to Davout on June 26, "yesterday [June 25] I reviewed the divisions of Friant, Morand. . . . The Viennese were astounded to see such superb troops" (*Corresp. Nap.*, No. 15317, to Davout, June 26, 1809, vol. 19, p. 101).

63] See Petre, *Napoleon and the Archduke Charles,* pp. 264, 271–72; de Renémont, *Campagne de 1809,* pp. 226–36; and Chandler, *Campaigns of Napoleon,* p. 711.

64] See "Ordres pour la Passage du Danube," *Corresp. Nap.*, No. 15481, July 2, 1809, vol. 19, pp. 240–46; and No. 15489, "Ordres," July 4, 1809, vol. 19, p. 252.

65] The figures given are from Esposito and Elting, *Military History and Atlas,* Map 104. Chandler, *Campaigns of Napoleon,* gives the figure at 155,000 men (pp. 714–15) while Petre, *Napoleon and the Archduke Charles,* puts the figure at 142,000 men and 414 guns (p. 352).

66] The figures are taken from Esposito and Elting, *Military History and Atlas,* Map 104. Chandler, *Campaigns of Napoleon,* generally agrees with them giving 188,000 men and "no less than 500 guns" (p. 709); while Petre, *Napoleon and the Archduke Charles,* gives the figures of 180,000 men and 554 guns (pp. 351–52) and de Renémont, *Campagne de 1809,* puts them at 188,000 men and 416 guns (p. 266).

67] Marbot gives a full account of the episode in his *Mémoirs,* 2: 270–75.

68] Bernadotte was given two administrative positions after the Battle of Wagram, but they did not involve the command of troops.

69] *Corresp. Davout,* No. 814, to Berthier, July 6, 1809, vol. 3, p. 83.

70] See Rivollet, *Morand, Friant et Gudin,* pp. 78–84, 285–86.

71] The first figure is given by Chandler, *Campaigns of Napoleon,* p. 729; the second by Esposito and Elting, *Military History and Atlas,* Map 106. Madelin writes: "In the single day of the 6th [July], 26,772 men were killed or wounded, of which 8,000 of the wounded did not live" (*Histoire du consulat,* 8: 83). Petre, *Napoleon and the Archduke Charles,* gives French losses at 27,000 (p. 379); while de Renémont, *Campagne de 1809,* puts them at the much too low figure of 18,000 (p. 301).

72] Esposito and Elting, *Military History and Atlas,* Map 106. Chandler, *Campaigns of Napoleon,* gives the Austrian losses at 37,146 (p. 729), while Madelin, *Histoire du consulat,* 8: 83, puts them at only 24,600 killed or wounded. Petre, *Napoleon and the Archduke Charles,* also gives the figure of 24,000 for Austrian losses (pp. 378–79) but de Renémont, *Campagne de 1809,* again gives the extremely low count of 18,000 (p. 301).

73] As quoted in Madelin, *Histoire du consulat,* 8: 85, 238.

74] Most notable of contemporary historians to hold this point of view is Chandler, *Campaigns of Napoleon.* At the end of his chapter on the campaign of 1809 he summarizes Napoleon's errors and concludes: "His genius for inspiring the conscripts of his rank and file and rallying the shaky loyalty of allied troops remained undimmed, and he was undoubtedly the best general on either side, his errors notwithstanding, yet something of the old energy and brilliance is lacking. Many of his orders are vaguely worded and more capable of misapprehension than ever before; he shows remarkable fits of lethargy, or sheer exhaustion, after both Aspern-Essling and Wagram; his summary treatment of Bernadotte, earned him an able man's enmity and falls short of the great *finesse* with which Napoleon customarily treated his subordinates. All this would seem to make the point that *Napoleon was past his military prime by 1809* [italics mine]" (p. 733).

CHAPTER 10

1] *Corresp. Davout,* No. 833, to Napoleon, Aug. 19, 1809, vol. 3, pp. 104–5; and *Corresp. Nap.,* No. 15607, to Davout, Aug. 3, 1809, vol. 19, p. 352.

2] *Corresp. Davout,* No. 834, to Napoleon, Sept. 14, 1809, vol. 3, p. 106.

3] *Corresp. Nap.,* No. 15825, to Prince Cambacérès, Sept. 19, 1809, p. 562; and *Corresp. Davout,* vol. 3, p. 107, n. 1.

4] *Corresp. Davout,* No. 827, to Napoleon, Aug. 6, 1809, vol. 3, p. 95; No. 828, to Napoleon, Aug. 8, 1809, vol. 3; No. 830, to Napoleon, Aug. 12, 1809, vol. 3, p. 101; and *Corresp. Nap.,* No. 15607, to Davout, Aug. 3, 1809, vol. 19, p. 352.

5] For the "Lettre Patente" see Blocqueville, 2: 453–56.

6] Ibid.

7] This treaty is also referred to as the Treaty of Vienna (October 14, 1809).

8] *Corresp. Nap.,* No. 15946, to Berthier, Oct. 14, 1809, vol. 19, pp. 677–79.

9] Ibid.

10] *Corresp. Davout,* No. 878, to Minister of War, Dec. 20, 1809, vol. 3, p. 148.

11] *Corresp. Davout,* No. 886, to Minister of War, Jan. 6, 1810, vol. 3, pp. 159–60.

12] *Corresp. Nap.,* No. 16146, to General Clarke, Jan. 18, 1810, vol. 20, pp. 151–52.

13] *Corresp. Nap.,* No. 16028, to Berthier, Nov. 28, 1809, vol. 20, p. 54.

14] *Corresp. Davout,* No. 888, to Minister of War, Jan. 11, 1810, vol. 3, pp. 161–62.

15] *Corresp. Davout,* No. 891, to Minister of War, Jan. 27, 1810, vol. 3, pp. 164–65.

16] *Corresp. Davout,* No. 893, to Minister of War, Jan. 29, 1810, vol. 3, pp. 166–67.

17] *Corresp. Davout,* No. 895, to Minister of War, Jan. 30, 1810, vol. 3, p. 167.

18] Henri Gratien Bertrand, *Napoleon at St. Helena,* trans. F. Hume (London: Cassell, 1953), pp. 54–55.

19] See the correspondence of Davout to his wife in Blocqueville, 2: 373–76.

20] Davout to wife, Mar. 23, 24, and 25, 1810, Blocqueville, 2: 373–75.

21] Davout to wife, Aug. 4, 1810, Blocqueville, 2: 384–85.

22] Davout to Alexandre, Aug. 8, 1810, Blocqueville, 2: 385–86.

23] Davout to wife, Jan. 7, 1811, Blocqueville, 3: 23.

24] Davout to wife, Jan. 14, 1811, Blocqueville, 3: 92.

25] Davout to wife, Jan. 16, 1811, Blocqueville, 3: 94.

26] Ibid.

27] Ibid.

28] The former Désirée Clary was the wife of Marshal Bernadotte, who accepted the Swedish offer to become crown prince and heir to the throne. She had been Napoleon's "first love" and was the sister of Julie, wife of Joseph Bonaparte.

29] Aimée Davout to Davout, mid-Nov. 1811, as quoted in Vigier, *Davout: maréchal d'empire,* 2: 65.

30] Davout to wife, 1812, Blocqueville, 3: 87–88.

31] Thiébault, *Mémoires,* 5: 50.

32] Ibid., p. 49.

33] See Blocqueville, 3: 30–32.

34] As quoted in Vachée, *Etude du charactère militaire du maréchal Davout,* p. 42; and *Corresp. Davout,* vol. 3, pp. 98–99, n. 1.

35] Ibid.

36] Davout to wife, Sept. 20, 1812, Blocqueville, 3: 172–73.

37] See for example Davout to wife, Feb. 2, 3, 1812, Blocqueville, 3: 111–12, 113–14.

38] Davout to wife, Aug. 11, 1812, Blocqueville, 3: 163.

39] Rivollet, *Morand, Friant et Gudin,* Davout to Morand, Feb. 23, 1806, p. 222.

40] Rivollet, *Morand, Friant et Gudin,* Davout to Morand, Jan. 4, 1808, p. 222.

41] Rivollet, *Morand, Friant et Gudin,* Morand to Clarke, Nov. 18, 1810, pp. 223–24.

42] See chapter 13.

43] Thiébault, *Mémoires,* 5: 25.

44] Ibid., p. 51.

45] *Corresp. Nap.,* No. 17516, to Davout, Mar. 24, 1811, vol. 21, pp. 594–98; and No. 17935, to Davout, July 20, 1811, vol. 22, pp. 396–97.

46] *Corresp. Davout,* No. 950, to Minister of War, Mar. 12, 1811, vol. 3, p. 220.

47] *Corresp. Davout,* No. 1004, to Minister of War, Nov. 24, 1811, vol. 3, p. 294.

48] *Corresp. Nap.,* No. 18259, to Davout, Nov. 14, 1811, vol. 23, pp. 16–17.

49] Bourrienne, *Memoirs of Napoleon,* 3: 165–66.

50] Vandal, *Napoléon et Alexandre,* 3: 328–29.

51] *Corresp. Davout,* No. 996, to Minister of War, Nov. 8, 1811, vol. 3, pp. 278–80; and *Corresp. Nap.,* No. 18253, to Minister of War, Nov. 12, 1811, vol. 23, pp. 10–12.

52] *Corresp. Davout,* No. 946, to Minister of War, Feb. 26, 1811, vol. 3, pp. 215–16.

53] Vandal, *Napoléon et Alexandre,* 3: 240–51.

54] *Corresp. Nap.,* No. 18447, to Davout, Jan. 19, 1812, vol. 23, pp. 212–13.

55] *Corresp. Davout,* No. 1008, to Friant, Jan. 21, 1812, vol. 3, pp. 298–303.

56] Ibid.

CHAPTER 11

1] Thompson, *Napoleon Bonaparte,* p. 256.

2] Davout to wife, Feb. 5, 1811, Blocqueville, 3: 117.

3] See *Corresp. Nap.,* Nos. 18363, 18399, 18400, and 18420, vol. 23; and *Corresp. Davout,* 3: 311–55.

4] See *Corresp. Nap.,* Nos. 18300, 18400, and 18422, vol. 23.

5] See *Corresp. Nap.,* Nos. 18413 and 18760, vol. 23.

6] The Emperor let it be known that he wished Madame Davout to give a ball early in 1812. Despite her pregnant condition and her general reluctance to entertain on a large scale, the Marshal convinced her that it was a necessity. (See Davout to wife, Feb. 12, 1812, Blocqueville, 3: 109–10.)

7] *Corresp. Nap.,* No. 18442, to Berthier, Jan. 16, 1812, vol. 23, p. 210.

8] *Corresp. Nap.,* No. 18427, to Davout, Jan. 10, 1812, vol. 23, pp. 190–91.

9] *Corresp. Nap.,* No. 18584, to Berthier, Mar. 16, 1812, vol. 23, pp. 367–68.

10] *Corresp. Nap.,* No. 18608, to Berthier, Mar. 25, 1812, vol. 23, pp. 396–97.

11] *Moniteur,* May 9, 1812.

12] Ibid.

13] See chapter 9.

14] Davout to wife, Feb. 9, 1812, Blocqueville, 3: 120.

15] Davout to wife, Apr. 19, 1812, Blocqueville, 3: 138.

16] Comte Paul Philip de Ségur, *History of the Expedition to Russia Undertaken by the Emperor Napoleon in the Year 1812,* 2 vols. (London: Treuttel and Wurtz, 1827), 1: 96. Ségur's account of the campaign was first published in December 1824. He had taken part in the expedition as a member of the Emperor's staff. In the years following the fall of the Empire he had gathered material for his work not only from his own personal experiences but from others who had survived the disastrous ordeal. To this end he had written to the Prince of Eckmühl on November 4, 1816: "I hope that you will not find me indiscreet if I dare to ask you to make for me several notes on the operations of your army [corps] during the Russian war of 1812? I have been gathering material necessary for the writing of the political, moral and military history of this campaign" (Blocqueville, 3: 82–83). There is no record of what information Davout sent Ségur at this time, nor of what use the author made of that which the Marshal sent him. However, it is necessary to read Ségur with caution, as he is not always historically accurate.

17] Ségur, *History of the Expedition to Russia,* 1: 97.

18] Ibid., pp. 97–98.

19] Blocqueville, Vigier, Joly, and Chenier.

20] Armand de Caulaincourt, *Mémoires du général Caulaincourt, duc de Vicence,* 3 vols. (Paris: Plon, 1933), 1: 342.

21] Esposito and Elting (*Military History and Atlas*) list the regiments and parts of regiments of each corps which were made up of foreign troops. See Map 107.

22] Though the foreign troops in Napoleon's army are credited with most of the plundering and marauding during the advance to Moscow, they fought well and cannot be singled out as a major cause for the failure of the campaign. In other words, even if the army had been one hundred percent French it is unlikely that the end result would have been any different.

23] The exact numbers of Napoleon's army have been the subject of debate over the years. The Russian historian Eugene Tarle wrote the following in his *Napoleon's Invasion of Russia 1812* (New York: Oxford University Press, 1942), pp. 50–51: "There are about ten different estimates of the size of the Grand Army that crossed the Niemen. Napoleon spoke of 400,000 men. His personal secretary, Baron Fain, mentioned 360,000; Ségur—375,000; Fezanzac [*sic*]—500,000. The figures given by St. Hilaire (614,000) and Labomme [*sic*] (680,000) clearly include the reserves stationed in Germany and Poland. Most of the estimates lie between 400,000 and 470,000. The number 420,000 is the most frequently mentioned in documents referring to the army that actually crossed the Niemen." The figure 430,000 used in the text is based on the calculations of Esposito and Elting (*Military History and Atlas,* Map 107) which they gave us as the number of men actually taking part in the invasion. Chandler, *Campaigns of Napoleon,* also gives a detailed breakdown of the

Grand Army and places its strength at 448,945 men. (See appendix G, pp. 1108–14.)

24] Here again there are as many different estimates of the strength of the Russian army as there are historians. The figures used in the text, and those below in this chapter, are the ones given by Esposito and Elting, *Military History and Atlas,* Map 107. The English General Wilson, who represented his government at Russian army headquarters, gave that army's strength at 220,050, while Clausewitz, who also took part in the campaign, figured the Tsar's field strength at 180,000 men.

25] For an excellent description and discussion of the fortified camp of Drissa see Karl von Clausewitz, *The Campaign of 1812 in Russia* (London: John Murray, 1843), pp. 17–27. Clausewitz was sent by the Tsar to inspect the camp at the opening of the campaign.

26] Clausewitz wrote of the Drissa position after he had thoroughly inspected it: "Had the Russians not abandoned this position, their numbers, whether 90,000 or 120,000, would have made no difference—they must, attacked from behind, have been driven into the half circle of their fortifications, and compelled to capitulate" (*Campaign of 1821,* pp. 24–25).

27] Blocqueville, 3: 135–36.

28] *Corresp. Nap.,* No. 18874, to Berthier, June 29, 1812, vol. 23, pp. 673–78.

29] *Corresp. Nap.,* No. 18879, to Davout, July 1, 1812, vol. 24, pp. 5–6. There is some confusion at this point in the numbering of the letters in the *Correspondance de Napoléon.* The numbers 18878, 18879, and 18880 are used for the last three letters of vol. 23 and the first three letters of vol. 24.

30] Arch. Guerre, C^2 290, Davout to Berthier, July 4, 1812.

31] Tarle, *Napoleon's Invasion of Russia,* pp. 89–92. Bagration had never liked Barclay and it was obvious even before the campaign opened that there would be a lack of cooperation. "One feels ashamed to wear the uniform," Bagration wrote to a friend on July 15, 1812, "honest to God, I feel sick . . . What a fool . . . Minister Barclay himself is running away, yet he orders me to defend all of Russia. I must confess, I'm so disgusted with the whole business that I'm nearly out of my wits." (Ibid., p. 91.)

32] See *Corresp. Nap.,* No. 18905, to Berthier, July 5, 1812, vol. 24, pp. 22–23. Frédéric Masson, *Napoléon et sa famille,* 7 vols. (Paris: Ollendorff, 1893) quotes Napoleon as writing to Jérôme on July 4, the following: "It is impossible to make war like this: you do not occupy yourself with it, you speak only of *babioles* and I see with pain that everything is petty in your camp. . . . You are compromising the success of the entire campaign on the right" (7: 311).

33] As quoted in Masson, *Napoléon,* 7: 313.

34] Ibid., p. 314.

35] *Corresp. Nap.,* No. 18911, vol. 24, p. 28.

36] Masson, *Napoléon,* 7: 317.

37] Ibid., p. 318.

38] Ibid., p. 319.

39] For a more detailed discussion of these events see Masson, *Napoléon,* 7: 286–90.

40] Ibid., p. 322.

41] Ségur, *History of the Expedition to Russia,* 1: 151.

42] Caulaincourt, *Mémoires,* 1: 372–73.

43] *Corresp. Nap.,* No. 18984, vol. 24, pp. 93–94.

44] Sir Robert T. Wilson, who gives a very good account of the Battle of Solta-Nawka in his *Narrative of Events During the Invasion of Russia by Napoleon Bonaparte, and the Retreat of the French Army, 1812* (London: John Murray, 1860), wrote: "Davoust [*sic*] and General Haxo, who were riding after the regiment, were themselves all but made prisoners" (p. 62). Wilson's account of this close escape is the only one that mentions it. Davout's lengthy description of the affair to Berthier makes no mention of his being with Bouistrys. (See *Corresp. Davout,* No. 1075, Aug. 7, 1812, vol. 3, pp. 375–79.)

45] Davout wrote to Berthier concerning his strength: "At Mohilew I had only the 57th, 61st and 111th infantry regiments of Compans' division, Valence's division and the 3rd regiment of chasseurs" (*Corresp. Davout,* No. 1075, Aug. 7, 1812, vol. 3, p. 376).

46] For the numerical strength of the Russian army see Wilson, *Narrative of Events During the Invasion of Russia,* p. 61 (35,000 foot, 10,000 cavalry, 6,000 Cossacks, and artillery); and Clausewitz, *Campaign of 1812,* p. 57 (45,000).

47] Caulaincourt, *Mémoires,* 1: 374.

48] The enemy's losses had been heavy. "He left on the battlefield more than 1,200 dead and more than 4,000 wounded, of which 700 or 800 remained in our hands along with 150 to 200 prisoners. Our losses . . . amounted to 900 men killed, wounded or captured." (*Corresp. Davout,* No. 1075, to Berthier, Aug. 7, 1812, vol. 3, p. 378.)

49] *Corresp. Davout,* No. 1069, to General Tharreau, July 27, 1812, vol. 3, pp. 370–72.

50] Both Ségur and Caulaincourt stress these aspects of the campaign even during its earliest stages. See Ségur, *History of the Expedition to Russia,* 1: 135–41, and Caulaincourt, *Mémoires,* 1: 370, 375–79.

51] Ségur, *History of the Expedition to Russia,* 1: 207.

52] Marbot, *Mémoires,* 2: 542.

53] Ségur, *History of the Expedition to Russia,* 1: 274–76.

54] *Corresp. Davout,* No. 1085, to Berthier, Aug. 30, 1812, vol. 3, pp. 389–91; Wilson, *Narrative of Events during the Invasion of Russia,* pp. 85–89; and Ségur, *History of the Expedition to Russia,* 1: 225–27.

55] See Wilson, *Narrative of Events During the Invasion of Russia,* pp. 91–95; Ségur, *History of the Expedition to Russia,* 1: 244–45; Caulaincourt, *Mémoires,* 1: 396–98; and *Corresp. Davout,* No. 1081, to Berthier, Aug. 21, 1812, vol. 3, p. 385.

56] Davout to wife, Aug. 11, 1812, Blocqueville, 3: 163.

57] Davout to wife, Aug. 20, 1812, Blocqueville, 3: 165–66. Shortly before the Russian campaign the Marshal and his wife had been godparents for the Gudins' youngest child, who was named after Madame Davout: Aimée-Louise Gudin. (Blocqueville, 3: 527.)

58] Maurice-Etienne Gérard (1773–1852) was named Marshal of France at the debut of the July Monarchy (Aug. 17, 1830) and Peer of France in 1833. It was Gérard to whom Davout turned over his command of Hamburg after the abdication of Napoleon in 1814.

59] *Corresp. Nap.,* No. 19115, to Davout, Aug. 22, 1812, vol. 24, pp. 191–92, and No. 19143, to Davout, Aug. 26, 1812, vol. 24, p. 209.

60] *Corresp. Nap.,* No. 19115, to Davout, Aug. 22, 1812, vol. 24, pp. 191–92.

61] *Corresp. Nap.,* No. 19143, to Davout, Aug. 26, 1812, vol. 24, p. 209.

62] Ségur, *History of the Expedition to Russia,* 1: 278.

63] Ibid., p. 281.

64] Ibid.

65] Ibid., pp. 282–83.

66] Ibid. Belliard said that as Murat strove to swallow the affront, tears of spite rolled down his cheeks and fell upon his uniform (Ségur, *History of the Expedition to Russia,* 1: 288).

67] See chapter 12.

68] Ibid.

69] Clausewitz, *Campaign of 1812,* pp. 131–35.

70] There is little dispute over these figures. Clausewitz gives them and most historians (see Tarle, *Napoleon's Invasion of Russia;* and Esposito and Elting, *Military History and Atlas*) have accepted them. Wilson, *Narrative of Events During the Invasion of Russia,* differs, mentioning 140,000.

71] Clausewitz, *Campaign of 1812,* p. 131.

72] Referring to Kutuzov's army as it arrived at Borodino, Tarle writes: "The soldiers were hungry, the army had nothing to eat. Kutuzuv was forced to ask Moscow for provisions; he exhorted Rostopchin [Governor-General of Moscow] to send the soldiers some food, lest the 'shortages' compromise every hope of success." And again further on: "Hunger and privations struck the Russian soldier harder than Napoleon's bullets and grapeshot" (*Napoleon's Invasion of Russia,* p. 117).

73] Clausewitz wrote the following on this subject: "Had he [Napoleon] only amused the center, which in respect of the ground was immeasurably stronger than the left wing, and endeavored to outflank the left with 50,000 men instead of with 10,000 [a reference to Poniatowski] the battle would have been sooner decided, and probably greater results obtained" (*Campaign of 1812,* p. 170).

74] Ségur, *History of the Expedition to Russia,* 1: 207–8. The reference was to the battles of Wagram and Eylau.

75] Baron Louis François Lejeune wrote in his *Memoirs* of this lack of support: "The Marshal [Davout], greatly put out at having to make an isolated assault in front on a position which he thought ought to be attacked simultaneously on three sides, said to me angrily, 'It's a confounded shame to make me take the bull by the horns' " (*Memoirs of Baron Lejeune, aide-de-camp to Marshals Berthier, Davout and Oudinot,* trans. and ed. Mrs. Arthur Bell, 2 vols. [London: Longmans, Green, 1897], 2: 181).

76] Lejeune, *Memoirs,* 2: 181.

77] The artillery of the Guard had been used and one regiment of the Young Guard had been sent forward to support the right in the event of a strong counterattack. But this unit had not been engaged.

78] Lejeune, *Memoirs,* 2: 183.

79] Davout to wife, Sept. 20, 1812, Blocqueville, 3: 171–73.

80] Ibid.

81] As quoted in Tarle, *Napoleon's Invasion of Russia,* p. 244.

82] The best care against Rostopchin is given by the Russian historian Tarle in his chapter entitled "The Burning of Moscow," in *Napoleon's Invasion of Russia,* pp. 205–55.

83] Clausewitz, *Campaign of 1812,* p. 192.

84] Davout to wife, Sept. 30, 1812, Blocqueville, 3: 177.

85] Louis F. Lejeune was named Davout's chief of staff following the Battle of Borodino in which General Romeuf, who previously held that post, was killed. Lejeune had been aide-de-camp to Marshal Berthier and had pleaded with him not to allow the new appointment. However, Napoleon and Davout both wished it to be and Lejeune joined the I Corps. In his *Memoirs* Lejeune complains, in a mild manner, that Davout was too demanding of him and his staff during the difficult days of the retreat. But he was also quick to point out that when he was injured in a fall from his horse at the height of the catastrophe—at a time when every man thought only of his personal safety—Davout befriended him by taking him into his own small carriage. (See Lejeune, *Memoirs,* 2: 190–91, 216.)

86] *Corresp. Davout,* No. 1092, to Berthier, Sept. 25, 1812, vol. 3, p. 396.

87] Blocqueville, 3: 175–76.

CHAPTER 12

1] On October 17 Napoleon ordered General Victor, now in command of the rear at Smolensk, to send troops and supplies to Elnay on the Kaluga road. This force was intended to support the main army as it retired from Kaluga. (*Corresp. Nap.,* No. 19281, to Berthier, vol. 24, pp. 313–14.)

2] Two thousand casualties and two thousand prisoners were taken by the Russians (Wilson, *Narrative of Events During the Invasion of Russia,* p. 211).

3] See *Corresp. Davout,* 3: 398–420.

4] *Corresp. Davout,* "Ordre du 16 octobre 1812," vol. 3, pp. 418–19; and No. 1130, to Berthier, Oct. 15, 1812, vol. 3, pp. 417–18.

5] *Corresp. Davout,* No. 1132, to Berthier, Oct. 18, 1812, vol. 3, pp. 420–21.

6] Caulaincourt, *Mémoires,* 2: 91–92.

7] The use of the term *decisive* may be debatable. Napoleon had already decided upon a strategic withdrawal. Thus the high point of the campaign had been the occupation of Moscow, and the fortunes of the French army had begun to decline. But after the stalemate at Maloyaroslavets the French strategic withdrawal became a retreat.

8] Wilson, *Narrative of Events During the Invasion of Russia,* pp. 224–33.

9] Ségur, *History of the Expedition to Russia,* 2: 109–10.

10] Wilson, *Narrative of Events during the Invasion of Russia,* pp. 231–34. Wilson quotes the old marshal as declaring to him that "he had determined to finish the war on that spot—to succeed or make the enemy pass over his body" (ibid., p. 231).

11] "The ultimate strategical error committed by Napoleon occurred a week after quitting Moscow. His decision to march south from the Russian capital towards the fertile and unspoiled areas of Kaluga Province was sound enough, but this wise and well-considered move was summarily abandoned when the army ran into resistance at Maloyaroslavets" (Chandler, *Campaigns of Napoleon,* pp. 857–58).

12] Clausewitz, *Campaign of 1812,* p. 199.

13] Ibid., pp. 199–200.

14] Lejeune, *Memoirs,* 2: 206–7.

15] *Corresp. Davout,* No. 1134, vol. 3, pp. 422–23; and Wilson, *Narrative of Events During the Invasion of Russia,* p. 239.

16] *Corresp. Nap.,* No. 19316, to Berthier, vol. 24, p. 344.

17] Eugene Labaume, *A Circumstantial Narrative of the Campaign in Russia* (London: Samuel Leigh, 1815), p. 275.

18] Ibid.

19] Labaume, who took part in the campaign under Prince Eugène and who fought at Vyazma, wrote the following defense of Davout's actions. "The marshal . . . might have replied, in his own justification, that too rapid a retreat would have redoubled the audacity of the enemy, who, strong in light cavalry, could at all times overtake us, and cut in pieces our rear-guard, if it had refused combat. That excellent officer had already, in more fortunate times, proved that we might confidently rely on his skill, and he could now have added this maxim of war;—'The more precipitate a retreat, the more fatal it becomes,' because the fear which it occasions in the minds of the soldiers, is more to be dreaded than any physical evils" (Labaume, *Campaign in Russia,* p. 275).

20] Ibid., p. 136.

21] *Corresp. Nap.,* No. 19316, to Berthier, vol. 24, p. 344.

22] Davout to wife, Oct. 6, 1812, Blocqueville, 3: 181.

23] Caulaincourt, *Mémoires,* 2: 119. Ségur, in his *History of the Expedition to Russia,* wrote the following on this disorder: "The hastiness of the maneuver, the surprise, so much wretchedness, and, above all, the fatal example of the multitude of dismounted cavalry, without arms, and running to and fro bewildered with fear, threw it [the I Corps] into confusion" (2: 140).

24] As quoted in Wilson, *Narrative of Events During the Invasion of Russia,* p. 248.

25] Caulaincourt, *Mémoires,* 2: 119.

26] It becomes increasingly difficult to establish the strength of the French army as it disintegrated during the retreat. The figure given here in the text is based on Esposito and Elting, *Military History and Atlas,* Map 122. Wilson, *Narrative of Events During the Invasion of Russia,* gives a figure of 45,300 (p. 262); and Ségur, *History of the Expedition to Russia,* 36,000 (2: 189).

27] *Corresp. Nap.,* No. 19337, to Berthier, Nov. 14, 1812, vol. 24, p. 359.

28] These events are described in Caulaincourt, *Mémoires,* 2: 151–52. Ségur, *History of the Expedition to Russia,* gives a slightly different version of the quarrel. "Ney was anxious immediately to evacuate Smolensk in the suite of the Viceroy [that is, on the fifteenth]; Davoust [*sic*] refused, pleading the orders of the Emperor, and the obligation to destroy the ramparts of the town. The two chiefs became warm, and Davoust [*sic*] persisting to remain until the following day, Ney, who had been appointed to bring up the rear, was compelled to wait for him" (2: 228).

29] "My cousin," wrote Napoleon to Berthier on November 14, "write to the Duke of Elchingen . . . that he should depart from the city [Smolensk] on the 16th after blowing it up; or if all is not ready, he should take up a position at the gate and blow up the city on the 17th" (*Corresp. Nap.*, No. 19337, vol. 24, p. 359).

30] Caulaincourt, *Mémoires,* 2: 151.

31] Ibid., p. 146.

32] Ibid., p. 152; and Ségur, *History of the Expedition to Russia,* 2: 228.

33] Caulaincourt, *Mémoires,* 2: 152; and Ségur, *History of the Expedition to Russia,* 2: 228. Caulaincourt suggests that it was for provisions that Ney remained the extra day: "Threatened on the one hand by the very real danger of his troops being demoralized through lack of food, and on the other of being attacked by superior enemy forces, he decided on the course of action most in keeping with his own daring and with the proven courage of his men" (*Mémoires,* 2: 152).

34] Labaume, *Campaign in Russia,* p. 350.

35] Raymond Aimery Philippe Joseph [Montesquiou] de Fezensac, *Journal de la campagne de Russie en 1812* (Paris: A. Maine, 1850), p. 103.

36] Ségur, *History of the Expedition to Russia,* 2: 230.

37] Caulaincourt, *Mémoires,* 2: 158.

38] "My cousin," wrote the Emperor to Berthier, "write to the Duke of Elchingen . . . that he will be supported by the Prince of Eckmühl" (*Corresp. Nap.*, No. 19337, Nov. 14, 1812, vol. 24, p. 359).

39] Caulaincourt, *Mémoires,* 2: 158.

40] de Fezensac, *Journal,* p. 121.

41] Ségur, *History of the Expedition to Russia,* 2: 220. Ségur goes on to quote Davout as saying "that none but men of iron constitutions could support such trials, that it was physically impossible to resist them [the trials]; that there were limits to human strength, the utmost of which had been exceeded."

42] Esposito and Elting, *Military History and Atlas,* Map 122, gives the effective strength of the army at between twenty and twenty-five thousand men. Lejeune also gives the strength of the I Corps at four thousand (*Memoirs,* 2: 221–22).

43] This figure is based on the following calculations: effective strength of the army under the Emperor's command as he approached the Berezina—25,000; stragglers with this army who could be brought back into ranks—20,000; Oudinot's II Corps—8,000; Dombrowski (cavalry) and

Bronkowski, who were with Oudinot—1,800; Victor's IX Corps—11,000; Wrede's VI Corps—12,000; Schwarzenberg's Austrian corps, and Reynier's VII Corps—42,000. (See Esposito and Elting, *Military History and Atlas,* Maps 122, 123.)

44] *Corresp. Davout.* No. 1139, to Berthier, Nov. 23, 1812, vol. 3, p. 428.

45] General Kreitz, *Notes* (St. Petersburg, 1903), as quoted in Tarle, *Napoleon's Invasion of Russia,* p. 343.

46] Baron Woldemar Hermann de Löwenstern, *Mémoires du général-major russe baron de Löwenstern (1776–1858),* ed. M. H. Weil, 2 vols. (Paris: A. Fontemoing, 1903), 1: 355–56.

47] Tarle, *Napoleon's Invasion of Russia,* p. 377.

48] Denis Davydov, as quoted in Constantin de Grünwald, *La Campagne de Russie* (Paris: René Julliard, 1964), p. 325; and Tarle, *Napoleon's Invasion of Russia,* p. 373.

49] On General Malet's unsuccessful attempt to overthrow the government in Napoleon's absence, see Madelin, *Histoire du consulat,* 12: 299–319; and Arthur de Lort de Serignan, *Un conspirateur militaire sur le premier empire: le général Malet* (Paris: Payot, 1925).

50] Ségur, *History of the Expedition to Russia,* 2: 314–15.

51] See *Corresp. Davout,* No. 1181, to duc de Frioul, Feb. 3, 1813, vol. 3, p. 484; and Ségur, *History of the Expedition to Russia,* 2: 350.

52] *Corresp. Davout,* No. 1181, to duc de Frioul, Feb. 3, 1813, vol. 3, p. 484.

53] Ibid.

CHAPTER 13

1] *Corresp. Davout,* No. 1146, to Berthier, Dec. 30, 1812, vol. 3, pp. 435–36; No. 1147, to Berthier, Jan. 1, 1813, vol. 3, pp. 435–36.

2] Davout acknowledged the arrival of Wrede's Corps of four to five thousand men on January 7, 1813. (See *Corresp. Davout,* No. 1154, to Berthier, vol. 3, p. 445.)

3] *Corresp. Davout,* No. 1177, to the Viceroy of Italy (Eugene), Jan. 31, 1813, vol. 3, pp. 475–76.

4] The letter in which Davout acknowledged the receipt of orders to assume command of the 32nd Military Division is missing—if indeed such a letter had been written. However, his transfer to the lower Elbe is mentioned in a letter to Eugène dated April 17, 1813 (*Corresp. Davout,* No. 1273, vol. 4, p. 46). In a letter to Eugène, dated March 18, Napoleon instructed the Viceroy to give Davout command of the 32nd Division and of the Elbe from Magdeburg to Hamburg (*Corresp. Nap.,* No. 19734, vol. 25, pp. 120–22).

5] For an account of the popular revolt in Hamburg and Carré St.-Cyr's withdrawal see Philip Paul Holzhausen, *Davout in Hamburg: Ein Beitrag zur Geschichte der Jahre 1813–1814* (Mulheim: Max Röder, 1892), pp. 40–41.

6] *Corresp. Nap.*, No. 19748, to General Clarke, Mar. 21, 1813, vol. 25, p. 136.

7] The entire letter is found in Blocqueville, 3: 208–11.

8] See Blocqueville, 3: 211–12.

9] In the defense of her father the Marquise of Blocqueville writes: "I have held in my hands, read and reread the answer to this barbarous order which begins thus: 'Your Majesty will never make of me a *duc d'Able*! I would rather break in two my marshal's baton than to obey orders which you yourself would be the first to regret. War is already horrible enough without adding to it unnecessary cruelties.'" (Blocqueville, 3: 207.) Unfortunately, this letter does not appear in Davout's correspondence, nor was this author able to find it in the Davout collection which is housed by the Ministry of War at the Château de Vincennes.

10] Blocqueville, 3: 215; and *Corresp. Davout,* vol. 4, pp. 156–57, n. 1. It should be pointed out that this letter and others which show Napoleon as the author of the stern measures taken by Davout in Hamburg at this time are conspicuously missing from the official *Correspondance de Napoléon I*[er]*,* which was published by order of Napoleon III during the Second Empire, or in any of the supplements.

11] Napoleon to Davout, June 17, 1813, Blocqueville, 3: 215.

12] "Your powers are unlimited," Madame Davout wrote the Marshal on May 8, 1813 concerning his command of the thirty-second military district, "but as for doing harm; you will do as little as possible." (Blocqueville, 3: 336.)

13] *Corresp. Nap.*, No. 19734, to Eugène, Mar. 18, 1813, vol. 25, p. 121.

14] *Corresp. Davout,* No. 1363, to Napoleon, June 11, 1813, vol. 4, pp. 152–53.

15] *Corresp. Davout,* No. 1382, to Napoleon, June 20, 1813, vol. 4, pp. 174–76.

16] Louis N. Davout, *Mémoire de m. le maréchal Davout, prince d'Eckmühl, au roi* (Paris: Crapelet, 1814), p. 65; and Blocqueville, 3: 217.

17] Davout used this expression in referring to the Hamburgese defending the city in the spring of 1813. See *Corresp. Davout,* No. 1338, to Berthier, May 26, 1813, vol. 4, pp. 124–25.

18] This report is referred to in Davout's letter to the Emperor of July 13, 1813 (*Corresp. Davout,* No. 1439, vol. 4, p. 225), and in the latter's reply of July 16 (*Corresp. Davout,* vol. 4, p. 230, n. 1).

19] *Corresp. Davout,* vol. 4, pp. 230–31, n. 1, and Blocqueville, 3: 220–21.

20] *Corresp. Davout,* vol. 4, pp. 220–21, n. 1. Mazade writes at the end of this lengthy letter: "This letter, which is important as evidence of the Emperor's intentions and as a direct expression of his orders with respect to the people of Hamburg, has not been reproduced in the *Correspondance de Napoléon Ier.*"

21] Ibid.

22] Davout, *Mémoire au roi,* p. 25.

23] Ibid., p. 66.

24] Ibid., pp. 66–67. The entire amnesty, eight articles, is printed in the *Mémoire au roi,* pp. 65–69.

25] Feb. 13, 1813, Blocqueville, 3: 268.

26] See *Corresp. Davout,* 3: 500–558 and 4: 5–105.

27] *Corresp. Nap.,* No. 20206, to Davout, July 1, 1813, vol. 25, pp. 519–20.

28] See Blocqueville, 3: 332–35.

29] Davout to wife, May 12, 1813, Blocqueville, 3: 314–15.

30] Ibid.

31] Davout to wife, Aug. 15, 1813, Blocqueville, 3: 357–58.

32] Davout to wife, Apr. 7, 1813, Blocqueville, 3: 297. Italics mine.

33] *Corresp. Nap.,* No. 20333, to Davout, Aug. 5, 1813, vol. 26, p. 8.

34] Hesse's Danish division was attached to Davout's command as part of his nation's contribution to the war. In return, Davout was to protect Holstein.

35] This figure is given by Gen. César de Laville, the Marshal's chief of staff during 1813–14, in his "Mémoire sur le siège et la défense de Hambourg." Laville's "Mémoire" is printed both in Blocqueville, 4: 5–124, and *Corresp. Davout,* 4: 288–349. In an introduction to Davout's *Correspondance,* Charles de Mazade refers to Laville's "Mémoire" as "a true account of the siege operations of Hamburg." (See *Corresp. Davout,* 4: 287.) All page references from Laville's "Mémoire" will be to volume 4 of Davout's *Correspondance.*

36] Laville, "Mémoire" p. 290.

37] Oudinot's action also left General Girard, whose regiment had advanced from Magdeburg toward Berlin to form somewhat of a link between Davout and Oudinot, in a dangerous position. The Prussian General Bülow took full advantage of the situation. He attacked the isolated regiment and threw it back across the Elbe with heavy losses.

38] *Corresp. Davout,* No. 1476, to Oudinot, Sept. 4, 1813, vol. 4, p. 274.

39] *Corresp. Davout,* No. 1477, to Chaban, Sept. 8, 1813, vol. 4, p. 275.

40] Davout, *Mémoire au roi,* pp. 14–15; and Laville, "Mémoire," p. 300.

41] Davout, *Mémoire au roi,* p. 16.

42] Ibid., p. 17.

43] Laville, "Mémoire," pp. 311–12.

44] Following the end of the siege there were a number of pamphlets and articles written condemning the actions of Marshal Davout during his command in Hamburg. Most of them were written in order to condemn Davout, or France, or both. Others were designed to justify the actions of leading citizens during the siege, and the Marshal was the most obvious scapegoat. None of them could be called objective history—even in nineteenth-century terms. The best work on the siege by a German is Holzhausen's *Davout in Hamburg.* In his introduction Holzhausen reviews the German literature about Davout and the siege of Hamburg.

45] Holzhausen, *Davout in Hamburg,* pp. 122–24.

46] Davout refers only to the "faubourg de Hambourg, dit le *Hamburgerberg*" in his *Mémoire au roi* (p. 21).

47] See the accounts in Laville, "Mémoire," pp. 315–16; and Holzhausen, *Davout in Hamburg,* pp. 126–28.

48] Holzhausen, *Davout in Hamburg,* p. 126.

49] Ibid., p. 129.

50] Davout, *Mémoire au roi,* pp. 26–27. Laville states that on Nov. 5, 1813, there were 13,500,000 francs in the Bank of Hamburg ("Mémoire," p. 303).

51] See *Corresp. Davout,* vol. 4, pp. 230–31, n. 1; and Blocqueville, 3: 220–21.

52] Davout, *Mémoire au roi,* pp. 27–28.

53] As quoted in Holzhausen, *Davout in Hamburg,* pp. 108–9.

54] Moltke to Blocqueville, June 9, 1890, Holzhausen, *Davout in Hamburg,* p. 109.

55] As quoted in Holzhausen, *Davout in Hamburg,* p. 145.

56] Ibid.

57] Davout, *Mémoire au roi,* p. 87; and Holzhausen, *Davout in Hamburg,* p. 140.

58] Davout, *Mémoire au roi,* pp. 22–23.

59] Ibid., pp. 15–16.

60] Ibid., p. 20.

61] Ibid., p. 23.

62] Laville, "Mémoire," p. 343.

63] Senator Abendroth, *Antwort auf das Memoire des Herrn Marschall's Davout, seine Verwaltung und Vertheidigung Hamburgs betreffend* (Germany, 1815), p. 43.

64] Davout, *Mémoire au roi,* p. 11.

65] Laville, "Mémoire," p. 343.

66] General Bennigsen, in a letter addressed to the "unhappy citizens of Hamburg," wrote: "There are more than 100,000 Russians, Swedes, Prussians and Saxons, inspired by their victories, before your walls" (Levin A. G. von Bennigsen, *Mémoires du général Bennigsen,* 3 vols. [Paris: Charles Lavauzelle, 1907–8], 3: 368). The figure 120,000 is given by Laville in his "Mémoire" (p. 317).

67] Laville, "Mémoire," p. 327.

68] Ibid., pp. 329–30.

69] Laville, "Mémoire," p. 339.

70] Ibid., p. 331.

71] Laville says that "we had constantly, since the beginning of February, 17,000 sick" ("Mémoire," p. 336).

72] Laville, "Mémoire," pp. 336, 343.

73] Ibid., p. 348.

74] Ibid., p. 338.

75] Davout, *Mémoire au roi,* Letter No. 40, Bennigsen to Davout, Apr. 1/13, 1814, p. 132.

76] Laville, "Mémoire," p. 344.

77] Davout, *Mémoire au roi,* Letter No. 41, Davout to Bennigsen, Apr. 14, 1814, p. 133.

78] As quoted in *Corresp. Davout,* vol. 4, p. 345, n. 1.

79] Bennigsen, *Mémoires,* 3: 370–71.

80] Davout, *Mémoire au roi,* p. 39.

81] Ibid., pp. 40–41.

82] The six signatures on the letter are: "le prince de Bénévent, François Jaucourt, l'abbé de Montesquiou, le duc d'Albert, le général Beurnonville [and] Dupont-de-Nemours." (Davout, *Mémoire au roi,* p. 41.)

83] Davout, *Mémoire au roi,* pp. 43–45.

84] François d'Avout had been a second lieutenant with Davout in the Royal-Champagne regiment when the Revolution broke out. He became an emigrant in October 1791 and served under the Comte d'Hargicout, former commander of the Royal-Champagne, in the war against France during 1793–95. He also saw service against France in Martinique; but following the Treaty of Amiens he became a captain in the French army and commanded the cavalry on the island until the English captured it in 1809. He returned to France in 1812 where he lived in retirement until the abdication of Napoleon. When Louis XVIII returned to France, François immediately took service with the king.

85] Davout, *Mémoire au roi,* pp. 45, 153–55; and Laville, "Mémoire," pp. 348–49.

86] Davout, *Mémoire au roi,* Letter No. 56, pp. 155–56.

87] Davout, *Mémoire au roi,* Letter No. 57, p. 157.

88] Davout, *Mémoire au roi,* p. 3. See also the letter from Bennigsen to Davout on this matter dated Apr. 17/20, 1814, in Bennigsen, *Mémoires,* 3: 374–75.

89] Bennigsen, *Mémoires,* 3: 368.

90] Davout, *Mémoire au roi,* p. 33.

91] Ibid., pp. 33–34.

92] Ibid., pp. 38–39.

93] Laville, "Mémoire," p. 349.

94] Davout, *Mémoire au roi,* p. 23.

95] Laville, "Mémoire," p. 349.

96] Davout, *Mémoire au roi,* Letter No. 1, pp. 51–52.

CHAPTER 14

1] Most noteworthy were Marshals Berthier, Oudinot, Masséna, and St.-Cyr.

2] See Mazade's introduction to chapter 11 in vol. 4 of Davout's *Correspondance,* p. 351.

3] Ibid., p. 352.

4] M. de Bourrienne writes the following in his *Memoirs of Napoleon:* "Davoust [*sic*] might have expected high command in the army, but to his annoyance, Napoleon fixed on him as War Minister. . . . Napoleon now wanted a man of tried devotion, and of stern enough character to overawe the capital and the restless spirits in the army. Much against his will Davoust [*sic*] was therefore forced to content himself with the organization of the forces being hastily raised, but he chafed in his position" (3: 275).

5] See *Corresp. Davout,* 4: 355–62.

6] See "Instruction au chef d'Escadrons LaLoy," Mar. 21, 1815, in *Corresp. Davout,* No. 1489, vol. 4, pp. 361–62.

7] See *Corresp. Davout,* vol. 4, pp. 369–426—particularly the correspondence to Generals Grouchy, Morand, and Solignac.

8] Madelin, *Histoire du consulat,* 16: 47–48.

9] See *Corresp. Davout,* Nos. 1490, 1635, 1649, 1651, vol. 4, pp. 362–63, 472–75, 586–88, 588–90; and *Corresp. Nap.,* particularly No. 21872, vol. 28, pp. 181–83.

10] Chandler, *Campaigns of Napoleon,* pp. 1014–15.

11] *Corresp. Nap.,* No. 21723, to Davout, Mar. 26, 1815, vol. 28, pp. 39–41.

12] The most popular explanation of Berthier's death is that he took his own life, but it is also claimed that it was accidental. The mystery surrounding this tragedy has never been solved.

13] *Corresp. Davout,* No. 1672, to Rapp, May 6, 1815, vol. 4, p. 502.

14] *Corresp. Nap.,* No. 21918, Note, May 16, 1815, vol. 28, p. 224.

15] *Corresp. Davout,* No. 1739, to Soult, May 22, 1815 vol. 4, p. 554.

16] As quoted in Blocqueville, 4: 133.

17] Ibid., pp. 132–33.

18] As quoted in Vigier, *Davout: maréchal d'empire,* 2: 270. Bourrienne wrote the following on Bourmont's appointment in his *Memoirs of Napoleon:* "It is characteristic of him [Davout] that Napoleon was eventually forced to send him the most formal orders before the surly Minister would carry out the Emperor's unlucky intention of giving a command to Bourmont, whom Davoust [*sic*] strongly and rightly suspected of treachery" (3: 275). See also Gustave Gautherot, *Un gentilhomme de grand chemin: le maréchal de Bourmont, d'après ses papiers inédits* (Paris: Presses Universitaires de France, 1926), pp. 246–47.

19] The *Fédérés* had sprung up as militant organizations which supported the Emperor in the cities in the west to protect themselves against the royalist countryside which surrounded them. The movement spread rapidly to the south, and was then given formal organization and direction from Paris. See Madelin, *Histoire du consulat,* 16: 133–37.

20] "You will make it known to him [General Rapp]," wrote Napoleon, "that it is my intention that there will not remain one soldier of the line in our fortified towns; that they be turned over to the national guard" (*Corresp. Nap.,* No. 21879, vol. 28, p. 188).

21] *Corresp. Davout,* 4: 488–566.

22] *Corresp. Nap.,* 28: 216.

23] *Corresp. Nap.,* No. 21948, to Davout, May 22, 1815, vol. 28, pp. 245–47; and *Corresp. Davout,* No. 1738, to General Saint-Sulpice, May 22, 1815, vol. 4, pp. 553–54.

24] *Corresp. Davout,* No. 1738, to Saint-Sulpice, May 22, 1815, vol. 4, pp. 553–54.

25] *Corresp. Davout,* vol. 4, p. 547, n. 1.

26] *Corresp. Davout,* No. 1746, to Lamarque, vol. 4, p. 559.

27] *Corresp. Davout,* No. 1751, to Lamarque, June 7, 1815, vol. 4, p. 563.

28] *Corresp. Davout,* No. 1721, vol. 4, p. 540.

29] Ibid.

30] *Corresp. Davout,* No. 1750, to Generals Vandamme, d'Erlon, Gérard, and Reille, vol. 4, p. 562.

31] *Corresp. Nap.,* No. 21851, vol. 28, p. 165.

32] Henri Lachouque, *The Last Days of Napoleon's Empire: From Waterloo to St. Helena,* trans. Lovett F. Edwards (New York: Orion, 1967), pp. 50–52.

33] See Henry Houssaye, *1815: la seconde abdication—la terreur blanche* (Paris: Perrin, 1905); and Lachouque, *The Last Days of Napoleon's Empire,* pp. 55–56.

34] Louis N. Davout, "Après Waterloo—Paris," *Revue de Paris,* Dec. 15, 1897, pp. 706–7.

35] Ibid., p. 707.

36] Lachouque, *The Last Days of Napoleon's Empire,* p. 64.

37] *Moniteur,* June 22, 1815.

38] Davout, "Après Waterloo—Paris," p. 709.

39] Ibid., pp. 709–10.

40] The seventeen supporting the Emperor were his two brothers, Joseph and Lucien, the ten ministers, the presidents of both chambers, and three Peers. (See Davout, "Après Waterloo—Paris," pp. 710–11.)

41] See Davout, "Après Waterloo—Paris," p. 710.

42] Henri Lachouque's recent work, *Les derniers jours de l'empire* (Paris: B. Arthaud, 1965), is an excellent example of a modern Bonapartist's views on the second abdication. It has been translated into English by Lovett F. Edwards as *The Last Days of Napoleon's Empire: From Waterloo to St. Helena* (New York: Orion, 1967).

43] "Procès-verbal de la séance de la commission de gouvernement," June 24, 1815 (Archives Nationales [hereafter cited as Arch. Nat.], AF, IV, 1933).

44] Ibid.

45] *Corresp. Davout,* No. 1763, to Grouchy, June 23, 1815, vol. 4, pp. 572–73.

46] Davout, "Après Waterloo—Paris," p. 717.

47] Ibid., p. 718.

48] Ibid.

49] Ibid.

50] *Corresp. Davout,* No. 1764, to Becker, June 25, 1815, vol. 4, pp. 573–74.

51] Lachouque, *The Last Days of Napoleon's Empire,* p. 121.

52] See General Becker's own account of this mission in Blocqueville, *Maréchal Davout: correspondance inédite,* pp. 145–262.

53] Davout, "Après Waterloo—Paris," p. 721.

54] Ibid.

55] Ibid.

56] Ibid.

57] Houssaye, *1815,* p. 180.

58] "Procès-verbal de la séance de la commission de gouvernement," June 27, 1815 (Arch. Nat., AF, IV, 1933).

59] Ibid.

60] Davout, "Après Waterloo—Paris," pp. 724–25.

61] Arch. Nat., AF, IV, 1936, and Davout, "Après Waterloo—Paris," p. 731.

62] *Corresp. Davout,* No. 1770, to Fouché, June 28, 1815, vol. 4, p. 578; and Davout, "Après Waterloo—Paris," p. 725.

63] Davout, "Après Waterloo—Paris," p. 726.

64] *Corresp. Davout,* to Marshal Blücher and Lord Wellington, vol. 4, pp. 581–82.

65] The delegation was made up of five representatives from the Chamber of Representatives: Arnaud, Jay, and Generals Pouget, Laguette-Mornay, and Dumoustier; from the Chamber of Peers: Marshal Lefebre and General Gazan.

66] *Moniteur,* June 29, 1815, *séance* of June 28, 1815.

67] Houssaye, *1815,* pp. 240–42.

68] Davout, "Après Waterloo—Paris," pp. 733–34.

69] Ibid.

70] *Moniteur,* July 2, 1815.

71] "Le ministre de la Guerre, commandant en chef l'armée à la Chambre des representants," quoted in Davout, "Après Waterloo—Paris," p. 735.

72] Henri Lachouque (*The Last Days of Napoleon's Empire*) states that Davout's retraction was the result of his learning that the Chamber of Representatives intended to print twenty thousand copies of the address, and concludes that "civil courage has nothing in common with military courage" (p. 157). Houssaye, *1815,* is more objective, but doubts the validity of the marshal's memoires (p. 253).

73] Davout, "Après Waterloo—Paris," p. 734.

74] In a letter to his wife dated June 30, 1815, he wrote: "The fate of our country will probably be decided tomorrow" (Blocqueville, 4: 248–49).

75] Davout, "Après Waterloo—Paris," p. 739; and Houssaye, *1815,* p. 262.

76] The best account of this day's fighting is found in Houssaye, *1815,* pp. 262–66.

77] "Procès-verbal de la commission de gouvernement," July 1, 1815, Arch. Nat., AF, IV, 1933; see also Davout, "Après Waterloo—Paris," p. 728.

78] "Procès-verbal de la commission de gouvernement," July 1, 1815, Arch. Nat., AF, IV, 1933.

79] Marshal Macdonald had been invited to attend the council but did not. Marshal Ney was not invited: "Accused of treason, said Caulaincourt (Sismondi, *Notes sur les Cent-Jours,* 6), he would probably not have been safe in the middle of these soldiers. Furthermore he held no command in the army, neither during the defense of Paris, nor the retreat to the Loire." (As quoted in Houssaye, *1815,* p. 277.)

80] "Procès-verbaux," Arch. Nat., AF, IV, 1936.

81] Davout, "Après Waterloo—Paris," pp. 738–39.

82] The other two members were the Count de Bondy, Prefect representing the city of Paris, and General Guilleminot, who, as Chief of Staff, represented the army.

83] Houssaye, *1815,* pp. 294–95.

84] See Houssaye, *1815,* on the capitulation of Paris (pp. 285–302).

85] Berthezène to Davout, July 7, 1815, Arch. Guerre, C^{15} 8.

86] "Procès verbal de la commission de gouvernement," July 6, 1815, Arch. Nat., AF, IV, 1933; and *Corresp. Davout,* No. 1779, to the Commission of Government, July 6, 1815, vol. 4, p. 588.

87] General Lamarque was ordered to march his small army (about ten thousand men) to Tours where it crossed the Loire and took up a position between Tours and Saumur forming Davout's left flank. (See *Corresp. Davout,* No. 1787, to Lamarque, July 11, 1815, vol. 4, pp. 595–96.)

88] It is very difficult to determine the size of the Army of the Loire because desertions continued throughout the month of July and there does not exist in the archives a general "situation" for the army. See Houssaye, *1815,* p. 406.

89] *Corresp. Davout,* No. 1780, to Generals Gérard, Haxo, and Kellermann, July 7, 1815, vol. 4, pp. 588–89.

90] Louis N. Davout, "Après Waterloo—L'Armée de la Loire," *Revue de Paris,* Jan. 1898, p. 154.

91] Ibid., p. 155.

92] Davout to Generals Gérard, Haxo, and Kellermann, July 9, 1815, Arch. Guerre, C^{15} 8. The document has the signatures of twenty-four senior officers.

93] Gérard, Kellermann and Haxo to Davout, July 10, 1815, Arch. Nat., F^{1c}, I. 26.

94] Milhaud to Gouvion St.-Cyr, Angerville, July 9, 1815, Archives of Foreign Affairs, 691, as footnoted in Houssaye, *1815,* p. 411; and Davout, "Après Waterloo—l'Armée de la Loire," p. 157.

95] *Corresp. Davout,* No. 1788, to Gérard, Haxo, de Valmy, July 13, 1815, vol. 4, pp. 596–97.

96] *Corresp. Davout,* No. 1790, to the King, July 14, 1815, vol. 4, pp. 598–99.

97] The son of General Dejean was one who refused to sign the document despite Davout's imploring him to do so for the sake of unanimity. (See Houssaye, *1815*, pp. 413–14.)

98] Davout, "Après Waterloo—l'Armée de la Loire," pp. 158–59.

99] See Davout's correspondence in the Arch. Guerre, C^{15} 8.

100] Davout, "Après Waterloo—l'Armée de la Loire," pp. 159, 163.

101] Ibid., pp. 161–64.

102] Quoted in Guillaume de Bertier de Sauvigny, *The Bourbon Restoration,* trans. Lynn M. Case (Philadelphia: University of Pennsylvania Press, 1966), p. 117.

103] Davout, "Après Waterloo—l'Armée de la Loire," p. 168.

104] Ibid., p. 167; and *Corresp. Davout,* No. 1824, to Minister of War, July 27, 1815, vol. 4, p. 632.

105] *Corresp. Davout,* No. 1824, to the Minister of War, July 27, 1815, vol. 4, pp. 629–32; and Davout, "Après Waterloo—l'Armée de la Loire," pp. 165–67.

106] Ibid.

107] Davout, "Après Waterloo—l'Armée de la Loire," p. 168. Bourrienne in his *Memoirs of Napoleon* blames Davout for the death of Ney: "If Davoust [*sic*] had restricted himself less closely to his duty as a soldier, if he had taken more on himself, with the 100,000 men he soon had under him, he might have saved France from much of her subsequent humiliation, or at least he might have preserved the lives of Ney and the brave men whom the Bourbons afterwards butchered" (3: 275).

CHAPTER 15

1] The "Procès-verbal" of the trial of Marshal Ney lists Davout's testimony as number thirty-six. See Arch. Guerre, MF, 12 (Ney). Vigier, *Davout: maréchal d'empire,* 2: 377, incorrectly states that Davout's testimony was thirty-eight.

2] "Procès-verbal" of the trial of Marshal Ney. Arch. Guerre, MF, 12 (Ney).

3] Ibid.

4] Ibid.

5] Blocqueville quotes her father as having made this statement before the Chamber of Peers (4: 282); but it does not appear in the "Procès-verbal" of the trial. (See Arch. Guerre, MF, 12 [Ney].) It nevertheless does express Davout's sentiment, whether said at the trial or afterwards.

6] Arch. Guerre, MF, 13, F^{0} 152.

7] Blocqueville quotes the greater part of this almost daily correspondence in 4: 309–69.

8] See Davout's correspondence to his wife, Feb. 29, 1816, Mar. 5, 1816, and Mar. 8, 1816, Blocqueville, 4: 318, 326, 329.

9] Arch. Guerre, MF, 13.

10] Davout to wife, May 23, 1816, Blocqueville, 4: 366.

11] Mayer was a Prussian who had been treated brutally by a drunken and violent master. Davout had rescued him and cared for him in 1806, and the man became passionately attached to the Marshal.

12] Madame Davout to husband, Apr. 5, 1816, Blocqueville, 4: 342.

13] Blocqueville, 4: 344.

14] Davout to wife, Blocqueville, 4: 330.

15] Madame Davout to husband, Blocqueville, 4: 336. On the surveillance of Davout while in exile at Louviers see Archives de la département de l'Eure, 8 M 8.

16] Davout to wife, Apr. 4, 1816, Blocqueville, 4: 337.

17] On the surveillance of Davout at Savigny during 1816–17, see Archives de la département de la Seine-et-Oise, iv. M. 1.

18] Ibid., iv. M. 1^{16}.

19] Blocqueville, 4: 379.

20] Ibid., 1: 183.

21] Arch. Guerre, MF, 13.

22] Ibid.

23] The manuscript is in Arch. Guerre, K^{100}. It was published by the Comte Vigier in two parts in *Revue de Paris* (December 1897 and January 1898) under the title "Après Waterloo."

24] Both of the manuscripts are in Arch. Guerre, K^{100}.

25] Blocqueville, 4: 267.

26] Théodule Pinard in his *Histoire de conton de Longjumeau* states that Achille Vigier was named count as the result of his marriage to Josephine Davout. (See Janvier, *Davout et sa famille,* p. 46, n. 111.)

27] See Etienne Denis, duc de Pasquier, *Histoire de mon temps: mémoires du chancelier Pasquier,* 6 vols. (Paris: Plon, 1893–95), 4: 460–61.

28] The document is given in Blocqueville, 4: 405–11.

29] The eulogy is given in Blocqueville, 4: 418–27.

BIBLIOGRAPHY

The official correspondence of Marshal Davout is housed in the Archives de la Guerre (Service historique de l'état-major de l'armée) at the château de Vincennes. This material, which is catalogued K^1 "Donation Davout," was given to the Ministry of War by Davout's family after the death of his wife. It is contained in one hundred cartons numbered K^1 1 through K^1 100. The first fifty cartons contain correspondence through 1815 which is arranged in chronological order. The cartons number K^1 51 through K^1 100 contain an assortment of correspondence, registers, reports, orders, and miscellaneous documents. Charles de Mazade edited four volumes of Davout's correspondence (*Correspondance du maréchal Davout*) which he took from the first fifty cartons. His work is accurate and reliable. I have, therefore, cited Mazade whenever the correspondence is published and the Archives de la Guerre for the correspondence and other documents not included by Mazade. The personal correspondence between Davout and his wife is found in five volumes published by his daughter Adélaïde-Louise de Blocqueville (*Le Maréchal Davout prince d'Eckmühl: raconté par les siens et par lui-même,* 4 vols.; and *Le Maréchal Davout prince d'Eckmühl: correspondance inédite 1790–1815: Pologne, Russie, Hambourg*).

The Archives de la Guerre (Service historique de l'état-major de l'armée) at the château de Vincennes proved the principal source of manuscript material. In addition to the "Donation Davout," the "Papiers Gudin" (K^2 1–9), a number of cartons from "Grande Armée" C^2 1–738) and other scattered cartons were very helpful. The Archives Nationales also provided indispensable documents (AF, IV, 1933, 1936, and F^{1c}, I. 26) on the events surrounding the second restoration of Louis XVIII. The Archives de la département de l'Yonne (Auxerre) yielded valuable material on Davout's early career, while the Archives de la département de la Seine-et-Oise (Versailles) and the Archives de la département de l'Eure (Evreux) were helpful with his later years.

Bibliography

Abendroth (Senator). *Antwort auf das Memoire des Herrn Marschall's Davout, seine Verwaltung und Vertheidigung Hamburgs betreffend.* Germany, 1815.

Almedingen, E. M. *The Emperor Alexander I.* London: Bodley Head, 1964.

Altrock, C. J. F. von. *Jena und Auerstedt.* Berlin, 1907.

André, Roger. *L'Occupation de la France par les alliés en 1815.* Paris: Boccard, 1924.

Askenazy, Szymon. *Le Prince Joseph Poniatowski, maréchal de France.* Translated by B. Kozakiewicz and Paul Cazin. Paris: Plon-Nourrit, 1921.

Avout, Auguste, Baron d'. "Davout et les événements de 1815," *Bulletin de la société des sciences historiques et naturelles de l'Yonne* 59 (1905).

———. *La Défense de Hambourg en 1813–1814.* Dijon, 1896.

Avout, Vicomte d'. *Les d'Avouts: étude généalogique d'une famille d'ancienne chevalerie du duché de Bourgogne.* N.p., 1952.

Barrow, John. *The Life and Correspondence of Admiral Sir William Sidney Smith.* 2 vols. London: Richard Bentley, 1848.

Belliard, Augustin Daniel. *Mémoires du comte Belliard.* Paris: Berquet et Pétion, 1842.

Bennigsen, Levin A. G. von. *Mémoires du général Bennigsen.* 3 vols. Paris: Charles Lavauzelle, 1907–8.

Benoist-Méchin, Jacques Gabriel Paul Michel, Baron. *Bonaparte en Egypte: ou le rêve inassouvi.* Lausanne: Clairefontaine, 1966.

Berthier, Louis Alexandre. *Campagne d'Egypte.* Paris: Baudouin Frères, 1827.

Bertier de Sauvigny, Guillaume de. *The Bourbon Restoration.* Translated by Lynn M. Case. Philadelphia: University of Pennsylvania Press, 1966.

Bertin, Ernest. *La Société du consulat de l'empire.* Paris, 1890.

Bertrand, Henri Gratien, Comte. *Cahiers de Sainte-Hélène.* 3 vols. Paris: A. Michel, 1949–59.

———. *Napoleon at St. Helena.* Translated by F. Hume. London: Cassell, 1953.

Blocqueville, Adélaïde-Louise de. *Le Maréchal Davout prince d'Eckmühl: correspondance inédite 1790–1815: Pologne, Russie, Hambourg.* Paris: Perrin, 1887.

———. *Le Maréchal Davout prince d'Eckmühl: raconté par les siens et par lui-même.* 4 vols. Paris: Didier, 1879–80.

Bonaparte, Jérôme. *Mémoires et correspondance du roi Jérome et de la reine Catherine.* 7 vols. Paris: Dentu, 1861–66.

Bonnal, Edmond. *Histoire de Desaix: armées du Rhin, expédition d'Orient, Marengo, d'après les Archives du Dépot de la Guerre.* Paris: Dentu, 1881.

BOURRIENNE, LOUIS ANTOINE FAUVELET DE. *Memoirs of Napoleon Bonaparte.* 4 vols. New York: Thomas Y. Crowell, 1885.

BRETT-JAMES, ANTONY. *The Hundred Days.* New York: St. Martin's Press, 1964.

CAMPAN, MADAME JEANNE LOUISE HENRIETTE. *Journal anecdotique de Mme. Campan ou souvenirs recueillis dans ses entretiens.* Edited by M. Maigne. Paris: Baudoin, 1824.

CAULAINCOURT, ARMAND DE. *Mémoires du général de Caulaincourt, duc de Vicence.* 3 vols. Paris: Plon, 1933.

CHANDLER, DAVID. *The Campaigns of Napoleon.* New York: Macmillan Co., 1966.

CHARDIGNY, LOUIS. *Les Maréchaux de Napoléon.* Paris: Flammarion, 1946.

CHELMINSKI, JAN V. *L'Armée du duché de Varsovie.* Paris: Leroy, 1913.

CHÉNIER, L.-J. GABRIEL DE. *Histoire de la vie politique, militaire et administrative du maréchal Davout.* Paris: Cosse, 1866.

CHUQUET, ARTHUR. "Davout en 1812," *Etudes d'histoire.* Series 5. Paris: Fontemoing, n.d.

———. *Les Guerres de la révolution.* 11 vols. Paris: L. Cerf, 1887–96.

———. *La Trahison de Dumouriez.* Paris: Léon Chailley, 1891.

CLAUSEWITZ, KARL VON. *The Campaign of 1812 in Russia.* London: John Murray, 1843.

———. *Notes sur la Prusse dans sa grande catastrophe: 1806.* Translated by A. Niessel. Paris: Chapelot, 1903.

———. *On War.* Translated by J. J. Graham. London: Routledge & Kegan Paul, 1908.

COLIN, JEAN LAMBERT ALPHONSE. *Campagne de 1805 en Allemagne.* 5 vols. Paris: Chapelot, 1902–4.

CONNELLY, OWEN. *Napoleon's Satellite Kingdoms.* New York: Free Press, 1965.

CONSTANT, LOUIS. *Recollections of the Private Life of Napoleon by Constant, premier valet de chambre.* Translated by Walter Clark. 3 vols. Akron: Saalfield, 1910.

CUBBERLY, RAY ELLSWORTH. *The Role of Fouché During the Hundred Days.* Madison: State Historical Society of Wisconsin, 1969.

D'ABRANTÈS, DUCHESSE [MME. LAURE SAINT-MARTIN PERMON JUNOT]. *Memoirs of Napoleon: His Court and Family.* 2 vols. London: 1836.

DARD, EMILE. *Un confident de l'empereur: le comte de Narbonne.* Paris: Plon, 1943.

DAVOUT, LOUIS NICOLAS, DUC D'AUERSTÄDT ET PRINCE D'ECKMÜHL. "Après Waterloo—l'Armée de la Loire." *Revue de Paris,* Jan. 1898, pp. 151–72.

———. "Après Waterloo—Paris." *Revue de Paris,* Dec. 15, 1897, pp. 705–43.

———. *Correspondance du maréchal Davout prince d'Ekmühl: ses commandements, son ministère, 1801–15.* Edited by Charles de Mazade. 4 vols. Paris: Plon, 1885.

———. *Mémoire de m. le maréchal Davout, prince d'Eckmühl, au roi.* Paris: Crapelet, 1814.

——. *Operations du 3e Corps, 1806–1807. Rapport du maréchal Davout, duc d'Auerstaedt.* Edited by Gen. Léopold Davout. Paris: Calmann Lévy, 1896.

DEDON, FRANÇOIS LOUIS. *Précis historique des campagnes de l'armée de Rhin et Moselle, pendant l'an IV et l'an V; contenant le récit de toutes les opérations de cette armée, sous le commandement du général Moreau, depuis la rupture de l'armistice conclu à la fin de l'an III, jusqu'à la signature des préliminaires de paix à Léoben.* Paris: Magimel, [1798].

DELDERFIELD, R. F. *Napoleon's Marshals.* Philadelphia: Chilton Books, 1966.

DE LORT DE SERIGNAN, ARTHUR. *Un conspirateur militaire sur le premier empire: le général Malet.* Paris: Payot, 1925.

DENON, DOMINIQUE VIVANT. *Voyage dans la basse et la haute Egypte, pendant les campagnes du général Bonaparte,* 3 vols. Paris, 1803.

DE RENÉMANT, C. *Campagne de 1809.* Paris: Charles-Lavauzelle, 1903.

DERRÉCAGAIX, VICTOR BERNARD. *Le Maréchal Berthier, prince de Wagram et de Neuchâtel.* 2 vols. Paris: R. Chapelot, 1905.

DESBRIÈRE, EDOUARD. *Projets et tentatives de débarquement aux Iles Britanniques.* 5 vols. Paris: R. Chapelot, 1900–1902.

[DESGENETTES, RENÉ NICOLAS]. *Souvenirs d'un médecin de l'expédition d'Egypte.* Paris: Calmann Lévy, 1892.

DESVERNOIS, NICOLAS PHILIBERT. *Mémoires du général baron Desvernois.* Paris: Plon-Nourrit, 1896.

DEVOUGES, O., ed. "Séance du 1er juin 1913," *Bulletin de la société des sciences historiques et naturelles de l'Yonne* 67 (1913): 42–49.

DODGE, THEODORE AYRAULT. *Napoleon: A History of the Art of War from the Beginning of the French Revolution to the End of the Eighteenth Century. With a Detailed Account of the Wars of the French Revolution.* 4 vols. London: Gay and Bird, 1904–7.

DU CASSE, ALBERT, BARON. *Le Général Vandamme et sa correspondance.* 2 vols. Paris: Didier, 1870.

———. *Mémoires pour servir à l'histoire de la campagne de 1812 en Russie.* Paris: Dumaine, 1852.

DUMAS, MATHIEU, COMTE. *Souvenirs du lieutenant général c[te] Mathieu Dumas, de 1770 à 1836*. 3 vols. Paris: C. Gosselin, 1839.

DUPONT, MARCEL. *Napoléon et la trahison des maréchaux, 1814*. Paris: Hachette, 1939.

ERNOUF, ALFRED AUGUSTE, BARON. *Histoire de la dernière capitulation de Paris:* Michel Lévy, 1859.

ESPOSITO, V. J. and J. R. ELTING. *A Military History and Atlas of the Napoleonic Wars*. New York: Praeger, 1964.

FABER DU FAUR, CHRISTIAN V. VON. *Campagne de Russe, 1812, d'après le journal illustré d'un temoin oculaire*. Paris: Flammarion, 1895.

FAIN, AGATHON JEAN FRANÇOIS, BARON. *Manuscrit de 1812, contenant le précis des événemens de cette année pour servir à l'histoire de l'empereur Napoléon*. 2 vols. Paris: Delaunay, 1927.

———. *Mémoires du baron Fain, premier secrétaire du cabinet de l'empereur*. Paris: Plon, 1884.

FEZENSAC, RAYMOND AIMERY PHILIPPE JOSEPH [MONTESQUIOU] DE. *Journal de la campagne de Russie en 1812*. Paris: A. Maine, 1850.

FLORIOT, RENÉ. *Le Procès du maréchal Ney*. Paris: Hachette, 1955.

FOUCHÉ, JOSEPH. *Les Mémoires de Fouché*. Paris: Flammarion, 1945.

GABARTI, ABD AL-RAHMAN AL. *Journal d'Abdurrahman Gabarti pendant l'occupation française en Egypte*. Paris, 1838.

GARROS, LOUIS. *Ney: le brave des braves*. Paris: Amiot-Dumont, 1955.

GAUTHEROT, GUSTAVE. *Un gentilhomme de grand chemin: le maréchal de Bourmont, d'après ses papiers inédits*. Paris: Presses Universitaires de France, 1926.

GENERAL SERVICE SCHOOL, GENERAL STAFF SCHOOL. *The Jena Campaign. Source Book*. Fort Leavenworth: General Service Schools Press, 1922.

GEYL, PIETER. *Napoleon: For and Against*. New Haven: Yale University Press, 1949.

GOURGAUD, GASPARD, BARON. *Journal de Sainte-Hélène, 1815–1818*. 2 vols. Paris: Flammarion, 1944.

GROHMANN, J. C. A. *Hamburgs Schicksale unter Davout und miene Auswanderung*. Gotha: Beckerschen, 1814.

GROUCHY, EMMANUEL, MARQUIS DE. *Mémoires du maréchal de Grouchy*. 5 vols. Paris: Dentu, 1873–74.

GRÜNWALD, CONSTANTIN DE. *La Campagne de Russie*. Paris: René Julliard, 1964.

HAUPT, THEODORE DE. *Réponse à un ecrit de m. d'Aubignosc, ex-directeur de la haute-police générale à Hambourg*. Paris: 1814.

HENNET, LÉON. *Le Maréchal Davout duc d'Auerstaedt, prince d'Eckmühl*. Paris: Baudoin, 1885.

HEROLD, J. CHRISTOPHER. *Bonaparte in Egypt.* New York: Harper & Row, 1962.

HOGENDORP, DIRK, GRAAF VAN. *Mémoires du général Dirk van Hogendorp.* La Haye: Nijhoff, 1887.

HOLZHAUSEN, PHILIP PAUL. *Davout in Hamburg: Ein Beitrag zur Geschichte der Jahre 1813–1814.* Mulheim: Max Röder, 1892.

HOUSSAYE, HENRY. *1815: la seconde abdication—la terreur blanche.* Paris: Perrin, 1905.

———. *Iéna et la campagne de 1806.* Paris: Perrin, 1912.

HUBERT, EMMANUELLE. *Les Cent-Jours.* Paris: Julliard, 1966.

IUNG, THEODORE. *Lucien Bonaparte et ses mémoires, 1775–1840 d'après les papiers déposes aux archives étrangères et d'autres documents inédits.* 3 vols. Paris: G. Charpentier, 1883.

JANVIER, JACQUES-ANDRÉ. *Le Maréchal Davout et sa famille à Savigny-sur-Orge.* Essonnes: Typolino, 1951.

JOLY, CHARLES. *Le Maréchal Davout: prince d'Eckmühl.* Auxerre: Gustave Perriquet, 1864.

JOMINI, ANTOINE HENRI DE, BARON. *Histoire des querres de la révolution.* 15 vols. Paris: Anselin et Pochard, 1820–24.

———. *Vie politique et militaire de Napoléon, racontée par lui-même; au tribunal de César, d'Alexandre et de Frédéric.* 4 vols. Paris: Anselin 1827.

JONQUIÈRE, CLÉMENT ETIENNE DE LA. *L'Expédition d'Egypte, 1798–1801.* 5 vols. Paris: Charles-Lavauzelle, 1899–1907.

KNAPTON, ERNEST JOHN. *Empress Josephine.* Cambridge: Harvard University Press, 1964.

LABAUME, EUGÈNE. *A Circumstantial Narrative of the Campaign in Russia.* London: Samuel Leigh, 1815.

LACHOUQUE, HENRI. *Iéna.* Besançon: Guy Victor, 1961.

———. *The Last Days of Napoleon's Empire: From Waterloo to St. Helena.* Translated by Lovett F. Edwards. New York: Orion, 1967.

LAS CASES, MARIE JOSEPH EMMANUEL, COMTE DE. *Le Mémorial de Sainte-Hélène.* 2 vols. Paris: Flammarion, 1951.

LAVILLE, CÉSAR DE. "Mémoire sur le siège et la défense de Hambourg." In *Correspondance du maréchal Davout prince d'Eckmühl: ses commandements, son ministère, 1801–1815.* Edited by Charles de Mazade. 4 vols. Vol. 4, pp. 288–349. Paris: Plon, 1885.

LEJEUNE, LOUIS FRANÇOIS, BARON. *Memoirs of Baron Lejeune, aide-de-camp to Marshals Berthier, Davout and Oudinot.* Translated and edited by Mrs. Arthur Bell. 2 vols. London: Longmans, Green, 1897.

LETTOW-VORBECK, OSCAR VON. *Der Krieg von 1806 und 1807.* 4 vols. Berlin: E. S. Mittler, 1892–99.

LEWAL, JULES LOUIS, GEN. *La Veillée d'Iéna: étude de stratégie de combat.* Paris: Chapelot, 1899.

LÖWENSTERN, WOLDEMAR HERMANN, BARON DE. *Mémoires du général-major russe baron de Löwenstern (1776–1858).* Edited by M. H. Weil. 2 vols. Paris: A. Fontemoing, 1903.

LUCAS-DUBERTON, JEAN. *Soldats de Napoléon.* Paris: Flammarion, 1948.

MADELIN, LOUIS. *Fouché.* 2 vols. Paris: Plon, 1941.

———. *Histoire du consulat et de l'empire.* 16 vols. Paris: Hachette, 1937–51.

MAHAN, A. T. *The Influence of Sea Power on the French Revolution and Empire.* 2 vols. Boston: Little, Brown, 1894.

MARBOT, JEAN BAPTISTE ANTOINE MARCELIN, BARON DE. *Mémoires du général baron de Marbot.* 3 vols. Paris: Plon, 1891.

MARMONT, AUGUSTE FRÉDÉRIC LOUIS VIESSE DE, DUC DE RAGUSE. *Mémoires du maréchal Marmont, duc de Raguse, de 1792 à 1841, imprimés sur le manuscrit original de l'auteur.* 9 vols. Paris: Perrotin, 1857.

MARSHALL CORNWALL, JAMES. *Marshal Masséna.* London: Oxford University Press, 1965.

———. *Napoleon as Military Commander.* Princeton: D. Van Nostrand, 1967.

MARTHA-BEKER, FÉLIX, COMTE DE MONS. *Le Général Desaix: étude historique.* Paris: Didier, 1852.

MASSÉNA, ANDRÉ, PRINCE D'ESSLING. *Mémoires d'André Masséna, duc de Rivole, prince d'Essling, maréchal d'empire, rédigés d'après les documents qu'il a laissés et sur ceux du dépot de la guerre et du dépot des fortifications.* 7 vols. Paris: J. de Bonnot, 1966–67.

MASSON, FRÉDÉRIC. *Napoléon et sa famille.* 7 vols. Paris: Ollendorff, 1893.

Les Mémoires d'une Soeur de Charité. Published by Madame Gagne (Elise Moreau). Paris: Didier, 1870.

MENEVAL, CLAUDE FRANÇOIS DE, BARON. *Souvenirs historiques du baron de Meneval.* Paris: A. Delahays, 1851.

MÉZERAY, FRANÇOIS EUDES DE. *Histoire de France.* 3 vols. Paris: M. Guillemot, 1643–51.

MOISET, CHARLES. "Le Collège royal militaire d'Auxerre," *Bulletin de la société des sciences historiques et naturelles de l'Yonne* 47 (1893): 5–22.

MONTÉGUT, EMILE. *Le Maréchal Davout: son caractère et son génie.* Paris: Quantin, 1882.

MURAT, JOACHIM. *Lettres et documents pour servir à l'histoire de Joachim Murat.* 8 vols. Paris: Plon-Nourrit, 1909–14.

NAPOLEON I. *Commentaires de Napoléon Ier.* 6 vols. Paris: Henri Charles-Lavauzelle, 1867.

———. *La Correspondance de Napoléon Ier.* 32 vols. Paris: Imprimerie Impériale, 1858–70.

———. *Supplement à la correspondance de Napoléon I: l'empereur et la Pologne.* Paris: Bureau de l'Agence Polonaise de Presse, 1908.

NEY, MICHEL LOUIS FÉLIX, DUC D'ELCHINGEN, PRINCE DE LA MOSKOWA. *Memoirs of Marshal Ney: Published by His Family.* 2 vols. Philadelphia: Carey, 1834.

NICOLAS TURC [MOU' ALLEM-NICOLAS-EL-TURKI]. *Chronique d'Egypte.* Translated by Gaston Wiet. Cairo, 1950.

OMAN, CAROLA. *Napoleon's Viceroy: Eugène de Beauharnais.* New York: Funk and Wagnalls, 1966.

O'MEARA, BARRY EDWARD. *Napoleon in Exile, or a Voice from St. Helena. The Opinions and Reflections of Napoleon on the Most Important Events of His Life and Government, in His Own Words.* 2 vols. New York: Worthington, 1890.

OUDINOT, NICOLAS CHARLES, DUC DE REGGIO. *Memoirs of Marshal Oudinot Duc de Reggio. Compiled from the Hitherto Unpublished Souvenirs of the Duchesse de Reggio.* Edited by Gaston Stiegler, translated by Alexander Teixeira de Mattos. London: H. Henry, 1896.

PASQUIER, ETIENNE DENIS, DUC DE. *Histoire de mon temps: mémoires du chancelier Pasquier.* 6 vols. Paris: Plon, 1893–95.

PELET, JEAN JACQUES GERMAINE, BARON. *Mémoires sur la guerre de 1809, en Allemagne, avec les opérations particulières des corps d'Italie, de Pologne, de Saxe, de Naples et de Walcheren; par le général Pelet, d'après son journal fort détaillé de la campagne d'Allemagne; ses reconnaissances et ses divers travaux; la correspondance de Napoléon avec le major-général, les marechaux, les commandans en chef, etc.; accompagnes de pièces justificatives et inédites.* 4 vols. Paris: Roret, 1824–26.

PETRE, FRANCIS LORAINE. *Napoleon and the Archduke Charles.* London and New York: J. Lane, 1909.

PHIPPS, RAMSAY WESTON. *The Armies of the First French Republic and the Rise of the Marshals of Napoleon I.* 5 vols. Oxford: At the Clarendon Press, 1935–39.

PONIATOWSKI, JOSEPH. *Correspondance du Prince Joseph Poniatowski avec la France.* Poznan: Ministère de l'Instruction Publique, 1921.

POTOCKA, ANNA. *Memoirs of the Countess Potocka.* Translated by Lionel Strachey. New York: Doubleday & McClure, 1900.

PRATT, FLETCHER. *The Empire and the Glory: Napoleon Bonaparte, 1800–1806.* New York: W. Sloane, 1949.

QUIMBY, R. S. *The Background of Napoleonic Warfare.* New York: Columbia University Press, 1957.

RAPP, JEAN. *Mémoires des contemporains, pour servir à l'histoire de France, et principalement à celle de la république et de l'empire.* Paris: Bossange, 1823.

———. *Mémoires du général Rapp, aide de camp de Napoléon, écrits par lui-même et publiés par sa famille.* Paris: Bossange, 1823.

REDDAWAY, W. F., PENSON, J. H., and HALECKI, O., eds. *The Cambridge History of Poland from Augustus II to Pilsudski.* 2 vols. Cambridge: At the University Press, 1951.

RIGAULT, GEORGES. *Le général Abdallah Menou et la dernière phase de l'expédition d'Egypte.* Paris: Plon-Nourrit, 1911.

RIVOLLET, GEORGES. *Général de bataille Charles Antoine Louis Morand, généraux Friant et Gudin du 3e Corps de la Grande Armée.* Paris: J. Peyronnet, 1863.

RIVOLLET, GEORGES and PAUL ALBERTINI. *Les Maréchaux d'empire et la première abdication.* Paris: Berger-Levrault, 1957.

RODGER, A. B. *The War of the Second Coalition, 1798–1801.* Oxford: At the Clarendon Press, 1964.

ROEDER, FRANZ. *The Ordeal of Captain Roeder, 1812–1813.* Translated and Edited by Helen Reeder. New York: St. Martin's Press, 1960.

ROOS, HENRI DE. *Avec Napoléon en russie: souvenirs de la campagne de 1812.* Translated by Lieutenant-Colonel Buat. Paris: Chapelot, 1913.

ROSSIGNEUX, ANDRÉ. "Officiers de la Grande Armée originaires du département de l'Yonne," *Bulletin de la société des sciences historiques et naturelles de l'Yonne* 66 (1912): 61–73.

ROUSSEAU, FRANÇOIS. *Kléber et Menou en Egypte, depuis le départ de Bonaparte, août 1799–septembre 1801.* Paris: A. Picard, 1900.

ST.-CYR, GOUVION. *Mémoires sur les campagnes des armées du Rhin et de Rhin-et-Moselle de 1792 jusqu'à la paix de Campo-Formio.* 4 vols. Paris: Anselin, 1829.

SASKI, CHARLES G. L. *Campagne de 1809 en Allemagne et en Autriche.* 3 vols. Paris: Berger-Levrault, 1899–1902.

SAUNDERS, EDITH. *The Hundred Days.* New York: W. W. Norton, 1964.

SAUZET, ARMAND. *Desaix: le "sultan juste."* Paris: Hachette, 1954.

SÉGUR, PAUL PHILIP, COMTE DE. *History of the Expedition to Russia Undertaken by the Emperor Napoleon in the Year 1812.* 2 vols. London: Treuttel and Wurtz, 1827.

SENKOWSKA, MONIKA. "Les Majorats français dans le duché Varsovie (1807–1813)," *Annales historic de la Révolution Frances,* July–Sept. 1964.

SHAW, STANFORD J. *Ottoman Egypt in the Age of the French Revolution.* Cambridge: Harvard University Press, 1966.

SIX, GEORGES. *Les généraux de la révolution et de l'empire.* Paris: Bordas, 1947.

SOUBIRAN, ANDRÉ. *Le baron Larrey chirurgien de Napoléon.* Paris: Fayard, 1966.

SPILLMAN, GEORGES. *Napoléon et l'Islam*. Paris: Perrin, 1969.

STIEGLER, GASTON and ALEXANDER T. DE MATTOS. *Memoirs of Marshal Oudinot, Duc de Reggio*. Translated by Alexander T. de Mattos. London: H. Henry, 1896.

TARLE, EUGENE. *Napoleon's Invasion of Russia 1812*. New York: Oxford University Press, 1942.

THIBAUDEAU, ANTOINE CLAIRE. *Mémoires du général A. C. Thibaudeau*. 5 vols. Paris: Plon-Nourrit, 1895.

THIÉBAULT, PAUL CHARLES, BARON. *Mémoires du général baron Thiébault*. 5 vols. Paris: Plon-Nourrit, 1895–97.

THIRY, JEAN. *La campagne de Russie*. Paris: Berger-Levrault, 1969.

———. *Les débuts de la seconde restauration*. Paris: Berger-Levrault, 1947.

———. *Eylau, Friedland, Tilsit*. Paris: Berger-Levrault, 1964.

———. *Iéna*. Paris: Berger-Levrault, 1964.

———. *La second abdication de Napoléon Ier*. Paris: Berger-Levrault, 1945.

THOMPSON, J. P. *Napoleon Bonaparte*. New York: Oxford University Press, 1952.

TITEUX, EUGÈNE, LT. COL. "Le Maréchal Bernadotte et la manoeuvre d'Jena," *Revue Napoléonienne* 4 (Apr.–Sept. 1903): 68–152.

TREUENFELD, BRUNO VON. *Auerstedt und Jena*. Hannover: Helwing'fche, 1895.

VACHÉE, LE COMMANDANT. *Etude du caractère militaire du maréchal Davout*. Paris: Berger-Levrault, 1907.

VANDAL, ALBERT. *Napoléon et Alexandre Ier: l'alliance russe sous le premier empire*. 3 vols. Paris: Plon-Nourrit, 1911.

VIGIER, JOSEPH, COMTE. *Davout: maréchal d'empire, duc d'Auerstaedt, prince d'Eckmühl*. 2 vols. Paris: Paul Ollendorff, 1898.

VITROLLES, EUGENE FRANÇOIS, BARON DE. *Mémoires et relations politiques du baron de Vitrolles*. 3 vols. Paris: Charpentier, 1884.

WELLINGTON, ARTHUR WELLESLEY, 1ST DUKE OF. *Dispatches, Correspondence, and Memoranda of Field Marshal Arthur Duke of Wellington*. 11 vols. London: John Murray, 1867–80.

WILSON, SIR ROBERT T. *Narrative of Events During the Invasion of Russia by Napoleon Bonaparte, and the Retreat of the French Army, 1812*. London: John Murray, 1860.

ZALUSKI, JÓSEF. *La Pologne et les polonais. Les erreurs et les injustices des écrivains français mm. Thiers, Ségur, Lamartine*. Paris: Dumineray, 1856.

INDEX

Aboukir, Battle of, 55
Aboukir Bay, Battle of, 47, 53, 63
Abrantès, Duchesse d'. *See* Junot, Madame
Additional Act, 305
Alexander I: and Third Coalition, 95; campaign of 1805, 103–14 passim; campaign of 1807; Battle of Eylau, 147; and Tilsit, 151, 152, 154, 172; and Duchy of Warsaw, 154, 167, 168; and Erfurt, 172–73; campaign of 1809, 177, 178; and Napoleon's second marriage, 208; Russian campaign, 219–53 passim
Allied Army: siege of Hamburg, 289
Allix, General: second restoration, 334
Ambert, General: Army of the Moselle, 28; capture of Heidelberg, 30; mentioned, 28
Amiens, Treaty of, 70, 78, 116, 219
Amyot: founder of "college" at Auxerre, 6
Anglo-Turkish Alliance, 58
Angoulême, Duchess of: and Hundred Days, 301
Angoulême, Duke of: and Hundred Days, 301
Ann of Russia, Princess: and Napoleon, 208
Armée des côtes de l'Océan, 100
Army, Austrian, 105, 111, 173, 177, 178, 181, 185, 186, 325, 333
Army, Grand: of 1805, 70, 100, 101, 106; of 1806, 132; of 1807, 138, 140, 148; of 1809, 175, 196; of 1812, 216–73 passim
Army, Prussian: campaign of 1806, 123–38 passim; campaign of 1807, 138; Waterloo Campaign, 308, 321, 322, 326, 328
Army, Russian: campaign of 1805, 103–14 passim; campaign of 1807, 139, 140; campaign of 1812, 227–71 passim; siege of Hamburg, 285; Waterloo Campaign, 325
Army of Egypt, 37, 39
Army of England, 39
Army of Germany, 176, 179
Army of Holland, 19
Army of Italy: First Italian Campaign, 12, 34, 36; Second Italian Campaign, 65, 66; *"Sans culottes"* of, 87; campaign of 1812, 223
Army of Observation of the Elbe, 216, 221
Army of Reserve, 63
Army of Spain, 224
Army of the Loire, 330–34
Army of the Moselle, 26, 27, 28
Army of the North: of 1815, 300, 306, 307, 310, 316; mentioned, 14, 17, 23
Army of the North (Allied), 275, 281
Army of the Rhine, 67
Army of the Rhine and Moselle, 28–30, 33–35
Army of the Sambre and Meuse, 27, 28, 30, 33, 34, 35
Army of the West, 21, 27, 67
Arnim, von: Battle of Auerstädt, 128
Arrighi, General: campaign of 1809, 198, 199, 201
Artois, Count of, 293, 294, 295
Aubert, Lieutenant Colonel: and siege of Hamburg, 292, 293

Auerstädt, Battle of, 126–34, 289
Auerstädt, Duke of. *See* Davout, Louis Nicolas, Marshal
Augereau, Pierre François Charles, Marshal (Duke of Castiglione): campaign of 1805, 100, 101; campaign of 1806, 124, 125, 126; campaign of 1807, 139, 141, 143, 145, 146; Battle of Eylau, 143, 145, 146; mentioned, 67, 87, 91
Aulic Council, 174
Austerlitz, Battle of, 103–13, 117, 123, 289
Austria: Treaty of Campo Formio, 63; Third Coalition, 95–96
Auxerre: military school of, 5, 6
Avout, César d', Capitan-Major, 4
Avout, François Claude d' (cousin of Marshal Davout), 8, 294, 389n*84*
Avout, François Jacques d', 4
Avout, Jacques-Edme d', Major (uncle of Marshal Davout), 10, 14
Avout, Jean François d' (father of Marshal Davout), 3, 4, 5, 209
Avout, Louis Nicolas d'. *See* Davout, Louis Nicolas, Marshal
Avout, Marie Adelaïde Minard d' (mother of Marshal Davout), 4, 5, 12, 24, 25
Avout, Nicolas d' (Lord of Annoux; grandfather of Marshal Davout), 4

Bagration, Peter, Prince: Battle of Austerlitz, 110; campaign of 1812, 227–48 passim; Battle of Borodino, 247, 248; mentioned, 130
Bâle, Treaty of, 29
Barclay de Tolly, Prince Michael: Campaign of 1812, 227–45 passim
Bastille: fall of, 8
Beauharnais, Alexandre de, 207
Beauharnais, Eugène de. *See* Eugène de Beauharnais
Beaumont, Bonnin de la Bonninière, Comte de, 29, 350n*10*
Becker, General, 318, 319
Bellart, M. (prosecutor of Marshal Ney), 337
Bellegrade, Heinrich, General: Austrian commander in Italy, 68; campaign of 1809, 178, 181, 182, 188, 197, 199; Battle of Wagram, 197, 199; mentioned, 68
Belliard, Auguste Daniel, General: Egyptian Campaign, 50, 51, 53; Battle of Borodino, 242, 243
Bender, Blaise Colomban, Marshal, 28
Bennigsen, Levin, Baron: campaign of 1807, 139–51 passim; Battle of Eylau, 143, 145, 147, 150; siege of Hamburg, 288, 289, 291, 292, 293, 294
Bentinck, Count, 212
Berezina: crossing of, 267, 268, 269, 270, 273
Bernadotte, Jean Baptiste Jules, Marshal (Prince of Ponte Corvo; Charles XIV, King of Sweden): campaign of 1805, 100, 101, 102, 103, 105, 110; campaign of 1806, 124, 125, 126, 134, 135, 136; and the maneuver at Jena-Auerstädt, 134, 135; campaign of 1807, 142, 149; Crown Prince of Sweden, 165, 218; campaign of 1809, 176, 190, 198, 199; Battle of Wagram, 198, 199; and the siege of Hamburg, 288, 289, 290; mentioned, 67, 78, 87, 91, 215, 272, 275, 281, 282
Bernadotte, Madame (Désirée Clary; Princess of Ponte Corvo), 210
Berry, Duke of: marriage of, 339
Berryer, M., 336
Berthezene, General, 334
Berthier, Louis-Alexandre, Marshal (Prince of Neufchatel; Prince of Wagram): campaign of 1805, 104, 115; 1809, 179, 180, 181, 182, 183; campaign of 1812, 221–72 passim; campaign of 1813, 275, 276, 277; death of, 305; Hundred Days, 305; mentioned, 87, 118, 123, 126, 134, 164, 215
Bessières, Jean Baptiste, Marshal (Duke of Istria): Battle of Austerlitz, 110; Battle of Wagram, 198, 200; campaign of 1809, 198, 200; mentioned, 75, 87, 90
Beurnonville, General, 34

Bignon, Baron, 329
Bisson, P. F. J. G., General, 100, 103
Blocqueville, Adélaïde-Louise de (daughter of Marshal Davout), 88, 165, 166, 287, 341
Blücher, Gebhard Leberecht von, General: Battle of Auerstädt, 127, 128, 138; Waterloo Campaign, 302, 311, 317, 323, 325, 328, 329, 330
Bonaparte, Jérôme (King of Westphalia): and kingship of Poland, 168; campaign of 1812, 226–42 passim; mentioned, 165, 207
Bonaparte, Joseph (King of Spain): Treaty of Lunéville, 69, Hundred Days, 311, 314; mentioned, 165
Bonaparte, Louis (King of Holland), 165
Bonaparte, Marie-Pauline (Princess Borghese): marriage to General Leclerc, 71
Bonaparte, Napoleon. *See* Napoleon I
Borodino, Battle of, 111, 243–50, 252, 253, 258
Boudet, General: Battle of Eckmühl, 186; campaign of 1809, 186, 198, 199; Battle of Wagram, 198, 199
Bouistry, General, 234
Bourbon, Duke of: Hundred Days, 301, 302
Bourcier, General: campaign of 1805, 106, 109, 111
Bourmont, Louis A. V., General: Hundred Days, 307
Bourrienne, Louis Antoine, General, 64, 166, 217
"Brigands of the Loire." *See* Army of the Loire
Bruges, camp at, 78, 80, 81, 82, 83, 100
Brumaire: eighteenth of, 314
Brune, Guillaume-Marie, Marshal: Second Italian Campaign, 67, 68, 69; Hundred Days, 304, 310; death of, 310; mentioned, 87
Brunswick, Charles F. W., Duke of: Battle of Valmy, 17; campaign of 1806, 124–33 passim; death of, 128
Bruyère, General, 218
Bucharest, Treaty of, 221
Buguet, General: campaign of 1812, 252
Bülow, Friedrich Wilhelm, Baron: shot as a spy, 82
Buxhöwden, General: campaign of 1805, 102, 104, 105, 106, 109, 110; commander of Russian army 1806, 140, 141

"Caesar's X Legion" (III Corps of the Grand Army): Battle of Eylau, 148; Battle of Wagram, 198
Caffarelli, Louis Marie, General: campaign of 1805, 103, 105, 114; mentioned, 90
Cambrai: Proclamation of, 333
Campaign of 1800. *See* Second Italian Campaign
Campaign of 1805, 100–120
Campaign of 1806, 119–38
Campaign of 1807, 138–50
Campaign of 1809, 175–203
Campaign of 1812, 222–72
Campaign of 1813, 172–283
Campaign of 1814, 308
Campaign of 1815. *See* Waterloo Campaign
Campo Formio, Treaty of (Peace of), 63–67
Canrobert, Marshal, 134
Carnot, Lazare, Count: Minister of War, 63–66; Hundred Days, 311, 313; second restoration, 316, 321; mentioned, 26
Castellane, M. de: Bishop of Mende, 15
Caulaincourt, Armand A. L. de (Duke of Vicenza): campaign of 1812, 225, 261, 265; Hundred Days, 311; second restoration, 316
Cazal, Major, 59
Cessac, Lacuée de: Battle of Wagram, 202
Chaban, Count de: campaign of 1813, 282
Charlemagne: relics of, 96
Charles, Archduke: campaign of 1805 (Italy), 99, 100, 102, 112; military reforms of, 174; campaign of 1809, 174–204 passim; Battle of Eckmühl,

Charles, Archduke (*continued*) 185–87; Battle of Aspern-Essling, 190–91; Battle of Wagram, 195–202 passim; mentioned, 34
Chartres, Duke of, 20
Chasseloup, François, General, 75–76
Clairfayt, François Sebastien Charles Joseph, General, 30
Clarke, General (Duke of Feltre; Minister of War), 215
Clausel, General: second restoration, 334
Clausewitz, Karl von, General, 157, 251
Coalition, Second, 69, 95, 106
Coalition, Third, 70, 95, 96, 106, 116, 117
Coburg, Prince of, 19
Code, Napoleonic: and Duchy of Warsaw, 157, 161
Combacérès, General: Hundred Days, 311
Compan, Jean Dominique, General: campaign of 1809, 192; chief of staff to Marshal Davout, 207; campaign of 1812, 229, 242, 246, 247, 248, 250; Battle of Borodino, 246, 247, 248, 250; wounded, 250
Confederation of the Rhine, 118
Constantine, Crown Prince: Battle of Austerlitz, 110
Constitution of the Year VIII, 85
Continental System, 152, 160, 164, 172, 220
Convention of El Arish, 58, 59, 60
Cossacks: campaign of 1812, 228–74 passim
Coutard, Colonel: command at Ratisbon, 184; surrender of Ratisbon, 186, 293; mentioned, 212

Dampierre, Auguste Henri Marie, General, 21, 22
Danish navy: English attack on, 70
Dargens, General: campaign of 1812, 252
Daultanne, General: campaign of 1805, 104; campaign of 1807, 141
Davot, Nicolas de: siegneur de Romanet, 4
Davou, Mille, Monsignor, 3
Davout, Adélaïde-Louise. *See* Blocqueville, Adélaïde-Louise de
Davout, Adèle Napoléonie: birth of, 168, 169; education of 340
Davout, Alexandre, 5, 14, 57, 60
Davout, Charles: birth of, 5; Egyptian campaign, 48; promotion of, 56
Davout, Josephine (first daughter of Marshal Davout): birth of, 89, 90; death of, 93
Davout, Josephine (second daughter of Marshal Davout): birth of, 89, 94; education of, 340; death of, 342, 343
Davout, Jules: illness of, 280; education of 281
Davout, Julie-Catherine-Charlotte-Françoise: birth of, 5; education of, 347n9; mentioned, 350n*10*
Davout, Louis: birth of, 210; death of, 210; education of, 281, 340–41
Davout, Louise-Aimée-Julie Leclerc (Duchess of Auerstädt; Princess of Eckmühl): marriage of, 71, 72; and Marshal Lannes, 72; education of, 74; and death of brother (General Leclerc), 76, 77; dislike of Napoleon Bonaparte, 77; and children, 89, 90, 93, 94, 118, 168, 278; attached to the household of Madame Mère, 91–93; visits husband in Poland, 170; and Napoleon's divorce, 208, 209; visits husband at Hamburg, 280; and siege of Hamburg, 294; second restoration, 337, 338, 339; mentioned, 88, 90, 119, 169, 210, 211, 239, 240, 281
Davout, Louis Nicolas, Marshal (Duke of Auerstädt, Prince of Eckmühl): genealogy of, 3–5; education of, 6–7; joins Army of the North, 14; first marriage, 14–15; joins Army of the West, 21; and the Jacobins, 21, 25, 26; arrested, 25; joins Army of the Moselle, 26; siege of Luxembourg, 27–28; prisoner of war, 31–32; first meets Napoleon, 37–39; influence of Desaix, 39; Egyptian campaign, 43–61 passim; Battle of Shubra Khit, 43–44;

Battle of the Pyramids, 46–47; campaign in Upper Egypt, 49–57 passim; Battle of Aboukir, 55; Convention of El Arish, 58–59; personal relationship with Napoleon, 63–64, 84, 164–66, 169, 205, 307, 316; Second Italian Campaign, 67–69; second marriage (Aimée Leclerc), 71, 72, 74; camp of Bruges, 80–83 passim, 89; named Marshal, 84, 85, 87, 88; campaign of 1805, 100–115 passim; Battle of Austerlitz, 106–11 passim; *ruse de guerre,* 112–13; campaign of 1806, 119–37 passim; Battle of Auerstädt, 126–34; campaign of 1807, 139–49 passim; Battle of Eylau, 143–47; military commander of Duchy of Warsaw, 153–70 passim; and the Polish people, 154, 155, 156; and Poniatowski, 157–60; named Duke of Auerstädt, 164; and the kingship of Poland, 165, 166; birth of Adèle Napoléonie, 168; campaign of 1809, 172–205 passim; Battle of Eckmühl, 185–87; Battle of Wagram, 195–202 passim; named Prince of Eckmühl, 205; and Jérôme Bonaparte, 207, 231, 234; and Napoleon's divorce, 208–9; character of, 211–16; campaign of 1812, 220–73 passim; Battle of Salta-Nawka, 233–35; death of Gudin, 239–40; conflict with Murat, 240, 241, 242, 243, 256–57, 272; Battle of Borodino, 243–50 passim; wounded, 250; command of 32nd Military Division, 274; campaign of 1813, 274–83 passim; siege of Hamburg, 284–96 passim; and Count von Moltke, 287; first restoration, 296–99; Hundred Days, 299–319 passim; Minister of War, 300–318 passim; second abdication, 312–18; second restoration, 320–42; surrender of Paris (1815), 327–29; Army of the Loire, 330–34; trial of Ney, 336; exiled to Louviers, 337–38; named Marshal of France, 340; sits in Chamber of Peers, 341; death of, 343; spelling of, 347n*4*

Davout, Napoleon, 176, 209

Debrun, General, 27

Decrees: Berlin and Milan. *See* Continental System

Dejean, Jean François Aime, General, 119

Delcambre, Victoire Joseph, General: siege of Hamburg, 294

Delort, General: campaign of 1812, 252

Delzons, Alexis Joseph, General: Battle of Borodino, 248

Demont, General: campaign of 1809, 180, 181, 183

Desailly, General: campaign of 1809

Desaix de Veygoux, Louis Charles Antoine, General: Army of the Rhine and Moselle, 30, 31, 33, 35; early life, 37, 38; meets Napoleon, 37, 38; influence on Davout, 39; Egyptian campaign, 43–60 passim; Battle of the Pyramids, 46, 47; Second Italian Campaign, 65; death of, 65; Napoleon on, 352n*4*, 355n*11;* mentioned, 63, 87, 88, 106, 351n*1*

Désirée Clary. *See* Bernadotte, Madame

Dessaix, J. M., General: campaign of 1812, 229, 247, 248, 250; wounded, 250

Destrées, General: Egyptian campaign, 54

Desvernois, Captain: Egyptian campaign, 52, 53

Dobeln, General: campaign of 1813, 275

Doctorov, D., General: campaign of 1807, 141; campaign of 1812, 255

Doudeauville, Duke of, 339

Drouet, Jean Baptiste (Comte d'Erlon): Hundred Days, 304

Drouot, A., General Count: surrender of Paris, 327

Droussier, General: Battle of Borodino, 248

Du Barry, Madame, 8

Dubois, François, Lieutenant Colonel, 14

Dufour, General, 30

Dumas, Madame: friend of Madame Davout, 94

Dumas, Mathieu, General: chief of staff to Marshal Davout, 80
Dumouriez, Charles François du Perier, General: Battle of Valmy, 17; Battle of Jemappes, 18; and the Girondins, 18; invasion of Holland, 18; Battle of Neerwinden, 19; and Davout, 19–20; treason of, 20
Duplessis, General: death of, 52
Dupont-de-Nemours: minister of war, 297
Duponthon, General: surrender of Paris (1815), 327
Duroc, Michel, General, 85, 90
Durutte, General, 80

Eckmühl, Battle of, 185–87, 289
Eckmühl, Prince of. *See* Davout, Louis Nicholas, Marshal
"Egypt, Men of," 87
Egyptian campaign, 31–61
El Arish, Convention of, 58, 59, 60, 64, 66
Emeriau, Vice-Admiral, 81
Enghien, Louis-Antoine-Henri de Bourbon, Duke of: kidnapping and execution of, 96 359n*1*
Erfurt, Meeting of, 172, 173
Erlon, J. B., General, 327
Eugène de Beauharnais (Viceroy of Italy): and Duchy of Warsaw, 168; campaign of 1809, 192, 196, 198; Battle of Wagram, 196, 198; campaign of 1812, 223–74 passim; Battle of Borodino, 246, 247, 248
Exelmans, Rémi-Joseph, General: Hundred Days, 304; second restoration, 322, 326, 328
Eylau, Battle of, 142–48, 250

Falcon, Colonel: Battle of Auerstädt, 132
Fédérés (1815), 309, 310, 391n*19*
Ferdinand, Archduke: campaign of 1805, 101
Flahaut, Count of, 307
Fleurus, Battle of, 27
Fontenay, Abbey of, 3
Fouché, Joseph (Duke of Otranto): treasonous plot of, 172, 173; Hundred Days, 311, 312, 316, 317; second restoration, 319–34 passim
Fournes, Marquis de, 8
Fox, Charles James (English foreign minister), 116
Foy, Maximilien, General, 81
Francis I: and the Second Coalition, 68, 69; and the Third Coalition, 96, 97; campaign of 1805, 103, 111; campaign of 1809, 179, 180; second marriage of Napoleon, 208; campaign 1812, 223; mentioned, 99, 300
Frederick Augustus (King of Saxony): and Duchy of Warsaw, 152, 154, 157, 160, 161, 167
Frederick of Hesse, Prince: campaign of 1813, 281
Fredericks, General: campaign of 1812, 252
Frederick the Great, 174
Frederick William III (King of Prussia): campaign of 1806, 117–38 passim; Battle of Auerstädt, 124, 128, 130, 133, 138; defeat of Prussia, 151; humiliation of, 152; mentioned, 217, 220
Friant, Louis, General: Egyptian campaign, 50; campaign of 1805, 100–111 passim; campaign of 1806, 120, 126, 127, 128, 130; Battle of Auerstädt, 126, 127, 128, 130; campaign of 1807, 139, 143, 145, 146; Battle of Eylau, 143, 145, 146; campaign of 1809, 175–200 passim; Battle of Wagram, 200; married to sister of Marshal Davout, 213, personal relationship with Marshal Davout, 214; campaign of 1812, 229, 238, 247, 249, 250; Battle of Borodino, 247, 249, 250; wounded, 250; mentioned, 80, 91, 119, 153
Friant, Madame (Claire Leclerc): sister of Madame Aimée Davout, 71
Friedland, Battle of, 71, 150, 250

Gazan, General: surrender of Paris (1815), 327
Gérard, Maurice-Etienne, General:

campaign of 1812, 240, 248, 250, 252; Battle of Borodino, 248, 250; siege of Hamburg, 295, 296; Hundred Days, 304; second restoration, 322; Army of the Loire, 330, 331, 332
Germinal: coup de'état of, 29
Gilly, General: second restoration, 334
Giza: pyramids of, 46
Goldback Brook, 110
Gordon, James (secretary to Marshal Davout), 340, 341
Gratien, General: campaign of 1812, 252
Grenier, General: second restoration, 316
Grouchy, Emmanuel, Marshal: named Marshal of the Empire, 87, 304; Battle of Eylau, 146; Battle of Wagram, 201, 202; campaign of 1812, 226, 229, 240, 246; Battle of Borodino, 246; Hundred Days, 304, 315, 316, 317; second restoration, 321, 322, 327, 334
Gudin, Charles Etienne César, General: campaign of 1805, 100, 103, 105, 112; campaign of 1806, 119, 120, 121, 126, 127, 128; Battle of Auerstädt, 126, 127, 128; campaign of 1807, 139, 141, 145, 146; Battle of Eylau, 145, 146, 148; campaign of 1809, 175–200 passim; Battle of Wagram, 200; personal relationship with Marshal Davout, 213, 239, 240; campaign of 1812; 229, 238, 239, 240; Battle of Kolodnia, 239; death of, 239, 240; mentioned, 91, 153
Gudin, Madame: death of husband, 239, 240; mentioned, 213
Gund, Joseph, 28

Hamburg, siege of: Bank of Hamburg, 286; expulsion of civilians, 287; mentioned, 284–96, 315
Hamelin: family, 77
Hanseatic Legion: campaign of 1813, 276, 277
Hargicourt, Colonel Count of, 8
Hassan Bey: Egyptian Campaign, 52
Haugwitz, Christian von: diplomatic mission, 117
Haxo, F. N., General: Army of the Loire, 330, 332
Hesdin (in Artois), 8
Heudelet, Etienne, General: Battle of Austerlitz, 108, 109, 111
Hoche, Lazare, General, 34, 35
Hohenlinden, Battle of, 67
Hohenlohe, Friedrich Ludwig, Prince: campaign of 1806, 124, 125, 126, 132, 133, 135, 138
Hohenzollern, General: campaign of 1809, 183, 184, 185, 186, 197
Hompesch, Baron von: Grand Master of Knights of Malta, 41
Hortense de Beauharnais Bonaparte: Queen of Holland, 94

Iberian Peninsula, 160, 172
Imperial Recess of 1803, 95

Jacquinot, General: campaign of 1809, 175, 184
Jellacic, General: campaign of 1805, 101
Jemappes, Battle of, 18
Jena, Battle of, 126, 133, 250
John, Archduke: campaign of 1805, 102; campaign of 1809, 179, 192, 193, 197, 198, 199
Josephine Tascher Beauharnais Bonaparte (Empress of France): divorced by Napoleon, 207, 209; mentioned, 94, 318
Jourdan, Jean Baptiste, Marshal: Battle of Fleurus, 27; capture of Düsseldorf, 30; second restoration, 340; mentioned, 33, 87, 91
Junot, Andoche, General (Duke of Abrantes): friendship with Marshal Davout, 63; campaign of 1812, 240, 249, 262; Battle of Borodino, 249
Junot, Madame (Duchess of Abrantes), 64, 91, 92

Kalkreuth, Friedrich Adolf, Count: Battle of Auerstädt, 128, 130
Kamenski, General: campaign of 1807, 140, 142

Keith, Admiral, 60
Kellermann, François Christophe, Marshal (Duke of Valmy): Battle of Valmy, 17, mentioned, 87, 327
Kellermann, François-Etienne, General: Hundred Days, 304; second restoration, 323; Army of the Loire, 330, 331, 332
Kienmaier, Michael, General: campaign of 1805, 102, 184
Kilmaine, Charles Joseph, General, 21
King of Rome (son of Napoleon): birth of, 210; mentioned, 317
Kister, General: Battle of Austerlitz, 108, 109, 111
Kléber, Jean-Baptiste, General: capture of Düsseldorf, 30; Egyptian campaign, 31–61 passim; given command of Army of Egypt, 56; Convention of El Arish, 57, 58, 59, 60, 64; mentioned, 66, 87, 293
Klein, Dominique Louis Antoine, General: campaign of 1805, 112
Klenau, General: Battle of Wagram, 196, 198, 199
Kobilinski, Colonel: campaign of 1812, 258, 259
Kollowart, John Charles, General: campaign of 1805, 105, 109; campaign of 1809, 182–99 passim; Battle of Wagram, 197, 198, 199
Kolodnia, Battle of, 239
Krasmy: combat at, 263, 264, 265
Kreitz, General: campaign of 1812, 269
Kuhnheim, General: Battle of Auerstädt, 128
Kutusov, Mikhail Golenischev, Prince: campaign of 1805, 102, 104, 109, 112, 113; campaign of 1812, 243–71 passim; Battle of Borodino, 243–250 passim

Labanoff, General, 151
La Barolière, General, 22
Labaume, General: campaign of 1812, 264
Labedoyere, General: second restoration, 334
Laboessière, General: Second Italian Campaign, 67
Laborde, General: second restoration, 334
Lafayette, Marie Joseph, Marquis de (General), 16, 17, 313
Lamarque, General: Hundred Days, 309; second restoration, 334
Lannes, Jean, Marshal (Duke of Montebello): campaign of 1805, 100, 103, 105, 110; campaign of 1806, 124, 125, 126, 138; campaign of 1807, 139, 140; campaign of 1809, 184–91 passim; death of, 191; mentioned, 72, 87
Laporte, Charles-Marie, Dom, 6, 93
La Rochefoucauld: family, 24
Lasalle, Antoine Charles Louis, General: campaign of 1809, 192
Latour, General, 35
La Tour du Pin Gouvernet: minister of war, 11, 12
Latour-Maubourg, Marie Victor Nicolas, General: campaign of 1812, 232, 233, 234, 235, 248, 267
Laudon, General, 68
Laville, César de, General: on the character of Marshal Davout, 211; siege of Hamburg, 290
League of Armed Neutrality, 70
Leclerc, Jean-Paul (father of Madame Davout), 71
Leclerc, Madame (mother of Madame Davout), 71, 280, 340
Leclerc, Victoire Emmanuel, General (brother of Madame Davout): married to Marie-Pauline Bonaparte, 71; expedition to Haiti, 72; death of, 76, 77; mentioned, 88
Leclerc Desessarts, Nicolas Marie (brother of Madame Davout), 71
Lecourbe, Claude Joseph, General, 35
Lefebvre, François Joseph, Marshal (Duke of Danzig): campaign of 1809, 180, 184, 185, 186, 190; mentioned, 87, 327, 340
Légion d'honneur: founding of, 84
Legrand, Claude-Juste-Alexandre, General: campaign of 1805, 105, 108, 109, 110

Leipzig, Battle of, 282, 283, 308, 315
Lejeune, Louis François, General: campaign of 1812, 249, 252, 258; mentioned, 381
Leoben, Armistice of, 35
Leon, Count of, 207
Lestocq, General: campaign of 1807, 140, 143, 146, 148, 149; Battle of Eylau, 143, 146
Lichtenstein, General: campaign of 1809, 183–200 passim; Battle of Wagram, 197, 299; mentioned, 110
Lison, Henri-Louis, General, 281
Lobau, General: Hundred Days, 304
Lochet, General: Battle of Austerlitz, 108, 109, 111
L'Orient: flagship of Napoleon, 41
Louis, Archduke: campaign of 1809, 184, 185
Louis, Prince: death of, 125
Louise: Queen of Prussia, 118
Louis-Ferdinand, Prince, 118
Louis XVI (King of France): founding of military schools, 5, 6, 7; and Marshal Davout, 8; flight to Varennes, 13; trial of, 18; mentioned, 15, 62
Louis XVIII (King of France): Marshal Davout and the siege of Hamburg, 283, 286, 294; first restoration, 292–305 passim; Hundred Days, 301, 302, 303, 316, 319; second restoration, 316–40 passim
Louvois, Madame de, 32
Lowenstern, Baron: campaign of 1812, 269
Lowicz, Duchy of: acquired by Marshal Davout, 164
Lunéville, Treaty of, 69, 70, 95

Macdonald, Jacques Etienne, Marshal (Duke of Taranto): Battle of Wagram, 197, 201; exile of Marshal Davout, 339; Army of the Loire, 344; mentioned, 67, 68, 87, 228
Mack, K., General: campaign of 1805, 99, 100, 101, 102; surrender of, 102
Maloyaroslavets, Battle of, 254, 255, 257, 259, 263, 269, 270
Malta: captured by French, 41; Knights of, 41; captured by English, 69
Mamelukes, 42–56 passim
Mantua: siege of, 33; surrender of, 34
Marat, J. P., 22
Marbot, General, 118, 236, 334
Marceau, General, 29
Marchand, Jean Gabriel, General: campaign of 1812, 232
Marengo, Battle of, 63, 65
Marie Antoinette: Queen of France, 208
Marie Louise: Empress of France, 207, 208, 209
Marmont, Auguste Frederic Louis Viesse, Marshal (Duke of Ragusa): Egyptian campaign, 55; campaign of 1805, 100, 102, 103; Battle of Wagram, 196; Hundred Days, 310; mentioned, 78, 87, 91
Masséna, André, Marshal (Duke of Rivoli; Prince of Essling): Second Italian Campaign, 67; campaign of 1805, 100, 102; campaign of 1807, 148; campaign of 1809, 176–200 passim; Battle of Wagram, 195, 196, 198, 199, 200; surrender of Genoa, 293; mentioned, 87, 127, 301
Massy, Lieutenant Colonel: Battle of Eylau, 146
Maulaz, Jacob François, General: campaign of 1809, 192
Mayer, M., 338
Meerfeldt, General: campaign of 1805, 103, 112
Mello, Guillaume de (Lord of Epoisses), 3
Menitz Pond, 110
Menou, General, 55, 57, 59
Mère, Madame (mother of Napoleon Bonaparte), 91, 92
Metternich, Klemens, Prince, 223
Milhaud, Edouard Jean Baptiste, General: campaign of 1807, 139, 146; Hundred Days, 304; Army of the Loire, 332
Miloradovich, M., General: campaign of 1812, 259, 260, 264

Minard, Antoine: Lord of Mongarneau, Bilemain, 4
Minard, Marie-Louise (grandmother of Marshal Davout), 4, 5
Minard de Velars, Etienne, (grandfather of Marshal Davout), 4
Minden, Battle of, 4
Mireaur, General, 43
Moltke, Count von (Field Marshal): on Marshal Davout and the siege of Hamburg, 287
Moncey, Bon Adrien Jeannot, Marshal (Duke of Conegliano): Second Italian Campaign, 68–69, 112; campaign of 1805, 114; mentioned, 87, 327, 340
Montaigu, Ann Charles Basset de, General, 31
Montbrun, L. P., General: campaign of 1809, 175, 180, 182, 184, 185, 187, 201
Morand, Charles Antoine Louis, General: campaign of 1806, 119–30 passim; Battle of Auerstädt, 126, 127, 128; campaign of 1807, 139–46 passim; Battle of Eylau, 143, 145, 146; and Duchy of Warsaw, 153; campaign of 1809, 175, 180, 181, 184, 187, 188, 190, 200; Battle of Wagram, 200; personal relationship with Marshal Davout, 214, 215; campaign of 1812, 228, 229, 238, 248, 250; Battle of Borodino, 248, 250; mentioned, 204, 205
Moreau, Jean Victor, General, 33, 34, 35, 38, 67, 68
Moreaux, General: commanded Army of the Moselle, 27; death of, 28
Mortier, Edouard Adolphe Casimer Joseph, Marshal (Duke of Treviso), 87, 327
Murad Bey: Battle of Shubra Khit, 43, 44; Egyptian campaign, 43–52 passim; Battle of the Pyramids, 46, 47
Murat, Joachim, Marshal (Grand Duke of Berg; King of Naples): campaign of 1805, 101, 110; campaign of 1807, 124, 125, 126, 134; campaign of 1807, 139–50 passim; Battle of Eylau, 143, 145; Duchy of Warsaw, 168; enemy of Marshal Davout, 215; campaign of 1812, 226–71 passim; Battle of Borodino, 243, 250; mentioned, 87, 88, 165
Musquinet, Marie-Jeanne-Louise. *See* Leclerc, Madame

Nansouty, M. A. C., General: campaign of 1809, 183, 184, 198, 199; Battle of Wagram, 198, 199; campaign of 1812, 229, 248; Battle of Borodino, 248
Napoleon I (Emperor of France): at the *Ecole militaire,* 7; Egyptian campaign, 31–61 passim; first campaign in Italy, 33, 34; first meets Marshal Davout, 37, 38, 39; departure from Egypt, 56; Convention of El Arish, 57, 58, 59, 60; feelings toward Marshal Davout, 63, 64; personal relationship with Marshal Davout, 63–64, 84, 164–66; Second Italian Campaign, 63, 67; and the marriage of Marshal Davout, 72, 74; Treaty of Amiens, 78; and the invasion of England, 80–83, 97, 99; coronation as Emperor, 91; and the Third Coalition, 95, 96; Battle of Trafalgar, 99; campaign of 1805, 100–113 passim; Battle of Austerlitz, 104–13 passim; campaign of 1806, 117, 137, et passim; battles of Jena and Auerstädt, 126–34 passim; campaign of 1807, 138–49 passim; Battle of Eylau, 143, 145, 147, 148; Treaty of Tilsit, 151, 152, 154; and the Duchy of Warsaw, 154–57, 164–66, 168; meeting at Erfurt, 173; Battle of Eckmühl, 185–87; campaign of 1809, 185–202 passim; Battle of Aspern Essling, 190, 191; Battle of Wagram, 200–202; the divorce, 207, 208; campaign of 1812, 217–72 passim; Battle of Borodino, 243–50 passim; departure from the army, 270, 271, 273; campaign of 1813, 275–83 passim; first abdication, 292,

293, 294, 298; at Elba, 298; Hundred Days, 299–316 passim; Battle of Waterloo, 311, 312; second abdication, 312–20 passim
Napoleon II. *See* King of Rome
Napoleonic Code. *See* Code, Napoleonic
Narbonne, Raymond Jacques Marie de, 8, 166, 169
Neerwinden, Battle of, 19
Nelson, Horatio, Admiral: Battle of Aboukir Bay, 47, 63; and the invasion of England, 97, 99; Battle of Trafalgar, 99; death of, 99; mentioned, 40, 41, 42, 56, 116
Ney, Michel, Marshal (Duke of Elchingen; Prince of Moskowa): campaign of 1805, 100, 101; campaign of 1806, 119, 124, 125, 126, 135; campaign of 1807, 139–49 passim; friendship with Marshal Davout, 215; campaign of 1812, 223–68 passim; Battle of Borodino, 246–49; Hundred Days, 304; second restoration, 334–37; trial of, 335–37; execution of, 337; mentioned, 35, 78, 87, 118

O'Moran, General, 17
Orange, Prince of: Battle of Auerstädt, 127, 128, 130
Ordinance of July 24, (1815), 333, 335
Orleans, Gaston d', 4
Oudinot, Nicholas Charles, Marshal (Duke of Reggio): Battle of Austerlitz, 110; campaign of 1809, 176–98 passim; Battle of Wagram, 195, 196, 198; friendship with Marshal Davout, 215; campaign of 1812, 223, 226, 267, 268; campaign of 1813, 282; second restoration, 319, 320, 322; surrender of Paris (1815), 327; mentioned, 31, 80, 87, 132, 153

Pajol, Claude-Pierre, General: campaign of 1809, 203; campaign of 1812, 229; Hundred Days, 304
Pelletier, General, 159
Perignon, Dominique Catherine, Marshal, 87
Petit, Madame: friendship with Madam Davout, 119
Phull, E. von, General: campaign of 1812, 228
Pichegru, Jean Charles, General: with the Army of the Rhine and Moselle, 29, 30
Pille, Louis-Antoine, General, 26, 350n*19*
Pino, Dominique, General: Battle of Borodino, 245
Pitt, William: and the Third Coalition, 96; and the Battle of Austerlitz, 116; death of, 116
Pius VII (Pope), 219
Platov, M. I., General: campaign of 1812, 227, 248, 259, 260, 261, 265
Polish campaign. *See* Campaign of 1807
Polish Constitution of 1791, 167
Polish Legions, 157, 158, 159, 160
"Polish Liberation, Second War of." *See* Campaign of 1812
Poniatowski, Joseph Anthony, Marshal (Prince): minister of war of Duchy of Warsaw, 157–60; on kingship of Poland, 166; and Madam Davout's visit to Poland, 170; campaign of 1809, 179; campaign of 1812, 227–62 passim; Battle of Borodino, 243–50 passim; mentioned, 87
Poniatowski, Stanislas Augustus: King of Poland, 157
Potocka, Countess, 170
Potsdam, Agreement of, 117
Poussielgue, Citizen: and the Convention of El Arish, 59
Pratzen: plains, 109; slopes, 110
Pressburg, Treaty of, 114, 173
Provisional Government (1814), 293, 294
Prschibitscheski, General: Battle of Austerlitz, 109
Puthod, Jacques Pierre Marie, General: Battle of Wagram, 200; mentioned, 213

Pyramids, Battle of the (Giza), 46, 47

Rapp, Jean, General: campaign of 1807, 141; campaign of 1812, 248, 250; Hundred Days, 305, 306
Recess of 1803, Imperial. *See* Imperial Recess of 1803
Reynier, Jean Louis, General: Battle of the Pyramids, 46; campaign of 1809, 198; campaign of 1812, 227; campaign of 1813, 282; Hundred Days, 304
Robespierre, Maximillien, 22, 26
Roer, Battle of, 27
Romeuf, General: death of, 250
Rosenberg, General: campaign of 1809, 183–202 passim; Battle of Wagram, 197, 198, 200, 201, 202
Rossbach, Battle of, 123
Rostopchin, Fedor Vassilievitch, Count: burning of Moscow, 251
Ruchel, Ernst Friedrich, General: campaign of 1806, 124, 125, 132
Russian campaign. *See* Campaign of 1812
Russo-Turkish War (1812), 221

Saalfeld, Battle of, 125
St.-Cyr, Carre, General: campaign of 1813, 274, 283
St.-Cyr, Gouvion, Marshal: campaign of 1805, 100; friendship with Marshal Davout, 215; surrender of Paris (1815), 327; second restoration, 331, 332; mentioned, 87
Saint-Germain, Claude Louis de: minister of war, 6
St. Hilaire, General: Battle of Austerlitz, 109; Battle of Eylau, 145; campaign of 1809, 175, 180, 181, 184, 185
St. Jean d'Acre: siege of, 53, 54
St. Sulpice, General: campaign of 1809, 175, 182, 184
Satschan Pond, 110
Savigny-sur-Orge: purchase of, 77
Saxe-Weimar, Duke of: campaign of 1806, 125
Schmettau, Friedrich Wilhelm Karl von, General: Battle of Auerstädt, 127, 128, 130
Schönbrunn, Treaty of, 117, 203, 204, 205
Schwarzenberg, Karl von, Prince: campaign of 1812, 227, 267, 268
Second Italian Campaign, 65–69
Ségur, Paul Philip, General (Count): campaign of 1812, 236, 242, 260, 264, 266, 270
Serurier, Jean Mathieu, Marshal, 87, 327
Seuguenot, Charles-Elie de, 14
Seuguenot, Madame (Marie-Magdelaine Cassons), 14
Seuguenot, Marie-Nicolle-Adelaïde de (first wife of Marshal Davout), 14, 15, 71
Seven Years' War, 4, 117, 125
Shubra Khit, Battle of, 43
Shuvalov, General: campaign of 1812, 229
Sieyès, Emmanuel Joseph, 64
Smith, Sir Sidney (Commodore): Egyptian campaign, 56, 58, 61; Convention of El Arish, 59, 60
Sohr, Colonel: second restoration, 325, 326
Solta-Nawka, Battle of, 233, 234, 235
Somme, Catherine de, 4
Songis, Nicolas Marie de, General, 75
Soul, General, 78
Soult, Madame: friend of Madame Davout, 94
Soult, Nicolas Jean de Dieu, Marshal (Duke of Dalmatia): campaign of 1805, 100–111 passim; Battle of Austerlitz, 108, 109, 110, 111; campaign of 1806, 124, 125, 126, 135; campaign of 1807, 139, 143, 149, 150; Hundred Days, 305, 306, 307, 316, 317; surrender of Paris (1815), 327; mentioned, 75, 87, 91
Stein, Karl von, Baron, 118
Suchet, Louis Gabriel, Marshal (Duke of Albufera): campaign of 1812, 225; Hundred Days, 304, 310; second restoration, 340; mentioned, 87

Tabor, Mount: Battle of, 53
Talleyrand, Charles-Maurice de (Bishop of Autun): Egyptian campaign, 39; treasonous plot of, 172, 173; second restoration, 333; mentioned, 133
Tettenborn, General: campaign of 1813, 275
Tharreau, General: Battle of Eckmühl, 186
Thermidor: ninth of, 25
Thermidorian Reaction, 26
Thibaudeau, General: second restoration, 321
Thiébault, Paul Charles, Baron: dislike of Marshal Davout, 170; on character of Marshal Davout, 211, 212; enemy of Marshal Davout, 216; campaign of 1813, 281; mentioned, 171
Tilsit, Treaty of, 151, 152, 155, 156, 163, 219
Tormassov, A. P., General: campaign of 1812, 227, 262
Tourton, General: Paris National Guard, 323
Trafalgar, Battle of Cape, 99, 116, 219
Travot, General: Hundred Days, 309
Trobriand, General, 135
Tshitshagov, Admiral: campaign of 1812, 267, 268, 271
Tuncq, General, 23
Turreau de Linieres, Louis (stepfather of Marshal Davout), 12, 26
Tyszkiewicz, Countess, 170

Ulm: siege and surrender of, 102
Uvarov, General: Battle of Borodino, 248

Valée, General: surrender of Paris (1815), 327
Valence, General: campaign of 1812, 229
Valmy, Battle of, 17
Vandamme, Dominique René, General: Battle of Austerlitz, 109; campaign of 1809, 180, 182, 190; campaign of 1813, 174, 215, 216, 275, 276, 280; campaign of 1812, 227; Hundred Days, 304; second restoration, 322, 327; mentioned, 35
Vanguard, 40
Vaubois, Charles Henri, General, 41
Vaubon, Madame, 158
Vechery, General: campaign of 1813, 281
Vendée: revolt of, 21, 22, 63; resistance in (1815), 301, 302, 309, 310; pacification of (1815), 334
Vialannes, General: campaign of 1805, 100; campaign of 1806, 120, 126, 137
Viceroy of Italy. *See* Eugène de Beauharnais
Victor, Claude, Marshal (Duke of Belluno): campaign of 1812, 267, 268; mentioned, 87, 149
Vigier, Achille Pierre Félix, Count: marriage to Josephine Davout, 342
Vigier, Joseph Louis Jules Achille (grandson of Marshal Davout): birth of, 342
Vigier, Pierre, 342
Vihiers, Battle of, 22
Villeneuve, Pierre Charles de, Admiral: and invasion of England, 97, 99; Battle of Trafalgar, 99
Vitrolles, Baron de: second restoration, 319, 320, 322, 323, 324
Vizier, Turkish Grand, 57, 58, 59, 61

Wagram, Battle of, 195–203
Wagram campaign. *See* Campaign of 1809
Walewska, Madame, 207
Walmoden, Count of: campaign of 1805, 112, 113
Warsaw, Grand Duchy of, 152, 153, 154, 155, 160, 161
Wartensleben, General: Battle of Auerstädt, 127, 128, 130
Waterloo, Battle of, 307, 310, 311, 312, 315, 316, 317, 322, 324, 336
Waterloo Campaign, 303–30
Wegesack, General: campaign of 1813, 282

Wellington, Arthur Wellesley, Duke of: Waterloo Campaign, 302–30 passim
Werneck, General: campaign of 1805, 101
"White Terror," 310
William I (King of Prussia), 133
William of Prussia, Prince: Battle of Auerstädt, 128
Wittgenstein, Ludwig, General: campaign of 1812, 227, 262, 267, 271, 274
Wrede, Karl Philipp von, General: campaign of 1805, 105; campaign of 1809, 183; campaign of 1812, 267, 274
Würmser, Dogobert Siegmund, General, 31
Württenberg, Prince of: campaign of 1806, 133, 136; mentioned, 95

Zajonczek, Joseph, General: campaign of 1807, 148